THE EMPEROR COMMODUS

THE EMPEROR COMMODUS
Gladiator, Hercules or a Tyrant?

GEOFF W. ADAMS

BrownWalker Press
Boca Raton

The Emperor Commodus: Gladiator, Hercules or a Tyrant?

BrownWalker Press
Boca Raton, Florida • USA
2013

ISBN-10: 1-61233-722-8
ISBN-13: 978-1-61233-722-7

www.brownwalker.com

Library of Congress Cataloging-in-Publication Data

Adams, Geoff W. (Geoffrey William)
The Emperor Commodus : gladiator, Hercules or a tyrant? / Geoff
W. Adams.
pages cm
Includes bibliographical references and index.
ISBN-13: 978-1-61233-722-7 (pbk. : alk. paper)
ISBN-10: 1-61233-722-8 (pbk. : alk. paper)
1. Commodus, Emperor of Rome, 161-192. 2. Emperors--Rome--
Biography. 3. Rome--History--Commodus, 180-192.
I. Title.

DG299.A33 2013
937.06092--dc23
[B]

2013038286

CONTENTS

ACKNOWLEDGEMENTS

This study originated out of a long-standing fascination with the Emperor Commodus, who has intrigued a large audience since antiquity. It has not been written to answer all of the questions surrounding the life of Gaius Caligula, which is an impossible task when the limited sources of information are taken into consideration. This book is intended to provide a different interpretation of this character, which will come across as being agreeable to some readers more than others. It has been structured to take into consideration as much of the ancient evidence as was possible in the hope of creating the most viable examination of this Emperor. The opinions surrounding how to interpret the life and reign of Commodus will continue to be divided within modern scholarship, but it is hoped that this *libellum* will provide some interesting ideas for most readers and topical debate among others.

I would initially like to thank several people and institutions that have been instrumental in their assistance for the production of this work. Firstly, I would like to thank my colleagues at the University of Tasmania for their support and opportunities for discussion about points of issue. I would also like to thank my family [Adams and Collie] friends for their support. I would also like to devote this study to my son and daughter, Callan and Charli, in the hope that in years to come you will find it both interesting and enlightening. Finally, I must thank my wife, Nicole, to whom I dedicate the following pages and thank deeply with love and gratitude for her patience and understanding throughout its development.

INTRODUCTION

The life and reign of Commodus has been the topic of much con-
troversy both in antiquity and modern times. The difficulty with any
evaluation of his life is that the literary sources who wrote about him
were from a social group that was diametrically opposed to almost
everything that he embodied. The surviving sources, and their anti-
Commodus stance, were written from just after his reign until long
after the assassination of Commodus and in many ways can be held
responsible for the confusion and lack of understanding that arises
when examining the life of this Roman *princeps*. Nevertheless, there
must be some factual basis for these portrayals of Commodus because otherwise there would have been little support for these representations in antiquity, regardless of the prevalent anti-Commodus
sentiment among both authors and their largely senatorial audience.
The 'reality' should be present somewhere within the extant evidence, which is only attainable through a critical and holistic approach to the available literary and archaeological sources.

This difficulty has in turn affected the interpretation of the evidence within several modern studies, which has largely resulted in
two schools of thought: those who have followed the line of the
ancient literary sources, and those who have rejected them. The first
interpretation is often criticised for taking the sources at face value
without any critical reading of the texts, whereas the second view has
been criticised as being a reactionary tendency that often results in a
'defensive' stance for the lives of so-called 'bad emperors'. In many
ways the latter is to be expected: the desire to study the life of an
historical figure in any depth indicates an initial interest in the figure
that usually results in a great deal of research and often a fair amount
of affection for (or at least interest in) the individual.

Nevertheless, neither of these methods are sound practices as
they tend to reflect the desire of each scholar to place their individual
interpretation upon the evidence. This is clearly a natural tendency,
illustrating the subjective interpretation that historians face which has

occurred since antiquity, as reflected in the ancient sources. It is impossible to write a purely objective historical work because the interpretation of historians is inherently subjective, particularly in relation to such a controversial historical character like Commodus Antoninus. But nevertheless, it is the responsibility of the researcher to weigh up the evidence and to present the most balanced analysis possible. It is for this reason that the prime focus of this book has been not only upon Commodus' actions, but also his heritage and the political climate that he lived in. This study has not been intended to serve as a biography, but rather as a thematic interpretation of the significant aspects of Gaius' life that provide insight into his personal inclinations and his approach to ruling Rome as Roman *princeps*.

The primary aim of the present study is to evaluate Commodus in light of his wider historical (and historiographical) context. He is often shown as being responsible for the end of a golden era[1] and is closely tied to other 'insane' emperors as well.[2] This could be entirely justified – or entirely fictional. The question remains about whether Commodus has simply suffered as an historical figure merely because his predecessors have been so loved in antiquity (or idealised for that matter). This is particularly plausible in view of the natural comparison that occurs between Commodus and his father, Marcus Aurelius. Commodus is also often attributed with being responsible for the decline of the Roman Empire in the 3rd Century AD,[3] but of course some questions remain about this assumption. This relies entirely upon the supposition that there was no sign of decline at all during the reigns of his predecessors, which naturally also needs to be considered in order to comprehensively evaluate Commodus as both an administrator and as a political leader.

All the same, it would be foolish to try and argue that he should be completely absolved of all responsibility for any ensuing political instability. As mentioned previously, this study is not intended to simply defend Commodus without question. It is evident that he was a flawed character, but it is also quite clear that he was not as inept or evil as shown in many of the ancient literary sources. The question about whether or not he should have attained the supreme political position in Rome remains, but in many ways this is irrelevant for the

---

[1] Dio 72.36.4; Herodian 1.1.4.

[2] *HA Marcus* 28.10 for example.

[3] Dio 72.36.4; Herodian 1.1.4.

present study. The main aim here is to establish the benefits and pitfalls of Commodus' reign in each instance and to contextualise his principate within a broader historical context. By doing this it should be possible to evaluate the reign of Commodus Antoninus as a ruler while hopefully limiting the preconceived notions or agendas of the modern scholar.

Previous Studies of Commodus

There are six previous studies that have been of particular use for the current analysis of the Emperor Commodus. These are works by: Traupman (1954), Grosso (1964), Gherardini (1974), Kaiser-Raiß (1980), Leunissen (1989) and Hekster (2002). All of these studies have contributed to the modern scholarship on the Emperor Commodus, but each has largely focused upon specific aspects rather than a holistic approach to the extant evidence. All the same, each of them has contributed to the present analysis, and each of them should be considered at this point in order to determine both their benefits and limitations that make the present study original and essential for an understanding of this *princeps*.

The first significant piece to be produced on Commodus was by Traupman,[4] which was largely intended as a defence of his reign. While the success of this line of argument is limited, this doctoral thesis still provides a good overview of the period from AD 180-192 and outlines the support structure that existed for Commodus during his principate. The next significant study, *La Lotta Politica al Tempo di Commodo*, by Grosso is probably the most protracted analysis of his reign, and largely focuses upon the literary representations and prosopographical evidence for Commodus' principate.[5] As Millar has noted,[6] the main benefit of this work is its use for reference material, with the actual argument of Grosso being lost within the expansive nature of the text itself. All the same, Millar's view that Commodus is unworthy of analysis[7] seems to underestimate the possible worth of

---

[4] J.C. Traupman, *The Life and Reign of Commodus*, PhD Diss., Princeton University, 1956.

[5] F. Grosso, *La Lotta Politica al Tempo di Commodo*, Accademia delle Scienze: Turin, 1964.

[6] F. Millar, "La Lotta Politica al Tempo di Commodo (Review)", *JRS* 56, 1966, p. 245.

[7] *ibid.*, p. 244.

considering Commodus as *princeps* during such a transitional phase of the Roman Empire.

Maria Gherardini's *Studien zur Geschichte des Kaisers Commodus*,[8] takes a different approach with the primary focus being upon the Praetorian Prefects and their relationship with Commodus during his reign. She also examines the question of the succession and the declaration of terms in AD 180, but the conclusions are not entirely different to those of the previous two scholars, Traupman and Grosso. Kaiser-Raiß (1980)[9] has taken another approach in *Die stadtrömische Münzprägung während der Alleinherrschaft des Commodus* by focusing almost entirely upon the numismatic material from Commodus' reign. While the inherent value of this form of evidence is unquestionable, the intention of the author is to provide another defence of Commodus, which highlights the limitations in its focus even further. Both of these texts provide additional analysis for the present study in these regards, but it is also evident that there is still more work to be done on Commodus' principate.

Konsuln und Konsulare in der Zeit von Commodus bis Severus Alexander (180-235 n. Chr.) by Paul Leunissen,[10] is another important study for the present analysis, which provides a survey of the consular positions during Commodus' reign. The intention of the work in general is not to analyse Commodus himself, but it does provide some useful insight into the administrative policies of his principate. Leunissen's scholarship is sound and has certainly added to the analysis of Commodus' role as *princeps* in the present study. The most recent study of Commodus is by Oliver Hekster (*Commodus: an Emperor at the Crossroads*),[11] which has largely focused upon the iconographic representations of this *princeps*. However, the limitations in this study are evident through the limited consideration taken for the other

---

[8] M. Gherardini, *Studien zur Geschichte des Kaisers Commodus*, Verband der wissenschaftlichen Gesellschaften Österreichs: Wien, 1974.

[9] M.R. Kaiser-Raiß, *Die stadtrömische Münzprägung während der Alleinherrschaft des Commodus: Untersuchungen zue Selbstdarstellung eines römisches Kaisers*, P.N. Schulten: Frankfurt, 1980.

[10] P.M.M. Leunissen, *Konsuln und Konsulare in der Zeit von Commodus bis Severus Alexander (180-235 n. Chr.): Prosopographische Untersuchungen zur senatorischen Elite im Römischen Kaiserreich*, J.C. Gieben: Amsterdam, 1989.

[11] O. Hekster, *Commodus: an Emperor at the Crossroads*, J.C. Gieben: Amsterdam, 2002.

forms of ancient evidence,[12] which should have been discussed in much greater detail. This study also attempts to defend Commodus, which seems to have been a consistent theme for the majority of modern works that have focused upon his principate. It is the contention of the present study that a complete absolution of Commodus' reign is entirely untenable, and that a more considered approach in relation to the ancient evidence is necessary for any analysis of this controversial historical figure.

Another significant text that has contributed greatly to the present work is *Fronto and Antonine Rome* by Edward Champlin.[13] This study not only considers the social and political contexts in which Fronto's correspondence was produced by examining the letters themselves, but he also commendably includes a large amount of epigraphic evidence,[14] which is very useful for the analysis of the careers of prominent figures throughout the period. A large part of its focus is upon the aristocratic world of Roman North Africa,[15] from which Fronto himself derived, thus illustrating the rising prominence of political and social figures from this province. Champlin's work here addresses this period, however, from a different angle to the current analysis of Commodus and his principate. All the same, it still provides an excellent source of insight and discussion about the workings of the Antonine imperial *consilium*.[16]

Following from these works, the present study is significant because it incorporates the most comprehensive amount of the available evidence in order to evaluate Commodus' principate. While previous studies have had clear focus points within the corpus of ancient sources of evidence, none of them have addressed all of them, which make the present analysis both unique and necessary. It is vital to critically consider as much of the available evidence as possible. While the ancient literary sources have provided the most vivid portrayal of Commodus as an emperor and as a person, it is also one of

---

[12] H. Elton, "Commodus: an Emperor at the Crossroads (Review)", *JRS* 93, 2003, p. 397.

[13] E. Champlin, *Fronto and Antonine Rome*, Harvard University Press: Cambridge, Mass., 1980.

[14] A.K. Bowman, "Fronto and Antonine Rome [Review]", *Phoenix* 36.3, 1982, p. 279.

[15] K.R. Bradley, "Fronto and Antonine Rome [Review]", *CJ* 77.4, 1982, p. 370.

[16] R. Mellor, "Fronto and Antonine Rome [Review]", *Journal of Philology* 103.4, 1982, p. 461.

the most affected by authorial subjectivity. Therefore, it is essential to weight these representations against the archaeological, numismatic, epigraphic and sculptural forms of evidence that can either support or reject the views of the ancient authors. All the same, each of these forms of evidence also requires different methods of analysis in order to determine their importance for an understanding of Commodus' principate.

Methods Used within this Study

In order to gain the most accurate and comprehensive understanding of Commodus Antoninus many different sources of information must be utilised. This entails use of the literary sources as well as archaeological, numismatic and epigraphic data. Archaeological evidence, such as the palaces on the Palatine Hill or the Villa of the Quintili on the *Via Appia*, can provide a further insight into both the public and domestic priorities of the emperor. Particularly in relation to the Imperial palace, a statistical method has been used to establish the social priorities of the Emperor,[17] which may in turn cast further light upon the principate of Commodus, when compared to the residences of his predecessors and successors. The numismatic evidence, when used as a corpus, can illustrate the public propaganda that was clearly important to Commodus. The epigraphic evidence can also illustrate aspects of the reign of Commodus, particularly in relation to his associations with the élite members of Roman society in the second half of the 2nd Century AD. This evidence adds significant amounts of information to this study in particular, with there certainly being good examples for his administration, and also in the form of religious dedications, such as the inscription showing a festival to Apollo at the Greek city of Acraephiae,[18] which can also provide some insight into the foreign and religious policies of the Emperor.

It is the numismatic evidence that is particularly important for this study. Numismatic sources provide one of the best portrayals of how Commodus wanted to be seen by the Roman public throughout the Empire, which in turn presents a view of how he may have wanted to (or did) see himself. However, this understanding can only be achieved if the historical and numismatic contexts for each issue are

---

[17] See G.W. Adams, *The Suburban Villas of Campania and their Social Function*, Archaeopress: Oxford, 2006.
[18] Bockh, Inscr. No. 1625.

taken into consideration; otherwise this can provide an unrealistic image of the significance of various numismatic issues. So in order for the context to be kept firmly in mind these issues have also been compared to the imagery on the coins of his predecessors and successors.

The aim of this study is to make comprehensive use of all of these varying forms of evidence in order to establish that there was some truth behind the portrayal of the ancient literary sources, such as Herodian, Cassius Dio and the *Historia Augusta*, but that it was their lack of understanding for his personal perspectives (or unwillingness to understand them) that resulted in such a biased representation. In addition to this, there was also the appeal of a simple 'good-bad' division within such representations. Being able to classify well-known figures in this fashion makes it easier to understand them, be it to an ancient or a modern audience. If a 'bad' emperor was evil from the very beginning of their life it makes the unpopularity of their later actions easier top comprehend. All the same, it is evident that individual personalities and their motives for acting in various ways are not always so black and white – in most instances there is a definite grey-scale that also exists between their various decisions. While it is quite clear that Commodus Antoninus may not have been the best candidate for the principate, it is also evident that he was not as consistently malicious as he was often portrayed.

The historical biographies of antiquity, particularly those written in relation to the Imperial household, frequently fall into two categories: 'good' emperors and the 'bad' emperors. These biographies were mostly intended to educate, instruct and entertain their audiences rather than to give accurate accounts of the emperors as they actually were. The 'good' emperors were often portrayed in such a positive light that they were 'super-humans' whereas the 'bad' emperors had evil, wicked dispositions often from the time of their births that were frequently accompanied by portents and omens of the ensuing wickedness that was about to be inflicted upon the world. The actual motives, intentions and desires of both 'good' and 'bad' emperors would seem to be somewhere between these views that exist between the various pieces of evidence about their reigns.

Overall Objectives of this Study
It is the intention of this work to undertake a comprehensive analysis of Commodus Antoninus that aims to understand this controversial figure, rather than simply defending or impeaching him for his ac-

tions. It is evident that he viewed his role within the political system of Antonine Rome in a different fashion to his predecessors, but this should not be taken as a definitive indictment against him either. This is not intended to be a defence of his actions or to provide an argument that he was in fact a highly efficient administrator and a brilliant general. Instead the intention is to examine the evidence: to view his more extreme actions in their historical and socio-political contexts in order to try and understand them. In his mind, Commodus would have viewed his position as *princeps* as being his birth-right and this would have in turn affected his view of how this power could be wielded. He was the son of the great Marcus Aurelius, which would have further accentuated the importance this birth-right.

Naturally, when it comes down to it all, this study is inflicted with the same difficulties that have beset all previous analyses of Commodus Antoninus: the reliance on the sources and the unfortunate subjectivity that exists in their interpretation. These difficulties are impossible to remove completely, but they have been abridged in this study. By using the widest possible array of evidence it has exhibited both the advantages and disadvantages that existed throughout the reign of Commodus. The second difficulty has been overcome by an acceptance of not only the evidence that complements this theme, but also the evidence that is at odds with it. Unfortunately, history will always be influenced by a degree of interpretation/argument – but it is the variance within its reading that makes it ultimately more personal.

But as mentioned previously, the primary aim of the present study is to consider as much of the extant evidence as possible in order to determine the general efficacy of Commodus' principate. The holistic approach in relation to the available ancient evidence should hopefully minimise the impact of the rather biased literary representations of him, but at the same time these opinions are not entirely ignored either. There must have been some grounding for these negative views of Commodus, so it would be negligent to entirely reject them on the basis of their pro-Senatorial sentiments. In all likelihood, Commodus' rejection (or persecution) of this social group was accentuated by the ultimate comparison that was drawn between himself and his father, Marcus Aurelius, and this would have in turn effected the accounts of this twelve year reign.

With that being recognised, it is also essential to note that Commodus was hardly a fitting character for the principate. His personal views seem to have brought about some of the more ex-treme elements within his policies, which in turn encouraged the opinions of him as a megalomaniac. So in many ways, neither the defensive nor the accusatory perspectives in his analysis are accurate, with Commodus' personal qualities as *princeps* probably being some-where in the middle of these widely contrasting views. All the same, this is difficult to argue – with it being natural to have either a posi-tive or negative opinion of such characters. Nevertheless, it is the intention of this study to simply evaluate the evidence, and to follow it wherever it leads. After all, it would be negligent to take a singular 'one-eyed' approach when considering such a figure and the ensuing reaction to him.

CHAPTER I

THE ANCIENT SOURCES OF EVIDENCE

Any in depth inquiry into the life of an historical figure such as the Emperor Commodus, needs to be undertaken based upon a well-founded understanding of the evidence within its historical context. There are several sources of information that can be used for an analysis of Commodus: the ancient literary texts, the archaeological data stemming from the reign of Commodus, the numismatic evidence and the epigraphic records that are dated from his reign. Each source of information has particular benefit for the insight that they can provide into the features of Commodus' reign, but none of them are perfect sources of historical reality. The best that can be achieved is through the combined use of each source, intending to balance their advantages and disadvantages while keeping the historical context firmly in mind. This requires the use of a varied number of methodologies which necessitates some caution

If these methods of historiography and archaeological theory are applied consistently, while not giving overt preference to a particular source of data, this will establish an optimal basis for any historical analysis. Naturally certain types of evidence provide a greater amount of detail for any understanding of Commodus, such as the ancient literary and numismatic evidence, but they must still be used in conjunction with the other sources in order to establish the most informed type of analysis possible. Therefore, to clearly evaluate the various sources on the life and reign of Commodus, each has been briefly scrutinised in order to establish their different benefits and difficulties, and thereby providing a solid foundation upon which to analyse this Emperor of Rome.

The Ancient Literary Sources
There are several ancient literary sources that provide evidence on the life and reign of Commodus, but there are six authors in particular who have focused more comprehensively upon him and provide the greatest

amount of information to be analysed. These authors are: Marcus Cornelius Fronto, Cassius Dio, Herodian and the *Historia Augusta*. There is evidence taken from other literary sources than these, but these authors provide the greatest amount of available evidence and need to be analysed both individually and collectively to successfully carry out a comprehensive analysis of Commodus. Each of these authors cover a wide period of time within their works and each of their works were written for different purposes. The intentions behind each piece must be kept in mind in order for each text to be used effectively. The time of composition is also an important factor with the temporal distance, or the lack thereof, having a clear effect upon the reliability of each text. This is also affected by the intended audience for each author, with each biographer or historian being influenced by the disposition of their particular audience. Each of these seven authors has been considered in order of both chronology (Fronto, Dio Cassius, Herodian) and importance to the study (The *Historia Augusta*), followed by a brief overview of other literary sources that provide further important information (Aurelius Victor, the *Epitomator*, Eutropius).

As mentioned previously, the prevailing attitude of these ancient sources was negative towards the Emperor Commodus. Therefore, it is imperative to use their accounts of his reign with some caution, but this does not preclude the importance of their opinions either. The lasting impressions from Commodus' reign are just as important for this study as the facts that are attainable from these various accounts. While this does not mean that the ancient literary sources can be taken as giving a precise portrayal of Commodus in the literal sense, it is still important to recognise that he was not popular within some circles – in fact, he was viewed as a vile, megalomaniac. Even with the senatorial parochialism being taken into consideration, there needed to have been some basis for these negative views to provoke such a fervent response against him. It should also be noted that there is a significant difference in the details of Commodus' behaviour as portrayed by these ancient authors, which highlights the degree of *interpretation* within these accounts. All the same, they all offer some insight not only into Commodus himself, but also how he was perceived by others.

Marcus Cornelius Fronto

Marcus Cornelius Fronto was originally from Numidia,[19] and he may have had some relationship with Plutarch.[20] He was clearly a leading

---

[19] C.R. Haines, "Fronto", *CR* 34, 1920, p. 14.

literary figure during his lifetime,[21] with his letters with Marcus Aurelius and Lucius Verus being published. These letters have been dated to the years between AD 161 and 176,[22] and they provide some useful evidence for the reign of Marcus Aurelius. This is evident through both his friendly relationship with Marcus and also as his *magister*.[23] This correspondence with the Imperial household has provided evidence that occasionally substantiates some of the episodes mentioned in the other ancient sources. These letters provide a useful insight into not only the principate of Marcus Aurelius, but they also give some indication of the familial relationship between him and his son, Commodus. While this literary source is not the most extensive form of evidence, it does provide some useful insight into this relationship, or at least some indication of how Marcus viewed his parental role. This is of course of great significance when considering how Marcus Aurelius influenced the development of his son and its possible later impact.

Cassius Dio

Cassius Dio was reportedly born around AD 164/5 at Nicaea in Bithynia.[24] Dio has also provided a great amount of information concerning the lead up to Commodus' reign, as well as the period of his rule. In structure his text is annalistic, but by the time it focuses upon the Imperial period it becomes essentially biographical,[25] focusing upon the major events surrounding each of the successive Roman Emperors. It has been argued that the outlook of Dio was essentially Roman,[26] and yet throughout the *Roman History* it is quite evident that he has combined sympathies: both Roman and Greek.[27]

---

[20] C.J. Webb, "Fronto and Plutarch", *CR* 11.6, 1879, pp. 305-6.

[21] E. Champlin, *Fronto and Antonine Rome*, Harvard University Press: Cambridge, Mass., 1980, p. 2; F. Portalupi, *Marco Cornelio Frontone*, Giappichelli: Turin, 1961, pp. 103-22.

[22] cf. E. Champlin, "The Chronology of Fronto", *JRS* 64, 1974, pp. 136-59.

[23] Champlin 1980, *op.cit.*, pp. 94-130.

[24] C.L. Murison, *Rebellion and Reconstruction*, Scholars Press: Atlanta, 1999, p. 6.

[25] C. Pelling, "Biographical History? Cassius Dio on the Early Principate", in M.J. Edwards and S. Swain (eds.), *Portraits: biographical representation in the Greek and Latin Literature of the Roman Empire*, Oxford University Press: Oxford, 1997, p. 117.

[26] Murison 1999, *op.cit.*, p. 6.

[27] S. Swain, *Hellenism and Empire*, Oxford University Press: Oxford, 1996, pp. 404-5.

This is exhibited not only through his use of Thucydidean style,[28] but also in his insistence about the influence and importance of Greek culture.[29] In relation to this research it is pertinent to note this duality in Dio's perspective; this is, for the most part, owing to the religious sympathies that Commodus himself possessed.

Considering that, in all likelihood, Dio probably spent a great amount of time in Rome,[30] he would have been intimately aware of the nature of Commodus' reign from an early stage and it is quite clear that his account of Commodus' principate would have been influenced by his own personal experiences. It is also important to note that the use of the *Roman History* by the biographer of the *Historia Augusta* is almost unquestionable.[31] The divergences between Cassius Dio and the author of the *HA* shows the different intentions behind their works,[32] so the impact of Dio's work on the later biographer still should not be doubted (even if it was unintentional). It is also significant that the later author Herodian also used Cassius Dio as a source of information,[33] which further illustrates the importance of his impact within the later historiographical tradition for Commodus Antoninus. Therefore, it is also quite evident that his views affected some of the most extensive sources on Commodus' reign used numerous other sources as well.

All the same, Cassius Dio was also quite selective in what he deemed worthy of comment throughout the *Roman History*.[34] While his early rise up the *cursus honorem* would have seemingly occurred during the reign of Commodus,[35] it is also evident that his writings were largely focused upon the decline of the Roman Empire with the

---

[28] F. Millar, *A Study of Cassius Dio*, Oxford University Press: Oxford, 1964, p. 7.

[29] Swain 1996, *op.cit.*, pp. 406-7.

[30] T.D. Barnes, *The Sources of the Historia Augusta*, Collection Latomus 155, Latomus Revue d'Etudes Latines: Brussels, 1978, p. 81.

[31] A.R. Birley, "Kolb, Literarische Beziehungen zwischen Cassius Dio und Herodian (Review)", *JRS* 64, 1974, p. 267; J. Straub, "Cassius Dio und die Historia Augusta", *HAC* 1970, 1972, pp. 271-85.

[32] Barnes 1978, *op.cit.*, p. 86.

[33] *ibid.*, p. 84.

[34] L. De Blois, "Volk und Soldaten bei Cassius Dio", *ANRW* 34.3, 1997, p. 2652.

[35] Millar 1964, *op.cit.*, pp. 15-16.

onset of his principate.[36] As Millar has noted,[37] one of the major themes that exists within Dio's portrayal of Commodus is the natural comparison with his father, Marcus Aurelius. For Cassius Dio, Marcus was the 'ideal' *princeps*, which was epitomized in his consideration for justice,[38] leniency,[39] and piety.[40] This is in direct contrast to the representation of Commodus in the *Roman History*, whereby he is depicted as being corrupt,[41] impious,[42] and murderous.[43] A similar approach is also noticeable in Herodian,[44] who is another vital historical source on the Emperor Commodus.

Herodian

One of the most important sources used for any analysis of Commodus is Herodian, who influenced the development of the various biographies in the later *Historia Augusta*.[45] As with Cassius Dio, Herodian wrote more from the perspective of an eye-witness,[46] which he emphasised with the claim that he confirmed all of his evidence personally.[47] It seems apparent that Herodian used Cassius Dio as a source,[48] which influenced the biographer of the *HA*.[49] It has already been established that Herodian was a major source for the Severan period in the *Historia Augusta*,[50] particularly in relation to the *Maximini Duo* and the *Maximus et Balbinus*.[51] It is important to note that Herodian was primarily used by the *HA* biographer for the period after

---

[36] W. Ameling, "Griechische Intellektuelle und das Imperium Romanum: das Biespiel Cassius Dio", *ANRW* 34.3, 1997, pp. 2472-96.

[37] Millar 1964, *op.cit.*, p. 122.

[38] Dio 72.6.1-2.

[39] Dio 72.28.3-4.

[40] Dio 72.34.2.

[41] Dio 73.6.1-5.

[42] Dio 73.16.1-3.

[43] Dio 73.4.1.

[44] Millar 1964, *op.cit.*, p. 122.

[45] G. Alfödy, "Eine Proskriptionsliste in der Historia Augusta", *HAC* 1968/9, 1970, pp. 1-11.

[46] Barnes 1978, *op.cit.*, p. 82.

[47] Herodian 1.1.3, 2.5.

[48] Barnes 1978, *op.cit.*, p. 84.

[49] cf. F. Kolb, *Literarische Beziehungen zwischen Cassius Dio und Herodian*, Bonn: *Antiquitas* Reihe 4.9, 1972.

[50] Barnes 1978, *op.cit.*, p. 85.

[51] T. Mommsen, "Die Scriptores Historiae Augustae", *Hermes* 25, 1890, pp. 260ff.

Marcus Aurelius' death,[52] which indicates that he was another influential scholar for the period of Commodus' principate and its negative tradition.

As mentioned previously, the portrayal of Commodus by Herodian was largely focused upon his comparison with Marcus Aurelius,[53] who was commonly viewed as the 'ideal' *princeps*. The use of Marcus as the initial focus in the text[54] served to provide a direct contrast with Herodian's account of Commodus' principate, which was shown as excessive and fantastical,[55] but also entirely deplorable. This representation is accentuated in Section 1.5.5, where Herodian epitomizes the arrogance of Commodus' reign:

ἔδωκε δὲ μετ' ἐκεῖνον ἐμὲ βασιλέα ἡ τύχη, οὐκ ἐπείσακτον, ὥσπερ οἱ πρὸ ἐμοῦ προσκτήτῳ σεμνυνόμενοι ἀρχῇ, ἀλλὰ μόνος τε ὑμῖν ἐγὼ ἐν τοῖς βασιλείοις ἀπεκυήθην, καὶ μὴ πειραθέντα με ἰδιωτικῶν σπαργάνων ἅμα τῷ τῆς γαστρὸς προελθεῖν ἡ βασίλειος ὑπεδέξατο πορφύρα, ὁμοῦ δέ με εἶδεν ἥλιος ἄνθρωπον καὶ βασιλέα.

'To follow him, Fortune has given the empire not to an adopted successor but to me. The prestige of those who reigned before me was increased by the empire, which they received as an additional honor, but I alone was born for you in the imperial palace. I never knew the touch of common cloth. The purple received me as I came forth into the world, and the sun shone down on me, man and emperor, at the same moment.'

Commodus was consistently shown as being excessive,[56] corrupt,[57] and murderous,[58] which was intended to further illustrate the depraved nature of his character. Herodian also explains the anti-senatorial sentiments of Commodus as being a result of a failed assassination attempt,[59] which may have been intended to absolve this élite group of any anti-Commodus responsibility. All the same, the main advantage of Herodian's account is that he was a contemporary of Commodus, but it is also evident that this did not preclude him from an entirely negative portrayal of this *princeps*. A similar theme is

---

[52] See Kolb 1972, *op.cit.*
[53] Millar 1964, *op.cit.*, p. 122.
[54] Herodian 1.1.1-4.8.
[55] cf. Kolb 1972, *op.cit.*, pp. 25-9.
[56] Herodian 1.12.4-5.
[57] Herodian 1.13.8.
[58] Herodian 1.12.6-9.
[59] Herodian 1.8.5-7.

also evident in the later biography of Commodus in the *Historia Augusta*.

The *Historia Augusta*

There are many difficulties that face modern scholars when approaching the *HA*, particularly in relation to the question of its authorship. This has been dealt with in numerous studies previously,[60] and will only be discussed briefly because it is not the prime aim of this examination. It is important for this rather significant question to be addressed. The presence of the six names of supposed authors (Aelius Spartianus, Julius Capitolinus, Vulcacius Gallicanus, Aelius Lampridius, Trebellius Pollio, Flavius Vospiscus) has been difficult to explain, but as argued by Dessau and Syme, the linguistic and stylistic similarities indicate a single author.[61] With this in mind, the dating of the *Historia Augusta* is difficult,[62] considering that at various stages the biographer addresses the Emperors Diocletian, Constantius and Constantine.[63] In response to this, Syme has also argued that an approximate date for its composition should be around AD 395,[64]

---

[60] P. White, "The Authorship of the HA", *JRS* 67, 1977, pp. 115-33; J.N. Adams, "The Authorship of the HA", *CQ* 22, 1972, pp. 186-94; "The Linguistic Unity of the HA", *Antichthon* 11, 1977, pp. 93 102; D. Den Hengst, "The Discussion of Authorship", *HAC* 2000, 2002, pp. 187-95; R. Syme, "The Secondary Vitae", *HAC* 1968/9, 1970, pp. 306-7; "The Composition of the Historia Augusta: recent theories", *JRS* 62, 1972, pp. 123-33; *Ammianus and the Historia Augusta*, Oxford University Press: Oxford, 1968, pp. 176-91; T. Marriott, "The Authorship of the Historia Augusta: two computer studies", *JRS* 69, 1979, pp. 65-77; D. Sansone, "The Computer and the Historia Augusta", *JRS* 80, 1990, pp. 174-7; J.H. Drake, "Studies in the Historia Augusta", *AJPh* 20.1, 1899, pp. 40-58; M. Meckler, "The Beginning of the Historia Augusta", *Historia* 45.3, 1996, pp. 364-75; T. Honore, "Scriptor Historiae Augustae", *JRS* 77, 1987, pp. 156-76.

[61] H. Dessau, 'Über Zeit und Persönlichkeit der Scriptores Historiae Augustae', *Hermes* 25, 1889, pp. 378ff; R. Syme, *Ammianus and the Historia Augusta*, Oxford University Press: Oxford, 1968, pp. 176ff.

[62] cf. H. Brandt, *Kommentar zur Vita Maximi et Balbini der Historia Augusta*, Antiquitas 4.2: Bonn, 1996, pp. 35-38.

[63] T.D. Barnes, *The Sources of the Historia Augusta*, Collection Latomus 155: Brussels, 1978, p. 13; "Some Persons in the Historia Augusta", *Phoenix* 26.2, 1972, p. 141.

[64] Syme, 1968, *op.cit.*, pp. 72-9; "Propaganda in the Historia Augusta", *Latomus* 37, 1978, p. 175; N.H. Baynes, *The Historia Augusta: its date and purpose*, Oxford University Press: Oxford, 1926; "The Historia Augusta: its date and

which appears most likely in view of the numerous correlations between the *HA* and other sources from this period.

Another difficulty with the *HA* as a literary and historical source is the nature of the extant evidence,[65] with the surviving manuscripts being quite different in their origins,[66] and erratic in their content.[67] The irregularities in the text have caused debate and discussion about how various passages should be interpreted,[68] which, in turn, has led to the legitimacy of its narrative being questioned, resulting in claims that it is a 'forgery'.[69] Nevertheless, for the purposes of this study, the episodes presented in the *Vita Commodi Antonini* have been compared to the other literary sources in order to ascertain their accuracy. It is also fortunate that in this regard there seems to be a fair amount of consensus about the text of the *Commodus*, which removes this problem for the most part in this study.

The author of the *Historia Augusta* also accentuated Commodus' indulgence,[70] debauchery,[71] impiety and cruelty,[72] but they seem to have focused upon these character traits even more than Cassius Dio and Herodian. One of the best examples of this is in the description of his physical appearance (*Commodus* 13.1-4):

---

purpose: a reply to criticism" *CQ* 22, 1928, pp. 166-71; "The Date of the Composition of the Historia Augusta", *CR* 38, 1924, pp. 165-9; J. Schwartz, "Sur la date de l'Histoire Auguste", *HAC* 1866/7, pp. 91-9; E. Birley, "Fresh Thoughts on the Dating of the Historia Augusta", *HAC* 1975/6, 1978, pp. 99-105; A. Cameron, "Education and Literary Culture", *CAH* 13, 1998, p. 685; B. Baldwin, "Some Legal Terms in the Historia Augusta", *Maia* 47, 1995, pp. 207-9; "Ausonius and the Historia Augusta", *Gymnasium* 88, 1981, p. 438; A. Momigliano, "Date et Destinataire de l'Histoire Auguste (Review)", *JRS* 44, 1954, pp. 129-31.

[65] cf. H.L. Zernial, *Akzentklausel und Textkritik in der Historia Augusta*, Antiquitas 4.18, 1986, pp.1-18.

[66] J. Hirstein, "L'Histoire du texte de l'Histoire Auguste: Egnazio et la Vita Marci", *HAC* 1996, 1998, pp. 167-89.

[67] Barnes, 1978, *op.cit.*, p. 32; J.P. Callu, "L'Histoire Auguste de Petrarque", *HAC* 1984/5, 1987, pp. 81-115.

[68] cf. R.J. Penella, "S.H.A. Commodus 9.2-3", *AJPh* 97.1, 1976, p. 39.

[69] cf. K.P. Johne, "Neue Beiträge zur Historia-Augusta-Forschung", *Klio* 58.1, 1976, pp. 255-62; R. Syme, "Bogus Authors", *HAC* 1972/4, 1976, p. 311.

[70] *HA Commodus* 1.1-2.4.

[71] *HA Commodus* 15.1-4.

[72] *HA Commodus* 5.5-14.

Fuit autem validus ad haec, alias debilis et infirmus, vitio etiam inter inguina prominenti, ita ut eius tumorem per sericas vestes populus Romanus agnosceret. versus in eo multi scripti sunt, de quibus etiam in opere suo Marius Maximus gloriatur. virium ad conficiendas fera tantarum fuit, ut elephantum conto transfigeret et orygis cornu basto transmiserit et singulis ictibus multa milia ferarum ingentium conficeret. impudentiae tantae fuit, ut cum muliebri veste in amphitheatro vel theatro sedens publice saepissime biberit.

'But, though vigorous enough for such exploits, he was otherwise weak and diseased; indeed, he had such a conspicuous growth on his groin that the people of Rome could see the swelling through his silken robes. Many verses were written alluding to this deformity; and Marius Maximus prides himself on preserving these in his biography of Commodus. Such was his prowess in the slaying of wild beasts, that he once transfixed an elephant with a pole, pierced a gazelle's horn with a spear, and on a thousand occasions dispatched a mighty beast with a single blow. Such was his complete indifference to propriety, that time and again he sat in the theatre or amphitheatre dressed in a woman's garments and drank quite publicly.'

The negative connotations of this description are highlighted when compared to the account of Herodian,[73] which epitomises the severity of the *HA* biographer. The entire biography of Commodus was intended to exemplify the negative aspects of his character. All the same, it is noteworthy that in this passage (*Commodus* 13.1-4) the biographer Marius Maximus is mentioned as a source, illustrating his importance as a source as well. Therefore, this important text must also be considered, despite the text itself having been lost.

---

[73] Herodian 1.7.5-6. γένους μὲν οὖν ὁ Κόμοδος οὕτως εἶχε, πρὸς δὲ τῇ τῆς ἡλικίας ἀκμῇ καὶ τὴν ὄψιν ἦν ἀξιοθέατος σώματός τε συμμετρίᾳ καὶ κάλλει προσώπου μετ' ἀνδρείας. ὀφθαλμῶν τε γὰρ †ἀρθμίαι καὶ πυρώδεις βολαί, κόμη τε φύσει ξανθὴ καὶ οὔλη, ὡς, εἴποτε φοιτῴη δι' ἡλίου, τοσοῦτον ἐκλάμπειν αὐτῷ πυροειδές τι, ὡς τοὺς μὲν οἴεσθαι ῥίνημα χρυσοῦ προιόντι ἐπιπάσσεσθαι, τοὺς δὲ ἐκθειάζειν, λέγοντας αἴγλην τινὰ οὐράνιον περὶ τῇ κεφαλῇ συγγεγενῆσθαι αὐτῷ· ἰουλοί τε αὐτοῦ κατιόντες ταῖς παρειαῖς ἐπήνθουν. τοιοῦτον δὴ θεασάμενοι βασιλέα οἱ Ῥωμαῖοι, εὐφημίαις τε παντοδαπαῖς καὶ στεφάνων καὶ ἀνθέων βολαῖς ὑπεδέχοντο. ὡς δ' ἐς τὴν Ῥώμην εἰσήλασεν, ἔς τε τοῦ Διὸς τὸ τέμενος καὶ τοὺς ἄλλους νεὼς ἀνελθὼν εὐθὺς τῇ τε συγκλήτῳ καὶ τοῖς ἐν Ῥώμῃ καταλειφθεῖσι στρατιώταις χαριστήρια ὁμολογήσας τῆς φυλαχθείσης πίστεως, ἐς τὴν βασίλειον αὐλὴν ἀνεχώρησεν.

Marius Maximus

The most obvious historical source for the *Vita Commodi* was Marius Maximus,[74] who was referred to in the text on two separate occasions by the biographer in this *vita*.[75] However, across all of the *vitae* in the *Historia Augusta* Marius Maximus has been referred to on twenty-six occasions.[76] Marius Maximus was a senator and wrote a series of biographies (or a history) from the reigns of Nerva to Elagabalus.[77] But the proposed career of Marius Maximus and his influences have been previously discussed at length by Birley.[78] For the purposes of the present discussion it is most important to note that the *Vita Commodi* has produced two direct references to the use of Marius Maximus as a source and that this is the only literary source mentioned within the entire *Vita*.[79] In view of the numerous direct references to Marius Maximus in the early biographies of the *HA*,[80] it is quite clear that his *Life of Commodus* had an influence on the creation of the *Vita Commodi* in the *Historia Augusta*.[81] Of course, the two references to Marius Maximus in the *Commodus* were associated with negative aspects of the emperor's character, and it is significant that both of these were associated with direct references in his text. This not only highlights the importance of this source for the *HA* biographer, but also exemplifies the inherent negativity towards Commodus in Marius' own biography of him. All the same, while noting the significance and influence of Marius Maximus is important, little else can be deduced about his writings on Commo-

---

[74] cf. F. Paschoud, "Propos sceptiques et iconoclasts sur Marius Maximus", *HAC* 1998, 1999, pp. 241-54.

[75] *HA Commodus* 13.3, 18.2.

[76] *HA Hadrian* 2.10, 12.4, 20.3, 25.4; *Aelius* 3.9, 5.5; *Pius* 11.3; *Marcus* 1.6, 25.11; *Avidius* 6.7; *Commodus* 13.3, 18.2; *Pertinax* 15.8; *Severus* 15.7; *Clodius Albinus* 3.4, 9.2; *Geta* 2.1; *Elagabalus* 11.6; *Alex. Sev.* 5.4, 15.8, 21.4, 30.6, 48.6, 65.4; *Quad. Tyr.* 1.1, 1.2.

[77] K.P. Johne, "Die Epitome de Caesaribus und die Historia Augusta", *Klio* 59.2, 1977, p. 498.

[78] A.R. Birley, "Marius Maximus: the consular biographer", *ANRW* 34.3, 1997, pp. 2678-757; See also R.P.H. Green, "Marius Maximus and Ausonius' Caesars", *CQ* 31.1, 1981, pp. 226-36.

[79] Against this view, see J.F. Matthews, "Marcus Aurelius", *JRS* 58, 1968, p. 263.

[80] Birley 1997, *op.cit.*, pp. 2684-93.

[81] cf. A.R. Birley, "Indirect Means of Tracing Marius Maximus", *HAC* 1992, 1995, pp. 57-74.

dus. The same can be said for the remaining three literary sources on him, who only provide cursory accounts of his principate: Aurelius Victor, the *Epitomator* and Eutropius. Each of these authors influenced the later *HA*, which gives a fuller account of his reign, but they also need to be considered in isolation.

Aurelius Victor

As stated previously, Aurelius Victor was another author who had an influence on the development of the *HA*,[82] which is shown by Dessau.[83] This influence makes a clear case for why the *HA* must be dated to the post-AD 360 period.[84] Aurelius Victor was born just after AD 320 in Africa,[85] and he stated that he was from quite modest origins.[86] The evidence for the use of the *Liber De Caesaribus* as a source by the biographer of the *HA* has been previously established,[87] which provides a strong indication of the late 4th Century dating for the *HA*.[88] As far as his sources are concerned, it is quite likely that Aurelius Victor used Suetonius as a source,[89] but it is also evident that he was not always careful with his sources either.[90] The *Liber De Caesaribus* was written in a biographical style and was also clearly intended as a platform by which Aurelius Victor could express his personal opinions about his subject matter.[91] This is particularly

---

[82] cf. A. Chastagnol, "L'Utilisation des 'Cesars' d'Aurelius Victor dans l'Histoire Auguste", *HAC* 1966/7, 1968, pp. 53-65.

[83] Dessau 1889, *op.cit.*, pp. 363ff; M. Festy, "Aurélius Victor, source de l'Histoire Auguste et de Nicomaque Flavien", *HAC* 1998, 1999, pp. 121-34.

[84] Barnes 1978, *op.cit.*, p. 17.

[85] H.W. Bird, *Sextus Aurelius Victor: a historiographical study*, Liverpool: Francis Cairns, 1984, p. 5.

[86] Aurelius Victor *Liber De Caesaribus*, 20.5.

[87] Bird 1993, *op.cit.*, pp. 122-6; *Liber De Caesaribus of Sextus Aurelius Victor*, Liverpool: Liverpool University Press, 1994, pp. xii-xiv; R. Syme, "The Historia Augusta: a call of clarity", *Antiquitas* 4, 1971, pp. 38-44; A. Chastagnol, "Le Problème de l'Histoire Auguste: état de la question", *HAC* 1963, 1964, pp. 43ff.

[88] A. Momigliano, "An Unsolved Problem of Historical Forgery: the *Scriptores Historiae Augustae*", in *Studies in Historiography*, London, 1966, p. 152.

[89] C.E.V. Nixon, *An Historiographical Study of the Caesares of Sextus Aurelius Victor*, diss. Michigan, 1971, p. 149.

[90] Bird 1984, *op.cit.*, p. 22; H.W. Bird, "The Sources of the De Caesaribus", *CQ* 31.2, 1981, pp. 457-63.

[91] Bird 1994, *op.cit.*, p. xv.

evident in relation to his brief, but scathing treatment of 'bad' emperors, such as Commodus Antoninus.[92]

As Bird has noted,[93] Aurelius Victor's treatment of Commodus was clearly tied to the author's view that great men produce bad offspring.[94] This fatalistic interpretation provides a different account to the other literary sources that have been previously discussed. For example, the biographer of the *Historia Augusta* attributed the early signs of depravity as being a sign of Commodus' rejection of his excellent tuition rather than as a direct result of Marcus' worth.[95] However, he does also claim in the *Vita Marci* that Commodus was actually the son of a gladiator,[96] which may have been an attempt to absolve Marcus of any 'blame' for Commodus' behaviour. All the same, Aurelius Victor still emphasises the base character of Commodus,[97] despite the comparative brevity of his account. Nevertheless, it should also be noted that he was also fully aware of the shortcomings that existed within the senatorial class,[98] so his account was more guided by his own idealism about how the state *should* be run than any class affiliations. Another brief but significant 4th Century literary source on Commodus Antoninus was the *Epitome De Caesaribus*.

The *Epitomator*

The *Epitome De Caesaribus* has previously been attributed to the authorship of Aurelius Victor, but it is quite clear that it was written by a different author.[99] Composition of the *Epitome* has been dated to just after AD 395,[100] which means that it was probably written slightly later than the *Historia Augusta*. As a historical source, this text is seemingly more accurate than the works of Aurelius Victor and Eu-

---

[92] Aurelius Victor *De Caesaribus* 17.1-7.

[93] Bird 1984, *op.cit.*, p. 85.

[94] Aurelius Victor *De Caesaribus* 3.5, 17.1.

[95] *Commmodus* 1.7-9, 2.6-9.

[96] *Marcus* 19.1-6.

[97] Aurelius Victor *De Caesaribus* 17.4-7.

[98] Bird 1984, *op.cit.*, pp. 24-40.

[99] J. Schlumberger, *Die Epitome de Caesaribus: Untersuchungen zur heidnischen Geschichtsschreibung des 4. jahrhunderts n. Chr.*, C.H. Beck: Munich, 1974, pp. 5-8.

[100] A. Cameron, "The *Epitome De Caesaribus* and the *Chronicle* of Marcellinus", *CQ* 51.1, 2001, p. 324.

tropius,[101] with the regular inclusion of exact periods for the reigns of various emperors.[102] All the same, it is quite clear that both Aurelius Victor and Marius Maximus were used as sources of information by the anonymous *Epitomator*.[103] Nevertheless, it is also evident that the number of sources used by them was quite limited,[104] with so many key details of Commodus' reign being omitted by the author.

As with the *De Caesaribus* by Aurelius Victor, the amount of space dedicated to Commodus in the *Epitome De Caesaribus* is quite limited. In fact only one section is dedicated to his principate,[105] and the amount of detail is incredibly selective by the *Epitomator*. Schlumberger has noted the similarities and differences between this account and those by other 4th Century authors,[106] but there are really only five themes mentioned by the *Epitomator*: the truce of AD 180, Commodus' base character, his gladiatorial combats, the conspiracies against him and his assassination.[107] These topics are frequently the dominating aspects in the other ancient literary sources, which illustrate both the consistently negative portrayal of Commodus and also the common sources that were used by these 4th Century writers. This also illustrates how the pervasive nature of this negative interpretation of Commodus was already well established by this time. A similar set of themes is also apparent in the *Breviarium Ab Urbe Condita* by Eutropius.

Eutropius

Eutropius[108] was probably used as a source for the composition of the *HA*,[109] judging from its similarities with the *Breviarium Ab Urbe Condita*. He served as *magister epistularum* for Constantius and was

---

[101] T.D. Barnes, "The *Epitome De Caesaribus* and its Sources", *CPh* 71.3, 1976, p. 263.

[102] Cameron 2001, *op.cit.*, p. 325.

[103] Barnes 1976, *op.cit.*, pp. 261, 263.

[104] Cameron 2001, *op.cit.*, p. 327.

[105] *Epitome* 17.1-5.

[106] Schlumberger 1974, *op.cit.*, pp. 105-7.

[107] *Epitome* 17.1-5.

[108] See J. Hellegouarc'h, *Eutrope: abrégé d'Histoire Romaine*, Belles Lettres: Paris, 1999, pp. vii-xi.

[109] Barnes 1978, *op.cit.*, pp. 95-7; W. Schmid, "Eutropsuren in der Historia Augusta", *HAC* 1963, 1964, pp. 123-33; J. Schwendemann, *Der historische Wert der Vita Marci bei den Scriptores Historiae Augustae*, C. Winter: Heidelberg, 1923, pp. 197-205.

probably born just after AD 320.[110] This is the only extant work attributed to Eutropius,[111] and it was clearly intended for a wide (populist?) audience in view of the brevity of the entries and the simplicity of his language.[112] All the same, as mentioned by Bird,[113] it is also possible that some political emphasis may have also been intended by the author, but this has also been questioned.[114] This makes it difficult to definitively ascertain the entire career of Eutropius,[115] but for the present discussion it is most important to note the breadth of the intended audience for the *Breviarium Ab Urbe Condita.*

As would be expected from the title of Eutropius' history, the amount of detail provided upon Commodus is suitable brief.[116] There are clear similarities between this passage and the other 4th Century historians, which may indicate some use of similar sources, even though he mentions them infrequently.[117] However, there are also points where he disagrees with the other authors in relation to Commodus, such as about his consecration,[118] although the confusion could be a result of the limited details in his account.[119] All the same, Eutropius clearly represents the continuation of the anti-Commodus tradition that is evident within all of the ancient literary sources. He continued to emphasise his lewd, depraved and cruel nature,[120] even though the brevity of his work precluded the inclusion of examples to support such statements.

When all of these literary sources are considered there is one theme that binds them together: their audience. For the most part the intended audience for these works would have been the social élites, particularly in Rome. This may have been slightly different for the later 4th Century historians, who seemingly also had the imperial audiences in mind, but, nonetheless, the influential members of Roman society (namely the Roman Senate) would have been the most

---

[110] Bird 1993, *op.cit.*, p. vii.

[111] R. Rees, "Eutropius", *CR* 48.1, 1998, p. 65.

[112] c.f. P.K. Marshall, "Eutropius", *CR* 51.2, 2001, p. 271.

[113] Bird 1993, *op.cit.*, pp. xix-xx.

[114] R.W. Burgess, "Eutropius v.c. *Magister Memoriae?*", *CPh* 96.1, 2001, pp. 76-81.

[115] W. Den Boer, *Some Minor Roman Historians*, Brill: Leiden, 1972, p. 115.

[116] Eutropius 15.

[117] Den Boer 1972, *op.cit.*, p. 116.

[118] Aurelius Victor *De Caesaribus* 20.30.

[119] Den Boer 1972, *op.cit.*, pp. 154-5.

[120] Eutropius 15.

likely group to have access to their works. Particularly in relation to an anti-senatorial figure like Commodus Antoninus this is highly significant. Their audiences would not have been entirely welcoming to a representation of Commodus that portrayed him as a well-respected and balanced *princeps*, which may explain part of the anti-Commodus stance that continued long after his assassination in AD 192. Nonetheless, the ancient literary sources provide a valuable source of evidence for an understanding of Commodus' perspectives, if these texts are analysed critically in order to gaze beyond their authors' predispositions.

Of course it is evident that the amounts of available evidence from these texts varies significantly, with Cassius Dio, Herodian and the *Historia Augusta* providing the most detail on Commodus' principate. All the same, it is vital to note the consistency in the themes across the board, regardless of the details on Commodus Antoninus. He is repeatedly shown as base, cruel, impious and corrupt by these authors, which illustrates the negative tradition that was well and truly established about Commodus by the 4th Century AD. Nevertheless, there must have been some basis for these claims, despite the clear influence that the 3rd Century sources had upon the succeeding texts that continued the tradition of these representations. It is for this reason that additional sources of information must be utilised for any study of Commodus Antoninus. The prosopographical, numismatic and sculptural evidence provides a different source of information (with their own corresponding set of interpretative issues), but the archaeological material from the period is also of great use for an analysis of this *princeps*.

The Archaeological Record

The archaeological evidence for the reign of Commodus is quite problematic due to the numerous changes that occurred to structures that he erected after the end of his reign. One of the most important archaeological features to be evaluated is the Villa of the Quintili, which was the suburban villa that Commodus acquired on the *Via Appia* outside of Rome. This building has been examined using a statistical methodology to analyse the areas that were potentially used for an entertainment function.[121] Firstly, the finds and

---

[121] For further discussion of the uses of this methodology see G.W. Adams, *The Suburban Villas of Campania and their Social Function*, Archaeopress: Oxford, 2006.

layout of each site are examined where possible, including their distance from the respective urban centres, as well as the levels of wealth displayed in the architecture and decoration of the building. This allows for further insight into the social standing and the activities of the owners of these structures.[122] The most important aspect is the variation in the percentage of space allocated for potential entertainment within the structures. This has been done in a similar way to the study of De Kind on townhouses in Herculaneum.[123] The statistics have derived from the potential entertainment space, in order to ascertain the possible social role of the residence. The statistical analysis is divided in three ways. The first was to gather all of the surface areas for potential entertainment space, including all known open areas, such as gardens and courtyards. The second method excludes all open areas from the potential entertainment space results. The third includes open areas with an element of decorative pretension. The information collected using these methods was then converted into percentages to determine the social emphasis placed upon the various Imperial residences.

There are four reasons why social space has been considered in these different ways. Firstly, owing to the varying roles that open areas served within many residences, by considering potential entertainment space in these ways, the most accurate results can be achieved. Secondly, the exclusion of open areas should avoid false interpretations at some sites with incomplete extant floor plans. It also indicates the amount of focus upon internal or external entertainment. Thirdly, due to the varying levels of extant remains at several Imperial residences it allows for greater interpretation at sites with limited information. Finally, the conversion of the results into percentages allows for a comparison of not only how much space was used for prospective entertainment, but also the varying emphasis placed upon entertainment by each Emperor. The results of this have been compared to the extant features from other Imperial villas, such as the villas of Livia, Domitian, Trajan, Hadrian and Antoninus Pius, which is intended to place the social emphasis of the structure within its historical context. Commodus would have ac-

---

[122] P.M. Allison, "The relationship between wall-decoration and room-type in Pompeian houses: a case study of the Casa della Caccia Antica", *JRA* 5, 1992, p. 248.

[123] De Kind, R.E.L.B., *Houses in Herculaneum: a new view on the town planning and the building of Insulae III and IV*, J.C. Gieben: Amsterdam, 1998.

quired these imperial properties as well, which provides an additional source of inquiry in relation to why he felt it was necessary to take this suburban residence in particular. In order to not only compare these structures within a broader context, but also to examine the priorities of Commodus, these structures have been measured against the imperial palace on the Palatine Hill. These analyses have been implemented in order to gain further insight into the provision for social activities that Commodus Antoninus sought in his Imperial residence, thereby ascertaining his socio-political priorities.

The Epigraphic, Sculptural and Numismatic Evidence

The epigraphic records taken from the reign of Commodus have significantly added to the development of this study as much as the numismatic evidence, providing valuable details that supports the other forms of information. The inscriptional evidence used in this study has been in relation to various different areas, such as career inscriptions, religious dedications and official decrees. Epigraphic evidence is important because it frequently predates many of the ancient literary texts that are used as evidence,[124] as well as being dated to the precise period under question, which is in this instance the reigns of Marcus Aurelius and Commodus Antoninus. They can also provide evidence that has not been mentioned in the literary sources,[125] or make mention of buildings that are no longer extant within the archaeological record. The provenance of these inscriptions is important to note,[126] but this significant piece of information is frequently undocumented, making this impossible. The majority of inscriptions used within this study have been published in the *Corpus Inscriptionum Latinorum* (*CIL*) or *Inscriptiones Latinae Selectae* (*ILS*) collections, which are the major sources of reference throughout the study.

One of the most useful texts for a prosopographical analysis of Commodus' principate is Leunissen (1989), which has traced the vast majority of consular positions between AD 180-192. However, the works of Alföldy and Hammond are also of great use for an under-

---

[124] J.E. Sandys, *Latin Epigraphy: an introduction to the study of Latin Inscriptions*, Ares Publishers: Chicago, 1927, p. 2.
[125] L. Keppie, *Understanding Roman Inscriptions*, Batsford: London, 1991, p. 9.
[126] A.E. Gordon, *Illustrated Introduction to Latin Epigraphy*, University of California Press: Berkeley, 1983, pp. 4-5.

standing of his administrative policies.[127] This form of analysis is also important because it is clear that Commodus introduce a change in the consular ranks during his reign,[128] which can provide further insight into his administrative priorities. This source of information is vital for any understanding of Commodus' efficacy as a ruler, and can further illustrate the difficulties in basing a view of him only on one type of evidence. But as far as the epigraphic evidence is concerned, Leunissen has compiled a large amount of information,[129] which has added greatly to the present study. All the same, it is also necessary to note the significance of other forms of ancient evidence, such as the sculptural works on Commodus Antoninus.

As Hekster has noted,[130] the use of sculptural evidence for the reign of Commodus is of some importance for the analysis of his principate. These representations were not only significant for the preservation of his historical portraits,[131] but were also vital for his imperial propaganda, which was essential for the delivery of his socio-political and religious themes to the wider population.[132] This process of conveying political messages through sculpture had been actively used since the reign of Augustus,[133] and comprised a variety of techniques that embodied the allegorical, symbolical and illustrative elements of these art forms and their symbolism.[134] All the same, it must also be noted that a large number of these sculptures were not directly commissioned by the emperor,[135] and were also indica-

---

[127] G. Alfody, *Konsulat und Senatorenstand unter den Antoninen: Prosopographische Untersuchungen zur Senatorischen Führungsschicht*, Antiquitas 1.27: Bonn, 1977; M. Hammond, *The Antonine Monarchy*, Papers and Monographs of the American Academy in Rome 19: Rome, 1959.

[128] Leunissen 1989, *op.cit.*, pp. 71-3.

[129] B.M. Levick, "Konsuln und Konsulare in der Zeit von Commodus bis Severus Alexander (Review)", *CR* 42.1, 1992, p. 116.

[130] Hekster 2002, *op.cit.*, pp. 3-4.

[131] J.M.C. Toynbee, *Roman Historical Portraits*, Thames and Hudson: London, 1978, p. 9.

[132] P. Stewart, *Statues in Roman Society: representation and response*, Oxford University Press: Oxford, 2003, p. 271.

[133] P. Zanker, *The Power of Images in the Age of Augustus*, University of Michigan Press: Ann Arbor, 1988.

[134] P.G. Hamberg, *Studies in Roman Imperial Art*, L'erma di Bretschneider: Rome, 1968, pp. 41-2.

[135] C.B. Rose, *Dynastic Commemoration and Imperial Portraiture in the Julio-Claudian Period*, Cambridge University Press: Cambridge, 1997, p. 51.

tive of the interpretation of these themes/policies (and of Commodus himself) by those beyond the imperial household. Nevertheless, much of their inspiration would have also derived from officially commissioned pieces, which in turn makes them an invaluable source of information.

In relation to Commodus and his portraiture there is some difficulty in view of the *damnatio memoriae* that was officially declared following his reign,[136] which was seemingly celebrated after his assassination according to the *HA* biographer (*Commodus* 18-19):

Adclamationes senatus post mortem Commodi graves fuerunt. ut autem sciretur quod iudicium senatus de Commodo fuerit, ipsas adclamationes de Mario Maximo indidi et sententiam senatus consulti: "Hosti patriae honores detrahantur. parricidae honores detrahantur. parricida trahatur. hostis patriae, parricida, gladiator in spoliario lanietur. hostis deorum, carnifex senatus, hostis deorum, parricida senatus; hostis deorum, hostis senatus. gladiatorem in spoliario. qui senatum occidit, in spoliario ponatur; qui senatum occidit, unco trahatur; qui innocentes occidit, unco trahatur. hostis, parricida, vere vere, qui sanguini suo non pepercit, unco trahatur. qui te occisurus fuit, unco trahatur. nobiscum timuisti, nobiscum periclitatus es. ut salvi simus, Iuppiter optime maxime, serva nobis Pertinacem. 8 fidei praetorianorum feliciter. praetoriis cohortibus feliciter. exercitibus Romanis feliciter. pietati senatus feliciter. Parricida trahatur. rogamus, Auguste, parricida trahatur. hoc rogamus, parricida trahatur. exaudi Caesar: delatores ad leonem. exaudi Caesar: Speratum ad leonem. victoriae populi Romani feliciter. fidei militum feliciter. fidei praetorianorum feliciter. cohortibus praetoriis feliciter. Hostis statuas undique, parricidae statuas undique, gladiatoris statuas undique. gladiatoris et parricidae statuae detrahantur. necator civium trahatur. parricida civium trahatur. gladiatoris statuae detrahantur. te salvo salvi et securi sumus, vere vere, modo vere, modo digne, modo vere, modo libere. Nunc securi sumus; delatoribus metum. ut securi simus, delatoribus metum. ut salvi simus, delatores de senatu, delatoribus fustem. te salvo delatorum ad leonem. te imperante delatoribus fustem. [19] Parricidae gladiatoris memoria aboleatur, parricidae gladiatoris statuae detrahantur. impuri gladiatoris memoria aboleatur. gladiatorem in spoliario. exaudi Caesar: carnifex unco trahatur. carnifex senatus more maiorum unco trahatur. saevior Domitiano, impurior Nerone. sic fecit, sic patiatur. memoriae innocentium serventur. honores innocentium restituas, rogamus. parricidae cadaver unco trahatur. gladiatoris cadaver unco trahatur. gladiatoris cadaver in spoliario ponatur. perroga, perroga: omnes censemus unco trahendum. qui omnes occidit, unco trahatur. qui omnem aetatem occidit, unco trahatur. qui utrumque sexum occidit, unco trahatur. qui sanguini suo non pepercit, unco trahatur. qui templa spoliavit, unco trahatur. qui testamenta delevit, unco trahatur. qui vivos spoliavit, unco trahatur. servis serviimus. qui pretia vitae exegit, unco trahatur. qui pretia vitae exegit et fidem non servavit, unco trahatur. qui senatum vendidit, unco trahatur. qui filiis abstulit hereditatem, unco trahatur. Indices de senatu, delatores de senatu, servorum subornatores de senatu. et tu nobiscum timuisti; omnia scis et bonos et malos nosti. omnia scis, omnia emenda; pro te timuimus. o nos felices, te vere imperante! de parricida refer, refer, perroga. praesentiam tuam rogamus. innocentes sepulti non sunt. parricidae cadaver trahatur. parricida sepultos eruit; parricidae cadaver trahatur."

Loud were the acclamations of the senate after the death of Commodus. And that the senate's opinion of him may be known, I have quoted from Marius Maximus the

---

[136] Stewart 2003, *op.cit.*, p. 273.

acclamations themselves, and the content of the senate's decree: "From him who was a foe of his fatherland let his honours be taken away; let the honours of the murderer be taken away; let the murderer be dragged in the dust. The foe of his fatherland, the murderer, the gladiator, in the charnel-house let him be mangled. He is foe to the gods, slayer of the senate, foe to the gods, murderer of the senate, foe of the gods, foe of the gods, foe of the senate. Cast the gladiator into the charnel-house. He who slew the senate, let him be dragged with the hook; he who slew the guiltless, let him be dragged with the hook – a foe, a murderer, verily, verily. He who spared not his own blood, let him be dragged with the hook; he who would have slain you, let him be dragged with the hook. You were in terror along with us, you were endangered along with us. That we may be safe, O Jupiter Best and Greatest, save for us Pertinax. Long life to the guardian care of the praetorians! Long life to the praetorian cohorts! Long life to the armies of Rome! Long life to the loyalty of the senate! Let the murderer be dragged in the dust. We beseech you, O Sire, let the murderer be dragged in the dust. This we beseech you, let the murderer be dragged in the dust. Hearken, Caesar: to the lions with the informers! Hearken Caesar: to the lions with Speratus! Long life to the victory of the Roman people! Long life to the soldiers' guardian care! Long life to the guardian care of the praetorians! Long life to the praetorian cohorts! On all sides are statues of the foe, on all side are statues of the murderer, on all sides are statues of the gladiator. The statues of the murderer and gladiator, let them be cast down. The slayer of citizens, let him be dragged in the dust. The murderer of citizens, let him be dragged in the dust. Let the statues of the gladiator be overthrown. While you are safe, we too are safe and untroubled, verily, verily, if in very truth, then with honour, if in very truth, then with freedom. Now at last we are secure; let informers tremble. That we may be secure, let the informers tremble. That we may be safe, cast informers out of the senate, the club for informers! While you are safe, to the lions with informers! While you are ruler, the club for informers! **[19]** Let the memory of the murderer and the gladiator be utterly wiped away. Let the statues of the murderer and the gladiator be overthrown. Let the memory of the foul gladiator be utterly wiped away. Cast the gladiator into the charnel-house. Hearken, Caesar: let the slayer be dragged with the hook. In the manner of our fathers let the slayer of the senate be dragged with the hook. More savage than Domitian, more foul than Nero. As he did unto others, let it be done unto him. Let the remembrance of the guiltless be preserved. Restore the honours of the guiltless, we beseech you. Let the body of the murderer be dragged with the hook, let the body of the gladiator be dragged with the hook, let the body of the gladiator be cast into the charnel-house. Call for our vote, call for our vote: with one accord we reply, let him be dragged with the hook. He who slew all men, let him be dragged with the hook. He who slew young and old, let him be dragged with the hook. He who slew man and woman, let him be dragged with the hook. He who spared not his own blood, let him be dragged with the hook. He who plundered temples, let him be dragged with the hook. He who set aside the testaments of the dead, let him be dragged with the hook. He who plundered the living, let him be dragged with the hook. We have been slaves to slaves. He who demanded a price for the life of a man, let him be dragged with the hook. He who demanded a price for a life and kept not his promise, let him be dragged with the hook. He who sold the senate, let him be dragged with the hook. He who took from sons their patrimony, let him be dragged with the hook. Spies and informers, cast them out of the senate. Suborners of slaves, cast them out of the senate. You, too, were in terror along with us; you know all, you know both the good and the evil. You know all that we were forced to purchase; all we have feared for your sake. Happy are we, now that you are the emperor in truth. Put it to the vote concerning the murderer, put it to the vote, put the question. We ask your presence. The guiltless are yet unburied; let the body of the murderer be dragged in the dust. The murderer dug up the buried; let the body of the murderer be dragged in the dust."

According to Cassius Dio (74.2.1), this was actively undertaken after his death as a symbolic damnation of his reign as well:[137]

καὶ οὕτως ὅ τε Περτίναξ αὐτοκράτωρ καὶ ὁ Κόμμοδος πολέμιος ἀπεδείχθη, πολλά γε ἐς αὐτὸν καὶ δεινὰ καὶ τῆς βουλῆς καὶ τοῦ δήμου συμβοησάντων. ἠθέλησαν μὲν γὰρ καὶ τὸ σῶμα αὐτοῦ σῦραι καὶ διασπάσαι ὥσπερ καὶ τὰς εἰκόνας, εἰπόντος δὲ τοῦ Περτίνακος τῇ γῇ ἤδη τὸν νεκρὸν κεκρύφθαι, τοῦ μὲν σώματος ἀπέσχοντο, τῶν δ' ἄλλων ἐνεφοροῦντο, οὐδὲν ὅ τι οὐκ ἐπιλέγοντες· Κόμμοδον μὲν γὰρ οὐδεὶς οὐδ' αὐτοκράτορα αὐτὸν ὠνόμαζεν, ἀλιτήριον δέ τινα καὶ τύραννον ἀποκαλοῦντες προσετίθεσαν ἐπισκώπτοντες τὸν μονομάχον, τὸν ἁρματηλάτην, τὸν ἀριστερόν, τὸν κηλήτην.

'In this way Pertinax was declared emperor and Commodus a public enemy, after both the senate and the populace had joined in shouting many bitter words against the latter. They wanted to drag off his body and tear it from limb to limb, as they did do, in fact, with his statues; but when Pertinax informed them that the corpse had already been interred, they spared his remains, but glutted their rage against him in other ways, calling him all sorts of names. For no one called him Commodus or emperor; instead they referred to him as an accursed wretch and a tyrant, adding in jest such terms as 'the gladiator,' 'the charioteer,' 'the left-handed,' 'the ruptured.'

Nevertheless, there is still a good amount of sculptural material to be considered in relation to both Commodus' principate and his socio-political propaganda.[138] One of the best examples of this is the Column of Marcus Aurelius, which was intended to commemorate the victories against the Marcomanni and the Sarmatians in AD 172 and 175.[139] While this column was intended to commemorate his father, it still holds important dynastic symbolism for his son, which is particularly significant because it was not completed until AD 193,[140] which means that Commodus would have been largely responsible for its construction. This monument provides a clearly different portrayal of Commodus' foreign policy to the ancient literary sources and illustrates why it is important to consider this form of evidence when undertaking a study of his principate.

---

[137] Stewart 2003, *op.cit.*, p. 275.

[138] Hekster 2002, *op.cit.*, p.3.

[139] D.E. Strong, *Roman Imperial Sculpture*, Alec Tiranti: London, 1961, p. 56.

[140] Strong 1961, *op.cit.*

The numismatic evidence from the reign of Commodus Antoninus has also been of great assistance to this study of his reign. The benefits of this source of information have been taken from not only the various Imperial and religious imagery on his issues, but also from the general monetary policies of Commodus. The use of numismatic imagery has proven to be of great use when determining the important and prevalent policies of various Roman Emperors,[141] with no exception the reign of Commodus Antoninus. Considering that the prime focus of this study is the autocratic/Hellenistic views of Commodus, this imagery is of great importance.[142] These images not only reflect how he himself wanted to be viewed by the Roman public, but also the socio-political themes advertised as being important to his regime. Ancient coinage after all was a useful tool for spreading propaganda,[143] throughout not only Rome, but also the entire Empire. The importance of numismatic imagery to Commodus is also shown through his general policies for the various issues from both the both Imperial and Senatorial mints.[144]

The importance of this numismatic imagery as a means of conveying political propaganda has been highlighted by Kaiser-Raiß (1980), which was clearly used by Commodus during his principate. As with many of his predecessors,[145] he emphasised the benefits of his reign by representing Jupiter,[146] *Securitas*,[147] and *Concordia*,[148] on his issues, but *Virtus*,[149] and *Fides*,[150] were other common themes on his coinage as well. However, it is also essential to note that he also ac-

---

[141] C.H.V. Sutherland, *History and Coinage 44BC-AD69*, Oxford University Press: Oxford, 1987; C. Foss, *Roman Historical Coins*, Seaby: London, 1990.

[142] c.f. W.E. Metcalf, "Coins as Primary Evidence", in G.M. Paul (ed.), *Roman Coins and Public Life under the Empire: E. Togo Salmon Papers II*, University of Michigan Press: Ann Arbor, 1999, p. 3.

[143] C. Howgego, *Ancient History from Coins*, Routledge: London, 1995, pp. 70-3.

[144] C.H.V. Sutherland, "Roman Coinage from Antoninus to Commodus", *CR* 55.2, 1941, p. 94.

[145] A. Wallace-Hadrill, "The Emperor and his Virtues", *Historia* 30.3, 1981, pp. 298-323.

[146] *BMC* 118; *RIC* 88, 101, 138, 152, 173, 187, 255.

[147] *RIC* 23, 179, 190.

[148] *RIC* 198b, 219.

[149] *RIC* 71, 160, 292; Kaiser-Raiß 1980, *op.cit.*, p. 45.

[150] *RIC* 75, 220, 232, 233, 608.

centuated his *nobilitas*,[151] and his good relations with the military,[152] who were clearly seen as a vital support base by him. Hercules was another significant character to be portrayed,[153] which may add some support to the literary representations of his affinity with this deity.[154] So as can be seen, these themes cover a wide range of aspects that are intrinsically connected to his principate and its subsequent interpretation, which makes them an invaluable source of information for the present study.

All the same, the production of these coins within the wider historical context of the Roman economy is also important to consider. This is a vital aspect to note in view of the later 3rd Century fiscal collapse,[155] which could be connected to Commodus' mismanagement of the empire.[156] It is significant to note that while commerce and industry saw a great amount of decentralisation in the 2nd Century AD,[157] the production of coinage remained largely centralised, which resulted in a strain on government resources.[158] This is particularly the case in relation to Commodus who actually reduced the number of mints outside the capital.[159] As shown by the gradual debasement of the precious metal issues, the state finances were

---

[151] *BMC* 216; *RIC* 155, 501.

[152] *RIC* 128.

[153] *RIC* 221, 253, 254a, 254b, 259, 365, 641.

[154] C.E. King, "Roman Portraiture: Images of Power?", in Paul, G.M. (ed.), *Roman coins and Public Life under the Empire: E. Togo Salmon Papers II*, University of Michigan Press: Ann Arbor, 1999, p. 133.

[155] S. Williams, *Diocletian and the Roman Recovery*, Batsford: London, 1985, pp. 15-23.

[156] Dio 72.36.4; Herodian 1.1.4; L. De Blois, "The Third Century and the Greek Elite in the Roman Empire", *Historia*, 33.3, 1984, pp. 363-6.

[157] M. Rostovtzeff, M., 1957, *The Social and Economic History of the Roman Empire*, Vol. 1, Oxford University Press: Oxford, 1957, pp. 165-9; K. Hopkins, "Taxes and Trade in the Roman Empire", *JRS* 70, 1980, pp. 101-25; G. Woolf, "Imperialism, empire and the integration of the Roman economy", *World Archaeology* 23.3, 1992, p. 283; P. Temin, "A Market Economy in the Early Roman Empire", *JRS* 91, 2001, p. 169.

[158] H. Mattingly, *Roman Coins: from the earliest times to the fall of the western empire*, Methuen: London, 1927, pp. 116.

[159] P. Bruun, "Coins and the Roman Imperial Government", in G.M. Paul (ed.), *Roman Coins and Public Life under the Empire: E. Togo Salmon Papers II*, University of Michigan Press: Ann Arbor, 1999, p. 32.

under a great deal of pressure throughout the 2nd Century AD,[160] and this may have been a controlling response by Commodus, although it could also be viewed as an indication of his personal insecurity about his position. It is for this reason that it is essential to consider Commodus' monetary policies within a wide historical context in order to ascertain his abilities as a fiscal administrator, and in turn his success as *princeps*. Therefore, all of these factors, including the interpretation of his choice of imagery[161] within the numismatic evidence clearly illustrate its great import for this study, thus making a significant contribution to its accuracy.

General Conclusions

The ancient literary evidence for the life and reign of Commodus has always been problematic due largely to the ensuing negative historical tradition that had its origins as early as the 2nd Century AD. The best illustration of how negative this tradition became in antiquity is the examination of how the name of Commodus has been associated with the most depraved or insane activities of other later Roman Emperors, which illustrates how he represented the embodiment of vice and immorality in the ancient mindset.[162] It would be erroneous for the modern viewer to simply take these literary opinions at face value. If these representations were correct it would seem highly unlikely that Commodus would have been viewed as an appropriate Roman Emperor, regardless of how well he hid his vices until after becoming *princeps*.

In order to gain the most accurate assessment of his life and his influences it is important to use all of the evidence available to us and to examine each piece critically and on its merits. The ancient literary evidence is of the greatest importance, but it should be used with the viewpoints of each author in mind. This involves evaluating their motives for writing about each episode and event that sur-

---

[160] Mattingly 1927, *op.cit.*, p. 125; R.P. Duncan-Jones, "The Monetization of the Roman Empire: Regional Variations in the Supply of Coin Types", in Paul, G.M. (ed.), *Roman coins and Public Life under the Empire: E. Togo Salmon Papers II*, University of Michigan Press: Ann Arbor, 1999, p. 79; C. Howgego, "The Supply and Use of Money in the Roman World 200 BC to AD 300", *JRS* 82, 1992, p. 30.

[161] B.M. Levick, "Messages on the Roman Coinage: Types and Inscriptions", in Paul, G.M. (ed.), *Roman coins and Public Life under the Empire: E. Togo Salmon Papers II*, University of Michigan Press: Ann Arbor, 1999, p. 44.

[162] For example see the *HA, Commodus*, 10.2-3.

rounded the life of Commodus. The ancient sources did not simply catalogue the events of the Roman principate; each author was writing with a specific purpose and audience in mind, which coloured their portrayal of him and must be heeded. The most effective way in which this can be achieved is to pay an equal amount of attention to the other forms of evidence. The epigraphic and numismatic data for example provides additional insight into the propaganda distributed by Commodus during his reign, as well as an important insight into the state of the Roman finances at the time of his reign. The epigraphic evidence has been useful to view the public interaction that Commodus had with the people of Rome, which emphasises his views on his role as *princeps*. The archaeological evidence from Rome has also added further insight into the life of Commodus, not only contributing to our understanding of his public image, but also his inclinations within the private domain.

It is through these methods that a greater understanding of Commodus is possible, removing the unnecessary historical stigma that has surrounded his reign and allowing for a clearer image of how such a character developed into the so-called 'bloodthirsty and cruel' Roman Emperor. All the same, such an insight is of course limited by the gaps in the available ancient evidence, but an improved perception of Commodus' principate should be possible. It is initially important to view his reign within its historical context, with Commodus being the last *princeps* of a successful phase of the Roman Empire. These Antonine predecessors would have not only affected the later perception of his reign by other people, but these 'good' emperors would have also had a significant impact upon his own views about what it was to be the emperor of Rome. Therefore, it is essential to consider this period prior to analysing Commodus as both a *princeps* and as a human being in general.

CHAPTER 2

THE ANTONINE ERA AND ITS IMPLICATIONS FOR COMMODUS

Introduction

The primary intention of the present chapter is to place Commodus and his principate within a broader historical context. This aims to place the analysis of his reign within the wider framework of the principate in general terms, which is intended to consider the various influences of his predecessors upon him. By considering the implications of the gradual progression of administrative themes during the various reigns prior to his rule, it can provide a more comprehensive perspective about the nature of Commodus' reign and its subsequent interpretation (both by ancient and modern scholars alike). In this regard one of the most pivotal aspects has been the consideration of how each *princeps* has been represented by the ancient sources and how this has affected the critical judgements made about Commodus' principate. However, it must be noted that the analysis has been primarily focused upon the ultimate impact upon Commodus and the anti-Commodus tradition in this regard.

This analysis has been limited to the six imperial predecessors of Commodus from the Antonine Dynasty: Nerva, Trajan, Hadrian, Antoninus Pius, Marcus Aurelius and Lucius Verus. These *principes* provide the most appropriate comparison with Commodus because of their temporal and dynastic connections with him, which is further accentuated by their largely positive portrayal (with only Lucius Verus being the most notable exception). The analysis of these emperors is not intended to be a comprehensive account of their reigns, but is instead simply considered on a purely comparative/influence level in relation to Commodus and his literary representation. In this regard more emphasis has been placed upon the literary sources of evidence because of their focus upon representation and characterisation, which often precludes an emphasis upon factual evidence, such as in the *Historia Augusta*. Epigraphic and numismatic sources have also been used, but this is largely a supplementary form of information for this chapter, which can provide a wider conception of the traditions surrounding the Emperor Commodus.

Nerva

While the Emperor Nerva has a very short reign (AD 96-98), the significance of his principate should not be underestimated.[163] Nerva symbolised an important transition for the imperial state,[164] whereby he was primarily a Senatorial candidate who was not entirely supported by the Roman military.[165] His age was also a significant factor, being sixty years old at the time of his accession.[166] This of course had a direct impact upon the issue of the succession, but this is discussed further below. The lack of political and military experience possessed by Nerva at the point of his accession[167] meant that he quickly sought the support of some influential military figures at the time, such as Licinius Sura,[168] and the future Emperor Trajan.[169] It is for this reason that Nerva becomes significant as a figure for the future of the Roman principate: the tenuous nature of his position within some circles required a delicate balance for the development of his promotion policies, which resulted in the innovative process that he undertook for securing the succession. This was of course absolutely vital for ensuring the overall stability of the State in general terms.

The ancient literary evidence for Nerva is brief and provides little detail. The most comprehensive account is provided by Cassius Dio, and even this section is rather short (68.1.1-4.2). This characterisation not only presented Nerva as old and weak (68.1.3), but also accentuated his respect for the views of his senatorial contemporaries (68.2.3-4). This contrast exhibits the general view presented of the Emperor Nerva: his old age made him weak and malleable, but he still sought to ensure the strength of the Roman State. This final aspect was clearly articulated by Cassius Dio just prior to the death notice for Nerva (68.4.1-2): οὕτω μὲν ὁ Τραϊανὸς Καῖσαρ καὶ μετὰ

---

[163] See Grainger 2003, *op.cit.*
[164] See Murison 2003, op.cit., p. 155.
[165] Grainger 2003, *op.cit.*, p. 32.
[166] *Epit.* 12.11.
[167] Grainger 2003, *op.cit.*, p. 28.
[168] PIR² L253; Jones 1979, *op.cit.*, no. 279; Adams 2001, *op.cit.*
[169] Plin. *Pan.* 5.2-4.

τοῦτο αὐτοκράτωρ ἐγένετο, καίτοι συγγενῶν τοῦ Νέρουα ὄντων τινῶν. ἀλλ' οὐ γὰρ τῆς τῶν κοινῶν σωτηρίας ὁ ἀνὴρ τὴν συγγένειαν προετίμησεν, οὐδ' αὖ ὅτι Ἴβηρ ὁ Τραϊανὸς ἀλλ' οὐκ Ἰταλὸς οὐδ' Ἰταλιώτης ἦν, ἧττόν τι παρὰ τοῦτο αὐτὸν ἐποιήσατο, ἐπειδὴ μηδεὶς πρόσθεν ἀλλοεθνὴς τὸ τῶν Ῥωμαίων κράτος ἐσχήκει· τὴν γὰρ ἀρετὴν ἀλλ' οὐ τὴν πατρίδα τινὸς ἐξετάζειν δεῖν ᾤετο. πράξας δὲ ταῦτα μετήλλαξεν, ἄρξας ἔτει ἑνὶ καὶ μησὶ τέσσαρσι καὶ ἡμέραις ἐννέα· προεβεβιώκει δὲ πέντε καὶ ἑξήκοντα ἔτη καὶ μῆνας δέκα καὶ ἡμέρας δέκα ['Thus Trajan became Caesar and later emperor, although there were relatives of Nerva living. But Nerva did not esteem family relationship above the safety of the State, nor was he less inclined to adopt Trajan because the latter was a Spaniard instead of an Italian or Italiot, inasmuch as no foreigner had previously held the Roman sovereignty; for he believed in looking at a man's ability rather than at his nationality. Soon after this act he passed away, having ruled one year, four months and nine days; his life prior to that time had comprised sixty-five years, ten months and ten days']. It is evident that this representation had little direct correlation with that of Commodus, but in real terms it is possible to view the impact of Nerva upon him. One poignant example was the selection of M. Annius Verus as a consul for AD 97.[170] This was the great-grandfather of Commodus and this appointment of a young man from Uccubi[171] saw his continued promotion under Hadrian,[172] and the gradual rise in prominence of this side of Commodus' ancestry.

The extent of Commodus' imperial inheritance can also be viewed through a comparison of their numismatic iconography. While there are clear differences in their representational emphases, such as Nerva's greater stress upon military harmony[173] and *libertas*,[174] it is evident that this form of iconography was of great importance to both leaders. There are some similarities in theme, such as *aequitas*,[175] Salus,[176] and Fortuna,[177] but it is evident that Nerva was much more

---

[170] PIR² A695; Jones 1979, *op.cit.*, no. 18.
[171] Gardiner 2003, *op.cit.*, p. 42.
[172] *Marcus* 1.
[173] BMC 27, 80; RIC 2-3, 14-15, 26, 48. c.f. Shotter 1983, *op.cit.*, p. 223.
[174] *RIC* 7, 19, 43, 65, 86, 100, 316.
[175] *RIC* Nerva 1, 13, 77; Commodus 120, 164d, 517, 517v.
[176] *RIC* Nerva 9, 20; Commodus 66, 169, 337, 512; Marcus 626, 641, 647, 649, 654, 663.

consistent in his imagery. Commodus did produce a greater variation in topic range, even with the lengths of their reigns being kept in mind, which suggests an attempt to communicate to a wide audience through this medium. However, for the purposes of the present discussion it is most important to note the continuation of particular iconographic traditions from the late First Century AD into the late Second Century AD, which exhibits Commodus' imperial heritage.

One of the most significant features that becomes apparent when considering Commodus' imperial inheritance is the general continuity in many Antonine policies, and this can be traced back to the reign of Nerva. While Gardiner has noted that Nerva largely maintained many of the administrative policies that had been established by Domitian,[178] it is the later continuation of some key official strategies that exhibits Commodus' inheritance. One excellent example of this tradition can be seen in the promotion of the *alimenta* policy that continued throughout the Second Century AD,[179] which was then revised by Pertinax, Commodus' successor.[180] However, what is important to note was the continuation of efficient administrative policy production from this time, particularly in light of the transitional nature of this period. Much of the credit for Nerva's work was ultimately given to Trajan, but it was the establishment and stability of these policies for the most part that would have had a significant impact upon Commodus' principate and its subsequent evaluation.

All the same, the most significant policy introduction by Nerva was in relation to the succession. It is evident that the selection of Trajan was a careful choice, tying in the elements of military connections, familial lineage, social ties and his age at the time.[181] He was adopted in October AD 97,[182] but it seems that there would have been a significant amount of consultation and planning previously in view of how smoothly the process advanced.[183] However, for the purposes of the present study, what is most notable is the introduc-

---

[177] *RIC* Nerva 16, 17, 28, 42, 60, 83, 84, 98-9; Commodus 2, 131, 166a, 172, 191a, 235, 513.

[178] Gardiner 2003, *op.cit.*, pp. 52-65.

[179] Gardiner 2003, *op.cit.*, p. 60.

[180] *Pertinax* 9.3.

[181] Gardiner 2003, *op.cit.*, p. 97.

[182] Plin. *Pan.* 6.3, 6.1-5, 10.1; Dio 68.2.3, 68.3.3-4; Eutr. 8.1.1-2; Victor 13.1.

[183] Gardiner 2003, *op.cit.*, pp. 96, 104.

tion of such an adoption process, which was seemingly based upon merit rather than just birth.[184] Of course in this instance this was largely brought about by necessity, but it is evident that Trajan's adoption was carefully considered in order to maintain the stability of the empire. The move away from hereditary and familial ties between *princeps* and successor was (and still often is) viewed as being a preferable selection option, which has significantly impacted upon the perception of Commodus: he was the first biological son to follow his father as *princeps*, which has been the primary reason for his perceived inability to reign effectively. Clearly this view needs to consider a much wider range of factors in order to be applied to any judgement made about Commodus' reign.

Trajan

When considering the impact/influence of Trajan upon Commodus' principate it is quite difficult to draw any significant connection between the two of them. This is particularly evident when viewing the ancient literary portrayals of both characters: Trajan was exhibited as an active, efficient and capable leader who consistently worked and fought for the advancement of the Roman State, whereas Commodus was largely shown as corrupt, inefficient and incapable of even maintaining the position of the empire in the state that he inherited it. The polarized nature of these characterizations is best presented by Cassius Dio (68.5.4; 73.4.1-4), who accentuates their principates from the outset:

Αἰλιανὸν δὲ καὶ τοὺς δορυφόρους τοὺς κατὰ Νέρουα στασιάσαντας, ὡς καὶ χρησόμενός τι αὐτοῖς, μεταπεμψάμενος ἐκποδὼν ἐποιήσατο. ἐς δὲ τὴν Ῥώμην ἐσελθὼν πολλὰ ἐποίει πρός τε διόρθωσιν τῶν κοινῶν καὶ πρὸς χάριν τῶν ἀγαθῶν, ἐκείνων τε διαφερόντως ἐπιμελούμενος, ὡς καὶ ταῖς πόλεσι ταῖς ἐν Ἰταλίᾳ πρὸς τὴν τῶν παίδων τροφὴν πολλὰ χαρίσασθαι, καὶ τούτους εὐεργετῶν. (68.5.4)

'He sent for Aelianus and the Praetorians who had mutinied against Nerva, pretending that he was going to employ them for some purpose, and then put them out of the way. When he came to Rome, he did much to reform the administration of affairs and much to please the better element; to the public business he gave unusual attention, making many grants, for example, to the cities in Italy for the support of their children, and upon the good citizens he conferred many favours.'

καὶ ἐπεβουλεύθη μὲν πολλάκις ὑπό τινων, πλείστους δὲ ἐφόνευσε καὶ ἄνδρας καὶ γυναῖκας, τοὺς μὲν φανερῶς τοὺς δὲ λάθρα φαρμάκοις, καὶ ὡς εἰπεῖν πάντας τοὺς ἐπὶ

---

[184] cf. Geer 1936, *op.cit.*, p. 47.

49

τοῦ πατρὸς αὐτοῦ καὶ ἐπ' αὐτοῦ ἐκείνου ἀνθήσαντας, πλὴν τοῦ τε Πομπηιανοῦ καὶ τοῦ Περτίνακος καὶ τοῦ Οὐικτωρίνου· τούτους γὰρ οὐκ οἶδ' ὅπως οὐκ ἀπέκτεινε. λέγω δὲ ταῦτά τε καὶ τὰ λοιπὰ οὐκ ἐξ ἀλλοτρίας ἔτι παραδόσεως ἀλλ' ἐξ οἰκείας ἤδη τηρήσεως. ἐλθὼν δὲ ἐς τὴν Ῥώμην καὶ πρὸς τὴν γερουσίαν διαλεχθεὶς ἄλλα τέ τινα ἀπελήρησε, καί τι καὶ τοιοῦτον ἐν τοῖς αὐτοῦ ἐπαίνοις εἶπεν, ὅτι τὸν πατέρα ποτὲ ἐς πηλὸν βαθὺν ἐμπεσόντα ἱππεύων ἐρρύσατο. τοιαῦτα μὲν τὰ σεμνολογήματα αὐτοῦ ἦν, ἐσιόντι δὲ αὐτῷ ἐς τὸ θέατρον τὸ κυνηγετικὸν Κλαύδιος Πομπηιανὸς ἐπεβούλευσε· ξίφος γάρ τι ἐν αὐτῇ τῇ τῆς ἐσόδου στενοχωρίᾳ ἀνατείνας, "ἰδού" ἔφη, "τοῦτό σοι ἡ βουλὴ [οὐ] πέπομφεν". (73.4.1-4)

'Many plots were formed by various people against Commodus, and he killed a great many, both men and women, some openly and some by means of poison, secretly, making away, in fact, with practically all those who had attained eminence during his father's reign and his own, with the exception of Pompeianus, Pertinax and Victorinus; these men for some reason or other he did not kill. I state these and subsequent facts, not, as hitherto, on the authority of others' reports, but from my own observation. On coming to Rome he addressed the senate, uttering a lot of trivialities; and among the various stories that he told in his own praise was one to this effect, that once while out riding he had saved the life of his father, who had fallen into a deep quagmire. Such were his lofty prattlings. But as he was entering the hunting-theatre, Claudius Pompeianus formed a plot against him: thrusting out a sword in the narrow entrance, he said: "See! This is what the senate has sent you."

In many ways Trajan's administration continued (or expanded upon) many of the policies that had been used during the principate of Nerva. He clearly continued the policy of *alimenta*, which was further accentuated by several laws that were concerned with the protection of children.[185] He was depicted as having a strong dedication to jurisprudence,[186] and its implementation was clearly of some importance to him.[187] Trajan's monetary policy also exhibits the continuing emphasis upon strict control that is shown in Nerva's finances. However, it is also evident that his own predilections did influence the recipients of some funding,[188] which exhibits that he was not strictly dedicated to frugality. All the same, one aspect that he did exhibit was a clear deference (or at least respect) to the status and wishes of the Senate.[189] It is in this regard that we can view another clear distinction between Trajan and Commodus, but it must also be noted that the diligent respect of Trajan (and his immediate successors) would only accentuate Commodus' disregard for them even more.

---

[185] Pliny *Ep.* 10.66-7; *Digest* 48.19.5.
[186] *Epit.* 13.
[187] Bennett 2001, *op.cit.*, pp. 120-1.
[188] Pliny *Pan.* 41.1.
[189] Bennett 2001, *op.cit.*, p. 126.

Nevertheless, the diligence and stability of Trajan's administrative policies must be noted as providing an effective inheritance for the succeeding *principes*.

When considering the direct impact of Trajan upon Commodus' ancestry it is possible to note two significant aspects. Firstly, when considering the maternal side of the *familia*, the impact upon Commodus is self-evident with the ancestral line being directly associated between them through the adoption of Antoninus Pius, Commodus' biological grandfather. However, the paternal line is much more significant with there being no consular appointments among the *Annii* during Trajan's reign. It seems notable that Annius Verus (Commodus' great-grandfather) received his first consulship in AD 97, but waited for his second until AD 121 and third consulship in AD 126. This is particularly notable when considering that the *Annii* were seemingly descended from Ulpia Marciana, the sister of Trajan. This not only illustrates the inter-connected nature of these prominent families at the time, but also exhibits the strength of Commodus' lineage and imperial inheritance as a descendant of such prestigious ancestral lines.

As far as the numismatic evidence is concerned, it is clear that Commodus continued to use similar imagery to that of his predecessors like Trajan, particularly with portrayals of *felicitas*,[190] *concordia*,[191] *providentia*,[192] *virtus*,[193] *pax*,[194] Mars,[195] *aequitas*,[196] Victory,[197] Salus,[198] and Fortuna.[199] All the same, it is evident that there was also some clear divergence in their numismatic propaganda, with Trajan having a

---

[190] *RIC* Trajan 13, 56, 120-1, 172, 271, 301, 332, 343-4; Commodus 15a, 15b, 29a, 74, 97, 108, 110, 137, 143, 159, 165.

[191] *RIC* Trajan 2, 12, 31, 33; Commodus 126, 198b, 219, 459c.

[192] *RIC* Trajan 358, 360-1, 364-5, 663, 665; Commodus 19, 44, 50, 65, 259, 312, 379, 641.

[193] *RIC* Trajan 202-4, 334, 353, 355; Commodus 71, 71v, 160, 292a, 505.

[194] *RIC* Trajan 6, 17, 30, 38, 102, 126, 187, 189; Commodus 17, 64, 64v, 86.

[195] *RIC* Trajan 52, 114, 154, 157, 161, 163, 269, 299; Commodus 46, 54, 174v, 175, 188, 257, 527.

[196] *RIC* Trajan 118, 119, 169, 495, 708; Commodus 120, 164d, 517, 517v.

[197] *RIC* Trajan 8, 22, 41, 57-61, 65, 113v, 114, 128; Commodus 4, 12, 49, 58, 69e, 90c, 93, 102, 110, 211.

[198] *RIC* Trajan 148v, 368v, 370, 515; Commodus 66, 169, 337, 512.

[199] *RIC* Trajan 4, 14, 122, 177, 254, 319, 321; Commodus 2, 131, 166a, 172, 191a, 235, 513.

much heavier emphasis upon *abundantia*,[200] Military trophies and standards,[201] building works,[202] and provinces/rivers.[203] This epitomizes the divergence in their principates, but it is also evident that Commodus produced a wider range of imagery that was influenced by later principates, such as those of Antoninus Pius and Marcus Aurelius. However, there are two topics that provide an interesting correlation between these two leaders: Hercules and Spes. Hope (Spes) had been a common motif used by previous emperors,[204] but it is most important to note the use of Hercules as a topic,[205] which was to become a fundamental feature of Commodus' reign.[206]

One other significant aspect to consider when viewing Commodus and Trajan is the topic of the succession. Unlike Nerva, Trajan decided to follow the tradition of naming a relative (albeit a distant one) as his successor, but it is also evident that he ensured that Hadrian had a great deal of experience prior to his accession. So while Trajan departed somewhat from this aspect of Antonine dynastic tradition, it is also evident that he made sure that Hadrian had enough training to be able to serve as a Roman *princeps*. The comparison of Trajan and Commodus is fruitful for the purposes of the present study owing to the stark contrast that exists between the fashions in which their reigns have been described by the ancient sources. The direct link between the two may be minimal, but it is evident that Commodus gained a great deal from the stability that he inherited from his predecessors.

Hadrian

The extant ancient literary evidence for Hadrian, which is most comprehensive in the works of Cassius Dio and the *HA* biographer, presents a mixed representation of his principate. Hadrian is commonly shown as being an adept *princeps*, but the execution of some prominent senatorial figures also brought a great deal of censure as well.[207] It is evident that upon his succession that there were a num-

---

[200] *RIC* Trajan 382, 385, 398, 411, 428, 429, 460, 492, 497.

[201] *RIC* Trajan 52, 114, 147, 154, 157, 220, 223, 225, 325,

[202] *RIC* Trajan 146, 256, 266, 292, 720.

[203] *RIC* Trajan 100, 220, 556v, 558, 621v, 623a.

[204] *RIC* Trajan 127, 191, 519-20.

[205] *RIC* Trajan 37, 45, 50, 689.

[206] *RIC* Commodus 221, 254a, 254b, 259, 365, 399b, 640-3.

[207] Dio 69.1.1-4, 69.2.5-6, 69.23.2-3; *Hadrian* 5.5-8, 23.1-24.13.

ber of threats to his position,[208] and that these were dealt with prior to his arrival in the capital in July AD 118.[209] All the same, this exhibits the difficulties that he faced throughout his reign with the dealings that he had with the Senate. Yet this also exhibits the impact that such divisions between *princeps* and Senate had upon ensuing literary traditions that were produced. A perfect example of this can be viewed in the final statements of Cassius Dio about his reign, which accentuates the hatred that existed towards him because of such executions, despite the evident benefits of his principate (Dio 69.23.2-3):

οὗτος ἐμισήθη μὲν ὑπὸ τοῦ δήμου, καίτοι τἆλλα ἄριστα αὐτῶν ἄρξας, διά τε τοὺς πρώτους καὶ τοὺς τελευταίους φόνους ἅτε καὶ ἀδίκως καὶ ἀνοσίως γενομένους, ἐπεὶ οὕτω γε ἥκιστα φονικὸς ἐγένετο ὥστε καὶ προσκρουσάντων αὐτῷ τινων ἀρκοῦν νομίζειν τὸ ταῖς πατρίσιν αὐτῶν αὐτὸ τοῦτο γράψαι, ὅτι αὐτῷ οὐκ ἀρέσκουσιν. εἴ τέ τινα τῶν τέκνα ἐχόντων ὀφλῆσαι πάντως τι ἔδει, ἀλλ᾽ οὖν πρός γε τὸν ἀριθμὸν τῶν παίδων καὶ τὰς τιμωρίας αὐτῶν ἐπεκούφιζεν. οὐ μέντοι ἀλλ᾽ ἡ γερουσία ἐπὶ πολὺ ἀντέσχε, τὰς τιμὰς μὴ ψηφίσασθαι ἐθέλουσα, καὶ αἰτιωμένη τινὰς τῶν ἐπ᾽ αὐτοῦ πλεονασάντων καὶ διὰ τοῦτο τιμηθέντων, οὓς καὶ κολασθῆναι ἔδει.

'Hadrian was hated by the people, in spite of his generally excellent reign, on account of the murders committed by him at the beginning and end of his reign, since they had been unjustly and impiously brought about. Yet he was so far from being of a bloodthirsty disposition that even in the case of some who clashed with him he thought it sufficient to write to their native places the bare statement that they did not please him. And if it was absolutely necessary to punish any man who had children, yet in proportion to the number of children he would lighten the penalty imposed. Nevertheless, the senate persisted for a long time in its refusal to vote him the usual honours and in its stricture upon some of those who had committed excesses during his reign and had been honoured therefore, when they ought to have been punished.'

Of course this vitriolic finale exhibits a clear point that impacts upon our reading of Commodus within the ancient literature – a character that was seemingly even more antagonistic towards his élite peers. When considering Hadrian's general administration it is easy to view not only his continuation of previous Antonine policy, but also well-founded reasons for his popularity. He introduced numerous policies that sought to alleviate financial stress for many social levels, such as in the case of taxation amnesties.[210] This is also exemplified in his

---

[208] Birley 2000, *op.cit.*, pp. 77-81.
[209] Smallwood n. 6.
[210] Birley 1997, *op.cit.*, p. 97.

strengthening of the *alimenta* scheme,[211] which was evidently a popular project[212] that continued for an extended period of time. All the same, it is important to note how his good work was cast by the ancient sources as a desire to win back his popularity after executions that he had ordered.[213] One significant policy that he did change was a definitive non-expansionist policy,[214] which was clearly a return to the principles followed by Augustus that sought to maintain the empire rather than to enlarge.

When considering this in light of the Hadrianic numismatic evidence, it is possible to view both symbolic continuation and policy divergence in the coin imagery of Hadrian and Commodus. Hadrian continued to emphasise similar themes of his predecessors, such as *felicitas*,[215] *concordia*,[216] *providentia*,[217] *pax*,[218] *aequitas*,[219] Victory,[220] Salus,[221] Fortuna,[222] *abundantia*,[223] and various building works.[224] He also continued other themes that became prominent under Commodus, such as Hercules,[225] *spes*,[226] and *fides*.[227] All the same, he also exhibited a new introduction of themes, particularly with the depiction of provinces,[228] which sought to exhibit his travels (and possibly his engagement with these communities as emperor) rather than military conquests. This was emphasised by the numerous depictions of galleys within this medium.[229] However, it is also notable that he introduced some themes that were later adopted by Commodus, such as

---

[211] *Hadrian* 7.8.

[212] Plin. *Pan.* 27.1.

[213] *Hadrian* 7.1-4.

[214] *Hadrian* 5.1-4.

[215] *RIC* Hadrian 83b, 120-1, 234a, 234d, 237a, 238a, 563a, 749.

[216] *RIC* Hadrian 4c, 9a, 9c, 17c, 39a, 82b, 118b, 172, 542, 550.

[217] *RIC* Hadrian 133, 261, 262a, 589b.

[218] *RIC* Hadrian 12c, 21, 44, 94b, 95b, 238a, 616b, 616c, 616v, 770a.

[219] *RIC* Hadrian 80, 228, 339e, 381b, 399c, 743d, 795e.

[220] *RIC* Hadrian 76, 77v, 78, 95b, 101a, 148d, 182, 282a, 286a, 499, 511.

[221] *RIC* Hadrian 46, 51v, 98b, 127a, 137a, 139b, 180, 267d, 268, 270d, 604a.

[222] *RIC* Hadrian 10c, 41a, 85, 86a, 242v, 244a, 245a, 248c, 379a, 530v.

[223] *RIC* Hadrian 146, 169c, 170d, 338.

[224] *RIC* Hadrian 156, 461a, 475a, 476.

[225] *RIC* Hadrian 56, 148d, 149c, 156.

[226] *RIC* Hadrian 4c, 9a, 17c, 39a, 100a, 181, 274a, 612b.

[227] *RIC* Hadrian 241, 241a.

[228] *RIC* Hadrian 324d, 326d, 327, 840, 849, 872, 884, 890, 897.

[229] *RIC* Hadrian 113a, 209, 240, 351, 352, 703v, 706v, 719, 796d.

liberalitas,[230] *hilaritas*,[231] and *libertas*,[232] which epitomises the evolution of this type of imagery. Therefore, this provides a clear indication of Commodus' continuation of his iconographic place within the Antonine tradition, which would have had a definitive impact upon the policies that he enacted, at least on a propagandistic level.

Another important aspect to consider between Hadrian and Commodus is the succession. Contrasting the amount of experience that both succeeding *principes* had provides an excellent insight into how prepared they were before assuming overall state power. In this regard it is clear that Hadrian was vastly more experienced in the role of government, which may explain some of Commodus' reckless (or autocratic) decisions. However, this does not excuse him entirely. All the same, it seems evident that Hadrian had a direct impact upon Commodus' succession, owing to his favourable view of Marcus Aurelius, which makes him an even more significant predecessor for understanding Commodus' principate. Of course there was no direct contact between these two *principes*, but there are some compelling similarities as far as their attitudes are concerned. However, for the purposes of the present discussion it is more important to note the impact that Hadrian's reign may have had upon the progression of Commodus' principate, especially in view of their apparent opinions about the senatorial class and its perceived value.

Antoninus Pius

The ancient literary evidence for Antoninus Pius is very limited in its scope, with only brief accounts really being available in the works of Cassius Dio and the *HA* biographer, which are then supplemented by the even more succinct accounts of the later Fourth Century authors. This has a definitive impact upon the way in which Antoninus Pius is recalled, providing only a limited amount of information upon the details of his principate. Much of this material presents him in an idealised nature,[233] which is often accentuated by his respectful attitude towards the Senate.[234] However, overall it does seem to sug-

---

[230] *RIC* Hadrian 132, 216a, 216v, 217d; Commodus 10, 22, 36a, 133, 202a, 239, 300.

[231] *RIC* Hadrian 126a, 970, 974i; Commodus 497; Marcus Aurelius 1547.

[232] *RIC* Hadrian 127c, 128, 175, 175c, 568, 538b; Commodus 135, 144, 168, 208d, 241, 619.

[233] See *HA Antoninus Pius* 2.1-11.

[234] *Antoninus Pius* 6.3-6.

gest that he was an effective *princeps*,[235] which is typified by his organisation of the frontier in northern Britain.[236] All the same, the idealism of the ancient evidence must still be taken with a critical approach, particularly when considering the later negativity that is used to compare him with his grandson, Commodus – a *princeps* who was evidently much less respectful to his senatorial peers.

When examining the general administrative policies of Antoninus Pius it is clear that there was a prevalent continuation of the established frameworks of his predecessors.[237] This need for continuity is epitomised in his need to secure senatorial support after the turbulence of Hadrian's final years,[238] and accentuates his prioritisation being upon stability.[239] Nevertheless, there was one significant difference in his method to that of Hadrian: once Antoninus Pius became *princeps* he never left Italian soil, which is a marked difference to the extensive travels of his adoptive father. This does not seem to have had a negative impact upon the provincial administrative processes,[240] and may have benefitted some judicial practices and developments in Rome,[241] through his direct involvement. This primacy of Italy over the other provinces may have had some impact upon Commodus' preference for residing close to the capital for extended periods of time as well, but this is impossible to prove definitively.

The continuity of Antonine numismatic imagery can also be viewed through the use of similar iconography by both Antoninus Pius and Commodus, such as with *felicitas*,[242] *concordia*,[243] *providentia*,[244]

---

[235] Hüttl 1975, *op.cit.*

[236] G.W. Adams, "An Analysis of Antoninus Pius' Frontier Policy in Northern Britain and its Representation of his Principate", *Journal of Ancient Civilizations* 23, 2008, pp. 119-37.

[237] Garzetti 1974 , *op.cit.*, pp. 445-8.

[238] Fronto *Ad. M. Caes.* 2.1.1, p. 24.

[239] Garzetti 1974, *op.cit.*, p. 447.

[240] Aelius Aristides *Or. Rom.* 33.

[241] Garzetti 1974, *op.cit.*, pp. 455, 459.

[242] *RIC* Antoninus Pius 11a, 130, 178, 298-9, 545a, 565, 658, 680v, 770, 936; Commodus 15a, 15b, 29a, 74, 97, 108, 110, 137, 143, 159, 165.

[243] *RIC* Antoninus Pius 65a, 66, 129, 453b, 600, 601, 678; Commodus 126, 198b, 219, 459c.

[244] *RIC* Antoninus Pius 80a, 618, 953, 957; Commodus 19, 44, 50, 65, 259, 312, 379, 641.

virtus,[245] *pax*,[246] *aequitas*,[247] Victory,[248] Salus,[249] and *fides*.[250] However, there were other images used by Antoninus Pius that were not adopted by Commodus, which exhibits different propagandistic priorities for each ruler, such as Antoninus Pius' depiction of the military handshake,[251] *pietas*,[252] Vesta,[253] and *tranquillitas*.[254] This epitomises how while numismatic traditions continued throughout this sequence of reigns that there was still a fair amount of personal prioritisation for each leader to communicate particular themes in their messages throughout the empire. So there was a clear connection between the issues of Antoninus Pius and Commodus, but this was not a simple matter of replication for the grandson. However, another important figure to be shown by Antoninus Pius was his successor Marcus Aurelius,[255] which has a direct impact upon Commodus' future legitimacy as *princeps*.

The succession of Marcus Aurelius was clearly of some importance to Antoninus Pius, which explains its frequent depiction on the numismatic evidence and epitomises his preference for the stable continuity of the succession. This association of course had a direct effect upon Commodus' future, despite that Antoninus Pius had passed away before the birth of his grandson. This would have seemingly had a definitive impact upon Commodus in view of not only Marcus Aurelius' personal admiration for Antoninus Pius as shown

---

[245] *RIC* Antoninus Pius 102c, 105c, 118, 154; Commodus 71, 71v, 160, 292a, 505.

[246] *RIC* Antoninus Pius 23a, 35, 42, 51, 78b, 117, 153, 200a, 200c, 216a, 246; Commodus 17, 64, 64v, 86.

[247] *RIC* Antoninus Pius 10a, 48, 61a, 127a, 169b, 177a, 855, 858; Commodus 120, 164d, 517, 517v.

[248] *RIC* Antoninus Pius 9a, 25, 111, 115b, 158, 266, 303, 654, 717a, 719, 724v, 780; Commodus 4, 12, 49, 58, 69e, 90c, 93, 102, 110, 112, 122a.

[249] *RIC* Antoninus Pius 82v, 167d, 181, 254, 264, 288, 304, 305, 635a, 749v; Commodus 66, 169, 337, 512.

[250] *RIC* Antoninus Pius 5a, 12a, 12c, 530b, 546, 716, 943a; Commodus 75, 220, 232, 608.

[251] *RIC* Antoninus Pius 26, 43, 54b, 136, 1088a.

[252] *RIC* Antoninus Pius 14b, 79, 217, 313c, 1031, 1035, 1045.

[253] *RIC* Antoninus Pius 203, 219, 229a, 238, 243, 285, 941v.

[254] *RIC* Antoninus Pius 202, 218.

[255] *RIC* Antoninus Pius 422, 424a, 426, 429, 432a, 432b, 434, 438, 445a, 456c, 457b, 481.

in the *Meditations*,[256] but also the numerous numismatic representations of him by Marcus Aurelius.[257] In this context the notable presence of Commodus' grandfather could have had an indirect impact upon not only his perception of how to serve as a *princeps*, but also his own sense of his legitimacy as a definitive imperial birthright. To extrapolate about what this impact would have been would be too speculative, but its presence seems to be undeniable regardless of its ultimate effects.

Marcus Aurelius

Unlike the previous emperors, the impact of Marcus Aurelius and the general reception of his principate would have made a direct and significant impression upon Commodus. Of course the actual nature of their private relationship is impossible to determine with any accuracy, but it is self-evident that Marcus Aurelius would have had a definite impact upon Commodus' development and his views of how to be a *princeps* (even if that hypothetically saw a rejection of his father's policies/methods, which is the view of the ancient literary sources). In addition to this, the range of ancient literary sources on Marcus Aurelius, such as Herodian and the *Meditations*, do provide some idea about how both of the emperors were perceived and possibly about the context in which they may have interacted. However, it must be noted that these sources are by no means perfect and there are still significant gaps in the available information for a modern audience. The primary focus must still be upon how each character is represented by the ancient authors and how these representations have impacted upon the way in which Commodus particularly has been judged as a Roman *princeps*.

One of the most significant aspects to note in this regard is the over-arching effect of the anti-Commodus tradition within the extant literary sources. Temporally this lasted from just after his reign, as exhibited by Herodian and Cassius Dio,[258] through into the Fourth Century AD, as seen in Eutropius and the *Historia Augusta*.[259] Of course in turn this has effected much of the modern scholarship on not only Commodus,[260] but it has also influenced the perceived relia-

---

[256] *Meditations* 1.16.
[257] *RIC* Marcus Aurelius 429, 430, 431, 435, 436, 438-42, 1265-9, 1272.
[258] Herodian 1.3.1-5; Dio 72.1.1-2.
[259] See Adams 2013, *op.cit.*
[260] Marasco 1998, *op.cit.*

bility of these authors.[261] However, the effect upon Marcus Aurelius' representation in this regard is paramount. Marcus has received such an idealised portrayal that ultimately it would have always tarnished the reception of any successor, regardless of their relationship with him. A perfect example of this is the *Histories* by Herodian. While the title directly invokes the remembrance and importance of Marcus Aurelius, very little of the work actually deals with him (Sections 1.1.2-1.4.8). Seemingly the primary reason for his prominence at the outset of the work was to accentuate Commodus' depravity through an implied comparison of their virtues and vices. This clearly epitomises the intentional contrast drawn by the ancient literary sources, but this also provides an excellent opportunity to consider the wider literary reception of both Marcus Aurelius and Commodus.

The ancient evidence for the relationship between Marcus Aurelius and Commodus is varied and quite often limited in its scope. There are three authors who provide the majority of the details: Cassius Dio, Herodian and the *HA* biographer. Cassius Dio does not accentuate the interaction between father and son greatly, but this would have been intended to minimise any emphasis upon their connection. His treatment of Commodus is stereotypically critical, which is epitomised by the statement that Faustina thought that her son was 'simple-minded'.[262] The first reference to Marcus' interaction with him focused upon his summoning to the German frontier and presentation with the *toga virilis*.[263] Commodus would have presumably been fourteen years old at the time, but Cassius Dio does not go into any detail about this period (unlike other authors) and instead focuses more upon the revolt of Avidius Cassius. The primary focus upon Marcus Aurelius and Commodus together is instead centred upon the events leading up to Marcus's death and his concerns surrounding Commodus' abilities to succeed him.[264] This appears to have been an attempt by Cassius Dio to absolve Marcus Aurelius for the perceived corruption of his son and clearly illustrates the persistent pro-Marcus/anti-Commodus sentiments that purvey the ancient literary tradition.

Herodian also continues this theme in his account, but goes to greater lengths to accentuate Marcus Aurelius' lack of responsibility

---

[261] Hekster 2002, *op.cit.*

[262] Dio 72.22.3.

[263] Dio 72.22.2.

[264] Dio 72.33.4-34.1; 73.1.2.

for Commodus' perceived later moral degradation. He emphasised this by mentioning the care with which Commodus was raised and his esteemed education,[265] but then follows a similar line to Cassius Dio, by stressing Marcus Aurelius' concerns about the succession.[266] However, Herodian accentuates this even further by inserting a directly quoted speech attributed to Marcus Aurelius about this issue and his concerns for the future.[267] This absolution of his perceived parental responsibilities ties in well with the authorial contrast drawn between father and son as mentioned previously, and epitomises the literary traditions surrounding both characters. This was further emphasised by Herodian in his account of the succession where another quoted speech was included that expressed Commodus' views about his filial love and his justifications for his accession to the army,[268] but this was quickly followed by the presentation of his rapid moral degradation.[269] Overall it is evident that Herodian sought to maintain the contrast in the pro-Marcus/anti-Commodus tradition.

The *HA* biographer provides one of the most comprehensive accounts of their interaction, which really provides useful information more about their literary traditions rather than a 'factual' account. However, this source has to be viewed in two parts: the *Vita Marci Antonini* and the *Vita Commodi*, owing to the different emphases within either biography. The author presents very similar themes to the previous writers in the *Vita Marci Antonini*, but with much greater detail.[270] The gradual promotion of Commodus is a key feature within this *vita*,[271] and this text also exhibits Marcus' concerns about the succession,[272] which is a clear theme within the literary tradition. However, unlike Herodian in particular, Commodus is exhibited by the *HA* biographer as having shown his cruel inclinations during Marcus' lifetime more explicitly,[273] despite a similar emphasis upon his later decline.[274] All the same, this biography illustrates the literary intentions of the author: the relationship between

---

[265] Herodian 1.2.1.

[266] Herodian 1.3.1-5.

[267] Herodian 1.4.1-6.

[268] Herodian 1.5.3-8.

[269] Herodian 1.6.1.

[270] See Adams 2013, *op.cit.*

[271] *Marcus* 12.8, 12.10, 22.12, 27.5, 27.8.

[272] *Marcus* 27.11, 28.1-10.

[273] *Marcus* 27.12.

[274] *Marcus* 27.9.

Marcus Aurelius and Commodus receives much more attention because of the greater emphasis upon characterisation rather than the wider historical events. In this sense, the *HA* biographer was further accentuating the all pervasive nature of the anti-Commodus tradition within the *Vita Marci Antonini.*

Within the *Vita Commodi* there is very little emphasis upon Marcus Aurelius at all, which instead predominantly focused upon the depravities and corruption of Commodus. This would have been largely intended to distance father from son within the minds of the intended audience. There are similar references to the promotions of Commodus during Marcus' reign,[275] but even these 'accolades' were used by the *HA* biographer as a means for ridiculing Commodus' later decision to change the names of the months.[276] The *Vita Commodi* also emphasises the attempts of Marcus Aurelius to provide Commodus with a good education,[277] but even this is used to exhibit the futility of denying his base nature.[278] There is one significant factual difference between the *Vita Commodi* and the *Vita Marci Antonini*,[279] where it states that Commodus joined Marcus on the journey to Syria at the outset.[280] However, the *HA* biographer does include some suggestions of Marcus as an indulgent father towards Commodus, such as the reinstatement of 'evil' custodians when he was young,[281] and that Commodus competed in three hundred and sixty five gladiatorial contests during Marcus' reign,[282] which contradicts previous statements of the author.[283] However, this simply illustrates how the *HA* biographer sought to maintain the portrayal of Commodus' 'evil' character rather than factual consistency.

As mentioned previously, the reliability of these ancient literary sources have been drawn into question owing to the consistency of the anti-Commodus tradition.[284] While one cannot view these sources as being entirely accurate on a factual level, this does not justify a definitive dismissal of what they can offer the modern

---

[275] *Commodus* 1.10-2.3, 2.4-5.
[276] *Commodus* 11.13-12.7.
[277] *Commodus* 1.5-6.
[278] *Commodus* 1.7.
[279] *Marcus* 25.11.
[280] *Commodus* 2.3.
[281] *Commodus* 2.6-7.
[282] *Commodus* 12.10.
[283] *Marcus* 27.6.
[284] Hekster 2002, *op.cit.*

scholar. One of the most prominent aspects that they exhibit is the breadth of the pro-Marcus/anti-Commodus tradition, which has had a clear impact upon how Commodus has been exhibited. This is most clearly shown by Cassius Dio and Herodian who were contemporaneous with Commodus' reign, whereas the *Historia Augusta* illustrates the longevity of this tradition. The comparative nature of these sources is one of the most compelling aspects that can be viewed as a result, be it as Marcus' disappointment in him, or as Commodus' rejection of his father's values. This has had a lasting impact upon the extant views of Commodus' principate, which clearly exhibits the strength of the continuing literary traditions that surround both *principes*.

Unfortunately the evidence provided in Marcus' *Meditations* and in his correspondence with Marcus Cornelius Fronto adds little to the picture of the father/son relationship. The *Meditations* simply states that Marcus was thankful that his children were neither born stupid nor deformed (*Meditations* 1.17.4: τὸ παιδία μοι ἀφυῆ μὴ γενέσθαι μηδὲ κατὰ τὸ σωμάτιον διάστροφα 'That my children are not without intelligence nor physically deformed'), and that he was grateful that they had competent teachers (*Meditations* 1.17.7: τὸ ἐπιτηδείων τροφέων εἰς τὰ παιδία εὐπορῆσαι 'That I had no lack of suitable teachers for my children').[285] Both statements exhibit somewhat of a distanced relationship, but this work was hardly the context in which Marcus would have exhibited a vast amount of parental affection. However, this attitude is also present in his correspondence with Fronto, where Marcus responds to a letter from Fronto that celebrates the good health of his twin sons (including Commodus),[286] with an expression of his love for Fronto (not the children) and an appreciation for his compositional skills.[287] A degree of separation between father and child was, however, to be expected in view of Marcus' lengthy periods of time outside the capital, which is epitomised in a letter to him from his wife, Faustina.[288] This text epitomises not only the vulnerability of the *familia* at times of crisis (in this instance during the revolt of Avidius Cassius), but also the practical limitations that existed for Marcus to have a continuing presence as a father in light of his official role as *princeps* of Rome.

---

[285] *Meditations* 1.17.
[286] Fronto *Ad. Ant. Imp.* 1.3.
[287] Fronto *Ad. Ant. Imp.* 1.4.
[288] Fronto *Ep. Faust. Ad Marc.* X.1.

One notable aspect that can be noted from the numismatic evidence is the frequent continuation of Marcus' imagery by Commodus, particularly in relation to topics such as *felicitas*,[289] *concordia*,[290] *providentia*,[291] *virtus*,[292] *pax*,[293] *aequitas*,[294] Victory,[295] Mars,[296] *securitas*,[297] *Salus*,[298] *liberalitas*,[299] Annona,[300] and Fortuna.[301] This clearly illustrates the continuation of a significant number of propaganda messages by Commodus, which exemplifies the importance of the Antonine numismatic tradition. However, it is also significant that some themes were continued by Marcus Aurelius that were also associated with his early career by his adoptive father Antoninus Pius, such as *hilaritas*,[302] and Spes.[303] All the same, it is important to note that Commodus did use some different concepts/deities that illustrate some deviation from the themes of Marcus' coinage, particularly through the promotion of *nobilitas*,[304] and Hercules as prominent motifs.[305] This form of evidence exhibits how Commodus not only continued the iconographic tradition established by his forebears, but also used this propaganda tool for his own reasons and personal incentives.

The most interesting aspect that becomes evident through this analysis is the varying impact of tradition and 'reality' upon what we know of Marcus' effect upon Commodus. This variance is epito-

---

[289] *RIC* Marcus 12v, 13b, 14, 110, 112, 132, 203, 357, 358v; Commodus 15a, 29a, 74, 97, 108, 110, 137, 143, 159, 165.

[290] *RIC* Marcus 1-3, 35, 37, 59-60, 62; Commodus 126, 198b, 219, 459c.

[291] *RIC* Marcus 20, 22-3, 50-1, 70, 73, 170, 176, 178, 186; Commodus 19, 44, 50, 65, 259, 312, 379, 641.

[292] *RIC* Marcus 91-2, 120, 123-4, 261, 262v, 276; Commodus 71, 71v, 160, 292a, 505.

[293] *RIC* Marcus 146, 164, 1202; Commodus 17, 64, 64v, 86.

[294] *RIC* Marcus 171, 171v, 189, 191-2, 252; Commodus 120, 164d, 517, 517v.

[295] *RIC* Marcus 162v, 163, 174, 225, 237, 273; Commodus 4, 12, 49, 58, 69e, 90c, 93, 98a, 102, 110, 112, 122a, 211.

[296] *RIC* Marcus 286, 310, 349; Commodus 46, 54, 174v, 175, 188, 257, 527.

[297] *RIC* Marcus 325, 1083; Commodus 23, 179, 190.

[298] *RIC* Marcus 77, 207, 216, 222; Commodus 66, 169, 337, 512.

[299] *RIC* Marcus 206, 1149, 1205; Commodus 10, 22, 36a, 133, 202a, 239.

[300] *RIC* Marcus 125, 126v, 142, 388; Commodus 14a, 28, 106, 307b, 325, 344, 350.

[301] *RIC* Marcus 185, 220, 409; Commodus 2, 131, 166a, 172, 191a, 235, 513.

[302] *RIC* Pius 432a, 432b, 1242a; Marcus 497, 1547.

[303] *RIC* Pius 431, 431v, 476; Marcus 620v, 622, 1545.

[304] *RIC* Commodus 155, 155a, 501.

[305] *RIC* Commodus 221, 254b, 259, 365, 399b, 640-1, 643.

mised in not only Commodus' combined acceptance and modification of his father's numismatic iconography, but also exhibited in general terms within the literary tradition. However, this exemplifies the difficulties in determining the correlation between the traditions that envelop both *principes* and the actual nature of their relationship. One element is certain within this overall issue: the positive perception of Marcus Aurelius had a clear impact upon the judgements that were made about Commodus' principate. Of course this is not intended to absolve him from any faults as a leader, but instead to simply note how the comparison of the two in antiquity has had a dramatic effect upon their portrayal and ultimately their assessment in modern times. One of the most significant differences between the two characters was their attitude towards the élite establishment within Roman society, which of course had a direct impact upon the styles of literary representation for them from the Second Century AD onwards.

All the same, while the ancient literary sources have attempted to disassociate Marcus Aurelius from his son as much as possible, the numismatic evidence still illustrates Commodus' clear place within the Antonine tradition. It would be undeniable that Marcus had a significant impact upon Commodus' reign, which is evident through the analysis of their shared numismatic iconography. So even if Marcus Aurelius was a relatively distant participant on a parental level, which is to be somewhat expected in view of his enormous responsibilities and frequent distance from the *familia*, the imperial inheritance that he provided Commodus for his own principate is indisputable. However, it must be noted that Commodus did not simply replicate the actions of his father unquestionably, but this has been dealt with consistently throughout this study. For the purposes of the present discussion it is simply important to note the consequence of Marcus Aurelius (and his later idealised symbolism) for an analysis of the reign of Commodus Antoninus.

Lucius Verus

Another significant feature during the lifetime of Commodus would have been Lucius Verus, who was co-emperor with Marcus Aurelius until AD 169. While it would be expected that Lucius Verus would have had a fair degree of contact with Commodus as a member of the imperial *familia*, the lack of ancient evidence exhibiting any kind of relationship is quite staggering. Of course this is largely owing to the ancient authorial preference to focus upon the contrast between

Marcus Aurelius and Commodus (as father and son), but it is notable that this topic is not dealt with by any ancient writer directly. This is particularly interesting with the hypothetical connection that *could* have been drawn by the sources: Verus influencing Commodus in his licentious ways,[306] which in turn could have further absolved Marcus Aurelius from any responsibility for his son's actions. However, in this regard the silence is quite deafening, which makes their possible relationship (or the lack thereof) even more intriguing.

While it must be recognized that Commodus would have only been seven years old at the time of Lucius Verus' death, and that they spent much of this period in separate locations, it appears unlikely that they had absolutely no contact with each other. However, when considering the ancient literary sources there are no direct references to any contact between them. The *HA* biographer provides the closest existing literary connection for them and this is an implied association rather than being an overt relationship. The first 'subtle' connection by the *HA* biographer was in their accentuation that prior to Marcus Aurelius' direct influence, that Lucius Verus had been called Commodus (*Verus* 4.1-3): *Dato igitur imperio et indulta tribunicia potestate, post consulatus etiam honorem delatum Verum vocari praecepit, suum in eum transferens nomen, cum ante Commodus vocaretur. Lucius quidem Marco vicem reddens si quid susciperet obsecutus ut legatus proconsuli vel praeses imperatori. iam primum enim pro ambobus ad milites est locutus et pro consensu imperii graviter se et ad Marci mores egit* ['After investing him the sovereignty, then, and installing him in the tribunician power, and after rendering him the further honour of the consulship, Marcus gave instructions that he be named Verus, transferring his own name to him, whereas previously he had been called Commodus. In return for this, Verus obeyed Marcus, whenever he entered upon any undertaking, as a lieutenant obeys a proconsul or a governor obeys the emperor. For, at the beginning, he addressed the soldiers in his brother's behalf as well as his own, and in consideration of the joint rule he conducted himself with dignity and observed the moral standard that Marcus had set up'].

The only other literary connection between them is in relation to the freedman Eclectus, who was the only one of Lucius' freedmen not to be sacked by Marcus, and that he later killed Commodus (*Verus* 9.6): *quos omnes Marcus post mortem Veri specie honoris abiecit Eclecto*

---

[306] See *Verus* 1.4, 4.4-10, 5.1-5, 6.1-6, 6.8-7.10. See *Commodus* 2-3, 9, 11 for examples of similar traits by the same author.

retento, qui postea Commodum filium eius occidit ['All of these Marcus dismissed after Verus' death, under pretext of doing them honour, with the exception of Eclectus, and he afterwards slew Marcus' son, Commodus']. Both of these statements by the *HA* biographer were seemingly intended to suggest a moral correlation between Lucius Verus and Commodus (particularly as being distinct from Marcus Aurelius), but it was clearly included to such a fashion that it did not remove the emphasis away from a father-son comparison too much.

The coinage of Lucius Verus is largely similar in its imagery to that of Marcus Aurelius, which is to be expected, but there was a clear emphasis upon Victory and *providentia* as themes that he is associated with.[307] However, this is to be expected in view of how Lucius Verus legitimized his role as *imperator* through his military activity. It is of note that Marcus Aurelius was associated with other concepts, such as *aequitas*,[308] *concordia*,[309] and *felicitas*[310] to a much greater extent, but this was largely owing to a division in imagery that symbolized their joint principate – each member fulfilled a specific role. All the same, the comparison of the numismatic imagery provided by Commodus and Lucius Verus highlights a similar emphasis upon Victory,[311] and Mars,[312] which further exemplifies their similar propaganda themes. However, for the purposes of the present discussion it is most important to note the continuity of the iconographic tradition from one generation to the next.

One of the most significant aspects concerning Lucius Verus for the present study is noting the similarly negative tradition surrounding him as that of Commodus. Both of these *principes* were viewed very critically by the ancient literary sources, which seems to have stemmed largely through their comparison with the highly idealized Marcus Aurelius. So in this sense it is possible to view a correlation between Lucius Verus and Commodus: both suffered a more critical audience owing to the inevitable comparisons drawn between them and the positive reception of Marcus Aurelius. This contrast is fur-

---

[307] *RIC* Marcus 463, 482, 485, 491, 522, 525, 551, 533, 566, 566v, 573v, 581, 1361, 1397, 1462.

[308] *RIC* Marcus 171, 171v, 189, 191-2, 252.

[309] *RIC* Marcus 1-3, 35, 37, 59-60, 62.

[310] *RIC* Marcus 12v, 13b, 14, 110, 112, 132, 203, 357, 358v.

[311] *RIC* Marcus 522, 525, 551, 533, 560, 566v, 573v; Commodus 4, 12, 49, 58, 69e, 90c, 93, 98a, 102, 110, 112, 122a, 211.

[312] *RIC* Marcus 286, 310, 349; Commodus 514, 515, 529.

ther highlighted by the absence of any direct literary reference to interaction between Lucius Verus and Commodus: their associations with Marcus were much more important from a comparative perspective. The actual nature of the relationship between Lucius Verus and Commodus is therefore impossible to quantify with any certainty, but it would be impossible to suggest that there was no connection between them. Both *principes* were clearly well entrenched within the Antonine imperial tradition, but have likewise been vilified for not epitomizing the ideals that have been attributed to Marcus Aurelius.

The Antonine Period before Commodus in General and its Impact

When considering the preceding *principes* in relation to the Emperor Commodus, one of the most compelling features was the general stability throughout the period, particularly in relation to the succession. While there were definite instances of insurgencies at the outset of some reigns, such as during the principates of Nerva, and Hadrian, and the general progression of these emperors has been largely shown in a positive light by the ancient literary sources. All the same, while this could also simply embody the traditions of the time and the effects of state-wide propaganda, it appears likely that this would have affected Commodus' view of the preceding periods. The exhibited stability with such transitions may have made him see it as being much more secure than it actually was in practice. After all, he was the direct descendant from a long line of well respected leaders who at the very least presented an image of *auctoritas* and state stability within the confines of the empire.

As has been noted previously, one of the most consistent aspects that can be viewed between the reigns of Nerva to Marcus Aurelius was that of administrative policy. One of the best examples of this can be seen in the case in point of the *alimenta* program, which was not only very popular,[313] but also would have been viewed as an effective propagandistic tool for exhibiting the benefits of the current administration. The general theme of administrative and legal continuity also accentuated the stability that each succeeding *princeps* sought to exemplify – thereby justifying their own position in turn. As has been discussed in greater detail further below, this general practice of administrative continuity was largely continued by Com-

---

[313] Plin. *Pan.* 27.1.

modus, who introduced very few radically different policies into the running of the Roman State. This could potentially be taken as representing his personal disinterest in state affairs or perhaps his administrative inexperience prior to becoming *princeps*, as much as a desire to replicate the continuity of the state policy of his predecessors.

The examination of numismatic iconography epitomises both dynastic continuity throughout the period as well as a personal prioritisation of particular themes and issues at different times. There seems to have been an evolution in topics used, while maintaining the continued presence of themes that were an effective means of conveying the idea of commercial and administrative stability/continuity. In this regard Commodus is no different to his predecessors. Themes such as safety, fortune, security, freedom and equality had been highlighted consistently by his predecessors, and they are also prominent during his principate. All the same, there are other topics/images that become much more conspicuous as well during Commodus' reign – notably Hercules,[314] and also *nobilitas*,[315] which had not been an advertised topic among his predecessors. While Hercules has been discussed further below (see Chapter Six) the promotion of the concept of *nobilitas* is more pertinent for the present discussion.

With the exemption of Hadrian at certain stages of his reign, emperor-Senate relations appear to have been largely positive between AD 98-181. This seems to have stemmed from a reciprocal relationship of respect and in turn support. The primary concern was the execution of senators without consultation by the *princeps*, which was viewed as a serious contravention of the respect that the Senate saw as a fundamental right. This convention was evidently not adhered to by Commodus, and clearly epitomises how he held a different perspective to that of his predecessors who are overtly praised by the ancient literary sources for not executing Senators. The reasoning behind this deviation of imperial practice may be explained by his use of *nobilitas* as a theme on his numismatic iconography, which was clearly worthy of being promoted as a propagandistic topic. This could suggest that instead of seeing himself as a person who was first among equals, Commodus viewed himself as the embodiment of *nobilitas*, and therefore above the 'petty' concerns of his senatorial peers. In turn, any repudiation levelled against him by this group

---

[314] *RIC* Commodus 221, 254b, 259, 365, 399b.
[315] *RIC* Commodus 155, 501.

could also have been seen as being not only unworthy or irrelevant, but also as a direct threat towards himself.

This possibility is quite tempting as a means for understanding Commodus' perceived place within Roman society. It is easy to imagine how his direct lineage back to Antoninus Pius affected his views about his position within the socio-political hierarchy of Rome, which was not a common occurrence in view of how infrequently the succession went from father to son previously. When this is combined with his youth at the time of his accession and his administrative inexperience there should be little surprise that his relationship with other élites was not entirely smooth. All the same, it is also important to note the pervasive nature of the idealism that surrounds his predecessors, which is clearly contrasted by his own portrayal. It is impossible to view Commodus' reign as being the sole reason for the downfall of the Roman Empire – there were prior, mitigating circumstances. However, for the purposes of the present discussion, the marked contrast between these representations not only serves to disparage his role as a *princeps*, but also glazes over some of the existing issues that were present prior to Commodus' succession. Nevertheless, this has been dealt with in greater detail in the ensuing chapters of this study.

CHAPTER 3

COMMODUS' EARLY LIFE AND EDUCATION

Introduction

The present section of this study is intended to analyse the early stages of Commodus' life in light of the available ancient evidence. This aims to examine the way in which Commodus' early life and familial heritage impacted upon his development and how this effected the later progression of his principate. This is, however, not intended to present a psychological analysis of Commodus' mindset, which is beyond the range of possibility in view of the limited nature of the ancient evidence. Instead it is the intention to focus upon the range of influences upon Commodus during his first fifteen years (until AD 176), and to examine how rapidly he was promoted through the array of symbolic and religious positions of Roman public life. This can allow for an examination of the level of administrative experience (or the lack thereof) possessed by Commodus at the point in which he was inducted as co-*princeps* in AD 177.

There are four primary forms of ancient evidence used throughout this chapter: inscriptions, coinage, sculptural representations and the ancient literature. The epigraphic sources (which are sometimes taken from the numismatic evidence as well) provide definitive evidence of key dates, which is particularly significant for the analysis of Commodus' rapid promotion at such an early age. This is particularly exhibited with the discovery of statue bases erected for him prior to AD 177 (see below). This can clearly establish the very public nature of his youth, which provides a clearer insight into the style of upbringing that he experienced. The public promotion of his position within the imperial *familia* is also accentuated by the imagery upon the coin evidence, which provides an additional source that can be analysed, particularly when considered in conjunction with the sculptural representations of the Antonine dynasty. All the same, these public sources have also been used in conjunction with the ancient literary evidence, which largely provide a more 'private' account of Commodus' upbringing. It is expected that by using such a wide range of evidence that the most accurate image possible of his youth may be achieved.

Nevertheless, the limitations of the ancient literary representations must also be noted. The portrayals of Commodus' early days are largely coloured by an evident 'future focus': his you is commonly cast in a negative light, which is intended to serve as a precursor or explanation of his later exhibited corruption as *princeps*.[316] This immediately suggests that such representations need to be taken with some caution. It is also vital to note the brevity of the accounts of his early days. The most detail is provided by the *HA* biographer in the *Commodus* (1.1-2.5), but this account is largely focused upon the anti-Commodus tendencies of the author. Other accounts, such as Cassius Dio,[317] Herodian,[318] and the *HA* biographer in the *Marcus Antoninus*,[319] simply make passing statements about his education and early career. This could be taken as either an indication of limited interest (with more emphasis being placed upon Commodus' later corruption) or basically as a means of separating Marcus Aurelius from his son's 'evil' nature. But either way it is imperative to note these limitations in the literary sources and the existent partialities within this source of evidence.

There are four general themes that are dealt with in this context: Commodus' parentage and the rumours surrounding his legitimacy (or albeit his illegitimacy), his familial relations and descent, his education, and his early career. Each of these topic areas uses a variety of source material as its evidence, which is intended to provide the most holistic examination possible. Through this analysis it is expected that a clearer perspective about his rise to the principate can be achieved. In this regard, the nature of the ancient evidence is varied in both quality and accuracy, but each source of information has been analysed critically. A perfect example of this can be viewed in the 3rd-4th Century rumours that surround Commodus' legitimacy (or illegitimacy) as being the son of Marcus Aurelius.

Parentage and the Rumours

One of the most significant aspects that needs to be considered when analysing the life of Commodus is his lineage. This was the

---

[316] Herodian 1.3.1; *Epit.* 17.2; *HA Commodus* 10.1.

[317] Dio 72.22.2.

[318] Herodian 1.3.1.

[319] *HA Marcus* 27.4-6.

sole basis for his position as *princeps*, which makes it a pivotal aspect for consideration. One important detail that is not highlighted by the ancient literary sources was his descendence from Antoninus Pius (this was through his mother, Faustina, which is important regardless of any perceived illegitimacy in connection with Marcus Aurelius), which ultimately legitimised his position as emperor despite it being an avoided subject by the subsequent ancient authors. Regardless, of this topical avoidance, it was still a pivotal issue, which provided Commodus with a perceived imperial birthright. This would have had a definitive impact upon Commodus' assessment of his own position within Roman society, and in turn his perceived role as a future *princeps*. The biological inheritance of such a position through Marcus Aurelius must have also had an impact: he was directly descended from two *principes* and would have been seen to have inherited their characters/successes. While the validity of the Roman adoption process is unquestionable, this does not mean that there was some residual primacy of biological parentage. This is particularly evident when considering that Commodus was the first succeeding *princeps* to be born while the father was an incumbent emperor. It is in this regard that Commodus must be viewed: the association between Marcus Aurelius and Commodus on a public or official level is vital for their parental and imperial symbolism.

The connection between Commodus and Marcus Aurelius in the literary sources is fascinating. A more contradictory and duopolistic relationship is hard to find in the Roman world. On one hand they are intrinsically connected; on the other – intentionally separated by the biographical and historical literary evidence. Firstly, the ancient authors connected Commodus to Marcus Aurelius (not Antoninus Pius) regardless of his direct lineage. So to them, it was the Commodus-Marcus Aurelius paradigm and association that mattered. This was counter-intuitive: while the succession needed to be explained, the literary sources also sought to create a clear distinction between them. The association, however, between Commodus and Marcus Aurelius is evident, which is clearly shown by the *Epitomator* where Marcus is shown as directly advising his son.[320] Of course, Commodus is represented as completely disregarding the advice of his father at this point, but the connection between the two (father and son) is seemingly undeniable.

---

[320] *Epit.* 17.2.

It is clearly evident that the ancient sources sought to separate Marcus and Commodus through a variety of literary motifs. One of the most notable examples of this is by Herodian, in his reference to another son (the twin of Commodus, Titus Aurelius Fulvus Antoninus), as *Verissimus*, who died in AD 165: τῷ βασιλεύοντι Μάρκῳ θυγατέρες μὲν ἐγένοντο πλείους, ἄρρενες δὲ δύο. τῶν δὲ ἀρρένων τούτων ὁ μὲν ἕτερος κομιδῇ νέος τὸν βίον μετήλλαξε (Βηρίσσιμος δ' ἦν ὄνομα αὐτῷ), τὸν δὲ περιόντα Κόμοδόν τε καλούμενον ὁ πατὴρ μετὰ πάσης ἐπιμελείας ἀνεθρέψατο ['The emperor Marcus Aurelius had a number of daughters but only two sons. One of them (his name was *Verissimus*) died very young; the surviving son, Commodus, his father reared with great care'].

While this reference appears somewhat innocuous, it is the name mentioned by Herodian, *Verissimus*, which is also mentioned as having been applied to Marcus Aurelius.[321] This 'pet-name' seems to indicate some preference for this child rather than Commodus, even though he was still a caring parent towards the latter. All the same, it is evident that this was a literary theme that was intended to distance father and son. This is not only illustrated through the simple fact that the other son's name was Titus Aurelius Fulvus Antoninus, but it can also be questioned by Marcus' own reference to his children in his letter to Marcus Cornelius Fronto (*Ad Antoninum Imp.* i.4): *Vidi filiolos meos, quom – eos vidisti; vidi et te, quom litteras tuas legerem. oro te, mi magister, ama me ut amas; ama me sic etiam quo modo istos parvolos nostros amas: nondum omne dixi quod volo: ama me quo modo amasti* ['I saw my little sons, when you saw them; I saw you too, when I read your letter. I beseech you, my master, love me as you do love me ; love me too even as you love those little ones of ours : I have not yet said all that I want to say : love me as you have loved me']. This exhibits his parental affection for both sons equally, but this was evidently not the primary literary motive for the subsequent ancient authors.

One of the most effective means by which the ancient texts attempt to distance Marcus Aurelius and Commodus was by including references to the rumours surrounding his illegitimacy. Before discussing these allegations of adultery by Faustina it is important to note the unusual nature of this invective. While this form of criticism

---

[321] *HA Marcus* 1.10; Dio 69.21.2. See G.W. Adams, *Marcus Aurelius in the Historia Augusta and Beyond*, Lanham: Lexington Books, 2013, p. 132, n. 167.

was typically intended to denigrate a particular individual directly,[322] in this instance Marcus Aurelius is almost completely absolved of any wrong-doing. While this is one of the few areas in which Marcus Aurelius is criticised by some ancient authors,[323] it is notable that it is generally only in relation o his compliance.[324] In some regards, he is almost even shown as being of a higher moral standing because of his forbearance, as exhibited by Cassius Dio (71.34.3): αὐτὸς μὲν γὰρ ἁπάντων τῶν ἁμαρτημάτων ἀπείχετο, καὶ οὔτε ἑκὼν οὔτ' ἄκων ἐπλημμέλει. τὰ δὲ δὴ τῶν ἄλλων ἁμαρτήματα, καὶ μάλιστα τὰ τῆς γυναικός, ἔφερε καὶ οὔτε ἐπολυπραγμόνει οὔτε ἐκόλαζεν ['He himself, then, refrained from all offences and did nothing amiss whether voluntarily or involuntarily; but the offences of the others, particularly those of his wife, he tolerated, and neither inquired into them nor punished them']. While it must be noted that Cassius Dio avoids being explicit in this instance, the implied failings of Faustina the Younger are still used by the author as being indicative of Marcus' personal strength. Nevertheless, as highlighted by Vinson,[325] the use of such sexual invective was a typically carefully targeted literary motif. In this instance the objective was not to besmirch the reputations of either Marcus Aurelius or his wife Faustina, but was instead directed towards the illegitimacy of Commodus as Marcus' heir.

Another example of this from the ancient sources is provided by Aurelius Victor (16.2): *Cuius divina omnia domi militiaeque facta consultaque; quae imprudentia regendae coniugia attaminavit, quae in tantum petulantiae proruperat, ut in Campania sedens amvena litorum obsideret ad legendes ex nauticis, quia plerumque nudi agunt, flagitiis aptiores* ['All of his deeds and verdicts, both civil and military, were inspired by the gods; but his inability to contain his wife ruined this for she had burst out in to such a level of brazenness that while residing in Campania she would frequent beautiful locations on the coast to select those sailors, because they predominantly labour naked, to choose who would be best suited for her shameful desires']. Judging from this passage there are two salient points: firstly, to note the prominence of this section within its context, and also the amount of detail provided by Aureli-

---

[322] A. Richlin, *The Garden of Priapus*, Oxford, Oxford University Press, 1992, pp. 81-104.

[323] Such as *HA Marcus* 29.1-3.

[324] See Adams 2013, *op.cit.*, p. 127.

[325] M.P. Vinson, "Domitia Longina, Julia Titi, and the Literary Tradition", *Historia* 38.4, 1989, p. 449.

us Victor in view of the overall brevity of the *Liber de Caesaribus*. So firstly, it must be highlighted that after briefly discussing the nobility and superiority of Marcus' character, Aurelius Victor launches into this diatribe against Faustina (and Commodus). The text is hardly subtle. This could have been an inclusion to simply make the text more interesting for Aurelius Victor's audience, or it may also be indicative of the prevalence of such rumours in the 4th Century AD. Considering the largely positive view of Marcus Aurelius in the 4th Century,[326] it would not be surprising to find such criticism of Faustina in order to explain the creation of such an 'evil' progeny from such a 'perfect' *princeps*.

Faustina's adultery would seem as the only 'logical' explanation for such corruption – hence the emphasis upon her lustful disposition by several of the ancient sources. All the same, the most virulent accusation against Commodus' legitimacy is presented in the *Historia Augusta*. Section 29.1-3 is one of the most overt passages: *Crimini ei datum est, quod adulteros uxoris promoverit, Tertullum et <T>utilium et Orfitum et Moderatum, ad varios honores, cum Tertullum et prandentem cum uxore depr[a]ehenderit. de quo mimus in sc<a>ena praesente Antonino dixit; cum stupidus nomen adulteri uxoris a servo quaereret et ille diceret ter 'Tullus', et adhuc stupidus quaereret, respondit ille: 'iam tibi dixi ter, Tullus dicitur.' et de hoc quidem multa populus, multa etiam alii dixerunt patientiam Antonini incusantes* ['It is regarded to Marcus' disrepute that he promoted the lovers of his wife, Tertullus, Tutilius, Orfitus and Moderatus, to various positions of respect, despite having caught Tertullus in the act of having breakfast with his wife. In relation to this fellow the following speech was announced on stage in the presence of Antoninus himself: The Fool asked the Slave the name of the lover of his wife, to which the Slave responded 'Tullus' three times; and when the Fool continued to ask, the Slave responded, 'I have already told you thrice Tullus is his name.' But the population of the city and others as well spoke greatly about this affair and saw fault with Antoninus for his tolerance'].

As mentioned previously, this allegation is one of the few criticisms levelled against Marcus Aurelius, but it would appear that this was largely undertaken by the author to discredit Commodus' legitimacy as the future *princeps*. There are definitely critical elements within this passage towards Marcus Aurelius, but in view of its textual

---

[326] See Adams 2013, *op.cit.*, pp. 213-33.

placement,[327] the primary focus was intended to lead into the criticism of Commodus and his principate.

The rumoured association between Commodus and his potential lineage from a gladiator is even more emphatic in the literary sources (*HA Marcus* 19.1-9):

Aiunt quidam, quod et verisimile videtur, Commodum Antoninum, successorem illius ac filium, non esse de eo natum sed de adulterio, ac talem fa<b>ellam vulgari sermone contexunt. Faustinam quondam, Pii filiam, Marci uxorem, cum gladiatores transire vidisset, unius ex his amore succensam, cum longa aegritudine laboraret, viro de amore confessa<m>. quod cum ad C<h>ald<a>eos Marcus ret<t>ulisset, illorum fuisse consilium, ut occiso gladiatore sanguine illius sese Faustina subl<a>varet atque ita cum viro concumberet. quod cum esset factum, solutum quidem amorem, natum vero Commodum gladiatorem esse, non principem, qui mille prope pugnas publice populo inspectante gladiatorias imperator exhibuit, ut in vita eius docebitur. quod quidem verisimile ex eo habetur, quod tam sancti principis filius his moribus fuit, quibus nullus lanista, nullus sc<a>enicus, nullus arenarius, nullus postremo ex omnium <de>decorum ac scelerum <c>onluvione concretus. multi autem ferunt Commodum omnino ex adultero natum, si quidem Faustinam satis constet apud Caietam condiciones sibi et nauticas et gladiatorias elegisse. de qua cum diceretur Antonino Marco, ut eam repudiaret, si non occideret, dixisse fertur: 'si uxorem dimittimus, reddamus et dotem.' dos autem quid habebatur <nisi> imperium, quod ille ab socero volente Hadriano adoptatus acceperat?

'Some say, and this seems likely, that Commodus Antoninus his son and successor, was not fathered by him, but conceived in adultery – and they fashion such a tale with a story current among the people. Supposedly – once upon a time – Faustina, the daughter of Pius and the wife of Marcus, saw some gladiators pass by and was inflamed with passion for one of them; while suffering from a long illness, she confessed this love to her husband. When Marcus reported this to the Chaldeans, it was their advice that the gladiator be killed and Faustina bathe in his blood from beneath and then lie with her husband. When this was done, the passion was indeed alleviated, but Commodus was born a gladiator, not a *princeps* for later as emperor he staged almost a thousand gladiatorial fights, with the general public looking on – as will be told in his life. This story, of course, is regarded as plausible, given that the son of so virtuous a *princeps* had traits possessed by no gladiator trainer, no actor, no performer in the arena and by nothing congealed from the filth of all vice and crime. Many say, however, that Commodus was really conceived in adultery, since it is generally known that Faustina would pick out lovers from among the sailors and gladiators while at Caieta. When Marcus Antoninus was told about this, so that he might divorce her (if not kill her) he is reported to have said: "If we send our wife away, we must return her dowry too." And what was this dowry, but the empire? – which Marcus had inherited from his father-in-law, after he had been adopted at the wish of Hadrian.'

Initially it is important to note the correlation with Aurelius Victor with the mention of sailors (even though this author of course ex-

---

[327] See Adams 2013, Chapter Four.

pands upon it), but in this instance there is a more direct reference towards Commodus being born out of adultery. This is another clear example of how the later ancient authors sought to explain Commodus' interests in gladiatorial combat, which was a favourite motif used to exemplify his base personality.[328] So it is clear that this instance of adulterous invective was not really intended to sully the representations of either Marcus Aurelius or Faustina the Younger, instead being intended to vilify the legitimacy of their son, Commodus.

Familial Relationships

The connection between Commodus and other members of the Antonine dynasty provide further insight into his place within Roman imperial history. It is apparent that he figured as a significant character within this dynastic context, seeing its demise ultimately with his assassination. This is important to note, particularly in light of the questions raised by some ancient sources in relation to his parentage and his legitimacy as the heir of Marcus Aurelius (suggesting that this was at least rumoured within the anti-Commodus elements of Roman society). Yet even with this being taken into consideration, the nature of his succession was also notable within the context of the Antonine *principes*: he was the first son to follow from his father.[329] In addition to this he was the first Roman emperor ever to be born while his father was already an established *princeps*.[330] This seemingly could have had a marked impact upon how Commodus would have perceived his place within Roman élite society. Therefore, it is prudent at this point within this study to consider the way in which Commodus is shown as a member of the Antonine dynasty.

One of the most fascinating aspects of Commodus' place within the Antonine dynasty can be taken in relation to his association with Antoninus Pius. This is best shown through the passage in the biography of Marcus Aurelius in the *Historia Augusta*, which exhibits the perceived connection between Commodus and Antoninus Pius (*Marcus* 19.8-9): *de qua cum diceretur Antonino Marco, ut eam repudiaret, si non occideret, dixisse fertur: 'si uxorem dimittimus, reddamus et dotem.' dos autem quid habebatur <nisi> imperium, quod ille ab socero volente Hadriano adopta-*

---

[328] Such as *HA Commodus* 11.10-12; Dio 73.19.1-6.

[329] Herodian 1.5.5-6.

[330] The only previous biological sons of emperors (Titus and Domitian) were born much earlier than their father's succession in AD 69.

tus acceperat? ['When Marcus Antoninus was told about this, so that he might divorce her (if not kill her) he is reported to have said: "If we send our wife away, we must return her dowry too." And what was this dowry, but the empire? – which Marcus had inherited from his father-in-law, after he had been adopted at the wish of Hadrian']. This statement epitomises a significant factor: the succession itself. This highlights the importance of Commodus as the son of Faustina – he was not only the son of Marcus Aurelius, but also the grandson of Antoninus Pius. So regardless of how his legitimacy was questioned by some, he was still the most legitimate heir to the principate. Nevertheless, there had been a precedent made by the earlier Antonine phases of succession for moving beyond simple 'blood' relations, which could draw this into question. However, the presence of a direct familial heir had previously not been available throughout the 2nd Century AD,[331] which is another pivotal point at hand. So while it seems that while the adoptive processes of succession were just as legitimate, the appeal (or at least acceptance) of biological inheritance (and in this case the succession) seems to have been quite compelling within Roman society.

The relationship between Commodus and his parents is equally compelling. The affiliation between father and son was seemingly close, but it is notable that both references by Marcus Aurelius in the *Meditations* towards his children were quite distant in character (*Meditations* 1.17.4, 1.17.7): τὸ παιδία μοι ἀφυῆ μὴ γενέσθαι μηδὲ κατὰ τὸ σωμάτιον διάστροφα ['That my children are not without intelligence nor physically deformed']; τὸ ἐπιτηδείων τροφέων εἰς τὰ παιδία εὐπορῆσαι ['That I had no lack of suitable teachers for my children']. It is clear that this would not have been the literary context for him to include remarks of doting affection, which seems more apparent in his correspondence with Marcus Cornelius Fronto (*Ad Antoninum Imp.* i.3):

Vidi pullulos tuos, quod quidem libentissime in vita mea viderim, tarn simili facie tibi ut nihil sit hoc simili similius. Feci prorsus compendium itineris Lorium usque, compendium viae lubricae, compendium clivorum arduorum : tamen vidi te non exadvorsum modo sed locupletius, sive me ad dexteram sive ad laevam convertissem. Sunt autem dis iuvantibus colore satis salubri, clamore forti. Panem alter tenebat bene candidum, ut puer regius, alter autem cibarium, plane ut a philosopho prognatus. Deos quaeso sit salvos sator, salva sint sata. salva seges sit, quae tarn similes procreat. Nam etiam voculas eorum audivi tarn dulces tarn venustas, ut orationis tuae lepidum ilium et

---

[331] The closest biological connection had been between Trajan and his nephew, Hadrian.

liquidum sonura nescio quo pacto in utriusque pipulo adgnoscerem. Iam tu igitur, nisi caves, superbiorem aliquanto me experiere ; habeo enim quos pro te non oculis modo amem sed etiam auribus.

'I have seen your little chicks, and a more welcome sight I shall never in my life see, so like in features to you that nothing can be more like than the likeness. I have absolutely taken a journey by short cut quite to Lorium, a short cut of the slippery road, a short cut of the steep ascents: nevertheless I have seen you not only opposite to me but in more places than one, whether I turned to the right hand or to the left. God be praised they have quite a healthy colour and strong lungs. One was holding a piece of white bread, like a little prince, the other a piece of black bread, quite in keeping with a philosopher's son. I beseech the Gods to bless the sower, bless the seed sown, bless the soil that bears a crop so true to stock. For even the sound of their little voices was so sweet, so winsome to my ear that I seemed, I know not how, to hear in the tiny piping of either the clear and charming tones of your own utterance. Now therefore, if you do not take care, you will find me holding my head a good deal higher, for I have those whom I can love instead of you, not with eyes only but with ears also'.

Firstly, it is notable that in this instance Marcus appears to exhibit more affection for the beauty of Fronto's prose than for his children. The letters between Faustina the Younger and Marcus Aurelius also highlight the frequent distance that would have occurred between the father and his children, which also would not have assisted in creating close ties between them (Fronto *xi.2. Rescriptum Marci ad Faustinam*): *Tu quidem, mea Faustina, religiose pro marito et pro nostris liberis agis. Nam relegi epistulam tuam in Formiano, qua me hortaris ut in Avidii conscios vindicem. Ego vero et eius liberis parcam et genero et uxori, et ad senatum scribam, ne aut proscriptio gravior sit aut poena crudelior. Non enim quicquam est quod imperatorem melius commendet gentibus quam dementia. Haec Caesarem deum fecit, haec Augustum consecravit, haec patrem tuum specialiter Pii nomine ornavit. Denique, si ex mea sententia de bello iudicatum esset, nee Avidius esset occisus. Esto igitur secura: Di me tuentur, dis pietas mea cordi est. Pompeianum nostrum in annum sequentem consulem dixi* ['The anxiety which you shew for your husband and our children, my Faustina, is natural. For I have read your letter again in the Formian Villa, in which you urge me to take vengeance on the accomplices of Cassius. But I intend to spare his children and son-in-law and wife, and I shall write to the Senate not to permit any severer persecution or harsher penalty being inflicted on them. For there is nothing that can commend an emperor to the world more than clemency. It was clemency that made Caesar into a God, that deified Augustus, that honoured your father with the distinctive title of Pius. Finally, if my wishes had been followed in respect to the war, not even Cassius would have been slain. So do not be troubled: *The Gods protect me, to the Gods my loyalty is dear.* I have named our Pompeianus 4 consul for the ensuing year'].

Figure 1 – Marcus and Faustina as Mars and Venus (Author's Photograph)

The relationship between the parents seems to have been quite close, despite the rumours of Faustina's infidelities. This is shown through letters from AD 175 between the two, whereby they are supporting each other at a time of great crisis with the uprising of Avidius Cassius (which is discussed further below) (Fronto x.1 *Epistula Faustinae ad Marcum*): (Fronto): *Ipsa in Albanum eras, ut iubes, veniam. Tamen iam hortor ut, si amas liberos tuos, istos rebelliones acerrime persequaris. Male enim adsueverunt duces et milites qui, nisi opprimuntur, oppriment* ['I will come myself as you suggest to Albana tomorrow. But in the meantime I urge you, as you love your children, take the severest measures against these rebels. For the morale of generals and soldiers is thoroughly bad, and unless you crush them they will crush us'].

This is also exhibited in the statue of Faustina the Younger and Marcus Aurelius in the guise of Venus and Mars from the Capitoline Museum (Figure 1), which has been dated to the reign of Commodus. Whether this is simply indicative of his dynastic propaganda or is symbolic of their actual relationship in his eyes is open to debate, but it is interesting to note how they are represented in such a fashion by him. Another indication of their union can also be viewed through the large number of children produced by Faustina the Younger. Some of the attestations of these children are somewhat problematic, which has resulted in some confusion to the actual number of children, but it would seem to have been at least eleven offspring, if not fourteen children.[332] Of course, such a high birth rate may have added to the rumours surrounding the questions of Commodus' legitimacy through Faustina's adulterous liaisons,[333] but this does appear to be quite unlikely because such overt promiscuity would have even tested the tolerance of even such a forbearing man as Marcus Aurelius.[334] All the same, for present purposes, it is most pertinent to note that at least from the perspective of Commodus there appears to have been a good relationship between his parents, hence their later commemoration by him, and he seems to have been cared for by both of them.

Another intriguing association, which is at least inferred by the ancient literary sources, is between Commodus and his predecessor, Lucius Verus. One of the best indicators is in relation to the succession, whereby both Commodus (aged five) and his brother Marcus Annius Verus (aged three) received the title of *Caesar* at the insistence of Lucius Verus.[335] This provides another excellent example of the early intentions behind the Antonine dynastic succession: both boys were being overtly linked with the principate at an early age. Unfortunately his younger brother, M. Annius Verus, died in AD 169, which left Commodus as the sole, designated male heir of Marcus Aurelius. The promotion of Commodus into the public sphere at such an age has been discussed further below, but for the present purposes of this discussion it is quite notable that this advancement was attributed to Lucius Verus. While this may have been attributable as another example by which the ancient literary sources sought to distance Commodus from his father (thereby removing Marcus Aurelius from the responsibility of his son's later actions), this ap-

---

[332] Birley 2000, *op.cit.*, p. 239.
[333] Such as *HA Marcus* 29.1-3.
[334] See Adams 2013, *op.cit.*, pp. 127-8.
[335] For further discussion of this see below. Also see Birley 2000, *op.cit.*, p. 147.

pears unlikely. Another vital aspect to consider, however, is the comparable representation of Commodus and Lucius Verus in the ancient sources. Both men are shown as lewd, corrupt, inclined towards gambling and lavish expense.[336] These representations epitomise how their faults were frequently intended to be viewed: they were embodiments of depravity that were of course naturally contrasted with the austerity and morality of Marcus Aurelius.[337] While this does not suggest any direct influence from Lucius Verus upon Commodus, it is still essential to note how both characterisations were constructed, which in turn affects our reading of the available ancient evidence.

Therefore, in general terms, it is possible to view the importance of these dynastic associations, not only upon Commodus' upbringing and childhood environment, but also in relation to his representation in the ancient sources, which were almost exclusively negative in his characterisation. It is therefore straightforward to establish that Commodus was directly descended from Antoninus Pius, which was of great importance for his future promotion. While this was hardly typical of the succession processed that had occurred during the 2nd Century AD in Rome, it is also important to recognise how symbolically significant it remained. This becomes even more apparent once it is noted how early Commodus received the title of *Caesar*: the (surviving) sons of Marcus Aurelius were already being presented as the succeeding generation of *principes*. Ideally this would have prepared these children from an early age and allowed for an extended period of guidance and tutelage prior to their succession. The naming of both Commodus and M. Annius Verus would of course add to the chances of this accession, which would have naturally been at the forefront of the mind of at least Marcus Aurelius, in view of having already lost children at early ages by AD 166. One of the most important guiding aspects to him would have also been the provision of an appropriate education for his children in order to prepare them for such public lives.

Education

One of the most significant aspects that Marcus Aurelius appears to have emphasised during Commodus' youth was that of his education. This comes as of no great surprise in view of Marcus' own keen

---

[336] See *HA Verus* 4.4-10; *Commodus* 10.1-11.

[337] Adams 2013, *op.cit.*, p. 64.

interest in scholarly activities.[338] This appears to have been at the foremost point in his mind as far as the upbringing of his children is concerned if the ancient literary sources are to be believed.[339] Not surprisingly the *Meditations* are probably the best source of information in this regard, which simply states: τὸ ἐπιτηδείων τροφέων εἰς τὰ παιδία εὐπορῆσαι ['That I had no lack of suitable teachers for my children']. As mentioned previously, this is one of two times that Marcus Aurelius mentions his children in the *Meditations*, which is probably to be expected in light of the philosophical and Stoic focus of the piece. All the same, for the present purposes of this study it is evident that Marcus did place a strong degree of emphasis upon the tuition of his children, including Commodus. This of course would not have only been in accordance with the views of Marcus Aurelius himself and his intellectual values, but would have also been seen as being essential among all of the Roman aristocracy at the time.

This view is also mentioned by Herodian (1.2.1-2): τῷ βασιλεύοντι Μάρκῳ θυγατέρες μὲν ἐγένοντο πλείους, ἄρρενες δὲ δύο. τῶν δὲ ἀρρένων τούτων ὁ μὲν ἕτερος κομιδῇ νέος τὸν βίον μετήλλαξε (Βηρίσσιμος δ' ἦν ὄνομα αὐτῷ), τὸν δὲ περιόντα Κόμοδόν τε καλούμενον ὁ πατὴρ μετὰ πάσης ἐπιμελείας ἀνεθρέψατο, πάντοθεν τοὺς ἐν τοῖς ἔθνεσιν ἐπὶ λόγοις δοκιμωτάτους ἐπὶ συντάξεσιν οὐκ εὐκαταφρονήτοις καλῶν, ὅπως συνόντες ἀεὶ παιδεύοιεν αὐτῷ τὸν υἱὸν ['The emperor Marcus Aurelius had a number of daughters but only two sons. One of them (his name was *Verissimus*) died very young; the surviving son, Commodus, his father reared with great care, summoning to Rome from all over the empire men renowned for learning in their own countries. He paid these scholars large fees to live in Rome and supervise his son's education']. The primary focus of his section is upon Marcus Aurelius, not Commodus, which is important to consider. There is no mention of how Commodus received his tuition: the primary emphasis is upon how loving and caring the father was towards his children. It is also notable that Herodian emphasises the expense of such tutors, possibly as a further example of how much he cared for his children, including Commodus of course. All the same, for present purposes, it is important to recognise that Commodus seemingly was given an excellent education in both Latin and Greek scholarship that would have

---

[338] *HA Marcus* 2.1-4.
[339] Such as Herodian 1.3.1.

been intended to instil in him the best opportunities and moral examples for a successful career in the future. The peer group of Commodus would have also expected such an education of him (considering that it is likely that he would have already received the title of *Caesar*).

The most comprehensive account of Commodus' education is provided by the *HA* biographer, especially in *Commodus* 1.6: *habuit litteratorem Graecum Onesicratem, Latinum Capellam Antistium; orator ei Ateius Sanctus fuit* ['In Greek literature he had Onesicrates as his teacher, in Latin, Antistius Capella; his instructor in rhetoric was Ateius Sanctus']. This passage refers to three teachers: Onesicrates, Capella Antistius and T. Aius Sanctus. Nothing is known about the first two tutors mentioned, but it appears that T. Aius Sanctus was an established orator who was seemingly Commodus' teacher in this discipline by AD 176 at the latest.[340] The sequence of when these three teachers taught Commodus is questionable, but there are other possible known tutors that he may have been taught by, such as Pitholaus, Cleander and Julius Pollux of Naucratis. Pitholaus was seemingly appointed as *tropheus*,[341] as Cleander but in more of a military guise.[342] Julius Pollux dedicated his literary work, the *Onomasticon*, to Commodus, while referring to him as *Caesar*, indicating that he would have taught him and written the text at some point between AD 166-176.[343] This wide ranging list of tutors and teachers further exemplifies the quality of Commodus' education, thereby preparing him for his future public career. It is also important to note how this form of tuition would have been expected among the élites within Rome, being seen as a vital aspect for the development of Commodus' future role in public life.

Therefore, it is evident that the education of Commodus Antoninus was of great importance to a variety of interested parties: his father, his social peers, and the later ancient sources. The importance of it for his father is almost completely self-evident as shown in his own words in the *Meditations*. The education of Commodus was also vital for his future career and the esteem in which he would have been held amongst hi social peers. The ancient sources of course provide a much more duplicitous representation of how he received

---

[340] Birley 2000, *op.cit.*, p. 197.

[341] Galen 16.650.

[342] Herodian 1.12.3.

[343] Grosso 1964, *op.cit.*, pp. 122-3.

his education. Commodus is never depicted as being particularly interested in his studies, whereas Marcus Aurelius was always represented by them as a diligent student. The ancient sources appear to seek to exhibit Marcus' own love and affection for his children through his attention towards their tuition. But the emphasis upon Commodus' education by the ancient authors can be summarised in two points: it was intended to show how Marcus and Commodus were entirely different (despite the best efforts and intentions of the father) and they also exemplified the boorish nature of Commodus – having received such an excellent education, he was still more inclined towards less reputable inclinations (such as gladiatorial combat). This illustrates the difficulty that the ancient sources had in relation to his parentage – how could such a depraved and licentious man like Commodus be the son of the 'great' Marcus Aurelius?

Early Career and his Positions

As mentioned previously, there have been many questions raised by the ancient sources about the legitimacy of Commodus' succession to the principate. All the same, similarly it has been established that he was the legitimate heir of Marcus Aurelius (and also Antoninus Pius), which makes such rumours somewhat irrelevant. Regardless of whether Faustina the Younger was adulterous or not, all of the children she bore were publically accepted by Marcus Aurelius, which made them all legitimate heirs. But Commodus was the only male heir to survive Marcus Aurelius, which unquestionably made him his direct heir to the principate. So in spite of the derisive comments made by the ancient literary sources that questioned Commodus' legitimacy, casting him as an entirely inappropriate successor, or had reservations about the decision of Marcus Aurelius and the whole concept of the dynastic succession – Commodus was still the heir of Marcus Aurelius and in turn this made him the next *princeps*. This had been recognised as being accepted for an extended period of time, and despite the reservations held by the later ancient authors, this was the reality of the Roman principate.

The firm establishment of dynastic succession is clearly indicated by the conferral of the title of *Caesar* upon Commodus and his younger brother in AD 166. This is mentioned by the *HA* biographer (*Commodus* 11.13): *Nominatus inter Caesares quartum iduum Octobrium, quas Herculeas postea nominavit, Pudente et Pollione consulibus* ['He received the name of Caesar on the fourth day before the Ides of the month usually called October, which he later named Hercules, in the consulship of Pudens and Pollio']. Both of these boys were young, being aged five and three respectively. Of course the naming of heirs for the principate at such a young age was not without precedent, clearly following the example set by Augustus in 17 BC with the declaration of both Gaius and Lucius (his grandsons) as *Caesares*.

However, the similarity does not end there: both dynasts (Augustus and Marcus Aurelius) had previously suffered the loss of more than one potential heir, which appears to have provoked both towards the conferral of such a prestigious title onto such young children. It was intended to secure the succession and the continuation of their respective dynasties (and possibly their own names for posterity). In the case of Marcus Aurelius in AD 166 it may have also been motivated by the loss of yet another son, Titus Aurelius Fulvus Antoninus – the twin of Commodus – in AD 165. The occasion of this declaration was of course linked with the triumphal celebration of the eastern victories with Lucius Verus, which was also celebrated with Marcus' other children in the triumphal procession.[344] This further accentuates the dynastic symbolism placed upon the conferral of these titles.

There have been several statue bases discovered throughout the Roman world that were erected in Commodus' honour during the earliest stages of his public career. One of the most notable examples[345] was dedicated to him between AD 164-6, and comprised a series of marble panels that depicted the imperial *familia*. It commemorated this group of Marcus Aurelius' children in Sabratha, in Roman North Africa. This style of representation epitomises how Commodus (and his other siblings) were actively promoted by Marcus Aurelius, with his dynastic aspirations being apparent to all (hence the appeal of such commemorations in the provinces). This is also indicated by another example discovered in Greece (*IG* VII, 1843), which is dated to sometime between AD 166-176. This statue base was presented by the entire city, illustrating how well recognised it had become that Commodus was going to succeed Marcus Aurelius. Another example (*CIL* 10.6001), dated to AD 172, was discovered at Minae. This was presented by the *decurions* (magistrates) of the town, and further exemplifies the dynastic processes at work here. While these inscriptions provide little detail about Commodus'

---

[344] Birley 2000, *op.cit.*, p. 147; *HA Marcus* 12.7-10.
[345] J.M. Hojte, *Roman Imperial Statue Bases: from Augustus to Commodus*, Aarhus University Press: Aarhus, 2005, p. 578, no. 55..

specific role at the time, they still provide a good source of evidence for the public acceptance of his future role (and Marcus' ambitions for him).

Several of the ancient literary sources provide details about Commodus' career up until AD 177, which was when he became co-emperor with his father, Marcus Aurelius. The conferral of most of these honours occurred in AD 175/6, in Commodus' fourteenth year.[346] One of the most detailed references to this is provided by the *HA* biographer (*Commodus* 1.10-2.2): *Appellatus est autem Caesar puer cum fratre suo Vero. quarto decimo aetatis anno in collegium sacerdotum adscitus est. cooptatus est inter trossulos principes iuventutis, cum togam sumpsit. adhuc in praetexta puerili congiarium dedi atque ipse in Basilica Traiani praesedit. indu-tus autem toga est Nonarum Iuliarum die, quo in terris Romulus non apparuit, et eo tempore quo Cassius a Marco* ['While yet a child he was given the name of Caesar, along with his brother Verus, and in his fourteenth year he was enrolled in the college of priests.[347] When he assumed the toga, he was elected one of the leaders of the equestrian youths, the *trossuli*, and even while still clad in the youth's *praetexta* he gave largess and presided in the Hall of Trajan. He assumed the toga on the Nones of July — the day on which Romulus vanished from the earth — at the time when Cassius revolted from Marcus'].

The enrolment of Commodus within the college of pontiffs[348] il-lustrates how he was being placed in a position for more prestigious future offices, with this position having been provided for potential future leaders for centuries,[349] but this is discussed in the next para-graph. Also in AD 175 he was elected *princeps iuventutis* ('prince of the youth'),[350] which was a customary position allocated to young men who were designated as future emperors. The distribution of the largess on Commodus' behalf was of course also intended to ingrati-ate him with the public and also sought to emphasise his future role within the Roman State. All the same, it is also important to not how the biographer of the *Historia Augusta* associates these accolades with the revolt of Avidius Cassius. This was seemingly intended to not

---

[346] *HA Marcus* 22.12.

[347] See I.C. Mantle, "The Roles of Children in Roman Religion", *G&R* 49.1, 2002, p. 105.

[348] See *HA Marcus* 16.1.

[349] D.E. Hahm, 1963, "Roman Nobility and the Three Major Priesthoods, 218-167 BC", *TAPA* 94, 1963, pp. 73-4.

[350] *HA Marcus* 6.3.

only besmirch the promotion of Commodus, but also seeks to connect him with the most serious occasion of insurrection throughout Marcus' reign. The connection between these elements is also inferred by Cassius Dio (71.22.2):

τοῦ δὲ Κασσίου κατὰ τὴν Συρίαν νεωτερίσαντος σφόδρα ἐκπλαγεὶς ὁ Μᾶρκος τὸν Κόμμοδον τὸν υἱὸν ἐκ τῆς Ῥώμης, ὡς καὶ ἐς ἐφήβους ἤδη τελεῖν δυνάμενον, μετεπέμψατο. ὁ δὲ δὴ Κάσσιος Σύρος μὲν ἐκ τῆς Κύρου ἦν, ἀνὴρ δὲ ἄριστος ἐγένετο, καὶ ὁποῖον ἄν τις αὐτοκράτορα ἔχειν εὔξαιτο, πλὴν καθ' ὅσον Ἡλιοδώρου τινὸς ἀγαπητῶς ἐς τὴν τῆς Αἰγύπτου ἡγεμονίαν ἐξ ἐμπειρίας ῥητορικῆς προχωρήσαντος υἱὸς ἦν.

'When Cassius rebelled in Syria, Marcus in great alarm summoned his son Commodus from Rome, as being now entitled to assume the *toga virilis*. Cassius, who was a Syrian from Cyrrhus, had shown himself an excellent man and the sort one would desire to have as an emperor, save for the fact that he was the son of one Heliodorus, who had been content to secure the governorship of Egypt as the reward of his oratorical ability'.

This also epitomises the consistency of the anti-Commodus sentiment implemented by the ancient literary sources. The vast majority of the previously mentioned honours were largely ceremonial, with his admittance to the *collegiums sacerdotum* being the only position that possessed any true (albeit largely symbolic) influence. These positions were intrinsically connected to the political activity of Rome, dating back to the Republican era.[351] The importance of this role was intended to place the incumbent (in this instance, Commodus) firmly within the public sphere. This was in keeping with his general advancement at the time whereby he gained more 'honorific' titles (such as *princeps iuventutis*), which also exemplifies how the prevailing authorities, particularly his father, were seeking to place him in direct line for the succession. While the ancient sources present this in the most questionable light, this theme is also supported by a variety of other evidence.

In this regard, one of the best indicators is provided by the numismatic corpus. The earliest coinage depicting Commodus was

---

[351] G.W. Houston, "The Priests of the Roman Republic: a study of interactions between priesthoods and Magistracies [Review]", *CW* 67.1, 1973, p. 52; T.R.S. Broughton, "The Priests of the Roman Republic: a study of interactions between priesthoods and Magistracies [Review]", *Gnomon* 47.4, 1975, pp. 383-4.

issued by Marcus Aurelius in AD 175/6.[352] The issues minted at this point that represented the young Commodus were produced in a variety of denominations (Aureus,[353] Denarius,[354] Sestertius,[355] As[356]), suggesting that the celebration of his taking of the *toga virilise* was intended to reach the widest audience possible. Commodus is presented on the obverse on all of these issues and in a variety of guises on the reverses. It is noteworthy that in some instances he was connected to symbols of military victory,[357] which is intriguing considering he was not directly involved in the Germanic campaigns at this stage. However, considering these were coins issued by Marcus Aurelius, it seems likely that he sought simply to promote not only the advancement of his son, but also the successes of his northern campaigns – the connection between the two was seemingly coincidental (and yet probably not undesired). Commodus was also linked on these issues with not only his role as *princeps iuventutis*,[358] but he was additionally directly connected with several deities, such as Jupiter,[359] *Hilaritas*,[360] Spes[361] and *Liberalitas*.[362] Of these issues two deserve particular comment: *RIC* 1516 and 1525. *RIC* 1516 is a Sestertius that on the reverse depicts Commodus fulfilling an administrative role (he is shown holding a coin counter) while seated on a platform above a citizen. This provides an excellent example of the role that he was intended to undertake within the Roman State from AD175/6 onwards. This is also suggested by *RIC* 1525, where Commodus is directly connected with Jupiter (the imperial deity) on the reverse in his guise as Jupiter Conservator, indicating how he was perceived as being the future protector of the Empire – and thereby the clear successor of Marcus Aurelius.

---

[352] Some issues, such as *RIC* Marcus Aurelius 1518, have been dated to AD 172/3, but this appears unlikely considering that Commodus had not been made *princeps iuventutis* at this point. A date of AD 175/6 appears much more likely.

[353] *RIC* Marcus 604, 615, 620v, 633.

[354] *RIC* Marcus 603, 606, 615, 617, 633, 1518, 1525.

[355] *RIC* Marcus 1516, 1518, 1525.

[356] *RIC* Marcus 1545, 1547.

[357] *RIC* Marcus 603, 606, 615, 617, 633, 1518, 1525.

[358] *RIC* Marcus603, 615, 617, 1518.

[359] *RIC* Marcus 1525.

[360] *RIC* Marcus 1547.

[361] *RIC* Marcus 620v, 622, 1545.

[362] *RIC* Marcus 1516.

The promotion of Commodus in AD 175, however, should come as of no great surprise though. This rapid advancement in social prominence for Commodus coincided with the rebellion of Avidius Cassius against Marcus' reign. This needs to be analysed in order to contextualise Commodus' promotion. The revolt of Avidius Cassius has often been discussed, and it is very problematic.[363] Syme's analysis is correct: 'Without the reports in Dio and Maximus, an alert student of men and government might arrive at the same conclusion. Otherwise the action of Avidius Cassius remains an enigma: blind ambition and a total miscalculation. No pretender insurgent in the Orient could hope to prevail against the armies of the Danube.'[364] This epitomises the highly complicated nature of the rebellion. Overall, the priorities of Avidius Cassius are quite obscure. This is vital to note because it gives a good perspective about the political and social contexts in which Commodus was promoted in AD 175/6. It is also essential to note how this influenced Marcus Aurelius and his dynastic ideals. The rebellion showed how even a successful *princeps* was still vulnerable to the ambitions of his social peers. Marcus' response to this sedition further characterises how his principate was primarily focused upon the security of the dynasty, his family and perhaps even his own place in history.

The advancement of Commodus in AD 175/6 is not to be viewed without considering the precarious military and political climate at that point. The rebellion of Avidius Cassius epitomises the last years of Marcus' reign. Avidius Cassius exhibited the problem of ambitious and essentially autonomous military generals. The understanding that *principes* could be replaced while separate from the capital had become well known within the Roman mentality. To position Avidius Cassius' revolt in its appropriate milieu and to analyse its importance, the purposes of Avidius Cassius, and the response of Marcus Aurelius, it is important to analyse the development of this prospective insurgent. This is vital to discuss as it has a clear impact upon Commodus' swift advancement in AD 175/6.

Before his revolt in AD 175, Avidius Cassius benefitted from the support of Marcus Aurelius. He had been rewarded for his successes in the Parthian War with a consulship, and by AD 172 was the overall military leader in the East.[365] His father was Avidius Heliodorus,

---

[363] Dio 72.17, 72.23; *HA Marcus* 24.6, 25.1; Birley 2000, *op.cit.*, pp. 184-98.
[364] Syme 1986, *op.cit.*, p. 701.
[365] Dio 71.3.1.

who had been prefect of Egypt under Hadrian and Antoninus Pius from 137-42.[366] Avidius Cassius was a praetorian during the Parthian War, but precisely when he appropriated his eastern position is unclear. The time of Avidius Cassius' consulship was probably in AD 166.[367]

The rebellion was in the East, especially in Syria and Egypt, which exhibits the seriousness of the entire state of affairs – if the idea of subversion multiplied further it could have created a calamitous condition for the impending period of the reign of Marcus Aurelius (and in turn the future of Commodus as emperor as well). There are a few representations of the details in this regard, but the most relevant characterisation is presented by the *HA* biographer (*Marcus* 24.5-25.3):

Voluit Marcomanniam provinciam, voluit etiam Sarmatiam facere et fecisset, nisi Avidius Cassius rebellasset sub eodem in Oriente; atque imperatorem se appellavit, ut quidam dicunt, Faustina volente, quae de mariti valetudine desperaret. alii dicunt ementita morte Antonini Cassium imperatorem se appellasse, cum divum Marcum appellasset. et Antoninus quidem non est satis motus defectione Cassii nec in eius affectus saevit. sed per senatum hostis est iudicatus bonaque eius proscripta per aerarium publicum. relicto ergo Sarmatico Marcomannicoque bello contra Cassium profectus est. Romae etiam turbae fuerunt, quasi Cassius absente Antonino adventaret. sed Cassius statim interfectus est caputque eius adlatum est ad Antoninum. Marcus tamen non exultavit interfectione Cassii caputque eius humari iussit.

'He wanted to create the province of Marcomannia and also of Sarmatia, and he would have done had not Avidius Cassius raised a revolt in the East. This man declared himself emperor, as some state, at the behest of Faustina, who was now in anguish over the health of her husband. But others say that Cassius proclaimed himself emperor after circulating bogus rumours of Antoninus' death, and actually had called him the Deified Marcus. Antoninus was not greatly perplexed by this insurgency, nor did he take on severe measures against Cassius' dear ones. But the Senate declared Cassius an enemy of the state and confiscated his property to the public treasury. Therefore, the Emperor, discarding the Sarmatian and Marcomannic campaigns, departed against him. In Rome there was panic in concern that Cassius would enter during Antoninus' absence; but he was quickly killed and his head was delivered to Antoninus. But even then, Marcus did not celebrate at Cassius' demise, and ordered that his head should be buried'.

This excerpt shows the seriousness of the predicament, which had a significant impact upon Commodus' career and future promotion. Marcus Aurelius is shown as having considered offering peace to Avidius Cassius, but the Senate had previously announced Avidius

---

[366] *PIR²* A 1405.
[367] Alföldy, pp. 181-2.

Cassius an 'Enemy of the State' and his land was taken by the public treasury. It is also significant that in their letters, Faustina II, the wife of Marcus Aurelius, also argued for a severe punishment of Avidius Cassius (Fronto x.1 *Epistula Faustinae ad Marcum*):

Mater mea Faustina patrem tuum Pium [eiusdem] in defectione Celsi cohortata est ut pietatem primum circa suos servaret, sic circa alienos. Non enim pius est imperator, qui non cogitat uxorem et filios. Commodus noster vides in qua aetate sit; Pompeianus gener et senior est et peregrinus. Vide quid agas de Avidio Cassio et de eius consciis. Noli parcere hominibus qui tibi non pepercerunt, et nee mihi nec filiis nostris parcerent, si vicissent. Ipsa iter tuum mox consequar. Quia Fadilla nostra aegrotabat, in Formianura venire non potui. Sed si te Formiis invenire non potuero, adsequar Capuam, quae civitas et meam et filiorum nostrorum aegritudinem poterit adiuvare. Soteridam medicum in Formianum ut dimittas rogo. Ego autem Pisitheo nihil credo, qui puellae virgini curationem nescit adhibere. Signatas mihi litteras Calpurnius dedit, ad quas rescribam, si tardavero, per Caecilium senem spadonem, hominem ut scis fideiem. Cui verbo mandabo quid uxor Avidii Cassii et filii et gener de te iactare dicantur.

'My mother Faustina exhorted your father Pius, on the revolt of [the same] Celsus, that he should shew loyalty in the first place to his own family and then to others. For an Emperor cannot be called Pius who does not think of wife and children. You see how young our Commodus is : Pompeianus, our son-in-law, is both aged and a provincial. See how you deal with Avidius Cassius and his accomplices. Spare not men who have not spared you, and would have spared neither me nor your children, had they succeeded. I will myself soon follow you on your journey. As our Fadilla was ill, I could not come to the Formian Villa. But if I cannot find you at Formiae, I will go on to Capua, a place which is likely to benefit my health and our children's. I beseech you send Soteridas the physician to the Formian Villa. I have no faith in Pisitheus, who does not know how to cure our little maid. Calpurnius gave me the sealed letter to which I will send an answer. If I fail to get it off at once, by Caecilius the old eunuch, a man, as you know, to be relied on, I will entrust him with an oral message of what the wife of Avidius Cassius and his children and son-in-law are reported to say about you.'

Marcus' journey to the East continued this aim. On one side, he affirmed the role of his son, Commodus, as heir and simultaneously secured the Antonine dynasty in the East – a region that he needed to secure for both military and economic reasons. The other reason for Marcus Aurelius' actions exhibits more nuance in his capacity as a leader, but this needs to be viewed as different from the more overt prospect of promoting his son, Commodus. The severity of the rebellion had destabilised Marcus Aurelius, and the trip throughout the eastern provinces was vital for him to view how important it was and to restore the control of his principate. The eastern journey was as much for the advantage and subsequent punishment of those areas that had promoted Avidius Cassius as it was for the benefit of Commodus – Antioch and its subsequent castigation is a perfect example.

So, in many ways, it is important not to underestimate the impact of the rebellion upon Commodus' future career. From this point on he was rapidly promoted (for someone so young particularly) in order to secure his succession, which of course culminated with him being appointed as joint *princeps* in AD 177, which is discussed in the next chapter. All the same, for the purposes of the present discussion it is important to simply observe how this rebellion actively accelerated a process that sought to continue the Antonine dynasty, which had been undertaken by Marcus Aurelius (and probably other members of the imperial *familia*) many years prior to the insurrection of Avidius Cassius. Yet it must also be noted how Commodus was still too young to take on any of the significant positions within the *cursus honorem*. This still left him quite inexperienced, despite the various honorific titles conferred upon him in AD 175/6.

Conclusions

Therefore, when considering the initial fifteen years of Commodus' life there are several notable elements that come to mind. One of the most prominent elements was of course the grandeur of his ancestry. Commodus was not only the son of Marcus Aurelius, the incumbent *princeps*, he was also the grandson of Antoninus Pius, which further legitimised his place as a future ruler of Rome. This should not be underestimated in its significance. While prior Antonine successions had occurred through adoption, this would not have happened if a male heir had existed. Even though this is entirely hypothetical, the hereditary nature of the imperial succession was well and truly established by the 2nd Century AD, despite the endeavours of some Roman aristocrats to circumvent this process (see Chapter Four for further discussion).

The acceptance of a hereditary dynastic succession was already problematic within the Roman mindset: it was unpalatable owing to its semblance of monarchy, and yet it had become frequently applied since the time of Augustus. There was clearly an element (largely aristocratic) within Roman society that sought to discredit such dynastic tendencies, which was owing to their own social or political ambitions. Changes in imperial families and dynasties had of course occurred previously.[368] This would also seemingly be connected to

---

[368] After all, consider the transition between the Julio-Claudian and Flavian dynasties – also the Flavian and Antonine dynasties. While the incumbent

the questions surrounding the legitimacy of Commodus' birth. Owing to his age, Commodus' position within Roman society was entirely reliant upon his ancestry – therefore the easiest way in which to tarnish his legitimacy (whether during his lifetime or after) was to question his parentage. This method applied by the ancient literary sources was also a means by which the illustrious (near perfect) Marcus Aurelius could also be distanced from such a disreputable successor – his own son. Nevertheless, this form of representation clearly contradicts the other ancient evidence – Commodus was actively promoted as a potential heir by his father.

The advancement of Commodus by Marcus Aurelius is best illustrated in the conferral of the title *Caesar* upon him and his younger brother Annius Verus in AD 166. The designation of such a title made an explicit declaration about the succession, which provides a further indication of the hereditary preferences that were tantamount for both Marcus Aurelius and Lucius Verus at the time. All the same, this may not have been a generally accepted opinion, as possibly shown through the revolt of Avidius Cassius. This epitomises the dominance of the emperors in this instance, and yet it also demonstrates the social and political confines of their position as well. Marcus Aurelius still did his utmost to place his children in the optimal position for their future careers, which is exemplified by the education of Commodus. Seemingly no lengths (or expense) were spared in this regard, which exhibits the value that he placed upon such tutelage. In light of Marcus' own devotion to such intellectual pursuits this is hardly surprising. It would have been seen as the ideal avenue by which a future *princeps* could be prepared for this type of public role. Regardless, it is clearly evident that Commodus was never going to be an 'average' Roman aristocrat.

The promotion of Commodus into public life during AD 175/6 exemplifies this point. While at the age of fourteen, Commodus was advanced into the public sphere, being provided with a series of largely honorific positions that further established his succession. At this point it is evident that Commodus was the only surviving male heir of Marcus Aurelius, which emphasises his dynastic importance. This would also have been drawn into stark reality following the sedition of Avidius Cassius, who had been a close and trusted member of Marcus' *consilium*. As has been discussed in Chapter Four (see

---

imperial family changed, the hierarchy within Roman society would have almost seamlessly continued.

below), Marcus Aurelius was hardly unprepared for the question of the succession, but the preference (or plan) was always that any surviving male heir of his would be the next *princeps* and continue the Antonine dynasty. The primary concern would have been Commodus' age – all of the somewhat honorific titles conferred upon him that designated him as Marcus' successor were unable to provide political experience, which was absolutely essential for a successful continuation of the Antonine dynasty.

This epitomises the expectations placed upon Commodus during his youth – he was ultimately the designated successor, regardless of his relative inexperience. So it seems that the strength behind a biological (as opposed to an adoptive) succession plan remained the preferred option. However, this had been in place since the time of Augustus, with the conferral of the title of Caesar upon his grandsons, Gaius and Lucius, at a much earlier age than Commodus.[369] This was not always accepted though, which is epitomised by Herodian (1.3.1-5):

γηραιὸν ὄντα Μᾶρκον, καὶ μὴ μόνον ὑφ' ἡλικίας, ἀλλὰ <καὶ> καμάτοις τε καὶ φροντίσι τετρυχωμένον διατρίβοντά τε ἐν Παίοσι νόσος χαλεπὴ καταλαμβάνει. ἐπεὶ δὲ αὐτῷ τὰς πρὸς σωτηρίαν ἐλπίδας φαύλως ἔχειν ὑπώπτευεν, ἑώρα τε τὸν παῖδα τῆς μειρακίων ἡλικίας ἀρχόμενον ἐπιβαίνειν, δεδιὼς μὴ νεότης ἀκμάζουσα καὶ ἐν ὀρφανίᾳ ἐξουσίαν αὐτοκράτορα καὶ ἀκώλυτον προσλαβοῦσα μαθημάτων μὲν καλῶν καὶ ἐπιτηδευμάτων ἀφηνιάσῃ, μέθαις δὲ καὶ κραιπάλαις ἐπιδῷ ἑαυτήν (ῥᾶστα γὰρ αἱ τῶν νέων ψυχαὶ ἐς ἡδονὰς ἐξολισθαίνουσαι ἀπὸ τῶν παιδείας καλῶν μετοχετεύονται), οἷα δὴ ἄνδρα πολυίστορα μάλιστα ἐτάραττε μνήμη τῶν ἐν νεότητι βασιλείαν παραλαβόντων, τοῦτο μὲν Διονυσίου τοῦ Σικελιώτου τυράννου, ὃς ὑπὸ τῆς ἄγαν ἀκρασίας καινὰς ἡδονὰς ἐπὶ μεγίστοις μισθοῖς ἐθηρᾶτο, τοῦτο δὲ αἱ τῶν Ἀλεξάνδρου διαδόχων ἐς τοὺς ὑπηκόους ὕβρεις τε καὶ βίαι, δι' ὧν τὴν ἐκείνου ἀρχὴν κατῄσχυναν, Πτολεμαῖος μὲν καὶ μέχρις ἀδελφῆς γνησίας ἔρωτος προχωρήσας παρὰ [τε] τοὺς Μακεδόνων καὶ Ἑλλήνων νόμους, Ἀντίγονος δὲ Διόνυσον πάντα μιμούμενος καὶ κισσὸν μὲν περιτιθεὶς τῇ κεφαλῇ ἀντὶ καυσίας καὶ διαδήματος Μακεδονικοῦ, θύρσον δὲ ἀντὶ σκήπτρου φέρων· ἔτι δὲ καὶ μᾶλλον αὐτὸν ἐλύπει τὰ μὴ πρὸ πολλοῦ <γενόμενα> ἀλλ' ὑπόγυον ἔχοντα τὴν μνήμην, τά τε Νέρωνι πεπραγμένα ὃς ἐχώρησε μέχρι μητρῴου φόνου παρεῖχέ τε τοῖς δήμοις ἑαυτὸν καταγέλαστον θέαμα, τά τε Δομετιανῷ τετολμημένα, τῆς ἐσχάτης ὠμότητος οὐδὲν ἀπολείποντα. τοιαύτας δὴ τυραννίδος εἰκόνας ὑποτυπούμενος ἐδεδίει τε καὶ ἤλπιζεν .... οὐ μετρίως δ' αὐτὸν ἐτάραττον καὶ οἱ Γερμανοὶ γειτνιῶντες, οὓς οὐδέπω πάντας ἐκεχείρωτο, ἀλλὰ τοὺς μὲν πειθοῖ ἐς συμμαχίαν προσηγάγετο, τῶν δὲ καὶ κρατήσας ἦν τοῖς ὅπλοις, ἦσαν δέ τινες οἳ διαδράντες πρὸς τὸ παρὸν ἀνακεχωρήκεσαν δέει τῆς παρουσίας τοιούτου βασιλέως. ὑπώπτευεν οὖν, μὴ τῆς ἡλικίας τοῦ μειρακίου καταφρονήσαντες ἐπιθῶνται αὐτῷ. ἐρᾷ δὲ τὸ βάρβαρον καὶ ἐπὶ ταῖς τυχούσαις ἀφορμαῖς ῥᾶστα κινεῖσθαι.

'When Marcus was an old man, exhausted not only by age but also by labors and cares, he suffered a serious illness while visiting the Pannonians. When the emperor suspected that there was little hope of his recovery, and realized that his son would become emperor while still very young, he was afraid that the undisciplined youth, deprived of parental advice, might neglect his excellent studies and good habits and turn to drinking and debauchery (for the minds of the young, prone to pleasures, are turned very easily from the virtues of education) when he had absolute and unrestrained power. This learned man was disturbed also by the memory of those who had become sole rulers in their youth. The Sicilian despot Dionysus, in his excessive licentiousness, had sought out new pleasures and paid the highest prices for them. The arrogance and violence of Alexander's successors against their subject peoples had brought disgrace upon his empire. Ptolemy, too, contrary to the laws of the Macedonians and Greeks, went so far as to marry his own sister. Antigonus had imitated Dionysus in every way, even wearing a crown of ivy instead of the Macedonian hat or the diadem, and carrying the thyrsus instead of a scepter. Marcus was even more distressed when he recalled events of recent date. Nero had capped his crimes by murdering his mother and had made himself ridiculous in the eyes of the people. The exploits of Domitian, as well, were marked by excessive savagery. When he recalled such spectacles of despotism as these, he was apprehensive and anticipated evil events. Then, too, the Germans on the border gave him much cause for anxiety. He had not yet forced all these tribes to submit; some he had won to an alliance by persuasion; others he had conquered by force of arms. There were some who, although they had broken their pact with him, had returned to the alliance temporarily because of the fear occasioned by the presence of so great an emperor. He suspected that, contemptuous of his son's youth, they would launch an assault upon him; for the barbarian is ever eager to revolt on any pretext.'

This passage establishes not only the later rejection of Commodus' own principate, but also the contradiction that is evident within the ancient evidence. It is clear that Commodus was being prepared to succeed Marcus Aurelius from an early stage, and yet Herodian here stresses the concerns of the father. This passage is more indicative of the way in which Herodian (and other ancient sources) sought to characterise both father and son – the 'ideal' as opposed to the 'depraved'. If this was the case, would Marcus Aurelius (being the astute Roman emperor as he is depicted) have taken on Commodus as his co-emperor? It is much more complex than this, but it is a salient point. Commodus was young and could not qualify for the traditional magistracies that were a vital source of training for any future *princeps* without a radical change in precedent. Nevertheless, all of this changes in AD 177, when Commodus becomes the partner of his father as co-emperor.

CHAPTER 4

THE ROLE OF COMMODUS AS JOINT
PRINCEPS WITH MARCUS AURELIUS

Introduction

The overall intent of this discussion follows on from the previous chapter. It aims to continue the general theme of considering Commodus within his social and political context. This has previously focused upon his rapid promotion up until AD 175/6, with particular emphasis upon his advancement in AD 166 through the conferral of the title of *Caesar* upon him. This epitomises how Commodus was already intended to succeed Marcus Aurelius and continue the Antonine dynasty, even if it was meant to originally have been in association with his brother, Marcus Annius Verus. This firmly establishes the dominance of the imperial succession within the Roman political scene. Experience from within the traditional *cursus honorem* was seemingly less important than dynastic hereditary descent at this point in time. This is a pertinent issue. It is symbolic of the position of the traditional Roman hierarchy and its general impotence politically (as compared to socially) when contrasted to the supremacy of the imperial *familia* and its *consilium*.

When examining this time period (AD 177-180) within the social and political contexts that surrounded Commodus' joint principate with Marcus Aurelius, it becomes evident that there is a wide variety of available ancient evidence that can be utilised in order to understand this era in the most comprehensive fashion. One of the most significant sources of evidence for this study is the numismatic corpus issued throughout the empire during this time period. The coin evidence presents a public (propagandistic?) representation of Commodus Antoninus as the joint emperor of Rome. This particularly emphasised the promotion of him in the public sphere with his first consulship, which coincided with his elevation to the role of joint *princeps*. This is also complimented by the epigraphic sources from the time, which further emphasise the prominence of the younger co-emperor. In particular the evidence from the statue bases discovered throughout the empire are especially useful – they definitively exhibit how Commodus was actively advanced as the sole successor of Marcus Aurelius between AD 177-180. The ancient literary sources do not accentuate this point, and yet they are also of great assistance as a means of determining Commodus' placement within the Roman principate during this period of transition. As would be expected these textual references are typically negative towards him, but this does not mean that they are not of use to the modern scholar, especially once their limited objectivity is not only recognised but also discounted.

All the same, one of the most important factors to be dealt with in this study is the general social context in which Commodus became emperor of the Roman Empire. It must be recognised that Commodus was no 'island' – the politics of his promotion extended far beyond the imperial *familia*. While the idea of the Roman imperial period being entirely focused upon one person is attractive for an author (be they ancient or modern), the reality of the situation is entirely different – the number of influences and extenuating factors that could be factored in are legion. Therefore, in this regard it is vital to examine the workings of the senatorial aristocracy at the time in order to gain a better perspective. This form of analysis exhibits a variety of elements that existed within both the social and political systems, providing a further contextualisation. This is also evident through the analysis of the other aspiring figures that could have been viewed as either supporters or rivals of Commodus at this stage. This was largely symbolic of the preparations made by Marcus Aurelius for the succession and the extension of the Antonine dynasty. All of these elements highlight the issues surrounding Commodus during this phase of the succession.

The historical context of Commodus' advancement and, in turn, the death of Marcus Aurelius is vital for any understanding of Commodus' principate. He cannot be examined in isolation – as no primary leader should be (they are responsible and answerable to the wider community). The question remains about why he was viewed as the most appropriate imperial colleague and ultimate successor of Marcus Aurelius. In many ways this decision epitomises the inadequacies of the system in general. Commodus was clearly chosen because of his birth, not his experience – unlike Trajan, Hadrian, and Antoninus Pius for example. All the same, was this the fault of Commodus? Or was it systemic? In many ways this epitomises the inadequacies of the system in general. It is also indicative of the limited powers of the Senate at this stage of the Roman principate – a group seemingly more interested in individual advancement rather than political consistency. The *princeps* (or in this case the co-*princeps*) was the dominant figure within the State, which made the choices and opinions of other Roman élites often largely redundant. All the same, this does not mean that the Senators (and other influential aristocrats) at the time did not hold onto their own imperial aspirations – as has already been discussed in relation to Avidius Cassius and his rebellion. The emperor(s) were clearly dominant politically, militarily, financially and socially – but there was always the prospect of potential sedition. Therefore, it is appropriate to consider the Senate and their role within Roman imperial politics at this point of the study.

The State of the Senate

The placement of the Senate within Roman society and its politics (both official and unofficial) has been the topic of much discussion within modern scholarship.[370] It is a highly complex topic,[371] one that is only dealt with here briefly. Of course these complexities can be traced back to before the creation of the principate – the *lex Titia* of the Second Triumvirate clearly establishes the difficulties of the Roman constitution in this regard as only one point of concern. All of the difficulties in this regard are best dealt with by Syme,[372] and are beyond the true focus of the present study. All the same, Augustus was the pivotal figure for the creation of the Roman principate of course, and he was clearly a smart operator. He recognised the importance of the Senate as both an institution and as a symbol for Roman society, and yet he also exploited the inherent weaknesses that existed within this group of aristocratic families at the time. This can be viewed by briefly examining two sources of evidence: Suetonius' biography of him (*Augustus* 56.3) and the *Res Gestae* (34):

Cum Asprenas Nonius artius ei iunctus causam veneficii accusante Cassio Severo diceret, consuluit senatum, quid officii sui putaret; cunctari enim se, ne si superesset, eripere legibus reum, sin deesset, destituere ac praedamnare amicum existimaretur; et consentientibus universis sedit in subsellis per aliquot horas, verum tacitus et ne laudatione quidem iudiciali data.

---

[370] Jones 1979, *op.cit.*; Syme 1958, *op.cit.*

[371] Traupman 1956, *op.cit.*, p. 45.

[372] R. Syme, *The Roman Revolution*, Oxford: Oxford University Press, 1939.

'When Nonius Asprenas, a close friend of his, was meeting a charge of poisoning made by Cassius Severus, Augustus asked the senate what they thought he ought to do; for he hesitated, he said, for fear that if he should support him, it might be thought that he was shielding a guilty man, but if he failed to do so, that he was proving false to a friend and prejudicing his case. Then, since all approved of his appearing in the case, he sat on the benches for several hours, but in silence and without even speaking in praise of the defendant.'

In consulátú sexto et septimo, bella ubi civilia exstinxeram per consénsum úniversórum potitus rerum omnium, rem publicam ex meá potestáte in senátus populíque Romani arbitrium transtulí. Quó pro merito meó senatus consulto Augustus appellátus sum et laureís postés aedium meárum vestiti publice coronaque civíca super iánuam meam fíxa est clupeusque aureus in cúriá Iúliá positus, quem mihi senatum populumque Romanum dare virtutis clementiae iustitiae pietatis caussa testatum est per eius clúpei inscriptionem. Post id tempus praestiti omnibus dignitate, potestatis autem nihilo amplius habui quam qui fuerunt mihi quoque in magistratu conlegae.

'In my sixth and seventh consulships, when I had extinguished the flames of civil war, after receiving by universal consent the absolute control of affairs, I transferred the republic from my own control to the will of the senate and the Roman people. For this service on my part I was given the title of Augustus by decree of the senate, and the doorposts of my house were covered with laurels by public act, and a civic crown was fixed above my door, and a golden shield was placed in the Curia Julia whose inscription testified that the senate and the Roman people gave me this in recognition of my valour, my clemency, my justice, and my piety. After that time I took precedence of all in rank, but of power I possessed no more than those who were my colleagues in any magistracy.'

Both of these ancient sources of evidence exhibit how while the opinion (or at least the respectability) of the Senate remained an important social and political consideration for most emperors, the real power was now placed in the hands of the *princeps*. This was Augustus' well considered creation, which he maintained both brilliantly and successfully. In view of the decline of its influence throughout the Second and First Centuries BC, the Senate clung to their vestiges of power but were ultimately unable to resist his dominance in 31 BC (let alone 27 or 23 BC). All the same, his does not make its constituent members an entirely placid and primarily unquestionably supportive element within the Roman community either. This was a difficult circumstance for Augustus – the *clementia* of Julius Caesar had clearly been ineffective, yet he knew there was resistance that was impossible to crush without a similar response. So therefore, Augustus sought to ingratiate himself with his social peers – his principate did little to suppress (if not encourage) the ambitions of many leading senators. This policy worked. Over time this of course led to less subtle *principes* dealing with this competitive group quite harshly, and yet at other points there were imperial demonstrations of both deference or compliancy (the reign of Hadrian actually exhibits both elements at different times). This was a fine line to tread for any emperor – but it is important to note that while the Senate were politically ineffective by the Second Century AD, they were by no means 'toothless' in social terms. So it is with this in mind that the Senate should be viewed as a significant factor in the analysis of Commodus' principate.

The placement of the Senate within the Roman social and political spheres of the Antonine Emperors is best shown by the differing levels of acceptance towards both Hadrian and Antoninus Pius. Hadrian placed himself in disfavour with the Senate at both the beginning and end of his reign by executing senators without their consultation. See the *Historia Augusta* for example:

usus Plotinae quoque favore, cuius studio etiam legatus expeditionis Parthicae tempore destinatus est. qua quidem tempestate utebatur Hadrianus amicitia Sosii Papi et Platorii Nepotis ex senatorio ordine, ex equestri autem Attiani, tutoris quondam sui, et Liviani et Turbonis. in adoptionis sponsionem venit Palma et Celso, inimicis semper suis et quos postea ipse insecutus est, in suspicionem adfectatae tyrannidis lapsis. secundo consul favore Plotinae factus totam praesumptionem adoptionis emeruit.

'He enjoyed, too, the favour of Plotina, and it was due to her interest in him that later, at the time of the campaign against Parthia, he was appointed the legate of the Emperor. At this same time he enjoyed, besides, the friendship of Sosius Papus and Platorius Nepos, both of the senatorial order, and also of Attianus, his former guardian, of Livianus, and of Turbo, all of equestrian rank. And when Palma and Celsus, always his enemies, on whom he later took vengeance, fell under suspicion of aspiring to the throne, his adoption seemed assured, and it was taken wholly for granted when, through Plotina's favour, he was appointed consul for the second time.' (*Hadrian* 4.1 4)

in senatu quoque excusatis quae facta erant iuravit se numquam senatorem nisi ex senatus sententia puniturum.

'In the senate, too, he cleared himself of blame for what had happened, and pledged himself never to inflict punishment on a senator until after a vote of the senate.'(*Hadrian* 7.4)

senatus fastigium in tantum extulit, difficile faciens senatores ut, cum Attianum ex praefecto praetorii ornamentis consularibus praeditum faceret senatorem, nihil se amplius habere quod in eum conferri posset ostenderit. equites Romanos nec sine se de senatoribus nec secum iudicare permisit. erat enim tunc mos ut, cum princeps causas agnosceret, et senatores et equites Romanos in consilium vocaret et sententiam ex omnium deliberatione proferret. exsecratus est denique principes qui minus senatoribus detulissent.

'In the appointment of senators he showed the utmost caution and thereby greatly increased the dignity of the senate, and when he removed Attianus from the post of prefect of the guard and created him a senator with consular honours, he made it clear that he had no greater honour which he could bestow upon him. Nor did he allow knights to try cases involving senators whether he was present at the trial or not. For at that time it was customary for the emperor, when he tried cases, to call to his council both senators and knights and give a verdict based on their joint decision. Finally, he denounced those emperors who had not shown this deference to the senators.' (*Hadrian* 8.7-10)

et mortuo Helio Vero Caesare Hadrianus ingruente tristissima valetudine adoptavit Arrium Antoninum, qui postea Pius dictus est, et ea quidem lege ut ille sibi duos adoptaret, Annium Verum et Marcum Antoninum. hi sunt qui postea duo pariter Augusti primi rem publicam gubernaverunt. et Antoninus quidem Pius idcirco appellatus dicitur quod socerum fessum aetate manu sublevaret, quamvis alii cognomentum hoc ei dicant inditum, quod multos senatores Hadriano iam saevienti abripuisset, alii, quod ipsi Hadriano magnos honores post mortem detulisset.

'After the death of Aelius Verus Caesar, Hadrian was attacked by a very severe illness, and thereupon he adopted Arrius Antoninus (who was afterwards called Pius), imposing upon him the condition that he adopt two sons, Annius Verus and Marcus Antoninus. These were the two who afterwards ruled the empire together, the first joint Augusti. And as for Antoninus, he was called Pius, it is said, because he used to give his arm to his father-in-law when weakened by old age. However, others assert that this surname was given to him because, as Hadrian grew more cruel, he rescued many senators from the Emperor; others, again, that it was because he bestowed great honours upon Hadrian after his death.' (*Hadrian* 24.1-5)

Each of these passages from the *Historia Augusta* illustrate how Hadrian was viewed by the senatorial élites – he paid respect to them, but at other times he superseded what was their traditional responsibility (at least as far as they were concerned). This has resulted in a somewhat 'mixed' representation of him by the ancient literary sources – Hadrian was an efficient emperor, but one who did not always play by their rules. This is contrasted with the representation of Antoninus Pius by the *HA* biographer (*Pius* 5.3): *Factus imperator nulli eorum quos Hadrianus provexerat successorem dedit fuitque ea constantia ut septenis et novenis annis in provinciis bonos praesides detineret* ['After his accession to the throne he removed none of the men whom Hadrian had appointed to office, and, indeed, was so steadfast and loyal that he retained good men in the government of provinces for terms of seven and even nine years']. Antoninus Pius is shown here as being almost extreme in his deference to the senatorial order. In his relations with the Senate, Antoninus Pius is depicted as being entirely respectful, which epitomises his general representation (regardless of its accuracy – the deification of Hadrian was clearly a sticking point and one where the new *princeps* got his way). In relation to the Emperor Commodus Antoninus, this exhibits how the Senate remained as an influential factor within Roman society.

Under Marcus Aurelius this continued.[373] By simply continuing to use the *Historia Augusta* this can be easily established, which is indicative of the majority of the ancient literary sources. In this regard he was clearly depicted as being a pro-senatorial figure, which would have been welcomed the intended audience.[374] The best way in which Marcus Aurelius was exhibited as possessing a respectful attitude towards the Senate was through the declaration that none of the order was executed by him without their consultation. This is mentioned three times by the *HA* biographer:

hoc quoque senatoribus detulit ut, quotiens de quorum capite esset iudicandum, secreto pertractaret atque ita in publicum proderet nec pateretur equites Romanos talibus interesse causis. semper autem, cum potuit, interfuit senatui, etiamsi nihil esset referendum, si Romae fuit; si vero aliquid referre voluit, etiam de Campania ipse venit. comitiis praeterea etiam usque ad noctem frequenter interfuit neque umquam recessit de curia nisi consul dixisset "nihil vos moramur patres conscripti". senatum appellationibus a consule factis iudicem dedit.

'He granted senators the further privilege that whenever any of them was to be tried on a capital charge, he would examine the evidence behind closed doors and only after so doing would bring the case to public trial; nor would he allow members of the equestrian order to attend such investigations. He always attended the meetings of the senate if he was in Rome, even though no measure was to be proposed, and if he wished to propose anything himself, he came in person even from Campania. More than this, when elections were held he often remained even until night, never leaving the senate-chamber until the consul announced, "We detain you no longer, Conscript Fathers". Further, he appointed the senate judge in appeals made from the consul.' (*Marcus* 10.6-9)

Maecianum etiam, socium Cassii, cui Alexandria erat commissa, exercitus occidit. nam et praefectum praetorio sibi fecerat, qui et ipse occisus est. in conscios defectionis vetuit senatum graviter vindicare. simul petiit, ne qui senator tempore principatus sui occideretur, ne eius pollueretur imperium. eos etiam qui deportati fuerant revocari iussit, cum paucissimi centuriones capite essent puniti.

'Maecianus, Cassius' ally, in whose charge Alexandria had been placed, was killed by the army; likewise his prefect of the guard — for he had appointed one — was also slain. Marcus then forbade the senate to impose any heavy punishment upon those who had conspired in this revolt; and at the same time, in order that his reign might escape such a stain, he requested that during his rule no senator should be executed. Those who had been exiled, moreover, he ordered to be recalled; and there were only a very few of the centurions who suffered the death-penalty.' (*Marcus* 25.4-7)

[373] A.R. Birely, *Marcus Aurelius: a biography*, London: Routeldge, 2000.
[374] See Adams 2013, *op.cit.*, p. 26.

Ante tempus sane mortis, priusquam ad bellum Marcomannicum rediret, in Capitolio iuravit nullum senatorem se sciente occisum, cum etiam rebelliones dixerit se servaturum fuisse si scisset. nihil enim magis et timuit et deprecatus est quam avaritiae famam, de qua se multis epistulis purgat.

'Previous to his death, and before he returned to the Marcomannic war, he swore in the Capitol that no senator had been executed with his knowledge and consent, and said that had he known he would have spared even the insurgents. Nothing did he fear and deprecate more than a reputation for covetousness, a charge of which he tried to clear himself in many letters.' (*Marcus* 29.4-5)

Each of these passages emphasise the consistent characterisation of Marcus Aurelius as being the dutiful *princeps* who respected the senatorial *ordo*. This is also shown in other honours and assistance he provided them (*HA Marcus* 10.3-7): *multos ex amicis in senatum adlegit cum aediliciis aut praetoriis dignitatibus. multis senatoribus verum pauperibus sine crimine dignitates tribunicias aediliciasque concessit. nec quemquam in ordinem legit, nisi quem ipse bene scisset. hoc quoque senatoribus detulit ut, quotiens de quorum capite esset iudicandum, secreto pertractaret atque ita in publicum proderet nec pateretur equites Romanos talibus interesse causis. semper autem, cum potuit, interfuit senatui, etiamsi nihil esset referendum, si Romae fuit; si vero aliquid referre voluit, etiam de Campania ipse venit* ['He enrolled in the senate many of his friends, giving them the rank of aedile or praetor; and on a number of poor but honest senators he bestowed the rank of tribune or aedile. Nor did he ever appoint anyone to senatorial rank whom he did not know well personally. He granted senators the further privilege that whenever any of them was to be tried on a capital charge, he would examine the evidence behind closed doors and only after so doing would bring the case to public trial; nor would he allow members of the equestrian order to attend such investigations. He always attended the meetings of the senate if he was in Rome, even though no measure was to be proposed, and if he wished to propose anything himself, he came in person even from Campania.']. All of these passages were intended to exhibit not only the equanimity of Marcus Aurelius towards his social peers,[375] but also their continued importance within Roman political life – thus being quite appealing to the intended author of the *HA* biographer.

The same cannot be said for the presentation of Commodus' character and his relationship with the Senate throughout the ancient literary sources.[376] These representations continually exhibited how

---

[375] Schwendemann 1923, *op.cit.*, p. 116.
[376] Grosso 1964, *op.cit.*

Commodus was at odds with the Senate. The *HA* biographer, for example, highlighted how the senatorial élite were persecuted by him: *Occisus est eo tempore etiam Claudius quasi a latronibus, cuius filius cum pugione quondam ad Commodum ingressus est, multique alii senatores sine iudicio interempti, feminae quoque divites* ['At this time Claudius also, whose son had previously come into Commodus' presence with a dagger, was slain, ostensibly by bandits, and many other senators were put to death, and also certain women of wealth']. This is also paralleled by Cassius Dio's portrayal of the fear among the senators that Commodus instilled (73.21.1-2):

οὗτος μὲν ὁ φόβος πᾶσι κοινὸς καὶ ἡμῖν καὶ τοῖς ἄλλοις ἦν· ἔπραξε δὲ καὶ ἕτερόν τι τοιόνδε πρὸς ἡμᾶς τοὺς βουλευτάς, ἐξ οὗ οὐχ ἥκιστα ἀπολεῖσθαι προσεδοκήσαμεν. στρουθὸν γὰρ ἀποκτείνας καὶ τὴν κεφαλὴν αὐτοῦ ἀποτεμὼν προσῆλθεν ἔνθα ἐκαθήμεθα, τῇ τε ἀριστερᾷ χειρὶ ἐκείνην καὶ τῇ δεξιᾷ τὸ ξίφος ἡματωμένον ἀνατείνας, καὶ εἶπε μὲν οὐδέν, τὴν δὲ κεφαλὴν τὴν ἑαυτοῦ σεσηρὼς ἐκίνησεν, ἐνδεικνύμενος ὅτι καὶ ἡμᾶς τὸ αὐτὸ τοῦτο δράσει. κἂν συχνοὶ παραχρῆμα ἐπ' αὐτῷ γελάσαντες ἀπηλλάγησαν τῷ ξίφει (γέλως γὰρ ἡμᾶς ἀλλ' οὐ λύπη ἔλαβεν), εἰ μὴ δάφνης φύλλα, ἃ ἐκ τοῦ στεφάνου εἶχον, αὐτός τε διέτραγον καὶ τοὺς ἄλλους τοὺς πλησίον μου καθημένους διατραγεῖν ἔπεισα, ἵν' ἐν τῇ τοῦ στόματος συνεχεῖ κινήσει τὸν τοῦ γελᾶν ἔλεγχον ἀποκρυψώμεθα.

'This fear was shared by all, by us senators as well as by the rest. And here is another thing that he did to us senators which gave us every reason to look for our death. Having killed an ostrich and cut off his head, he came up to where we were sitting, holding the head in his left hand and in his right hand raising aloft his bloody sword; and though he spoke not a word, yet he wagged his head with a grin, indicating that he would treat us in the same way. And many would indeed have perished by the sword on the spot, for laughing at him (for it was laughter rather than indignation that overcame us), if I had not chewed some laurel leaves, which I got from my garland, myself, and persuaded the others who were sitting near me to do the same, so that in the steady movement of our armies we might conceal the fact that we were laughing'.

Even when the inherent anti-Commodus sentiment by these authors is factored in when viewing these texts, there is one clear sentiment: Commodus and the Senate did not work well together.[377] All the same, this did not make either side 'right' or 'wrong' – it is more indicative of a variance in priorities and their respective ambitions. Commodus sought to promote himself (and his *consilium*) as he saw fit, which he viewed as being well within his own prerogative. The Senate had differing ideas and motives – they sought to maintain the

---

[377] Traupman 1956, *op.cit.*

dignitas and relevance of their social (and political) position, which was clearly incompatible with the perspective of Commodus. The one thing that they had in common can be summarised in one word – ambition.[378]

In many ways the Senate (and its constituent members) at this time was somewhat of a dichotomy. They adhered to sentiments of the Roman Republican system, and yet there was an acceptance of what was effectively a monarchical system. If this was not the case, why accept two children as *Caesares* in AD 166, and an inexperienced youth as joint *princeps* in AD 177? While the ancient literary sources portray the Senate as hating the imperial autocracy, its more ambitious members would have seemingly greedily accepted it for themselves if the chance was provided. There were always contenders for the role as well as imperial supporters, which epitomises the complexity of the position of *princeps* – who could be trusted. The possibility of insurrection against an emperor had been exhibited many times before, which would have been known to all involved. It is for this reason that the other significant personages need to be considered at this point of the present analysis. Commodus may have been groomed for the principate from an early age, but that did not make his position entirely secure either. The joint principate was intended to ensure a smooth succession upon the death of Marcus Aurelius, but there were still other significant personages within élite circles that played their part.

The Other 'Players'

The analysis of the other significant 'players' within Roman politics at this time can be interpreted in a variety of ways. This influential group could be viewed as being promoted and brought into the imperial *familia* (or *consilium*) in order for Marcus Aurelius to secure Commodus' succession. This would suggest that they were intended to be his supporters after Marcus' death. All the same, this collection of powerful and influential people could also be seen as potential competitors for the imperial position of Commodus as well. What is important, however, is to initially recognise that each 'player' held a significant position during the joint principate of Marcus Aurelius and Commodus, and continued to perform a prominent role within the imperial administration after the death of Marcus Aurelius in AD 180. There are five individuals to be considered here in this regard:

---

[378] Grosso 1964, *op.cit.*

Lucius Antistius Burrus, Marcus Petronius Sura Mamertinus, Marcus Peducaeus Plautius Quintillus, Cnaeus Claudius Severus and Tiberius Claudius Pompeianus.

Lucius Antistius Burrus was clearly of some influence during the joint principate of Marcus Aurelius and Commodus Antoninus, with him being given his first consulship (as *ordinaries*) in AD 181 as the colleague of the *princeps*. He was also influential as he married Commodus' sister, Vibia Aurelia Sabina. Considering he was from a newly promoted family from the African provinces, this makes Lucius Antistius Burrus quite significant. Although this may appear remarkable, it is evident that he had been part of a vital supporting group for both emperors following the revolt of Avidius Cassius.

All the same, it must be noted that he was ultimately executed on the charge of conspiring against Commodus: *qui tantum per stultitiam Commodi potuit, ut Burrum, sororis Commodi virum, reprehendentem nuntiantemque Commodo quae fiebant in suspicionem regni adfectati traheret et occideret, multis aliis, qui Burrum defendebant, pariter interemptis* ['Indeed, because of Commodus' utter degeneracy, his power was so great that he brought Burrus, the husband of Commodus' sister, who was denouncing and reporting to Commodus all that was being done, under the suspicion of pretending to the throne, and had him put to death; and at the same time he slew many others who defended Burrus.']. This highlights two significant elements in particular – firstly, the prominence of Lucius Antistius Burrus as a member of the imperial *familia*, who was clearly ambitious and seemingly a threat to Commodus' position (well at least as far as the *princeps* was concerned). Secondly, the rise (and ultimate demise) of Lucius Antistius Burrus epitomises how during the joint principate Marcus Aurelius sought to secure the position of his son, Commodus, by allying himself with his most prominent supporters, although this may not have always turned out as he would have planned – Lucius Antistius Burrus seemingly may have had his own ambitions.

Marcus Petronius Sura Mamertinus was another African who became another member of the imperial *familia* through his marriage to another of Commodus' sisters, which in this case was Cornificia.[379] Another indication of his prominence is shown through his appointment as *consul ordinarius* in AD 182.[380] As with Lucius Antistius Burrus, this is probably indicative of Commodus Antoninus promot-

---

[379] This seems to have occurred in AD 175. See Birley 2001, *op.cit.*, p. 182.
[380] *PIR*² P 311, 312.

ing members of the imperial *familia* who had been advanced during his joint principate with his father, Marcus Aurelius.[381] The connection with the influential group of *nobiles* from the African provinces would have also in turn strengthened his own position at the time.[382] But it may have also brought some concerns for Commodus as well. He was seemingly seen as a threat. At some point between AD 190-192 Commodus had both Marcus Petronius Sura Mamertinus and his son, Antoninus, executed:[383] *his occisis interemit Servilium et Dulium Silanos cum suis, mox Antium Lupum et Petronios Mamertinum et Suram filiumque Mamertini Antoninum ex sorore sua genitum* ['After these men had been put to death he slew the two Silani, Servilius and Dulius, together with their kin, then Antius Lupus and the two Petronii, Mamertinus and Sura, and also Mamertinus' son Antoninus, whose mother was his own sister.']. The *HA* biographer provides little detail here about the reasoning behind this decision (favouring to simply establish Commodus' innate cruelty),[384] but it may have been another example of his relatives through marriage becoming too prominent for his liking.

Marcus Peducaeus Plautius Quintillus derived from an aristocratic family,[385] and was connected to the imperial *familia* through his marriage to Commodus' sister, Fadilla. His prominence also becomes very apparent when his appointment as *consul ordinarius* in AD 177 (as Commodus' colleague) is factored in.[386] The introduction of Peducaeus Plautius Quintillus into the imperial nexus was seemingly owing to his strong links with the Roman aristocracy. As with the other promotions of such figures, this appears to have come as a direct result of the rebellion of Avidius Cassius. The swift promotion of Commodus at the time to that of joint *princeps* in such uncertain circumstances required the securing of these prominent figures as supporters for this largely inexperienced young man. In view of his familial connection to Commodus Antoninus prior to his marriage to Fadilla (as being the nephew of Lucius Verus)[387] it would have seemed to Marcus Aurelius that he was a trustworthy supporter for

---

[381] Grosso 1964, *op.cit.*

[382] Champlin 1979, *op.cit.*, p. 306.

[383] Traupman 1956, *op.cit.*

[384] Grosso 1964, *op.cit.*

[385] For example, see *PIR²* C 603-605.

[386] Traupman 1956, *op.cit.*

[387] *CIL* 14.328.

Commodus – hence his appointment as Commodus' consular colleague in AD 177.[388] All the same, this was also indicative of how his ambitions would have also required attention to ensure his support.

Cnaeus Claudius Severus[389] was another *nobilis* during the joint principate of Marcus Aurelius and Commodus Antoninus who was married to another sister of Commodus, in this case Annia Aurelia Galeria Faustina.[390] Cnaeus Claudius Severus came from a consular family that had strong prior connections to Marcus Aurelius, who had actively promoted them. He attained his second consulship in AD 173 (as *consul ordinarius* and consular colleague of Tiberius Claudius Pompeianus – which is discussed below) and it is notable that his name appears first on the *fasti*.[391] While with the previous 'players' there was an over (and pivotal) African connection,[392] it is important to note that Cnaeus Claudius Severus possessed a strong connection to the East – particularly in Ancyra and Paphlagonia. This is particularly significant because, following the revolt of Avidius Cassius, this region would have been of some concern for both *principes*. It would appear that the Claudii Severii maintained their elevated position throughout the reign of Commodus, so it seems that they performed a supportive role – or at least avoided the ire of the young *princeps*. Yet, the *ambitio* of Cnaeus Claudius Severus would have remained as a significant factor within the perspective of the emperor.

Tiberius Claudius Pompeianus was clearly the most influential group of 'players' in this regard. He was married to the daughter of Marcus Aurelius, Lucilla, in AD 169 following the death of Lucius Verus.[393] He was vital following the revolt of Avidius Cassius not only because of his prominent military role, but also for his Antioch connections.[394] The ancient literary sources provide a laudatory representation – often distancing him from the future sole emperor, Commodus:

οὐδὲν ἧττον μέντοι καὶ ὁ Κόμοδος ἐφύλαττε τὰς τιμὰς τῇ ἀδελφῇ· καὶ γὰρ ἐπὶ τοῦ βασιλείου θρόνου καθῆστο ἐν τοῖς θεάτροις, καὶ τὸ πῦρ προεπόμπευεν αὐτῆς. ἐπεὶ δὲ ὁ Κόμοδος γυναῖκα ἠγάγετο, Κρισπῖναν ὄνομα, ἀνάγκη τε ἐγένετο τὴν προεδρίαν

---

[388] Grosso 1964, *op.cit.*
[389] *PIR*² C 1004.
[390] Birley 2001, *op.cit.*, p. 247.
[391] Pflaum 1961, p. 30.
[392] Champlin 1980, *op.cit.*
[393] *HA Marcus* 20.6-7.
[394] *PIR*² C 973.

ἀπονέμεσθαι τῇ τοῦ βασιλεύοντος γυναικί, δυσφόρως τοῦτο φέρουσα ἡ Λουκίλλα, καὶ
τὴν ἐκείνης τιμὴν ἑαυτῆς ὕβριν νομίζουσα, τὸν μὲν ἑαυτῆς ἄνδρα Πομπηιανὸν εἰδυῖα
ἀγαπῶντα τὸν Κόμοδον, οὐδὲν αὐτῷ περὶ ἐπιθέσεως τῆς ἀρχῆς ἀνακοινοῦται,
Κοδράτου δέ, νεανίσκου εὐγενοῦς τινος καὶ πλουσίου, ἐφ' οὗ καὶ λανθανούσῃ
συνουσίᾳ διεβάλλετο, πεῖραν τῆς γνώμης λαμβάνουσα, περί τε τῆς προεδρίας συνεχῶς
ἀπωδύρετο, καὶ κατ' ὀλίγον ἀνέπεισε τὸν νεανίσκον ὀλέθρια βουλεύσασθαι αὐτῷ τε καὶ
πάσῃ τῇ συγκλήτῳ.

'Commodus, too, allowed his sister to retain the imperial honors; she continued to
occupy the imperial seat at the theaters, and the sacred fire was carried before her.
But when Commodus married Crispina, custom demanded that the front seat at the
theater be assigned to the empress. Lucilla found this difficult to endure, and felt
that any honor paid to the empress was an insult to her; but since she was well aware
that her husband Pompeianus was devoted to Commodus, she told him nothing
about her plans to seize control of the empire. Instead, she tested the sentiments of
a wealthy young nobleman, Quadratus, with whom she was rumored to be sleeping
in secret. Complaining constantly about this matter of imperial precedence, she soon
persuaded the young man to set in motion a plot which brought destruction upon
himself and the entire senate.' (Herodian 1.8.4)

Despite the complaints of Faustina the Younger (Marcus' wife) and
Lucilla, Tiberius Claudius Pompeianus was viewed as being of great
value to Marcus Aurelius owing to his military skill and political connections.[395] Herodian's reference to this reasoning speaks volumes
(1.2.1): τῷ βασιλεύοντι Μάρκῳ θυγατέρες μὲν ἐγένοντο πλείους,
ἄρρενες δὲ δύο. τῶν δὲ ἀρρένων τούτων ὁ μὲν ἕτερος κομιδῇ νέος
τὸν βίον μετήλλαξε (Βηρίσσιμος δ' ἦν ὄνομα αὐτῷ), τὸν δὲ περιόντα
Κόμοδόν τε καλούμενον ὁ πατὴρ μετὰ πάσης ἐπιμελείας ἀνεθρέψατο,
πάντοθεν τοὺς ἐν τοῖς ἔθνεσιν ἐπὶ λόγοις δοκιμωτάτους ἐπὶ συντάξεσιν
οὐκ εὐκαταφρονήτοις καλῶν, ὅπως συνόντες ἀεὶ παιδεύοιεν αὐτῷ τὸν
υἱόν ['The emperor Marcus Aurelius had a number of daughters but
only two sons. One of them (his name was Verissimus) died very
young; the surviving son, Commodus, his father reared with great
care, summoning to Rome from all over the empire men renowned
for learning in their own countries. He paid these scholars large fees
to live in Rome and supervise his son's education']. While the connection to such a seemingly austere general like Tiberius Claudius
Pompeianus had its short term benefits, it is also likely that Marcus
Aurelius also saw a long term advantage for the succession of Commodus.[396] He would definitely need the assistance of a strong, com-

---

[395] Traupman 1956, *op.cit.*
[396] Grosso 1964, *op.cit.*

petent military commander to ensure the continuation of the Antonine dynasty. Tiberius Claudius Pompeianus was clearly a highly influential figure during the joint principate of Marcus Aurelius and Commodus Antoninus.

The significance of these figures cannot be underestimated. Each candidate was brought into the imperial *familia* through marriage and they became increasingly more pivotal figures during the transitional phase that was the joint principate. It is notable to recognise how each character was clearly selected because of their connection to quite influential sectors of the Roman state and its social establishment. Both prominent provincials and other ambitious aristocratic leaders from Rome itself are present within this group who were welcomed into the imperial *familia* – thus epitomising the nature of the Roman state at the time. Primarily this reflects how Marcus Aurelius wanted to prepare for the succession. All the same, it also reflects the inexperience of Commodus – otherwise he would not have required such a wide range of both factional and provincial support bases for him upon the accession of his son. This appears to be indicative of the general nature of the joint principate – it sought to verify Commodus as the successor of Marcus Aurelius, which was a difficult task in view of the circumstances (the constant conflict on the northern frontier was a severe hindrance). Nevertheless, these important 'players' were intended to help Commodus with this role. Their efficacy or success is entirely up to conjecture.

Commodus as Joint Emperor

As noted previously, the advancement of Commodus Antoninus to the role of joint *princeps* can be directly connected to the aftermath of the revolt of Avidius Cassius.[397] That being stated, it could also be viewed as being that Commodus' promotion may have been inspired by the impending death of Marcus Aurelius. There are two problems with this view: firstly, Commodus was appointed as joint emperor roughly four or five years prior to the death of his father; secondly, it is important not to overly stress such a point owing to the precarious nature of historical hindsight – we know the events, the individuals involved at the time did not. The advancement of Commodus to the position of joint *princeps* coincided with his first consulship – a notable accolade with him being the youngest consul ever at the time.[398]

---

[397] See A.K. Bowman, "A letter of Avidius Cassius?", *JRS* 60, 1970, pp. 20-6.
[398] Grosso 1964, *op.cit.*

This is also indicative of both the inefficacy of the Senate and the serious establishment of what was in effect a hereditary political succession at this point. To put it bluntly he was entirely inexperienced. He may have learnt some aspects by watching his father in the role throughout his lifetime, but he had not experienced the onus of the position personally. Essentially, the necessity for the joint principate was stimulated by the circumstances at the time – the rebellion of Avidius Cassius highlighted how tenuous the position of Marcus Aurelius actually was – a trusted advisor and supporter had moved against him for his own ambitions. But as far as the *princeps* was concerned the Antonine dynasty needed to be maintained, and this 'ideal' meant that in order to ensure its survival Marcus Aurelius needed to guide it through his son – hence the joint principate.

The irony here is that Marcus is moving in a different direction to his Antonine predecessors clearly – birth was more important than experience or worth as a leader.[399] This negation of prior tradition is also exhibited in how Commodus had been designated as a potential successor to Marcus Aurelius from as early as AD 166 (this was a first for the principate). Yet the prevailing circumstances of AD 175, despite his youth, necessitated his appointment which required his education, a role his father sought to fill, but this still did not make Commodus entirely prepared for his sole principate from AD 180.[400]

The ancient literary sources do not provide a large amount of information about the nature of Commodus' role as joint *princeps*. This was seemingly because they did not seek to emphasise his advancement in any form that could be remotely construed as being either effective or positive. This is best highlighted by Cassius Dio (72.22.2-3), where he draws a direct connection between the revolt of Avidius Cassius and the promotion of Commodus Antoninus: τοῦ δὲ Κασσίου κατὰ τὴν Συρίαν νεωτερίσαντος σφόδρα ἐκπλαγεὶς ὁ Μᾶρκος τὸν Κόμμοδον τὸν υἱὸν ἐκ τῆς Ῥώμης, ὡς καὶ ἐς ἐφήβους ἤδη τελεῖν δυνάμενον, μετεπέμψατο. ὁ δὲ δὴ Κάσσιος Σύρος μὲν ἐκ τῆς Κύρου ἦν, ἀνὴρ δὲ ἄριστος ἐγένετο, καὶ ὁποῖον ἄν τις αὐτοκράτορα ἔχειν εὔξαιτο, πλὴν καθ' ὅσον Ἡλιοδώρου τινὸς ἀγαπητῶς ἐς τὴν τῆς Αἰγύπτου ἡγεμονίαν ἐξ ἐμπειρίας ῥητορικῆς προχωρήσαντος υἱὸς ἦν.

---

[399] See R.M. Geer, "Second Thoughts on the Imperial Succession from Nerva to Commodus", *TAPA* 67, 1936, p. 54.
[400] Grosso 1964, *op.cit.*

τοῦτο δὲ δὴ δεινῶς ἥμαρτεν ὑπὸ Φαυστίνης ἀπατηθείς· αὕτη γὰρ τὸν ἄνδρα ἀρρωστήσαντα (ἦν δὲ τοῦ Εὐσεβοῦς Ἀντωνίνου θυγάτηρ) προσδοκήσασα ὅσον οὐκ ἤδη τελευτήσειν, ἐφοβήθη μὴ τῆς ἀρχῆς ἐς ἄλλον τινά, ἅτε τοῦ Κομμόδου καὶ νέου καὶ ἁπλουστέρου τοὺς τρόπους ὄντος, περιελθούσης ἰδιωτεύσῃ, καὶ ἔπεισε τὸν Κάσσιον δι᾽ ἀπορρήτων παρασκευάσασθαι ἵν᾽, ἄν τι ὁ Ἀντωνῖνος πάθῃ, καὶ αὐτὴν καὶ τὴν αὐταρχίαν λάβῃ. ['When Cassius rebelled in Syria, Marcus in great alarm summoned his son Commodus from Rome, as being now entitled to assume the toga virilis. Cassius, who was a Syrian from Cyrrhus, had shown himself an excellent man and the sort one would desire to have as an emperor, save for the fact that he was the son of one Heliodorus, who had been content to secure the governorship of Egypt as the reward of his oratorical ability. But Cassius in rebelling made a terrible mistake, due to his having been deceived by Faustina. The latter, who was the daughter of Antoninus Pius, seeing that her husband had fallen ill and expecting that he would die at any moment, was afraid that the throne might fall to some outsider, inasmuch as Commodus was both too young and also rather simple-minded, and that she might thus find herself reduced to a private station. Therefore she secretly induced Cassius to make his preparations so that, if anything should happen to Antoninus, he might obtain both her and the imperial power'].

In this regard it is also vital to note how Faustina, his mother, was cast by Cassius Dio as being pivotal in the rebellion. One of the key elements of this characterisation by Cassius Dio is the simple perspective (or implied stupidity) of Commodus, which is also emphasised in Book 73.1.1-2: ὅτι οἱ Μαρκομάνοι οὔτε τροφὴν οὔτ᾽ ἄνδρας συχνοὺς ὑπό τε τοῦ πλήθους τῶν ἀπολλυμένων καὶ ὑπὸ τῆς ἀεὶ τῶν χωρίων κακώσεως ἔτι εἶχον· δύο γοῦν μόνους τῶν πρώτων καὶ δύο ἄλλους τῶν καταδεεστέρων πρέσβεις πρὸς αὐτὸν ὑπὲρ τῆς εἰρήνης ἔπεμψαν. καὶ ἐξεργάσασθαι αὐτοὺς δυνάμενος ῥᾳδίως, μισόπονος δὲ δὴ ὢν καὶ πρὸς τὰς ἀστικὰς ῥαστώνας ἐπειγόμενος ἐσπείσατο αὐτοῖς ἐπί τε τοῖς ἄλλοις ἐφ᾽ οἷς ὁ πατὴρ αὐτοῦ συνετέθειτο, καὶ ἵνα τούς τε αὐτομόλους καὶ τοὺς αἰχμαλώτους, οὓς μετὰ ταῦτα ἔλαβον, ἀποδῶσιν αὐτῷ, καὶ σῖτόν τινα κατ᾽ ἔτος τακτὸν τελῶσιν, ὃν ὕστερον αὐτοῖς ἀφῆκεν. ὅπλα τέ τινα παρ᾽ αὐτῶν ἔλαβε, καὶ στρατιώτας παρὰ μὲν τῶν Κουάδων μυρίους καὶ τρισχιλίους, παρὰ δὲ τῶν Μαρκομάνων ἐλάττους· ἀνθ᾽ ὧν ἀνῆκεν αὐτοῖς τῶν κατ᾽ ἔτος διδόναι τινάς· προσεπέταξε μέντοι σφίσιν ἵνα μήτε πολλάκις μήτε πολλαχοῦ τῆς χώρας ἀθροίζωνται, ἀλλ᾽ ἅπαξ ἐν ἑκάστῳ μηνὶ καὶ ἐς τόπον ἕνα ἑκατοντάρχου τινὸς Ῥωμαίου παρόντος, πρὸς δὲ καὶ ἵνα μήτε τοῖς Ἰάζυξι μήτε τοῖς Βούροις μήτε τοῖς Οὐανδίλοις πολεμῶσιν. ἐπὶ μὲν τούτοις συνηλλάγη, καὶ τά τε φρούρια πάντα τὰ ἐν τῇ χώρᾳ αὐτῶν ὑπὲρ τὴν μεθορίαν τὴν ἀποτετμημένην ὄντα ἐξέλιπεν. ['This man [Commodus] was not naturally wicked, but, on the contrary, as guileless as any man that ever lived. His great simplicity, however, together with his cowardice, made him the slave of his companions, and it was through them that he at first, out of ignorance, missed the better life and then was led on into lustful and cruel habits, which soon became second nature. And this, I think, Marcus clearly perceived beforehand. Commodus was nineteen years old when his father died, leaving him many guardians, among whom were numbered the best men of the senate. But their suggestions and counsels Commodus rejected, and after making a truce with the barbarians he rushed to Rome; for he hated all exertion and craved the comfortable life of the city']. It is for this reason that the author does not dwell upon what Commodus actually did as joint *princeps*.[401] All the same, it must also be acknowledged that there is also the possibility that while Commodus was nominally (and officially) joint emperor, the vast majority of unofficial power (particularly the *auctoritas*) remained with his father – which may in turn explain the reputation of Commodus for indolence.

When the joint principate was characterised by Herodian there was a similar avoidance of reference to what Commodus actually did. The focus remained upon the concerns of Marcus Aurelius towards what Commodus would become without his guidance (Herodian 1.3.1-4.8):

γηραιὸν ὄντα Μᾶρκον, καὶ μὴ μόνον ὑφ᾽ ἡλικίας, ἀλλὰ <καὶ> καμάτοις τε καὶ φροντίσι τετρυχωμένον διατρίβοντά τε ἐν Παίοσι νόσος χαλεπὴ καταλαμβάνει. ἐπεὶ δὲ αὐτῷ τὰς πρὸς σωτηρίαν ἐλπίδας φαύλως ἔχειν ὑπώπτευεν, ἑώρα τε τὸν παῖδα τῆς μειρακίων ἡλικίας ἀρχόμενον ἐπιβαίνειν, δεδιὼς μὴ νεότης ἀκμάζουσα καὶ ἐν ὀρφανίᾳ ἐξουσίαν αὐτοκράτορα καὶ ἀκώλυτον προσλαβοῦσα μαθημάτων μὲν καλῶν καὶ ἐπιτηδευμάτων ἀφηνιάσῃ, μέθαις δὲ καὶ κραιπάλαις ἐπιδῷ ἑαυτήν (ῥᾶστα γὰρ αἱ τῶν νέων ψυχαὶ ἐς ἡδονὰς ἐξολισθαίνουσαι ἀπὸ τῶν παιδείας καλῶν μετοχετεύονται), οἷα δὴ ἄνδρα πολυίστορα μάλιστα ἐτάραττε μνήμη τῶν ἐν νεότητι βασιλείαν παραλαβόντων, τοῦτο μὲν Διονυσίου τοῦ Σικελιώτου τυράννου, ὃς ὑπὸ τῆς ἄγαν ἀκρασίας καινὰς ἡδονὰς ἐπὶ μεγίστοις μισθοῖς ἐθηρᾶτο, τοῦτο δὲ αἱ τῶν Ἀλεξάνδρου

---

[401] Grosso 1964, *op.cit.*

διαδόχων ἐς τοὺς ὑπηκόους ὕβρεις τε καὶ βίαι, δι' ὧν τὴν ἐκείνου ἀρχὴν κατῇσχυναν, Πτολεμαῖος μὲν καὶ μέχρις ἀδελφῆς γνησίας ἔρωτος προχωρήσας παρὰ [τε] τοὺς Μακεδόνων καὶ Ἑλλήνων νόμους, Ἀντίγονος δὲ Διόνυσον πάντα μιμούμενος καὶ κισσὸν μὲν περιτιθεὶς τῇ κεφαλῇ ἀντὶ καυσίας καὶ διαδήματος Μακεδονικοῦ, θύρσον δὲ ἀντὶ σκήπτρου φέρων· ἔτι δὲ καὶ μᾶλλον αὐτὸν ἐλύπει τὰ μὴ πρὸ πολλοῦ <γενόμενα> ἀλλ' ὑπόγυον ἔχοντα τὴν μνήμην, τά τε Νέρωνι πεπραγμένα ὃς ἐχώρησε μέχρι μητρῴου φόνου παρεῖχέ τε τοῖς δήμοις ἑαυτὸν καταγέλαστον θέαμα, τά τε Δομετιανῷ τετολμημένα, τῆς ἐσχάτης ὠμότητος οὐδὲν ἀπολείποντα. τοιαύτας δὴ τυραννίδος εἰκόνας ὑποτυπούμενος ἐδεδίει τε καὶ ἤλπιζεν .... οὐ μετρίως δ' αὐτὸν ἐτάραττον καὶ οἱ Γερμανοὶ γειτνιῶντες, οὓς οὐδέπω πάντας ἐκεχείρωτο, ἀλλὰ τοὺς μὲν πειθοῖ ἐς συμμαχίαν προσηγάγετο, τῶν δὲ καὶ κρατήσας ἦν τοῖς ὅπλοις, ἦσαν δέ τινες οἳ διαδράντες πρὸς τὸ παρὸν ἀνακεχωρήκεσαν δέει τῆς παρουσίας τοιούτου βασιλέως. ὑπώπτευεν οὖν, μὴ τῆς ἡλικίας τοῦ μειρακίου καταφρονήσαντες ἐπιθῶνται αὐτῷ. ἐρᾷ δὲ τὸ βάρβαρον καὶ ἐπὶ ταῖς τυχούσαις ἀφορμαῖς ῥᾷστα κινεῖσθαι. κυμαίνουσαν οὖν ἔχων τοσαύταις φροντίσι τὴν ψυχήν, συγκαλέσας τε τοὺς φίλους ὅσοι τε παρῆσαν τῶν συγγενῶν, καὶ τὸν παῖδα παραστησάμενος, ἐπειδὴ πάντες συνῆλθον, ἡσυχῇ τοῦ σκίμποδος κουφίσας ἑαυτὸν τοιούτων λόγων ἤρξατο· "ἄχθεσθαι μὲν ὑμᾶς ἐφ' οἷς ὁρᾶτέ με διακείμενον, θαυμαστὸν οὐδέν· φύσει τε γὰρ τὸ ἀνθρώπινον ἐλεεινὸν ἐν ταῖς τῶν ὁμοφύλων συμφοραῖς, τά τε δεινὰ ὑπ' ὄψιν πεσόντα οἶκτον προκαλεῖται μείζονα. ἐμοὶ δέ τι καὶ πλέον ὑπάρχειν παρ' ὑμῶν οἴομαι· ἐκ γὰρ ὧν αὐτὸς διάκειμαι πρὸς ὑμᾶς, ἀμοιβαίαν εὔνοιαν εἰκότως ἤλπικα. νῦν δὲ καιρὸς εὔκαιρος ἐμοί τε αἰσθέσθαι μὴ μάτην ἐς ὑμᾶς τοσούτου χρόνου τιμήν τε καὶ σπουδὴν κατατεθεῖσθαι, ὑμῖν τε ἀποδοῦναι χάριν, δείξασιν ὅτι ὑπὲρ ὧν ἐτύχετε οὐκ ἀμνημονεῖτε. ὁρᾶτε δή μοι τὸν υἱὸν ὃν αὐτοὶ ἀνεθρέψασθε, ἄρτι τῆς μειρακίων ἡλικίας ἐπιβαίνοντα καὶ δεόμενον ὥσπερ ἐν χειμῶνι καὶ ζάλῃ τῶν κυβερνησόντων, μή ποι φερόμενος ὑπ' ἀτελοῦς τῆς τῶν δεόντων ἐμπειρίας ἐς φαῦλα ἐπιτηδεύματα προσαραχθῇ. γένεσθε δὴ οὖν αὐτῷ ὑμεῖς ἀνθ' ἑνὸς ἐμοῦ *πατέρες πολλοί*, περιέποντές τε καὶ τὰ ἄριστα συμβουλεύοντες. οὔτε γὰρ χρημάτων πλῆθος οὐδὲν αὔταρκες πρὸς τυραννίδος ἀκρασίαν, οὔτε δορυφόρων φρουρὰ ἱκανὴ ῥύεσθαι τὸν ἄρχοντα, εἰ μὴ προσυπάρχοι ἡ τῶν ὑπηκόων εὔνοια. μάλιστα δὲ ἐκεῖνοι ἐς ἀρχῆς μῆκος ἀκινδύνως ἤλασαν, ὅσοι μὴ φόβον ἐξ ὠμότητος, πόθον δὲ <ἐκ> τῆς αὑτῶν χρηστότητος ταῖς τῶν ἀρχομένων ψυχαῖς ἐνέσταξαν. οὐ γὰρ οἱ ἐξ ἀνάγκης δουλεύοντες ἀλλ' οἱ μετὰ πειθοῦς ὑπακούοντες ἀνύποπτα καὶ ἔξω κολακείας προσποιήτου δρῶντές τε καὶ πάσχοντες διατελοῦσι καὶ οὐδέ ποτε ἀφηνιάζουσιν, ἢν μὴ βίᾳ καὶ ὕβρει ἐπὶ τοῦτο ἀχθῶσι. χαλεπὸν δὲ μετριάσαι τε καὶ ὅρον ἐπιθεῖναι ἐπιθυμίαις ὑπηρετούσης ἐξουσίας. τοιαῦτα δὴ συμβουλεύοντες αὐτῷ, καὶ ὧν ἀκούει παρὼν ὑπομιμνήσκοντες, ὑμῖν τε αὐτοῖς καὶ πᾶσιν ἄριστον ἀποδείξετε βασιλέα, τῇ τε ἐμῇ μνήμῃ χαριεῖσθε τὰ μέγιστα, οὕτω τε μόνως ἀΐδιον αὐτὴν ποιῆσαι δυνήσεσθε." τοσαῦτα εἰπόντα τὸν Μᾶρκον ἐπιπεσοῦσα λιποθυμία κατεσίγασεν· ὑπὸ δὲ ἀσθενείας τε καὶ ἀθυμίας αὖθις ὑπτίαζεν. οἶκτος δὲ πάντας ἐλάμβανε τοὺς παρόντας, ὡς μηδὲ κατασχόντας αὐτῶν τινὰς ἐς οἰμωγὴν ἀναβοῆσαι. ὃ μὲν οὖν νυκτός τε καὶ ἡμέρας ἐπιβιώσας μιᾶς ἀνεπαύσατο, πόθον τε τοῖς καθ' αὑτὸν ἀνθρώποις ἐγκαταλιπὼν ἀρετῆς τε ἀΐδιον μνήμην ἐς τὸν ἐσόμενον αἰῶνα. τελευτήσαντος δὲ Μάρκου, ἐπειδὴ διεφοίτησεν ἡ φήμη, πᾶν τε τὸ παρὸν στρατιωτικὸν καὶ τὸ δημῶδες πλῆθος ὁμοίως πένθει κατείχετο, οὐδέ τις ἦν ἀνθρώπων τῶν ὑπὸ τὴν

Ῥωμαίων ἀρχὴν ὃς ἀδακρυτὶ τοιαύτην ἀγγελίαν ἐδέχετο. πάντες δ᾽ ὥσπερ ἐκ μιᾶς φωνῆς, οἱ μὲν πατέρα χρηστόν, οἱ δ᾽ ἀγαθὸν βασιλέα, γενναῖον δὲ ἕτεροι στρατηγόν, οἱ δὲ σώφρονα καὶ κόσμιον ἄρχοντα ἀνεκάλουν, καὶ οὐδεὶς ἐψεύδετο.

'When Marcus was an old man, exhausted not only by age but also by labors and cares, he suffered a serious illness while visiting the Pannonians. When the emperor suspected that there was little hope of his recovery, and realized that his son would become emperor while still very young, he was afraid that the undisciplined youth, deprived of parental advice, might neglect his excellent studies and good habits and turn to drinking and debauchery (for the minds of the young, prone to pleasures, are turned very easily from the virtues of education) when he had absolute and unrestrained power. This learned man was disturbed also by the memory of those who had become sole rulers in their youth. The Sicilian despot Dionysus, in his excessive licentiousness, had sought out new pleasures and paid the highest prices for them. The arrogance and violence of Alexander's successors against their subject peoples had brought disgrace upon his empire. Ptolemy, too, contrary to the laws of the Macedonians and Greeks, went so far as to marry his own sister. Antigonus had imitated Dionysus in every way, even wearing a crown of ivy instead of the Macedonian hat or the diadem, and carrying the thyrsus instead of a scepter. Marcus was even more distressed when he recalled events of recent date. Nero had capped his crimes by murdering his mother and had made himself ridiculous in the eyes of the people. The exploits of Domitian, as well, were marked by excessive savagery. When he recalled such spectacles of despotism as these, he was apprehensive and anticipated evil events. Then, too, the Germans on the border gave him much cause for anxiety. He had not yet forced all these tribes to submit; some he had won to an alliance by persuasion; others he had conquered by force of arms. There were some who, although they had broken their pact with him, had returned to the alliance temporarily because of the fear occasioned by the presence of so great an emperor. He suspected that, contemptuous of his son's youth, they would launch an assault upon him; for the barbarian is ever eager to revolt on any pretext. Troubled by these thoughts, Marcus summoned his friends and kinsmen. Placing his son beside him and raising himself up a little on his couch, he began to speak to them as follows: "That you are distressed to see me in this condition is hardly surprising. It is natural for men to pity the sufferings of their fellow men, and the misfortunes that occur before their very eyes arouse even greater compassion. I think, however, that an even stronger bond of affection exists between you and me; in return for the favors I have done you, I have a reasonable right to expect your reciprocal good will. And now is the proper time for me to discover that not in vain have I showered honor and esteem upon you for so long, and for you to return the favor by showing that you are not unmindful of the benefits you have received from me. Here is my son, whom you yourselves have educated, approaching the prime of youth and, as it were, in need of pilots for the stormy seas ahead. I fear that he, tossed to and fro by his lack of knowledge of what he needs to know, may be dashed to pieces on the rocks of evil practices. You, therefore, together take my place as his father, looking after him and giving him wise counsel. No amount of money is large enough to compensate for a tyrant's excesses, nor is the protection of his bodyguards enough to shield the ruler who does not possess the good will of his subjects. The ruler who emplants in the hearts of his subjects not fear resulting from cruelty, but love occasioned by kindness, is most likely to complete his reign safely. For it is not those who submit from necessity but those who are persuaded to obedience who continue to serve and to suffer without suspicion and without pretense of flattery. And they never rebel unless they are driven to it by violence and arrogance. When a man holds absolute power, it is difficult for him to control his desires. But if you give my son proper advice in such matters and constantly remind him of what he has heard here, you will make him the best of emperors for yourselves and for all, and you will be paying the greatest tribute to my memory. Only in this way can you make my memory immortal." At this point Marcus suffered a severe fainting spell and sank back on his couch, exhausted by weakness and worry. All who were present pitied him, and some cried out in their grief, unable to control themselves. After living another night and day, Marcus died, leaving to men of his own time a legacy of regret; to future ages, an eternal memorial of excellence. When the news of his death was made public, the whole army in Pannonia and the common people as well were grief-stricken; indeed, no one in the Roman empire received the report without weeping. All cried out in a swelling chorus, calling him "Kind Father," "Noble Emperor," "Brave General," and "Wise, Moderate Ruler," and every man spoke the truth.'

While Cassius Dio focused upon the stupidity of Commodus in his characterisation, the view of Herodian was more inclined towards his youth, inexperience and susceptibility to corruption. It is also notable how the ancient numismatic evidence can provide a different perspective. While the literary evidence has focused upon the characterisation of Commodus Antoninus, the ancient coinage presents how he was publically presented throughout the Empire. One example of this is an *aureus* (*RIC* Marcus 648) (AD 177/8), which depicts a young Commodus in association with Castor, one of the Dioscuri, who mythlogically assisted at a time of great crisis. Another *aureus* (*RIC* Marcus 659) (AD 179) has a direct military correlation through his association with Mars and a military trophy. The celebration of his promotion is depicted one two *denarii* for example (*RIC* Marcus 651, 627), dated to AD 177, and in this instance Commodus was exhibited as being connected to Salvus, the Roman goddess of health and prosperity. It is notable that with all of these numismatic issues Commodus was being directly associated with deities of success, military strength and prosperity. This seems to be intended to promote the idea of a smooth transition at the time during the joint principate and beyond – the Empire was being told that all was safe and secure in the hands of the young Commodus.

The epigraphic evidence is equally instructive, and highlights a different aspect – how the new joint *princeps* was honoured throughout the Empire. It is notable how many commemorative statue bases were erected from AD 177-180. In total sixteen examples have survived. The vast majority of these (ten examples)[402] were constructed on behalf of various cities throughout the Empire, celebrating the introduction of the joint principate and the continuation of the dynasty. Another statue was also constructed on behalf of two leading citizens of Osilipo for example (*CIL* 2.187), who were named as Quintus Coelius Cassianus and Marcus Fabius Tuscus. This dedication was clearly intended as a public statement of their fealty to the new *princeps* and the dynasty in general.[403] It is evident that the whole reality of the joint principate at the time could be epitomised in the dedication erected in Avan-Tesvikiye (ancient Phrygia), which has been dated to AD 177-180.[404] This statue (or possibly statues) commemorates both *principes* seemingly as equals, which exhibits how they were intended to be viewed throughout the Empire in general. This was unlikely to be the case in the practical running of State. It would hardly be surprising to judge that Marcus Aurelius was still the dominant party within the imperial principate at the time.[405]

Therefore, judging from the range of available sources of ancient evidence, it is clear that there are a range of plausible interpretations available to us. Each source of evidence has provided a different perspective about this changing period (AD 177-180), but none of them really give an entirely coherent view of Commodus' actual (or official) role – in many ways he was still subservient to his father, Marcus Aurelius. That he was joint *princeps* is not to be questioned, but what he actually did in this capacity is almost impossible to discern. He was actively promoted by Marcus Aurelius as his imperial colleague, but there is no indication of any significant administrative role. The ancient numismatic evidence attests to this. The ancient epigraphic sources have also shown how he was recognised as joint *princeps* from this time throughout the Roman Empire. All the same, both Marcus Aurelius and Commodus Antoninus were seemingly rarely within the capital during this tumultuous period – most of their time was spent on the German frontier from AD 177/8. The problems on the Germanic frontier had become a significant problem throughout the later stages of Marcus Aurelius' life, which makes

---

[402] Such as *CIL* 3.3968; 8.99; 8.12095; 8.26253; 8.26254 for example. See Hojte 2005, *op.cit.*, pp. 571-89.

[403] See Traupman 1956, *op.cit.*

[404] Hojte 2005, *ibid.*, pp. 582-3, no. 80.

[405] Grosso 1964, *op.cit.*

the implications of this particular region an important point of consideration.

War in Germania until AD 180

The relationship between Rome and the various Germanic tribes had often been problematic for centuries prior to the Antonine dynasty, which sometimes erupted into open conflict, such as during the period of Caius Marius in the late Second Century BC.[406] From the time of Augustus *Germania* was largely a military zone that was divided between two distinct Roman commands – those of Upper and Lower Germany.[407] The importance of controlling this region (as a potential threat for a military incursion) is shown by the fact that fourteen legions were stationed on the Rhine consistently between 13 BC – AD 70.[408] The impact that this region had upon the Roman Empire itself can simply be illustrated through the prominence of both the Rhine and Danubian legions as supporters of various imperial candidates from AD 68-69.[409] These legions viewed themselves as being 'king makers'- but with such a proliferation of Roman legions throughout the region at the time this comes as of little surprise. All the same, it also establishes the highly tenuous nature of Roman 'control' throughout this area over time. It is of little surprise that Vespasian reorganised the legions here on the point of his accession in order to place these military units firmly under his control.[410]

The next significant period of activity that Rome undertook in the Germanic region was under the Emperor Domitian, who undertook a significant campaign against the Chatti.[411] The ancient literary sources are highly critical of the motives behind this campaign,[412] but this is indicative of their anti-Domitianic sentiment (one that was rather similar to the anti-Commodus perspective that has been noted previously).[413] The success (and necessity) of this military campaign should not be questioned,[414] but this also highlights the tenuous nature of Roman authority within this region. All the same, this result-

---

[406] Plutarch *Marius* 23-28.

[407] Tacitus *Annals* 1.3.

[408] Schonberger 1985, *op.cit.*, pp. 345-7.

[409] Ruger 2000, *op.cit.*, pp. 496-7.

[410] *ibid.*, p. 497.

[411] B.W. Jones 1991, *op.cit.*, pp. 144-50.

[412] See Adams 2001, *op.cit.*

[413] Grosso 1964, *op.cit.*

[414] See Jones 1991, *op.cit.*

ed in the conversion of this area from being two militarised zones into the official provinces of Upper and Lower Germany.[415] While this could be viewed as being indicative of how Rome had completely subjugated the region, this was definitely not the case.[416] The Germanic tribes continued to periodically resist Roman dominion, despite the flattery of some ancient literary sources towards more favourable *principes*, such as the Emperor Trajan. There was no continual open rebellion in the region, but it was certainly a continual concern that directly affected the prospects of every incumbent Roman *princeps* from this time. The events of AD 169 certainly epitomise the instability of the region. See the *Historia Augusta*:

sed Marcus tanta fuit moderatione ut, cum simul triumphasset, tamen post mortem Lucii tantum Germanicum se vocaret, quod sibi bello proprio pepererat. in triumpho autem liberos Marci utriusque sexus secum vexerunt, ita tamen ut et puellas virgines veherent. ludos etiam ob triumphum decretos spectaverunt habitu triumphali. inter cetera pietatis eius haec quoque moderatio praedicanda est: funambulis post puerum lapsum culcitas subici iussit. unde hodieque rete praetenditur. Dum Parthicum bellum geritur, natum est Marcomannicum, quod diu eorum qui aderant arte suspensum est, ut finito iam Orientali bello Marcomannicum agi posset. et cum famis tempore populo insinuasset de bello, fratre post quinquennium reverso in senatu egit, ambos necessarios dicens bello Germanico imperatores.

'But Marcus was so free from love of display that though he triumphed with Lucius, nevertheless after Lucius' death he called himself only Germanicus, the title he had won in his own war. In the triumphal procession, moreover, they carried with them Marcus' children of both sexes, even his unmarried daughters; and they viewed the games held in honour of the triumph clad in the triumphal robe. Among other illustrations of his unfailing consideration towards others this act of kindness is to be told: After one lad, a rope-dancer, had fallen, he ordered mattresses spread under all rope-dancers. This is the reason why a net is stretched them to-day. While the Parthian war was still in progress, the Marcomannic war broke out, after having been postponed for a long time by the diplomacy of the men who were in charge there, in order that the Marcomannic war might not be waged until Rome was done with the war in the East. Even at the time of the famine the Emperor had hinted at this war to the people, and when his brother returned after five years' service, he brought the matter up in the senate, saying that both emperors were needed for the German war.' (*HA Marcus* 12.9-14)

Cum Mauri Hispanias prope omnes vastarent, res per legatos bene gestae sunt. et cum Aegyptum Bucolici milites gravia multa fecissent, per Avidium Cassium retunsi sunt, qui postea tyrannidem arripuit.

---

[415] Ruger 2000, *op.cit.*, pp. 498-9.
[416] Traupman 1956, *op.cit.*

'Against the Mauri, when they wasted almost the whole of Spain, matters were brought to a successful conclusion by his legates; and when the warriors of the Bucolici did many grievous things in Egypt, they were checked by Avidius Cassius, who later attempted to seize the throne.' (*HA Marcus* 21.1-2)

et multi nobiles bello Germanico sive Marcomannico immo plurimarum gentium interierunt. quibus omnibus statuas in foro Ulpio collocavit. quare frequenter amici suaserunt, ut a bellis discederet et Romam veniret, sed ille contempsit ac perstitit nec prius recessit quam omnia bella finiret. provincias ex proconsularibus consulares aut ex consularibus proconsulares aut praetorias pro belli necessitate fecit. res etiam in Sequanis turbatas censura et auctoritate repressit. compositae res et in Hispania, quae per Lusitaniam turbatae erant. filio Commodo accersito ad limitem togam virilem dedit, quare congiarium populo divisit et eum ante tempus consulem designavit.

'And because in this German, or Marcomannic, war, or rather I should say in this "War of Many Nations," many nobles perished, for all of whom he erected statues in the Forum of Trajan, his friends often urged him to abandon the war and return to Rome. He, however, disregarded this advice and stood his ground, nor did he withdraw before he had brought all the wars to a conclusion. Several proconsular provinces he changed into consular, and several consular provinces into proconsular or praetorian, according to the exigencies of war. He checked disturbances among the Sequani by a rebuke and by his personal influence; and in Spain, likewise, he quieted the disturbances which had arisen in Lusitania. And having summoned his son Commodus to the border of the empire, he gave him the *toga virilis*, in honour of which he distributed largess among the people, and appointed him consul before the legal age.' (*HA Marcus* 22.7-12)

It is clearly evident that the German frontier was a significant point of consideration for both foreign policy and military strategies under Marcus Aurelius throughout the second half of his reign. In AD 178 the Germanic campaign (the *expeditio Germanica secunda*) was seemingly against the Quadi,[417] a tribe that had previously been a serious problem during the reign of Domitian.[418] The previous campaigns of Marcus Aurelius (in AD 169 and 172) had been prompted through inter-tribal conflicts involving the Chatti,[419] but this reflects the turbulent nature of the region in general (both within and beyond the *limes*). While it could be argued that this region was almost brought under control during this period by Marcus Aurelius,[420] this appears to be highly speculative and ties in with the pro-Marcus Aurelius tendencies of the ancient literary sources.[421] All the same, for the

---

[417] Dio 71.33.3-4.
[418] Jones 1991, *op.cit.*
[419] Ruger 2000, *op.cit.*, p. 503.
[420] Birley 2001, *op.cit.*, p. 209.
[421] See Adams 2013, *op.cit.*, p. 232.

purposes of the present discussion, the Germanic campaign was the primary focus during the joint principate of Marcus Aurelius and Commodus.[422] This pivotal point of attention that was directed towards the northern frontier was important for Commodus, but it also reduced the amount of time he spent in the capital – and his experience of how to deal with internal politics was clearly reduced accordingly.[423]

The ancient literary sources for this period have highlighted the significance (or seriousness) of this campaign, as noted previously. The way in which Commodus has been presented in this regard is best epitomised by the *HA* biographer (*Commodus* 3.5): *bellum etiam quod pater paene confecerat legibus hostium addictus remisit ac Romam reversus est* ['He abandoned the war which his father had almost finished and submitted to the enemy's terms, and then he returned to Rome.']. This exhibits the way in which both emperors were depicted – one was good and efficient whereas the other was not. All the same, the best ancient literary source for such detail is Cassius Dio. The seriousness of the situation is best epitomised by him in Book 72.20.1-2. The way in which Cassius Dio presents Marcus Aurelius is unquestionably that of the great leader – Commodus is depicted as being the complete opposite. All the same, this is indicative of their general historiographical and biographical representations (and traditions). The most common comment by the ancient literary sources is that Commodus failed to defeat the various Germanic tribes, which seems to have been a highly unlikely result even if the war had continued to be pursued in AD 180 (Dio 73.2.1-4):

ὅτι οἱ Μαρκομάνοι οὔτε τροφὴν οὔτ' ἄνδρας συχνοὺς ὑπό τε τοῦ πλήθους τῶν ἀπολλυμένων καὶ ὑπὸ τῆς ἀεὶ τῶν χωρίων κακώσεως ἔτι εἶχον· δύο γοῦν μόνους τῶν πρώτων καὶ δύο ἄλλους τῶν καταδεεστέρων πρέσβεις πρὸς αὐτὸν ὑπὲρ τῆς εἰρήνης ἔπεμψαν. καὶ ἐξεργάσασθαι αὐτοὺς δυνάμενος ῥᾳδίως, μισόπονος δὲ δὴ ὢν καὶ πρὸς τὰς ἀστικὰς ῥᾳστώνας ἐπειγόμενος ἐσπείσατο αὐτοῖς ἐπί τε τοῖς ἄλλοις ἐφ' οἷς ὁ πατὴρ αὐτοῦ συνετέθειτο, καὶ ἵνα τούς τε αὐτομόλους καὶ τοὺς αἰχμαλώτους, οὓς μετὰ ταῦτα ἔλαβον, ἀποδῶσιν αὐτῷ, καὶ σῖτόν τινα κατ' ἔτος τακτὸν τελῶσιν, ὃν ὕστερον αὐτοῖς ἀφῆκεν. ὅπλα τέ τινα παρ' αὐτῶν ἔλαβε, καὶ στρατιώτας παρὰ μὲν τῶν Κουάδων μυρίους καὶ τρισχιλίους, παρὰ δὲ τῶν Μαρκομάνων ἐλάττους· ἀνθ' ὧν ἀνῆκεν αὐτοῖς τῶν κατ' ἔτος διδόναι τινάς. προσεπέταξε μέντοι σφίσιν ἵνα μήτε πολλάκις μήτε πολλαχοῦ τῆς χώρας ἀθροίζωνται, ἀλλ' ἅπαξ ἐν ἑκάστῳ μηνὶ καὶ ἐς τόπον ἕνα ἑκατοντάρχου τινὸς Ῥωμαίου παρόντος, πρὸς δὲ καὶ ἵνα μήτε τοῖς Ἰάζυξι μήτε τοῖς Βούροις μήτε τοῖς Οὐανδίλοις πολεμῶσιν. ἐπὶ μὲν τούτοις συνηλλάγη, καὶ τὰ

---

[422] Traupman 1956, *op.cit.*
[423] Grosso 1964, *op.cit.*

τε φρούρια πάντα τὰ ἐν τῇ χώρᾳ αὐτῶν ὑπὲρ τὴν μεθορίαν τὴν ἀποτετμημένην ὄντα ἐξέλιπεν.

'The Marcomani by reason of the multitude of their people that were perishing and the constant ravishing of their lands no longer had an abundance of either food or men. At any rate they sent only two of their chief men and two others of inferior rank as envoys to sue for peace. And, although Commodus might easily have destroyed them, yet he made terms with them; for he hated all exertion and was eager for the comforts of the city. In addition to the conditions that his father had imposed upon them he also demanded that they restore to him the deserters and the captives that they had taken in the meantime, and that they furnish annually a stipulated amount of grain — a demand from which he subsequently released them. Moreover, he obtained some arms from them and soldiers as well, thirteen thousand from the Quadi and a smaller number from the Marcomani; and in return for these he relieved them of the requirement of an annual levy. However, he further commanded that they should not assemble often nor in many parts of the country, but only once each month and in one place, and in the presence of a Roman centurion; and, furthermore, that they should not make war upon the Iazyges, the Buri, or the Vandili. On these terms, then, he made peace and abandoned all the outposts in their country beyond the strip along the frontier that had been neutralized.' (Dio 73.2.1-4)

The ancient numismatic evidence also exhibits how important the Germanic campaign was within the Roman mindset. There are numerous issues that Commodus directly with the advertised successes of the Roman military on the German frontier[424] — even before his involvement on the northern *limes*. Commodus' connection to the success of the Germanic wars was established early within the realm of public propaganda during the joint principate, as shown by *RIC* (Marcus) 1518 which represents Commodus in association with a trophy from this conflict – a coin that is dated to AD 172/3.[425] This is further established through his public commemoration with *Victory* as depicted on *RIC* (Marcus) 615. This coin (dated to AD 175/6) shows a young Commodus in direct association with the vestiges of military victory – an attribution that he could not have really claimed through his involvement in the northern wars. This iconography was more about his advancement and public persona rather than his martial acumen. It seems unlikely that even between AD 177-180 that he played an active military role – this would have been undertaken by others, such as Marcus Aurelius and Commodus' brother-in-law, Tiberius Claudius Pompeianus. Commodus would have

---

[424] *RIC Commodus* 604, 606, 615, 633.
[425] Traupman 1956, *op.cit.*

probably been expected to simply watch and learn from these more experienced figures.[426]

Judging from the extant ancient evidence in general, Commodus Antoninus plays the role of a somewhat diminutive figure in this regard. While it must be taken that the ancient literary sources have always downplayed his role in this regard, there is little else in the early record to show that Commodus was either an active (or able) military campaigner at this point in time. This is exhibited (if not emphasised) by Herodian (1.6.1-9) who sought to stress how Commodus differed from his father:

ὀλίγου μὲν οὖν τινὸς χρόνου πάντα ἐπράττετο τῇ γνώμῃ τῶν πατρῴων φίλων, οἳ πανημέριοι συνῆσαν αὐτῷ τὰ βέλτιστα συμβουλεύοντες, καὶ τοσοῦτον ἐνδιδόντες χρόνον, ὅσον ἐνόμιζον αὐτάρκη πρὸς σώφρονα τοῦ σώματος ἐπιμέλειαν. παρεισδύντες δέ τινες τῶν ἐπὶ τῆς αὐλῆς οἰκετῶν διαφθείρειν ἐπειρῶντο νέον ἦθος βασιλέως, ὅσοι τε κόλακες τραπέζης [καὶ] τὸ εὔδαιμον γαστρὶ καὶ τοῖς αἰσχίστοις μετροῦσιν, ὑπεμίμνησκον αὐτὸν τῆς ἐν Ῥώμῃ τρυφῆς, θεάματά τε καὶ ἀκούσματα τερπνὰ διηγούμενοι τήν τε τῶν ἐπιτηδείων δαψίλειαν καταριθμοῦντες διαβάλλοντές τε πᾶσαν τὴν ἐπὶ ταῖς ὄχθαις τοῦ Ἴστρου ὥραν, μήτε ὀπώρας εὔφορον κρυεράν τε ἀεὶ καὶ συννεφῆ. "οὐ παύσῃ" δὲ ἔλεγον "ὦ δέσποτα, πηγνύμενόν τε καὶ ὀρυττόμενον πίνων ὕδωρ; ἄλλοι δὲ ἀπολαύσουσι πηγῶν τε θερμῶν καὶ ψυχροῦ νάματος ἀτμίδων τε καὶ ἀέρων, ὧν Ἰταλία μόνη εὔφορος." τοιαῦτα δή τινα τῷ μειρακίῳ ὑποτυπούμενοι ἤγειρον αὐτοῦ τὰς ὀρέξεις ἐς τὴν ἡδονῶν ἐπιθυμίαν. αἰφνιδίως δὲ καλέσας τοὺς φίλους ποθεῖν ἔλεγε τὴν πατρίδα· ὁμολογεῖν δὲ τὰς αἰτίας τῆς αἰφνιδίου ὁρμῆς αἰδούμενος, δεδιέναι προσεποιεῖτο, μή τις ἐκεῖσε προκαταλάβοι τὴν βασίλειον ἑστίαν τῶν εὐπατριδῶν πλουσίων, εἶθ' ὥσπερ ἐξ ὀχυρᾶς ἀκροπόλεως δύναμιν καὶ περιβολὴν συγκροτήσας ἐπιθῆται τῇ ἀρχῇ. αὐτάρκης δὲ ὁ δῆμος χορηγῆσαι πλῆθος ἐπιλέκτων νεανιῶν. τοιαῦτά τινα προφασιζομένου τοῦ μειρακίου οἱ μὲν ἄλλοι συνεστάλησάν τε τὴν ψυχήν, καὶ σκυθρωπαῖς ταῖς ὄψεσιν ἐς γῆν ἔνευσαν. Πομπηιανὸς δέ, ὃς πρεσβύτατός τε ἦν ἀπάντων καὶ κατ' ἐπιγαμίαν προσήκων αὐτῷ (συνῴκει γὰρ τῇ πρεσβυτάτῃ τῶν ἀδελφῶν τοῦ Κομόδου), "ποθεῖν μέν σε", ἔφη, "τέκνον καὶ δέσποτα, τὴν πατρίδα εἰκός· καὶ γὰρ αὐτοὶ τῶν οἴκοι ὁμοίᾳ ἐπιθυμίᾳ ἑαλώκαμεν. ἀλλὰ τὰ ἐνταῦθα προυργιαίτερα ὄντα καὶ μᾶλλον ἐπείγοντα ἐπέχει τὴν ἐπιθυμίαν. τῶν μὲν γὰρ ἐκεῖσε καὶ ὕστερον ἐπὶ πλεῖστον αἰῶνα ἀπολαύσεις, ἐκεῖ τε ἡ Ῥώμη, ὅπου ποτ' ἂν ὁ βασιλεὺς ᾖ. τὸν δὲ πόλεμον ἀτελῆ καταλιπεῖν μετὰ τοῦ ἀπρεποῦς καὶ ἐπισφαλές. θάρσος γὰρ ἐμβαλοῦμεν τοῖς βαρβάροις, οὐκ ἐπανόδου πόθον ἀλλὰ φυγὴν καὶ δέος ἡμῶν καταγνοῦσι. καλὸν δέ σοι χειρωσαμένῳ πάντας αὐτοὺς καὶ τῷ ὑπὸ τὴν ἄρκτον ὠκεανῷ τὴν ἀρχὴν ὁρίσαντι ἐπανελθεῖν οἴκαδε θριαμβεύοντί τε καὶ δεσμίους ἀπάγοντι καὶ αἰχμαλώτους βασιλεῖς τε καὶ σατράπας βαρβάρους. τούτοις γὰρ οἱ πρὸ σοῦ Ῥωμαῖοι μεγάλοι τε καὶ ἔνδοξοι γεγόνασι. δεδιέναι δέ σε οὐ χρή, μή τις ἐκεῖ τοῖς πράγμασιν ἐπιθῆται. οἵ τε γὰρ ἄριστοι τῆς βουλῆς ἐνταῦθα σὺν σοί, ἥ τε στρατιωτικὴ

δύναμις παροῦσα πᾶσα τῆς σῆς ἀρχῆς προασπίζει· ταμιεῖά τε χρημάτων βασιλικῶν ἐνταῦθα πάντα· ἥ τε τοῦ πατρὸς μνήμη αἰώνιόν σοι πίστιν καὶ εὔνοιαν παρὰ τῶν ἀρχομένων ἐβεβαίωσεν." τοιαῦτά τινα ἐς προτροπὴν καὶ τὴν πρὸς τὰ κρείττονα ὁρμὴν ὁ Πομπηιανὸς εἰπὼν διέτρεψε πρὸς ὀλίγον τὸ μειράκιον. αἰδεσθεὶς γὰρ ὁ Κόμοδος τὰ λεχθέντα, οὐδέν τε οἷός τε ὢν εὐλόγως ἀποκρίνασθαι, τοὺς φίλους ἀπεπέμψατο, φήσας ἀκριβέστερον καθ᾽ αὑτὸν ἐπισκέψεσθαι τὸ πρακτέον. ἐγκειμένων δὲ τῶν περὶ αὐτὸν θεραπόντων οὐκέτι μὲν τοῖς φίλοις οὐδὲν ἐκοινώσατο, ἐκπέμψας δὲ γράμματα, καὶ διανείμας οἷς ἐδοκίμασε τῆς ὄχθης τοῦ Ἴστρου τὴν πρόνοιαν προστάξας τε αὐτοῖς ἀνέχειν τὰς τῶν βαρβάρων ἐπιδρομάς, ἐπαγγέλλει τὴν ἔξοδον. οἱ μὲν οὖν διῴκουν τὰ ἐγκεχειρισμένα· οἳ καὶ οὐ πολλῷ χρόνῳ πλείστους τῶν βαρβάρων ὅπλοις ἐχειρώσαντο, τοὺς δὲ ἐπὶ μεγάλαις συντάξεσιν ἐς φιλίαν ἐπηγάγοντο ῥᾶστα πείσαντες. φύσει γὰρ τὸ βάρβαρον φιλοχρήματον, καὶ κινδύνων καταφρονήσαντες ἢ δι᾽ ἐπιδρομῆς καὶ ἐφόδου τὸ χρειῶδες πρὸς τὸν βίον πορίζονται, ἢ μεγάλων μισθῶν τὴν εἰρήνην ἀντικαταλλάσσονται. ἅπερ ὁ Κόμοδος εἰδὼς καὶ τὸ ἀμέριμνον ὠνούμενος ἀφειδῶς τε ἔχων χρημάτων, πάντα ἐδίδου τὰ αἰτούμενα.

'Then, for a short time, the emperor did everything as the advisers appointed by his father suggested. They were with him every day, giving him wise counsel; they allowed him only as much leisure as they thought necessary for the sensible care of his body. But some of his court companions interfered and tried to corrupt the character of the naive emperor. All the sycophants at his table, men who gauge their pleasure by their bellies and something a little lower, kept reminding him of the gay life at Rome, describing the delightful spectacles and musical shows and cataloguing the abundance of luxuries available there. They complained about wasting their time on the banks of the Danube, pointing out that the region was not productive in summer and that the fog and cold were unending. "Master," they said again and again, "when will you stop drinking this icy liquid mud? In the meantime, others will be enjoying warm streams and cool streams, mists and fine air too, all of which only Italy possesses in abundance." By merely suggesting such delights to the youth, they whetted his appetite for a taste of pleasures. And so he immediately summoned his advisers and informed them that he longed to see his native land. But, ashamed to admit the real reason for his sudden interest in returning, he pretended to be fearful that one of the wealthy aristocrats in Rome would seize the empire and, after raising an army and a rampart, take control of the empire, as if from an impregnable fortress. For the Roman populace was sufficiently large to supply numerous picked young men for such an army. While the youth was alleging such specious excuses, the rest, sick at heart, kept their eyes fixed on the ground in dismay. But Pompeianus, the oldest of his advisers and a relation to the emperor by marriage (his wife was Commodus' eldest sister), said to him: "Child and master too, it is entirely reasonable for you to long to see your native land; we too are gripped by hunger to see those we left at home. But more important and more urgent matters here put a curb on that yearning. For the rest of your life you will have the enjoyment of things at home; and for that matter, where the emperor is, Rome is. But to leave this war unfinished is both disgraceful and dangerous. That course would increase the barbarians' boldness; they will not believe that we long to return to our home, but will rather accuse us of a cowardly retreat. After you have conquered all these barbarians and extended the boundaries of the empire to the northern seas, it will be glorious for you to return home to celebrate your triumph, leading as fettered captives barbarian kings and governors. The Romans who preceded you became famous and gained renown in this way. There is no reason to fear that someone at home may seize control. The most distinguished senators are right here with you; the imperial troops are here to protect you; all the funds from the imperial depositories are here; and finally, the memory of your father has won for you the eternal loyalty and good will of your subjects." Eager to improve the situation, Pompeianus, by his exhortations, restrained the youth for a short time. Commodus, shamed by his words and unable to make a suitable reply, dismissed the group, saying that he would consider personally and at greater length what he should do. Then, yielding to his companions, he no longer consulted his advisers about anything. He sent off letters and, after assigning command of the Danube to men whom he considered capable, ordering them to block the barbarians' attacks, he announced his departure for Rome. Those left behind carried out their assignments; soon they subdued most of the barbarians by force of arms, and easily won the friendship of the rest by substantial bribes. The barbarians are by nature fond of money; contemptuous of danger, they obtain the necessities of life either by pillaging and plundering or by selling peace at a huge price. Commodus was aware of this practice; since he had plenty of money, he bargained for release from care and gave them everything they demanded.'

This representation of Commodus by Herodian is clearly quite negative towards him, but it also epitomises the general circumstances in which he came to not only become a joint *princeps*, but also eventually taking the role of sole ruler of the Roman Empire (one that the author viewed as being entirely inappropriate). All the same, the question remains about how much experience Commodus Antoninus had with the running of the State in general. Most of the time during the joint principate was spent on the Germanic campaign on the northern frontier. So while Marcus Aurelius' guidance would have been invaluable for his son's future imperial prospects, it still left him sorely under prepared for the rigours of political life in Rome itself. This was beyond the control of Marcus Aurelius, but it also signifies the attempts that he made in order to leave his son, Commodus, as prepared and able to lead the empire as possible.[427]

The campaigns against the Germanic tribes symbolises the significance of the joint principate in many ways – Commodus Antoninus was thrust into a serious circumstance with little experience, but a situation that was also dominated by his father (the experienced campaigner). The gravity of the Germanic campaigns cannot be overstated – there was a significant threat in the region at the time. This has been discussed more fully in Chapter Seven, but for the purposes of the present discussion it is simply sufficient to note the importance of the northern (Germanic) frontier at this stage. Com-

---

[427] Grosso 1964, *op.cit.*

modus had an intended role at this point in time, but it still remained uncertain that he would be capable of fulfilling the role of *princeps*. The death of Marcus Aurelius, however, was a fundamental turning point. Not only because Commodus Antoninus was left to his own devices (a point that the ancient literary sources went at length to have us believe), but primarily because this saw a complete change in northern frontier policy for a variety of reasons. This also epitomised the transition from the leadership of an experienced (steady?) *princeps* to that of one who was much more inexperienced. This became apparent to all almost instantaneously.

The Death of Marcus Aurelius

The death of Marcus Aurelius was of great significance to all – even despite the introduction of the joint principate in AD 177. His influence not only as a leader, but also as a father should not be underestimated. The ancient literary sources provide several accounts of his death, mostly focusing upon not only his exemplary (and highly idealised) character, but also upon his concern over Commodus' future. Cassius Dio (72.20-34.1), Herodian (1.4.7-5.8) and the *HA* biographer (*Marcus* 18.1-3; 19.1-5; 27.11-12; 28.10) all present Marcus Aurelius in the most positive light possible:

τοσαῦτα εἰπόντα τὸν Μᾶρκον ἐπιπεσοῦσα λιποθυμία κατεσίγασεν· ὑπὸ δὲ ἀσθενείας τε καὶ ἀθυμίας αὖθις ὑπτίαζεν. οἶκτος δὲ πάντας ἐλάμβανε τοὺς παρόντας, ὡς μηδὲ κατασχόντας αὐτῶν τινὰς ἐς οἰμωγὴν ἀναβοῆσαι. ὁ μὲν οὖν νυκτός τε καὶ ἡμέρας ἐπιβιώσας μιᾶς ἀνεπαύσατο, πόθον τε τοῖς καθ' αὑτὸν ἀνθρώποις ἐγκαταλιπὼν ἀρετῆς τε ἀίδιον μνήμην ἐς τὸν ἐσόμενον αἰῶνα. τελευτήσαντος δὲ Μάρκου, ἐπειδὴ διεφοίτησεν ἡ φήμη, πᾶν τε τὸ παρὸν στρατιωτικὸν καὶ τὸ δημῶδες πλῆθος ὁμοίως πένθει κατείχετο, οὐδέ τις ἦν ἀνθρώπων τῶν ὑπὸ τὴν Ῥωμαίων ἀρχὴν ὃς ἀδακρυτὶ τοιαύτην ἀγγελίαν ἐδέχετο. πάντες δ' ὥσπερ ἐκ μιᾶς φωνῆς, οἱ μὲν πατέρα χρηστόν, οἱ δ' ἀγαθὸν βασιλέα, γενναῖον δὲ ἕτεροι στρατηγόν, οἱ δὲ σώφρονα καὶ κόσμιον ἄρχοντα ἀνεκάλουν, καὶ οὐδεὶς ἐψεύδετο. ὀλίγων δὲ διελθουσῶν ἡμερῶν, ἐν ὅσαις περὶ τὴν κηδείαν τοῦ πατρὸς τὸν υἱὸν ἀπησχόλουν, ἔδοξε τοῖς φίλοις προαγαγεῖν τὸ μειράκιον ἐς τὸ στρατόπεδον, ὡς ἂν διαλεχθείη τε τοῖς στρατιώταις, καὶ χρήματα δωρησάμενος, ὡς ἔθος ἐστὶ τοῖς βασιλείαν διαδεχομένοις, μεγαλόφρονι ἐπιδόσει οἰκειώσηται τὸ στράτευμα. παρηγγέλθη τε δὴ πᾶσιν ἐλθεῖν ἐς τὸ εἰωθὸς πεδίον αὐτοὺς ὑποδέξεσθαι. προελθὼν δὲ ὁ Κόμοδος τάς τε βασιλείους θυσίας ἐπετέλει, καὶ βήματος αὐτῷ ἐς ὕψος ἀρθέντος ἐν μέσῳ τῷ στρατοπέδῳ ἀνελθὼν ἐπ' αὐτὸ καὶ περιστησάμενος τοὺς πατρῴους φίλους (πολλοὶ δὲ καὶ λόγιοι παρῆσαν αὐτῷ) ἔλεξε τοιάδε· "κοινὴν εἶναί μοι πρὸς ὑμᾶς τὴν ἐπὶ τοῖς καταλαβοῦσιν ἀλγηδόνα καὶ μηδέν τι ἧττον ὑμᾶς ἐμοῦ δυσφορεῖν ἐμαυτὸν ἀκριβῶς πέπεικα. οὐδὲ γὰρ περιόντος μοι τοῦ πατρὸς πλεονεκτεῖν ὑμῶν ἠξίουν. ἐκεῖνος γὰρ πάντας ἡμᾶς ὡς ἕνα ἠγάπα. ἔχαιρε γοῦν μᾶλλον συστρατιώτην με ἢ υἱὸν καλῶν· τὴν μὲν γὰρ προσηγορίαν ἡγεῖτο φύσεως, τὴν δ' ἀρετῆς κοινωνίαν. φέρων τέ με πολλάκις ἔτι νήπιον ὄντα ταῖς ὑμετέραις ἐνεχείρισε πίστεσι. διόπερ καὶ ῥᾶστα πάσης εὐνοίας μεθέξειν πρὸς ὑμῶν ἤλπικα, τῶν μὲν πρεσβυτέρων τροφεῖά μοι ταῦτα ὀφειλόντων, τοὺς δ᾽ ἡλικιώτας εἰκότως ἂν καὶ συμφοιτητὰς τῶν ἐν ὅπλοις ἔργων ἀποκαλοίην· πάντας γὰρ ἡμᾶς ὡς ἕνα ὁ πατὴρ ἐφίλει τε καὶ πᾶσαν ἀρετὴν ἐπαίδευεν. ἔδωκε δὲ μετ᾽ ἐκεῖνον ἐμὲ βασιλέα ἡ τύχη, οὐκ ἐπείσακτον, ὥσπερ οἱ πρὸ ἐμοῦ προσκτήτῳ σεμνυνόμενοι ἀρχῇ, ἀλλὰ μόνος τε ὑμῖν ἐγὼ ἐν τοῖς βασιλείοις ἀπεκυήθην, καὶ μὴ πειραθέντα με ἰδιωτικῶν σπαργάνων ἅμα τῷ τῆς γαστρὸς προελθεῖν ἡ βασίλειος ὑπεδέξατο πορφύρα, ὁμοῦ δέ με εἶδεν ἥλιος ἄνθρωπον καὶ βασιλέα. εἰκότως δ᾽ ἂν ταῦτα λογιζόμενοι στέργοιτε οὐ δοθέντα ὑμῖν ἀλλὰ γεννηθέντα αὐτοκράτορα. ὁ μὲν οὖν πατὴρ ἐς οὐρανὸν ἀναπτὰς ὀπαδὸς ἤδη καὶ σύνεδρός ἐστι θεῶν· ἡμῖν δὲ χρὴ μέλειν τῶν ἐν ἀνθρώποις καὶ τὰ ἐπὶ γῆς διοικεῖν. κατορθοῦν δὲ αὐτὰ καὶ βεβαιοῦν ὑμέτερον ἔργον, εἰ τά τε τοῦ πολέμου λείψανα μετὰ πάσης ἀνδρείας ἀπαλείψαιτε καὶ τὴν Ῥωμαίων ἀρχὴν μέχρις ὠκεανοῦ προαγάγοιτε. ὑμῖν τε γὰρ ταῦτα δόξαν οἴσει καὶ τὴν τοῦ κοινοῦ πατρὸς μνήμην χάρισιν ἀξίαις οὕτως ἀμείψεσθε· ὃν ἐπακούειν τε τῶν λεγομένων καὶ τὰ πραττόμενα ἐφορᾶν ἡγεῖσθε. εὐδαιμονοίημεν δ᾽ ἂν τὰ δέοντα πράττοντες ὑπὸ τοιούτῳ μάρτυρι. καὶ τὰ μὲν πρότερον ὑμῖν ἀνδρείως κατορθωθέντα ἐς τὴν ἐκείνου σοφίαν τε καὶ στρατηγίαν τὴν ἀναφορὰν ἔχει· ὅσα δ᾽ ἂν σὺν ἐμοὶ βασιλεῖ νέῳ προθύμως ἐπιδείξησθε, τούτων <αὐτοὶ> τὴν δόξαν πιστεώς τε ἀγαθῆς καὶ ἀνδρείας ἀποίσεσθε. τό τε ἐν ἡμῖν νέον σεμνότητος πληρώσετε τῇ τῶν ὑμετέρων ἔργων ἀνδραγαθίᾳ. τὸ βάρβαρον δὲ ἐν ἀρχῇ νέας ἡγεμονίας κολασθὲν οὔτε ἐς τὸ παρὸν καταθαρσήσει τῆς <ἡμετέρας> ἡλικίας [καταφρονῆσαν], τά τε μέλλοντα φοβήσεται δέει τῶν πεπειραμένων."

'At this point Marcus suffered a severe fainting spell and sank back on his couch, exhausted by weakness and worry. All who were present pitied him, and some cried out in their grief, unable to control themselves. After living another night and day, Marcus died, leaving to men of his own time a legacy of regret; to future ages, an eternal memorial of excellence. When the news of his death was made public, the whole army in Pannonia and the common people as well were grief-stricken; indeed, no one in the Roman empire received the report without weeping. All cried out in a swelling chorus, calling him "Kind Father," "Noble Emperor," "Brave General," and "Wise, Moderate Ruler," and every man spoke the truth. During the next few days Commodus' advisers kept him busy with his father's funeral rites; then they thought it advisable to bring the youth into the camp to address the troops and, by distributing money to them — the usual practice of those who succeed to the throne—to win the support of the army. Accordingly, all the soldiers were ordered to proceed to the assembly field to welcome them. After performing the imperial sacrifices, Commodus, surrounded by the advisers appointed by his father (and there were many learned men among them), mounted the high platform erected for him in the middle of the camp and spoke as follows: "I am fully persuaded that you share in my grief over what has occurred, and that you are no less distressed by it than I. At no time when my father was with me did I see fit to play the despot with you. He took greater delight, I am convinced, in calling me 'fellow soldier' than in calling me 'son,' for he considered the latter a title bestowed by Nature, the former, a partnership based on excellence. While I was still an infant he often brought me to you and placed me in your arms, a pledge of the trust he had in you. And for that reason I have every hope that I shall enjoy your universal good will, since I am indebted to you old soldiers for rearing me, and I may properly call you young soldiers my fellow students in deeds of arms, for my father loved us all and taught us every good thing. To follow him, Fortune has given the empire not to an adopted successor but to me. The prestige of those who reigned before me was increased by the empire, which they received as an additional honor, but I alone was born for you in the imperial palace. I never knew the touch of common cloth. The purple received me as I came forth into the world, and the sun shone down on me, man and emperor, at the same moment. And if you consider the matter properly, you will honor me as an emperor born to you, not presented to you. Assuredly, my father has gone up to heaven, where he is already companion and counselor of the gods. But it is our task to devote ourselves to human affairs and to the administration of earthly matters. To set these affairs in order and make them secure is for you to undertake, if with resolute courage you would finish what is left of the war and carry forward to the northern seas ⁵ the boundaries of the Roman Empire. These exploits will indeed bring you renown, and in this way you will pay fitting respect to the memory of our mutual father. You may be sure that he hears and sees what we do. And we may count ourselves fortunate to have such a man as a witness when we do what has to be done. Up to now, all that you have courageously accomplished is attributable to his wisdom and his generalship. But now, whatever zeal you display in further exploits under me, your new emperor, will gain for you a reputation for praiseworthy loyalty and bravery. By these dauntless exploits you will confer upon us added dignity. Crushed at the beginning of a new imperial reign, the barbarian will not be so bold to act at the present, scorning our youth, and will be cautious and fearful in the future, mindful of what he has suffered."' (Herodian 1.4.7-5.8)

Cum igitur in amore omnium imperasset atque ab aliis modo frater, modo pater, modo filius, ut cuiusque aetas sinebat, et diceretur et amaretur, octavo decimo anno imperii sui, sexagensimo et primo vitae, diem ultimum clausit. tantusque illius amor eo die regii funeris claruit ut nemo illum plangendum censuerit, certis omnibus quod ab diis commodatus ad deos redisset. denique, priusquam funus conderetur, ut plerique dicunt, quod numquam antea factum fuerat neque postea, senatus populusque non divisis locis sed in una sede propitium deum dixit.

'After he had ruled, then, with the good-will of all, and had been named and beloved variously as brother, father, or son by various men according to their several ages, in the eighteenth year of his reign and the sixty-first of his life he closed his last day. Such love for him was manifested on the day of the imperial funeral that none thought that men should lament him, since all were sure that he had been lent by the gods and had now returned to them. Finally, before his funeral was held, so many say, the senate and people, not in separate places but sitting together, as was never done before or after, hailed him as a gracious god.' (*Marcus* 18.1-3)

Aiunt quidam, quod et veri simile videtur, Commodum Antoninum, successorem illius ac filium, non esse de eo natum sed de adulterio, ac talem fabellam vulgari sermone contexunt: Faustinam quondam, Pii filiam, Marci uxorem, cum gladiatores transire vidisset, unius ex his amore succensam, cum longa aegritudine laboraret, viro de amore confessam. quod cum ad Chaldaeos Marcus rettulisset, illorum fuisse consilium, ut occiso gladiatore sanguine illius sese Faustina sublavaret atque ita cum viro concumberet. quod cum esset factum, solutum quidem amorem, natum vero Commodum gladiatorem esse, non principem, qui mille prope pugnas publice populo inspectante gladiatorias imperator exhibuit, ut in vita eius docebitur.

'Some say, and it seems plausible, that Commodus Antoninus, his son and successor, was not begotten by him, but in adultery; they embroider this assertion, moreover, with a story current among the people. On a certain occasion, it was said, Faustina, the daughter of Pius and wife of Marcus, saw some gladiators pass by, and was inflamed for love of one of them; and afterwards, when suffering from a long illness, she confessed the passion to her husband. And when Marcus reported this to the Chaldeans, it was their advice that Faustina should bathe in his blood and thus couch with her husband. 4 When this was done, the passion was indeed allayed, but their son Commodus was born a gladiator, not really a prince; 5 for afterwards as emperor he fought almost a thousand gladiatorial bouts before the eyes of the people, as shall be related in his life.' (*Marcus* 19.1-5)

ante biduum quam exspiraret, admissis amicis dicitur ostendisse sententiam de filio eandem quam Philippus de Alexandro, cum de hoc male sentiret, addens nimium se aegre ferre filium superstitem relinquentem. nam iam Commodus turpem se et cruentum ostentabat.

'Two days before his death, it is said, he summoned his friends and expressed the same opinion about his son that Philip expressed about Alexander when he too thought poorly of his son, and added that it grieved him exceedingly to leave a son behind him. For already Commodus had made it clear that he was base and cruel.' (*Marcus* 27.11-12)

fertur filium mori voluisse, cum eum talem videret futurum qualis exstitit post eius mortem, ne, ut ipse dicebat, similis Neroni Caligulae et Domitiano esset.

'It is said that he foresaw that after his death Commodus would turn out as he actually did, and expressed the wish that his son might die, lest, as he himself said, he should become another Nero, Caligula, or Domitian.' (*Marcus* 28.10)

These accounts are of course highly romanticised in their depiction of the event. Marcus Aurelius was typically shown as the epitome of the 'perfect' *princeps*, often as a result of the hatred levelled against his son, Commodus. This appears somewhat unjustified in both regards. Neither of these characters were entirely 'good' or 'evil' respectively as leaders of the Roman State – despite the ancient literary sources finding a more 'black and white' approach much more easier to deal with in their characterisations of them.[428] If only life was as simple as they portray. It is not. The death of Marcus Aurelius had a profound effect not only upon Commodus, but upon the empire in general. Marcus Aurelius had provided a long period of stability throughout the realm, and while the joint principate with his son sought to maintain this sense of constancy, it also saw quite radical changes within the administration as of AD 180 as Commodus sought to create his own interpretation of the Roman principate (*HA Commodus* 2.6-3.9):

---

[428] Traupman 1956, *op.cit.*

Adhibitos custodes vitae suae honestiores ferre non potuit, pessimos quosque detinuit et summotos usque ad aegritudinem desideravit. quibus per patris mollitiem restitutis popinas et ganeas in Palatinis semper aedibus fecit neque umquam pepercit vel pudori vel sumptui. in domo aleam exercuit. mulierculas formae scitioris ut prostibula mancipia per speciem lupanarium et ludibrium pudicitiae contraxit. imitatus est propolas circumforanos. equos currules sibi comparavit. aurigae habitu currus rexit, gladiatoribus convixit, atque se gessit ut lenonum minister, ut probris natum magis quam ei loco eum crederes, ad quem fortuna provexit. Patris ministeria seniora summovit, amicos senes abiecit. filium Salvii Iuliani, qui exercitibus praeerat, ob impudicitiam frustra temptavit atque exinde Iuliano tetendit insidias. honestissimos quosque aut per contumeliam aut per honorem indignissimum abiecit. appellatus est a mimis quasi obstupratus eosdemque ita ut non apparerent subito deportavit. bellum etiam quod pater paene confecerat legibus hostium addictus remisit ac Romam reversus est. Romam ut rediit, subactore suo Saotero post se in curro locato ita triumphavit ut eum saepius cervice reflexa publice oscularetur. etiam in orchestra hoc idem fecit. et cum potaret in lucem helluareturque viribus Romani imperii, vespera etiam per tabernas ac lupanaria volitavit. misit homines ad provincias regendas vel criminum socios vel a criminosis commendatos. in senatus odium ita venit ut et ipse crudeliter in tanti ordinis perniciem saeviret fieretque e contempto crudelis.

'The more honourable of those appointed to supervise his life he could not endure, but the most evil he retained, and, if any were dismissed, he yearned for them even to the point of falling sick. When they were reinstated through his father's indulgence, he always maintained eating-houses and low resorts for them in the imperial palace. He never showed regard for either decency or expense. He diced in his own home. He herded together women of unusual beauty, keeping them like purchased prostitutes in a sort of brothel for the violation of their chastity. He imitated the hucksters that strolled about from market to market. He procured chariot-horses for his own use. He drove chariots in the garb of a professional charioteer, lived with gladiators, and conducted himself like a procurer's servant. Indeed, one would have believed him born rather to a life of infamy than to the high place to which Fortune advanced him. His father's older attendants he dismissed, and any friends that were advanced in years he cast aside. The son of Salvius Julianus, the commander of the troops, he tried to lead into debauchery, but in vain, and he thereupon plotted against Julianus. He degraded the most honourable either by insulting them directly or giving them offices far below their deserts. He was alluded to by actors as a man of depraved life, and he thereupon banished them so promptly that they did not again appear on the stage. He abandoned the war which his father had almost finished and submitted to the enemy's terms, and then he returned to Rome. After he had come back to Rome he led the triumphal procession with Saoterus, his partner in depravity, seated in his chariot, and from time to time he would turn around and kiss him openly, repeating this same performance even in the orchestra. And not only was he wont to drink until dawn and squander the resources of the Roman Empire, but in the evening he would ramble through taverns and brothels. He sent out to rule the provinces men who were either his companions in crime or were recommended to him by criminals. He became so detested by the senate that he in his turn was moved with cruel passion for the destruction of that great order, and from having been despised he became bloodthirsty.'

As shown by the previous passage, Commodus Antoninus sought to create his own principate following the death of his father, Marcus

Aurelius.[429] While this image may be a result of the views of the ancient literary sources (and their inherent anti-Commodus biases) it would seem more likely that the administration did not change greatly at this point in time.[430] The ancient authors would have us believe that there was a radical shift in policy in AD 180 – this was largely a result of their desire to distance the father and the son in their characterisations. The reality, however, was that not too much actually changed. The Germanic campaign ended (which was a major change, but not an unexpected one), but this was more of a result of the necessity for Commodus Antoninus to return to Rome in order that he could consolidate his position there. Roman politics was always a fickle creature (and still is). The ancient literary sources instead represented Commodus as introducing a fundamental change in imperial policy – seemingly to the detriment of northern frontier security. This was not the case. In addition to this there was no depiction by any of these authors of grief after his father's passing on the part of the new sole *princeps*, which epitomises their negative characterisation by them.

In general terms, owing to the introduction of the joint principate in AD 177, the transition to Commodus' sole rule went relatively smoothly. Through the period of their joint principate Marcus Aurelius had introduced a number of 'reliable' (and politically, socially, militarily) influential figures into the imperial *familia* that allowed for a solid continuation of the Antonine administration. The ancient literary sources have naturally provided an entirely different perspective. All the same, these opinions do not reflect the reality of the situation in early AD 180. The years of preparation undertaken by Marcus Aurelius for the succession of Commodus saw him becoming sole *princeps* without any resistance. The desire and plan of Marcus Aurelius had clearly paid off in this regard – despite the narratives of his regret expressed by the ancient literary sources. Commodus was firmly entrenched as sole *princeps* at this point, which had been the plan for the Antonine dynasty ever since Ad 166 when he was only aged five. Nevertheless, it must also be recognised that the position of Roman *princeps* was always of a tenuous nature. As has been noted previously, the capital was filled with other aristocratic and influential aspirants who also coveted the supreme imperial posi-

---

[429] Grosso 1964, *op.cit.*
[430] Traupman 1956, *op.cit.*

tion for themselves. Such 'vipers' would have already been ready and waiting at this point.

The ancient numismatic corpus provides some excellent early evidence in this regard. While the transition from the joint to sole principate saw a minimal number of fundamental changes in the administrative running of the empire, Commodus still needed to clearly exhibit the introduction of a new era within his public propaganda. It was the dualistic role of continuity and change at the same time. In relation to his representation on the imperial coinage, up until this point he had always been shown as a youth. This style of portrayal was also quite reminiscent of those depicting a young Marcus Aurelius – thus presenting his connection as an established and familial member of the Antonine dynasty. All the same, it is additionally notable that the introduction of the sole principate under Commodus Antoninus also saw a change in his depiction on these issues. The beardless youth was replaced with a bearded *princeps* (such as upon *RIC* Commodus 4),[431] which represented his not only his age, maturity, and leadership, but also his Antonine heritage. It is unlikely that such a dramatic change in his appearance occurred so quickly in reality, but it is more indicative of his new social and political advancement in AD 180.

The death of Marcus Aurelius would have had a dramatic impact upon Commodus Antoninus in more ways than one.[432] Not only had he just lost his father – who had clearly been a pivotal influence upon him – but the young Commodus was now thrust into the solitary (and often lonely or precarious) limelight of being the sole Roman *princeps*. This would have been a very difficult period of time for him. Regardless of all the preparations by Marcus Aurelius, such as through the creation of the joint principate and also the installed support network that surrounded him, this was never going to be an easy task for the son. The ancient literary sources would have us believe that Commodus simply rejected all of Marcus Aurelius' tutelage and guidance – preferring to move towards idleness and depravity. This is not only too simplistic, but also indicative of their anti-Commodus sentiments. The fact remains that Commodus was very young and largely inexperienced, despite the best efforts of his father, Marcus Aurelius. 'Good' emperors like Trajan, Hadrian, Antoninus Pius, and Marcus Aurelius himself had a wealth of experi-

---

[431] See also *RIC* (Commodus) 9a, 291, 300v for example.
[432] See Traupman 1956, *op.cit.*

ence on many different levels prior to their reigns – this was not afforded to Commodus owing to circumstances beyond the control of both himself and his father.

Conclusions

The joint principate of Marcus Aurelius and Commodus Antoninus has illustrated a number of important points for the benefit of the present study. Firstly, the succession of a son of Marcus Aurelius was always the plan, which highlights how dynasticism seems o have been more of a priority for the father rather than practical experience. Commodus (and his other siblings probably) were groomed from an early age for public office without question. He simply just happened to be the sole surviving male heir. Secondly, it is also quite evident that the roles of Marcus Aurelius and Commodus Antoninus were not entirely 'equal' during the joint principate. The father was clearly the dominant partner during this period, which was not only owing to his far greater experience (and *auctoritas*), but also because this would have allowed Commodus to ideally 'learn on the job' as it were. The expectations upon him would have been extremely high at this point. All the same, Commodus seemingly did not possess the illustrious *auctoritas* of his father. It must also be noted that he also possessed less military, political and social experience (and in all likelihood the essential élite connections) that other members of the imperial *familia* (or *consilium*) enjoyed throughout the joint principate.

As has been noted previously, there could have been several leading figures connected to the imperial *familia* by the father, Marcus Aurelius. It is evident that this was another method by which Marcus Aurelius sought to secure the transition from the joint to sole principates of Commodus Antoninus. If he was sounded by trusted and well connected advisors, the succession would have been easier upon Commodus – and much more likely to be unchallengeable. All the same, this is also indicative of Commodus' youth and inexperience – Marcus Aurelius sought to protect his son and ensure the succession of another Antonine *princeps* evidently for a variety of motives. With this in mind it is vital to also note that these prominent figures within the imperial *familia* and *consilium* could have also been viewed as potential threats to the principate of his son, Commodus. All of them were both influential and very well connected to significant factions within the Roman State – an area that neither Marcus Aurelius nor Commodus had possessed time to pay particular attention to with the conflict on the northern frontier. So while these persons were intended to assist Commodus in this transitional phase there was always the potential for insurrection if their ambitions got the better of them – as shown though Marcus Aurelius' experiences with Avidius Cassius.

Another aspect to consider in this regard is how this would have been viewed by Commodus Antoninus himself. He may have been young and inexperienced, but this would not have either precluded him from having feelings of his own ambitions either. Despite all of the preparations undertaken by Marcus Aurelius, Commodus was not really prepared for the principate in real terms. He had previously been promoted to the consulship in AD 177, but this was seemingly more of a result of his appointment as joint *princeps* – hardly an ideal situation. Importantly Commodus had not held any of the primary magistracies of the *cursus honorem* prior to this extraordinary appointment, which of course left him ill prepared for the sole principate. Essentially this is the case of holding a position without really experiencing its ramifications – not an ideal scenario. All the same, this would not have really hampered the ambitions of Commodus either – in his mind he would have been 'destined' to be the successor of his father (he would have no reason to think otherwise since AD 166). This would have resulted in a large part of his upbringing after all – he had become *Caesar* at the ripe old age of five after all.

The context in which Commodus Antoninus became sole *princeps* was hardly ideal, the Germanic campaign had lasted for years and it had also ultimately taken Marcus Aurelius away from Rome for an extended period of time, which would have made the social and political climates there quite unknown. Commodus himself had not been there either. Secondly, the war in *Germania* was seemingly at a crucial point, which would have made the transition less than ideal. Finally, as mentioned previously, Commodus was not an experienced replacement as sole *princeps*. This was a difficult situation. While the ancient literary sources prefer to place all of the emphasis upon Commodus' 'evil' character, it is evident that the reality was much more complicated than this simplistic viewpoint. The circumstances and social perspectives among the Roman aristocracy are seriously important to consider. All the same, this is discussed further in the next chapter.

CHAPTER 5

COMMODUS AS SOLE EMPEROR OF ROME

Introduction

In general terms, this chapter aims to consider the reign of Commodus Antoninus with particular reference towards how he reigned as *princeps* (without the guidance of his father, Marcus Aurelius). As would be expected, this is not the context in which an all encompassing analysis of his almost thirteen year sole administration can be achieved, but this is not the intent of the current work. The present study seeks to focus upon themes primarily. In addition to this the most important concentration has also been upon the ancient evidence (in a variety of forms) and how they relate (or inform us) about particular aspects of his reign – such as the Roman economy, public architecture, private architecture, and his relationship with the senatorial aristocracy for example. Other aspects on his reign have been discussed in the subsequent two chapters (focusing upon social, military and foreign policy aspects). All the same, there is a prominent theme within all of the points of consideration – namely the general question about the difference between Roman autocracy and imperialism (a question that is by no means limited to Commodus Antoninus). Therefore, this analysis has not been limited to an isolated focus upon Commodus in his role as sole *princeps*, but instead it has also entailed some analysis of other prominent figures (and their representation in the ancient literary sources) from this time period.

There are several types of ancient evidence used within this chapter as should be expected, which is intended to provide the widest possible source of early evidence for consideration, and in turn allowing for the optimal perspective of the AD 180-192 period. One of the most notable aspects is the use of the archaeological record – primarily through the use of various architectural structures (be they public or domestic). This analysis examines both civic and private complexes in order to consider just how Commodus Antoninus sought to represent (or commemorate, depending on the context) his sole principate in such a wide range of architectural guises. A variety of interpretative methods have been used in this regard, particularly in relation to the domestic structures, in order to gain more of a coherent idea about how Commodus sought to construct his 'ideal' residence.

In addition to this though it must be noted that this does not directly exactly exhibit how each structure functioned – this analysis is focused upon how they were *intended* to be used. The same variety of approaches has also been applied to the numismatic corpus. These ancient coins have similarly been used to examine just how Commodus Antoninus sought to represent himself through this form of imperial propaganda. All the same, the various weights of the different types of valuable issues have also been considered in order to ascertain the consistency (and in turn the strength) of the Roman economy throughout the reign of Commodus (it is historical perspective of course). It must also be noted that in order to efficiently contextualise these numismatic issues, the coins of Commodus have also been compared with those of Marcus Aurelius (as of AD 169). This is intended to provide a visualisation of the general stability (or instability) of the economy during the late Second Century AD.[433]

The impact of Commodus Antoninus' sculptural representations has been dealt with here briefly. The work of Olivier Hekster (2002) has already focused upon this form of evidence in much greater detail than suits the purposes of the present study, but with this in mind a few comments have still been provided for the extension of the present analysis. This type of ancient evidence has been particularly considered in light of how Commodus presented himself throughout the Roman Empire. This has also been complimented through a further consideration of the statue bases that have been discovered throughout the region. This is intended to establish how commonly Commodus was commemorated in the provinces, which represented not only an immense section of the empire, but also a significant (largely non-senatorial élite faction) that sought to express their loyalty to him - a different influential group to those influencing the ancient authors. Of course, the extant literary sources also provide an important source of information about Commodus' reign. While their perspectives are largely negative about him, they still need to be considered, and they still provide an excellent source of information about how Commodus was perceived by his social

---

[433] Grosso 1964, *op.cit.*

peers in Rome at the time (and by the succeeding generations of this group).

At this point, it is also important to consider the general context in which Commodus Antoninus became the sole *princeps* of the Roman Empire. As mentioned in the previous chapter, the perceived stability provided by his father, Marcus Aurelius had now seemingly been removed. This would have created a great deal of uncertainty within the senatorial élite in the capital. The primary question would have been what would this well-born, but largely unproven young man do? This was complimented by the uncertainty surrounding the northern imperial frontier. The lengthy period in which the imperial power had not been in Rome was a significant factor. So the succession of Commodus Antoninus was loaded with one primary concern for a variety of reasons.[434] In essence the new emperor was needed in two locations at one time. The departure of the new *princeps* from the northern frontier (for politically internal reasons – and those unacknowledged motives by the early authors) while trying to continue the northern campaign would have been disastrous. Yet he needed to return to the capital. This would have also exposed a weakening of morale within the military, potentially leading to the possibility of rebellion among them (an unquestionably impossible choice), which is discussed further in Chapter Seven. All the same, to not return to Rome and secure his position was also untenable. This explains the rapid terms provided to the various Germanic tribes in AD 180 and his imminent return to the capital.[435] So initially, the social and political considerations in Rome need to be analysed.

Political Climate

When considering the general political environment surrounding the succession of Commodus Antoninus as sole *princeps*, there are numerous elements that need to be considered. With this in mind, the only appropriate means by which to examine this period effectively is to do so thematically (as distinct from a chronological approach). In many ways, a thematic method will continue throughout the remainder of the present study. A chronological approach will also be maintained whenever possible, but in general terms the overall themes have been followed as the primary focus of the text. There are two fundamental reasons for this methodology. Firstly, this allows for the

---

[434] Traupman 1956, *op.cit.*
[435] Herodian 1.5.1-8.

opportunity to holistically examine the changing nature of Commodus' principate (of which it certainly did) while focusing upon each individual aspect at a time. Secondly, this also allows for the interpretation and comparison of Commodus' role as both a popularist and as an elitist. These were two prominent, and albeit conflicting, elements that were highly prominent during his principate (ones that were also emphasised in the ancient literary sources as well).

Once Commodus returned to the capital from the Germanic campaign even the ancient literary sources had to present his as receiving a rapturous welcome to Rome. One of the best accounts of the joyous nature of his arrival in the capital is provided by Herodian (1.7.2-6):

ἀνύσας δὲ τὴν ὁδοιπορίαν ὁ Κόμοδος μετὰ νεανικῆς σπουδῆς καὶ διαδραμὼν τὰς ἐν μέσῳ πόλεις, ὑποδεχθείς τε πανταχοῦ βασιλικῶς καὶ δήμοις ἑορτάζουσιν ἐπιφανείς, ἀσπαστός τε καὶ ποθεινὸς πᾶσιν ὤφθη. ὡς δὲ πλησίον ἐγένετο τῆς Ῥώμης, πᾶσά τε ἡ σύγκλητος βουλὴ καὶ πανδημεὶ ὅσοι τὴν Ῥώμην κατῴκουν ἄνθρωποι, μὴ κατασχόντες αὐτῶν ἀλλ' ἕκαστος φθάσαι θέλων, δαφνηφόροι τε καὶ πάντα ἐπιφερόμενοι ἄνθη τότε ἀκμάζοντα, ὡς ἕκαστος οἷός τε ἦν, πόρρω τῆς πόλεως ὑπήντων, θεασόμενοι τὸν νέον καὶ εὐγενῆ βασιλέα. ἐπόθουν γὰρ αὐτὸν ἀληθεῖ ψυχῆς διαθέσει ἅτε παρ' αὐτοῖς γεννηθέντα τε καὶ τραφέντα καὶ ἄνωθεν ἐκ τριγονίας βασιλέα τε καὶ εὐπατρίδην ὄντα Ῥωμαίων. τὸ μὲν γὰρ πρὸς πατρὸς αὐτῷ γένος ἐκ τῶν τῆς συγκλήτου βουλῆς ἐπισήμων ἦν· Φαυστῖνα δ' ἡ μήτηρ βασίλισσα γεγένητο θυγάτηρ τε οὖσα Ἀντωνίνου τοῦ εὐσεβοῦς ἐπικληθέντος, καὶ Ἀδριανοῦ ἔκγονος κατὰ θηλυγονίαν, ἀνήνεγκε δὲ τὸ γένος αὕτη ἐπὶ Τραϊανὸν πρόπαππον. γένους μὲν οὖν ὁ Κόμοδος οὕτως εἶχε, πρὸς δὲ τῇ τῆς ἡλικίας ἀκμῇ καὶ τὴν ὄψιν ἦν ἀξιοθέατος σώματός τε συμμετρίᾳ καὶ κάλλει προσώπου μετ' ἀνδρείας. ὀφθαλμῶν τε γὰρ †ἀρθμίαι καὶ πυρώδεις βολαί, κόμη τε φύσει ξανθὴ καὶ οὔλη, ὡς, εἴποτε φοιτῴη δι' ἡλίου, τοσοῦτον ἐκλάμπειν αὐτῷ πυροειδές τι, ὡς τοὺς μὲν οἴεσθαι ῥίνημα χρυσοῦ προιόντι ἐπιπάσσεσθαι, τοὺς δὲ ἐκθειάζειν, λέγοντας αἴγλην τινὰ οὐράνιον περὶ τῇ κεφαλῇ συγγεγενῆσθαι αὐτῷ· ἴουλοί τε αὐτοῦ κατιόντες ταῖς παρειαῖς ἐπήνθουν. τοιοῦτον δὴ θεασάμενοι βασιλέα οἱ Ῥωμαῖοι, εὐφημίαις τε παντοδαπαῖς καὶ στεφάνων καὶ ἀνθέων βολαῖς ὑπεδέχοντο. ὡς δ' ἐς τὴν Ῥώμην εἰσήλασεν, ἔς τε τοῦ Διὸς τὸ τέμενος καὶ τοὺς ἄλλους νεὼς ἀνελθὼν εὐθὺς τῇ τε συγκλήτῳ καὶ τοῖς ἐν Ῥώμῃ καταλειφθεῖσι στρατιώταις χαριστήρια ὁμολογήσας τῆς φυλαχθείσης πίστεως, ἐς τὴν βασίλειον αὐλὴν ἀνεχώρησεν. χρόνου μὲν οὖν τινος ὀλίγων ἐτῶν τιμὴν πᾶσαν ἀπένεμε τοῖς πατρῴοις φίλοις, πάντα τε ἔπραττεν ἐκείνοις συμβούλοις χρώμενος.

'When the emperor's decision was announced, the army was in turmoil; all the soldiers wanted to leave with him, so that they might stop wasting their time in the war and enjoy the pleasures at Rome. When the news was circulated and messengers arrived to report the approach of the emperor, the Roman people were overjoyed; they had the highest hopes for the reign of the young emperor, believing that he would rule as his father had ruled. Speeding with the vigor of youth, Commodus passed quickly through the cities between Pannonia and Rome. Received everywhere with imperial pomp, he appeared in person before the celebrating crowds, a pleasing sight to all. As he drew near Rome, the entire senate and the people of the city cast aside all restraint. Bearing laurel branches and every kind of flower then in bloom, each man carrying as much as he could manage and eager to be first, they came out some distance from the city to welcome their young and nobly born emperor. For they did indeed give him all their affection, since he was born and reared among them and was of imperial ancestry through three generations of distinguished Romans. His father's family tree included a number of distinguished senators; his mother, the empress Faustina, was the daughter of Antoninus Pius; she was the granddaughter of Hadrian on her mother's side and traced her ancestry to Trajan, her great-grandfather. Such was Commodus' family background. At this time he was in the prime of youth, striking in appearance, with a well-developed body and a face that was handsome without being pretty. His commanding eyes flashed like lightning; his hair, naturally blond and curly, gleamed in the sunlight as if it were on fire; some thought that he sprinkled his hair with gold dust before appearing in public, while others saw in it something divine, saying that a heavenly light shone round his head. To add to his beauty, the first down was just beginning to appear on his cheeks. This was the emperor upon whom the Romans feasted their eyes and welcomed with garlands and showers of blossoms. Entering the city, Commodus went immediately to the temple of Jupiter and the other shrines.'

This reflects the optimism that was seemingly felt throughout the population of Rome at the time, although this was probably included by Herodian in order to accentuate Commodus' fall from grace with the people (or at least many of the *nobiles*), as shown by Herodian (1.14.7-8):

πολλῶν δὴ καὶ δεινῶν συνεχῶς κατειληφότων τὴν πόλιν οὐκέτι ὁ Ῥωμαίων δῆμος μετ' εὐνοίας τὸν Κόμοδον ἐπέβλεπεν, ἀλλὰ καὶ τὰς αἰτίας τῶν ἀλλεπαλλήλων συμφορῶν ἐς τοὺς ἐκείνου ἀκρίτους φόνους καὶ τὰ λοιπὰ τοῦ βίου ἀνέφερεν ἁμαρτήματα. οὐδὲ γὰρ ἐλάνθανε τὰ πραττόμενα πάντας, ἀλλ' οὐδὲ αὐτὸς λανθάνειν ἤθελεν· ἃ δὲ πράττων οἴκοι διεβάλλετο, ταῦτα καὶ δημοσίᾳ δεῖξαι ἐτόλμησεν· ἐς τοσοῦτόν τε μανίας καὶ παροινίας προὐχώρησεν, ὡς πρῶτον μὲν τὴν πατρῴαν προσηγορίαν παραιτήσασθαι, ἀντὶ δὲ Κομόδου καὶ Μάρκου υἱοῦ Ἡρακλέα τε καὶ Διὸς υἱὸν αὐτὸν κελεύσας καλεῖσθαι ἀποδυσάμενός τε τὸ Ῥωμαίων καὶ βασίλειον σχῆμα λεοντῆν ἐπεστρώννυτο καὶ ῥόπαλον μετὰ χεῖρας ἔφερεν· ἀμφιέννυτό τε ἁλουργεῖς καὶ χρυσουφεῖς ἐσθῆτας, ὡς εἶναι καταγέλαστον αὐτὸν ὑφ' ἑνὶ σχήματι καὶ θηλειῶν πολυτέλειαν καὶ ἡρώων ἰσχὺν μιμούμενον.

'With so many disasters befalling the city in rapid succession, the Roman people no longer looked with favor upon Commodus; they attributed their misfortunes to his illegal murders and the other mistakes he had made in his lifetime. He no longer concealed his activities, nor did he have any desire to keep them secret. What they objected to his doing in private he now had the effrontery to do in public. He fell into a state of drunken madness. First he discarded his family name and issued orders that he was to be called not Commodus, son of Marcus, but Hercules, son of Zeus. Abandoning the Roman and imperial mode of dress, he donned the lion skin, and carried the club of Hercules. He wore purple robes embroidered with gold, making himself an object of ridicule by combining in one set of garments the frailty of a woman and the might of a superman.'

All the same, the celebration (and of course the ensuing expectation) surrounding the accession of Commodus was not purely limited to Rome. This is exhibited through the discovery of five statue bases that have been dated to the earliest period of Commodus' sole principate,[436] thus illustrating the welcome that he generally received throughout the provinces at this point (AD 180-182).[437]

Of course the popularity of Commodus throughout the Roman Empire would have been welcomed by some, but not by all. This mixed response would have been most pronounced within the Senate.[438] Elements of this group (or perhaps factions) would have welcomed Commodus as sole Roman emperor, but this cannot be said for the entire group. The accession of Commodus Antoninus to the role of sole *princeps* would have also created a great deal of insecurity among this order of *nobiles* – who would have wondered about both the nature of the new political circumstances, but also through their harbouring of their own personal social (or imperial) ambitions. The Senate would have been feeling largely insecure for either reason – Commodus was an unknown quantity in many regards. This group of nobles had seemingly accepted the imperial rule of Marcus Aurelius, largely because he allowed the smooth continuation of their elevated status. Commodus did not play this political game as effectively. It was important to give the senatorial élite the respect that they felt they deserved, simply for the stability of the State (and in turn the principate), but Commodus sought other avenues in this regard.

ὀλίγου μὲν οὖν τινὸς χρόνου πάντα ἐπράττετο τῇ γνώμῃ τῶν πατρῴων φίλων, οἳ πανημέριοι συνῆσαν αὐτῷ τὰ βέλτιστα συμβουλεύοντες, καὶ τοσοῦτον ἐνδιδόντες χρόνον, ὅσον ἐνόμιζον αὐτάρκη πρὸς σώφρονα τοῦ σώματος ἐπιμέλειαν. παρεισδύντες δέ τινες τῶν ἐπὶ τῆς αὐλῆς οἰκετῶν διαφθείρειν ἐπειρῶντο νέον ἦθος βασιλέως, ὅσοι τε κόλακες τραπέζης [καὶ] τὸ εὔδαιμον γαστρὶ καὶ τοῖς αἰσχίστοις μετροῦσιν, ὑπεμίμνησκον αὐτὸν τῆς ἐν Ῥώμῃ τρυφῆς, θεάματά τε καὶ ἀκούσματα τερπνὰ διηγούμενοι τήν τε τῶν ἐπιτηδείων δαψίλειαν καταριθμοῦντες διαβάλλοντές τε πᾶσαν τὴν ἐπὶ ταῖς ὄχθαις τοῦ Ἴστρου ὥραν, μήτε ὀπώρας εὔφορον κρυεράν τε ἀεὶ καὶ συννεφῆ. "οὐ παύσῃ" δὲ ἔλεγον "ὦ δέσποτα, πηγνύμενόν τε καὶ ὀρυττόμενον πίνων ὕδωρ; ἄλλοι δὲ ἀπολαύσουσι πηγῶν τε θερμῶν καὶ ψυχροῦ νάματος ἀτμίδων τε καὶ ἀέρων, ὧν Ἰταλία μόνη εὔφορος." τοιαῦτα δή τινα τῷ μειρακίῳ ὑποτυπούμενοι

---

[436] *CIL* 8.8468; 8.23828; *IGRR* 4.1201; Hojte 2005, *op.cit.*, pp. 577, 582.
[437] Grosso 1964, *op.cit.*
[438] Traupman 1956, *op.cit.*

ἤγειρον αὐτοῦ τὰς ὀρέξεις ἐς τὴν ἡδονῶν ἐπιθυμίαν. αἰφνιδίως δὲ καλέσας τοὺς φίλους ποθεῖν ἔλεγε τὴν πατρίδα· ὁμολογεῖν δὲ τὰς αἰτίας τῆς αἰφνιδίου ὁρμῆς αἰδούμενος, δεδιέναι προσεποιεῖτο, μή τις ἐκεῖσε προκαταλάβοι τὴν βασίλειον ἑστίαν τῶν εὐπατριδῶν πλουσίων, εἶθ᾽ ὥσπερ ἐξ ὀχυρᾶς ἀκροπόλεως δύναμιν καὶ περιβολὴν συγκροτήσας ἐπιθῆται τῇ ἀρχῇ. αὐτάρκης δὲ ὁ δῆμος χορηγῆσαι πλῆθος ἐπιλέκτων νεανιῶν. τοιαῦτά τινα προφασιζομένου τοῦ μειρακίου οἱ μὲν ἄλλοι συνεστάλησάν τε τὴν ψυχήν, καὶ σκυθρωπαῖς ταῖς ὄψεσιν ἐς γῆν ἔνευσαν. Πομπηιανὸς δέ, ὃς πρεσβύτατός τε ἦν ἁπάντων καὶ κατ᾽ ἐπιγαμίαν προσήκων αὐτῷ (συνῴκει γὰρ τῇ πρεσβυτάτῃ τῶν ἀδελφῶν τοῦ Κομόδου), "ποθεῖν μέν σε", ἔφη, "τέκνον καὶ δέσποτα, τὴν πατρίδα εἰκός· καὶ γὰρ αὐτοὶ τῶν οἴκοι ὁμοίᾳ ἐπιθυμίᾳ ἑαλώκαμεν. ἀλλὰ τὰ ἐνταῦθα προυργιαίτερα ὄντα καὶ μᾶλλον ἐπείγοντα ἐπέχει τὴν ἐπιθυμίαν. τῶν μὲν γὰρ ἐκεῖσε καὶ ὕστερον ἐπὶ πλεῖστον αἰῶνα ἀπολαύσεις, ἐκεῖ τε ἡ Ῥώμη, ὅπου ποτ᾽ ἂν ὁ βασιλεὺς ᾖ. τὸν δὲ πόλεμον ἀτελῆ καταλιπεῖν μετὰ τοῦ ἀπρεποῦς καὶ ἐπισφαλές. θάρσος γὰρ ἐμβαλοῦμεν τοῖς βαρβάροις, οὐκ ἐπανόδου πόθον ἀλλὰ φυγὴν καὶ δέος ἡμῶν καταγνοῦσι. καλὸν δέ σοι χειρωσαμένῳ πάντας αὐτοὺς καὶ τῷ ὑπὸ τὴν ἄρκτον ὠκεανῷ τὴν ἀρχὴν ὁρίσαντι ἐπανελθεῖν οἴκαδε θριαμβεύοντί τε καὶ δεσμίους ἀπάγοντι καὶ αἰχμαλώτους βασιλεῖς τε καὶ σατράπας βαρβάρους. τούτοις γὰρ οἱ πρὸ σοῦ Ῥωμαῖοι μεγάλοι τε καὶ ἔνδοξοι γεγόνασι. δεδιέναι δέ σε οὐ χρή, μή τις ἐκεῖ τοῖς πράγμασιν ἐπιθῆται. οἵ τε γὰρ ἄριστοι τῆς βουλῆς ἐνταῦθα σὺν σοί, ἥ τε στρατιωτικὴ δύναμις παροῦσα πᾶσα τῆς σῆς ἀρχῆς προασπίζει· ταμιεῖά τε χρημάτων βασιλικῶν ἐνταῦθα πάντα· ἥ τε τοῦ πατρὸς μνήμη αἰώνιός σοι πίστιν καὶ εὔνοιαν παρὰ τῶν ἀρχομένων ἐβεβαίωσεν." τοιαῦτά τινα ἐς προτροπὴν καὶ τὴν πρὸς τὰ κρείττονα ὁρμὴν ὁ Πομπηιανὸς εἰπὼν διέτρεψε πρὸς ὀλίγον τὸ μειράκιον. αἰδεσθεὶς γὰρ ὁ Κόμοδος τὰ λεχθέντα, οὐδέν τε οἷός τε ὢν εὐλόγως ἀποκρίνασθαι, τοὺς φίλους ἀπεπέμψατο, φήσας ἀκριβέστερον καθ᾽ αὑτὸν ἐπισκέψεσθαι τὸ πρακτέον. ἐγκειμένων δὲ τῶν περὶ αὐτὸν θεραπόντων οὐκέτι μὲν τοῖς φίλοις οὐδὲν ἐκοινώσατο, ἐκπέμψας δὲ γράμματα, καὶ διανείμας οἷς ἐδοκίμασε τῆς ὄχθης τοῦ Ἴστρου τὴν πρόνοιαν προστάξας τε αὐτοῖς ἀνέχειν τὰς τῶν βαρβάρων ἐπιδρομάς, ἐπαγγέλλει τὴν ἔξοδον. οἱ μὲν οὖν διώκουν τὰ ἐγκεχειρισμένα· οἳ καὶ οὐ πολλῷ χρόνῳ πλείστους τῶν βαρβάρων ὅπλοις ἐχειρώσαντο, τοὺς δὲ ἐπὶ μεγάλαις συντάξεσιν ἐς φιλίαν ἐπηγάγοντο ῥᾷστα πείσαντες.

Then, for a short time, the emperor did everything as the advisers appointed by his father suggested. They were with him every day, giving him wise counsel; they allowed him only as much leisure as they thought necessary for the sensible care of his body. But some of his court companions interfered and tried to corrupt the character of the naive emperor. All the sycophants at his table, men who gauge their pleasure by their bellies and something a little lower, kept reminding him of the gay life at Rome, describing the delightful spectacles and musical shows and cataloguing the abundance of luxuries available there. They complained about wasting their time on the banks of the Danube, pointing out that the region was not productive in summer and that the fog and cold were unending. "Master," they said again and again, "when will you stop drinking this icy liquid mud? In the meantime, others will be enjoying warm streams and cool streams, mists and fine air too, all of which only Italy possesses in abundance." By merely suggesting such delights to the youth, they whetted his appetite for a taste of pleasures. And so he immediately summoned his advisers and informed them that he longed to see his native land. But, ashamed to admit the real reason for his sudden interest in returning, he pretended to be fearful that one of the wealthy aristocrats in Rome would seize the empire and, after raising an army and a rampart, take control of the empire, as if from an impregnable fortress. For the Roman populace was sufficiently large to supply numerous picked young men for such an army. While the youth was alleging such specious excuses, the rest, sick at heart, kept their eyes fixed on the ground in dismay. But Pompeianus, the oldest of his advisers and a relation of the emperor by marriage (his wife was Commodus' eldest sister), said to him: "Child and master too, it is entirely reasonable for you to long to see your native land; we too are gripped by hunger to see those we left at home. But more important and more urgent matters here put a curb on that yearning. For the rest of your life you will have the enjoyment of things at home; and for that matter, where the emperor is, Rome is. But to leave this war unfinished is both disgraceful and dangerous. That course would increase the barbarians' boldness; they will not believe that we long to return to our home, but will rather accuse us of a cowardly retreat. After you have conquered all these barbarians and extended the boundaries of the empire to the northern seas, it will be glorious for you to return home to celebrate your triumph, leading as fettered captives barbarian kings and governors. The Romans who preceded you became famous and gained renown in this way. There is no reason to fear that someone at home may seize control. The most distinguished senators are right here with you; the imperial troops are here to protect you; all the funds from the imperial depositories are here; and finally, the memory of your father has won for you the eternal loyalty and good will of your subjects." Eager to improve the situation, Pompeianus, by his exhortations, restrained the youth for a short time. Commodus, shamed by his words and unable to make a suitable reply, dismissed the group, saying that he would consider personally and at greater length what he should do. Then, yielding to his companions, he no longer consulted his advisers about anything. He sent off letters and, after assigning command of the Danube to men whom he considered capable, ordering them to block the barbarians' attacks, he announced his departure for Rome. Those left behind carried out their assignments; soon they subdued most of the barbarians by force of arms, and easily won the friendship of the rest by substantial bribes.' (Herodian 1.6.1-8)

As seen in the previous passage by Herodian (1.6.1-8), the emphasis was placed upon how Commodus rejected the advice of the well established network that had been formulated by Marcus Aurelius. There were two reasons for this. Firstly, one of Herodian's primary literary aims was to distance the characterisations of Marcus Aurelius and Commodus,[439] after all how could such a 'great' father have such a cruel and debased son. Secondly, it was intended to show how Commodus sought to reject the advisors (and in turn, the advice) of Marcus Aurelius – of course to his own detriment. As would be expected the reasoning behind this decision by Commodus is quite complex, but in many ways it is seemingly understandable.[440] After previously being placed in the footsteps of his illustrious father, the youthful Commodus would have wanted to create his own path.

[439] See Adams 2013, *op.cit.*, p. 194.
[440] Grosso 1964, *op.cit.*

How is this not to be expected from such a young man with such an elevated birthright? One of the persons that he seemingly regaled against was Tiberius Claudius Pompeianus, who provides an excellent example in this regard.

μέχρι μὲν οὖν τινὸς ἐπεῖχε τὸν νεανίσκον ἥ τε τοῦ πατρὸς μνήμη καὶ ἡ πρὸς τοὺς φίλους αἰδώς. ἀλλὰ γάρ, ὥσπερ τινὸς πονηρᾶς καὶ βασκάνου τύχης ἀνατρεπούσης αὐτοῦ τὸ ἔτι σῶφρον καὶ κόσμιον, συνέβη τι τοιοῦτον. Λουκίλλα ἦν τῷ Κομόδῳ πρεσβυτάτη πάντων ἀδελφή. αὕτη πρότερον Λουκίῳ Βήρῳ αὐτοκράτορι συνῴκει, ὃν κοινωνὸν τῆς βασιλείας Μᾶρκος ποιησάμενος, ἐκδοὺς [τε] αὐτῷ τὴν θυγατέρα, δεσμὸν εὐνοίας ἐχυρώτατον τὴν πρὸς αὐτὸν ἐπιγαμίαν ἐποιήσατο. ἀλλ᾽ ἐπεὶ συνέβη τὸν Λούκιον τελευτῆσαι, μενόντων τῇ Λουκίλλῃ τῶν τῆς βασιλείας συμβόλων Πομπηιανῷ ὁ πατὴρ ἐξέδοτο αὐτήν. οὐδὲν ἧττον μέντοι καὶ ὁ Κόμοδος ἐφύλαττε τὰς τιμὰς τῇ ἀδελφῇ· καὶ γὰρ ἐπὶ τοῦ βασιλείου θρόνου καθῆστο ἐν τοῖς θεάτροις, καὶ τὸ πῦρ προεπόμπευεν αὐτῆς. ἐπεὶ δὲ ὁ Κόμοδος γυναῖκα ἠγάγετο, Κρισπῖναν ὄνομα, ἀνάγκη τε ἐγένετο τὴν προεδρίαν ἀπονέμεσθαι τῇ τοῦ βασιλεύοντος γυναικί, δυσφόρως τοῦτο φέρουσα ἡ Λουκίλλα, καὶ τὴν ἐκείνης τιμὴν ἑαυτῆς ὕβριν νομίζουσα, τὸν μὲν ἑαυτῆς ἄνδρα Πομπηιανὸν εἰδυῖα ἀγαπῶντα τὸν Κόμοδον, οὐδὲν αὐτῷ περὶ ἐπιθέσεως τῆς ἀρχῆς ἀνακοινοῦται, Κοδράτου δέ, νεανίσκου εὐγενοῦς τινος καὶ πλουσίου, ἐφ᾽ οὗ καὶ λανθανούσῃ συνουσίᾳ διεβάλλετο, πεῖραν τῆς γνώμης λαμβάνουσα, περί τε τῆς προεδρίας συνεχῶς ἀπωδύρετο, καὶ κατ᾽ ὀλίγον ἀνέπεισε τὸν νεανίσκον ὀλέθρια βουλεύσασθαι αὐτῷ τε καὶ πάσῃ τῇ συγκλήτῳ.

'For the present, however, the memory of his father and his respect for his advisers held Commodus in check. But then a disastrous stroke of ill fortune completely altered his previously mild, moderate disposition. It happened this way. The oldest of the emperor's sisters was Lucilla. She had formerly been married to Lucius Verus Caesar, whom Marcus had made his associate in governing the empire; by marrying Lucilla to Lucius, Marcus had made her marriage to his Caesar the strongest bond of mutual good will. But after Lucius died, Lucilla, who retained all the privileges of her imperial position, was married by her father to Pompeianus. Commodus, too, allowed his sister to retain the imperial honors; she continued to occupy the imperial seat at the theaters, and the sacred fire was carried before her. But when Commodus married Crispina, custom demanded that the front seat at the theater be assigned to the empress. Lucilla found this difficult to endure, and felt that any honor paid to the empress was an insult to her; but since she was well aware that her husband Pompeianus was devoted to Commodus, she told him nothing about her plans to seize control of the empire. Instead, she tested the sentiments of a wealthy young nobleman, Quadratus, with whom she was rumored to be sleeping in secret. Complaining constantly about this matter of imperial precedence, she soon persuaded the young man to set in motion a plot which brought destruction upon himself and the entire senate.' (Herodian 1.8.3-4)

This statement by Herodian exhibits how initially Commodus wielded some restraint in his persecutions.[441] Or at the very least this is

---

[441] See Traupman 1956, *op.cit.*

what we are meant to believe judging from the following extracts of Herodian (1.6.4-7) (see above) and Cassius Dio (73.4.1-6):

ὅτι ὁ Κόμμοδος πολλὰ μὲν καὶ ἀπρεπῆ ἔπραξε, πλείστους δὲ ἐφόνευσε. καὶ πεβουλεύθη μὲν πολλάκις ὑπό τινων, πλείστους δὲ ἐφόνευσε καὶ ἄνδρας καὶ γυναῖκας, τοὺς μὲν φανερῶς τοὺς δὲ λάθρα φαρμάκοις, καὶ ὡς εἰπεῖν πάντας τοὺς ἐπὶ τοῦ πατρὸς αὐτοῦ καὶ ἐπ' αὐτοῦ ἐκείνου ἀνθήσαντας, πλὴν τοῦ τε Πομπηιανοῦ καὶ τοῦ Περτίνακος καὶ τοῦ Οὐικτωρίνου· τούτους γὰρ οὐκ οἶδ' ὅπως οὐκ ἀπέκτεινε. λέγω δὲ ταῦτά τε καὶ τὰ λοιπὰ οὐκ ἐξ ἀλλοτρίας ἔτι παραδόσεως ἀλλ' ἐξ οἰκείας ἤδη τηρήσεως. ἐλθὼν δὲ ἐς τὴν Ῥώμην καὶ πρὸς τὴν γερουσίαν διαλεχθεὶς ἄλλα τέ τινα ἀπελήρησε, καί τι καὶ τοιοῦτον ἐν τοῖς αὐτοῦ ἐπαίνοις εἶπεν, ὅτι τὸν πατέρα ποτὲ ἐς πηλὸν βαθὺν ἐμπεσόντα ἱππεύων ἐρρύσατο. τοιαῦτα μὲν τὰ σεμνολογήματα αὐτοῦ ἦν, ἐσιόντι δὲ αὐτῷ ἐς τὸ θέατρον τὸ κυνηγετικὸν Κλαύδιος Πομπηιανὸς ἐπεβούλευσε· ξίφος γάρ τι ἐν αὐτῇ τῇ τῆς ἐσόδου στενοχωρίᾳ ἀνατείνας, "ἰδού" ἔφη, "τοῦτό σοι ἡ βουλὴ [οὐ] πέπομφεν". οὗτος ἠγγύητο μὲν τὴν θυγατέρα Λουκίλλης, ἐχρῆτο δὲ καὶ αὐτῇ ταύτῃ καὶ τῇ τῆς κόρης μητρί, καὶ διὰ ταῦτα τῷ Κομμόδῳ ᾠκείωτο ὡς καὶ συνεστιᾶσθαι καὶ συννεανιεύεσθαι αὐτῷ. ἡ γὰρ Λουκίλλα οὐδὲν ἐπιεικεστέρα οὐδὲ σωφρονεστέρα τοῦ ἀδελφοῦ Κομμόδου ὑπάρχουσα ἤχθετο μὲν τῷ ἀνδρὶ αὐτῆς τῷ Πομπηιανῷ· ὅθεν καὶ ἀνέπεισε τὸν εἰρημένον ἐπιθέσθαι τῷ Κομμόδῳ, καὶ αὐτόν τε ἀπώλεσε καὶ αὐτὴ φωραθεῖσα ἐπανῃρέθη. ἀπέκτεινε δὲ καὶ τὴν Κρισπῖναν ὁ Κόμμοδος, ἐπὶ μοιχείᾳ δή τινι ὀργισθεὶς αὐτῇ. πρὸ δὲ τοῦ ἀναιρεθῆναι καὶ ἀμφότεραι ἐς τὴν νῆσον τὴν Καπρίαν ὑπερωρίσθησαν.

'Commodus was guilty of many unseemly deeds, and killed a great many people. Many plots were formed by various people against Commodus, and he killed a great many, both men and women, some openly and some by means of poison, secretly, making away, in fact, with practically all those who had attained eminence during his father's reign and his own, with the exception of Pompeianus, Pertinax and Victorinus; these men for some reason or other he did not kill. I state these and subsequent facts, not, as hitherto, on the authority of others' reports, but from my own observation. On coming to Rome he addressed the senate, uttering a lot of trivialities; and among the various stories that he told in his own praise was one to this effect, that once while out riding he had saved the life of his father, who had fallen into a deep quagmire. Such were his lofty pratings. But as he was entering the hunting-theatre, Claudius Pompeianus formed a plot against him: thrusting out a sword in the narrow entrance, he said: "See! This is what the senate has sent you." This man had been betrothed to the daughter out of Lucilla, but had intimate relations both with the girl herself and with her mother; in this way he had become friendly with Commodus, so that he was his companion both at banquets and in youthful escapades. Lucilla, who was no more modest or chaste than her brother Commodus, detested her husband, Pompeianus. It was for this reason that she persuaded him to make the attack upon Commodus; and she not only caused his destruction but was herself detected and put out of the way. Commodus also put Crispina to death, having become angry with her for some act of adultery. But before their execution both women were banished to the island of Capreae.' (Dio 73.4.1-6)

These passages were not only intended to represent the distinguished character of Tiberius Claudius Pompeianus, but also the depravity of Commodus Antoninus as well – such a devoted supporter who ultimately sought to reject the *princeps*. Herodian 1.6.4-7 illustrates the earliest stages of Commodus' principate – a point where Claudius Pompeianus was entirely supportive of the young emperor in accordance with the wishes of Marcus Aurelius. This contrasts with the representation of Cassius Dio (73.4.1-6) where Tiberius Claudius Pompeianus is depicted as actively plotting the downfall of Commodus. This was in accordance with the view that Claudius Pompeianus was disillusioned with Commodus' corruption and how the author sought to establish the ultimate virtues of Pompeianus as a character.

In many ways the ancient literary sources characterise Tiberius Claudius Pompeianus as being a highly symbolic figure during this period. Pompeianus was a highly respected member of the Roman aristocracy,[442] which epitomises the significance of (and subsequent attention towards) such textual representation of him by Herodian and Cassius Dio. The use of his characterisation should not be surprising. Both authors sought to identify Tiberius Claudius Pompeianus with the opinion of the conservative elements within the Senate at the time.[443] This is hardly to be unexpected in view of not only his elevated social position but also his political connections. Claudius Pompeianus was used as an example by these early authors in order to provide a commentary about how while the principate was initially welcomed by the aristocratic circles in Rome it did not last and ultimately resulted in both suspicion and derision. All the same, it is difficult to determine which party was at fault – in all likelihood it was probably the responsibility of both of them.

Inter haec Commodus senatu semet inridente, cum adulterum matris consulem designasset, appellatus est Pius; cum occidisset Perennem, appellatus est Felix, inter plurimas caedes multorum civium quasi quidam novus Sulla. idem Commodus, ille Pius, ille Felix, finxisse etiam quandam contra se coniurationem dicitur, ut multos occideret. nec alia ulla fuit defectio praeter Alexandri, qui postea se et suos interemit, et sororis Lucillae. appellatus est Commodus etiam Britannicus ab adulatoribus, cum Britanni etiam imperatorem contra eum deligere voluerint.

'Meanwhile, because he had appointed to the consulship a former lover of his mother's, the senate mockingly gave Commodus the name Pius; and after he had executed Perennis, he was given the name Felix, as though, amid the multitudinous executions of many citizens, he were a second Sulla. And this same Commodus, who was

---

[442] Grosso 1964, *op.cit.*
[443] Traupman 1956, *op.cit.*, p. 49.

called Pius, and who was called Felix, is said to have feigned a plot against his own life, in order that he might have an excuse for putting many to death. Yet as a matter of fact, there were no rebellions save that of Alexander, who soon killed himself and his near of kin, and that of Commodus' sister Lucilla. He was called Britannicus by those who desired to flatter him, whereas the Britons even wished to set up an emperor against him.' (*HA Commodus* 8.1-4)

As seen by the previous passages the relationship between Commodus Antoninus and the Senate had clearly disintegrated. The passage by the *HA* biographer was clearly intended to establish how much antagonism existed between the *princeps* and his senatorial peers.[444] The reliability of the extract is of course somewhat questionable, but the execution of senators without their approval was never a popular action by any *princeps*. All the same, Cassius Dio (73.21.1-3) was even more explicit in this regard. He emphasises the public antagonism of Commodus Antoninus and the resulting fear of the senatorial élite. It is particularly important to note how Cassius Dio directly associated himself with the senatorial *ordo*, which overtly characterises not only his own literary biases but also his intended audience. These references clearly demonstrate how the relationship between the emperor and his aristocratic peers had become toxic, which would have made the general administration of the Roman Empire less effective.

The general political climate definitely changed throughout Commodus' reign – what had begun with a strong sense of optimism had degenerated into mutual suspicion and fear among the Roman aristocracy and their *princeps*. Commodus Antoninus feared the ambitions of other *nobiles*, and this resulted in a series of élite persecutions (without consulting the Senate) and in turn this increased their burgeoning animosity towards him. Of course this resulted in a strong anti-Commodus theme throughout the ensuing literary sources that were produced about his reign. One of the most prominent aspects that dominated his characterisation was that of his overt corruption. This theme has been dealt with in the next section.

Corruption

If the ancient literary sources are to be believed in an unquestioning fashion, Commodus was among one of the worst Roman *principes* ever.[445] All the same, as noted previously, this is not the approach taken here – all the textual sources have been read and interpreted

---

[444] Grosso 1964, *op.cit.*
[445] See Traupman 1956, *op.cit.*, p. 66.

with some degree of caution. The primary aim of this section is to examine the various themes of vice and corruption that are emphasised by them. It is, however, important to note that the executions ordered by Commodus Antoninus have been dealt with in another section below. This methodology is intended to provide a clearer perspective about how the ancient authors sought to emphasise the depravity of the young emperor almost to the exclusion of everything else. A good example of this is shown by the *Epitomator* (17.3). Despite the brevity of this reference, it is indicative of the overall work. It is also important to note the almost complete lack of detail provided by the author. All the same, this was deemed to have been necessary to the *Epitomator* – the emphasis upon his corruption was all that was deemed necessary to him – the general theme was more important than the details.

This was not a new literary innovation. The use of various types of authorial invective against an unpopular Roman *princeps* was a long standing compositional tradition. Previous Roman imperial historians and biographers, such as Tacitus and Suetonius, had gone to great lengths to emphasise the corruption of earlier notorious (or 'evil') *principes*.[446] Caligula provides an excellent example of this tradition. Owing to his largely autocratic perspective towards his imperial role, Caius Caligula came into constant conflict with his senatorial peers, which in turn has affected the fashion in which he was depicted by the resulting ancient authors.[447] Another Roman emperor who received a similar focus upon his vice and corruption was Nero,[448] who also had a rather antagonistic relationship with some elements of the social nobility. Domitian also received a great deal of invective surrounding his corruption and his unpopularity among the political élites, which was intended to remove attention from his favourable accomplishments.[449] As far as Commodus Antoninus is concerned, one author who sought to undermine his reputation in particular was the historian, Herodian.[450]

τὸν μὲν οὖν ἀνδριάντα μετὰ τὴν ἐκείνου τελευτὴν καθελοῦσα ἡ σύγκλητος Ἐλευθερίας εἰκόνα ἵδρυσεν· ὁ δὲ Κόμοδος μηκέτι κατέχων ἑαυτοῦ δημοσίᾳ θέας ἐπετέλεσεν,

---

[446] Grosso 1964, *op.cit.*
[447] See Adams 2007, *op.cit.*
[448] See Champlin 1980, *op.cit.*
[449] Adams 2005, *op.cit.*
[450] Traupman 1956, *op.cit.*

ὑποσχόμενος τά τε θηρία πάντα ἰδίᾳ χειρὶ κατακτενεῖν καὶ τοῖς ἀνδρειοτάτοις τῶν νεανιῶν μονομαχήσειν. διαδραμούσης δὲ τῆς φήμης συνέθεον ἔκ τε τῆς Ἰταλίας πάσης καὶ τῶν ὁμόρων ἐθνῶν, θεασόμενοι ἃ μὴ πρότερον μήτε ἑωράκεσαν μήτε ἠκηκόεσαν. καὶ γὰρ διηγγέλλετο αὐτοῦ τῆς χειρὸς τὸ εὔστοχον, καὶ ὅτι ἔμελεν αὐτῷ ἀκοντίζοντι καὶ τοξεύοντι μὴ πταίειν. συνῆσαν δὲ παιδεύοντες αὐτὸν Παρθυαίων οἱ τοξικὴν ἀκριβοῦντες καὶ Μαυρουσίων οἱ ἀκοντίζειν ἄριστοι, οὓς πάντας εὐχειρίᾳ ὑπερέβαλλεν. ἐπεὶ δὲ κατέλαβον αἱ τῆς θέας ἡμέραι, τὸ μὲν ἀμφιθέατρον πεπλήρωτο, τῷ δὲ Κομόδῳ περίδρομος κύκλῳ κατεσκεύαστο, ὡς μὴ συστάδην τοῖς θηρίοις μαχόμενος κινδυνεύοι, ἄνωθεν δὲ καὶ ἐξ ἀσφαλοῦς ἀκοντίζων εὐστοχίας μᾶλλον ἢ ἀνδρείας παρέχοιτο δεῖξιν. ἐλάφους μὲν οὖν καὶ δορκάδας ὅσα τε κερασφόρα πλὴν ταύρων, συνθέων αὐτοῖς καὶ καταδιώκων ἔβαλλε φθάνων τε αὐτῶν τὸν δρόμον καὶ πληγαῖς καιρίοις ἀναιρῶν· λέοντας δὲ καὶ παρδάλεις ὅσα τε ζῷα γενναῖα περιθέων ἄνωθεν κατηκόντιζεν. οὐδέ τις εἶδεν ἀκόντιον δεύτερον οὐδὲ τραῦμα ἄλλο πλὴν τοῦ θανατηφόρου· ἅμα γὰρ τῇ τοῦ ζῴου ὁρμῇ κατὰ τοῦ μετώπου ἢ κατὰ καρδίας ἔφερε τὴν πληγήν, καὶ οὐδέποτε σκοπὸν ἄλλον ἔσχεν οὐδὲ ἐπ᾽ ἄλλο μέρος ἦλθε τὸ ἀκόντιον τοῦ σώματος, ὡς μὴ ἅμα τε τρῶσαι καὶ φονεῦσαι. τὰ δὲ πανταχόθεν ζῷα ἠθροίζετο αὐτῷ. τότε γοῦν εἴδομεν ὅσα ἐν γραφαῖς ἐθαυμάζομεν· ἀπό τε γὰρ Ἰνδῶν καὶ Αἰθιόπων, εἴ τι πρότερον ἄγνωστον ἦν, μεσημβρίας τε καὶ τῆς ἀρκτῴας γῆς ζῷα πάντα φονεύων Ῥωμαίοις ἔδειξε. τὸ δ᾽ εὔστοχον τῆς χειρὸς αὐτοῦ πάντες ἐξεπλήττοντο. λαβὼν οὖν ποτὲ βέλη ὧν αἱ ἀκμαὶ ἦσαν μηνοειδεῖς, ταῖς Μαυρουσίαις στρουθοῖς ὀξύτατα φερομέναις καὶ ποδῶν τάχει καὶ κολπώσει πτερῶν ἐπαφιεὶς τὰ βέλη κατ᾽ ἄκρου τοῦ τραχήλου ἐκαρατόμει, ὡς καὶ τῶν κεφαλῶν ἀφῃρημένας ὁρμῇ τοῦ βέλους ἔτι περιθεῖν αὐτὰς ὡς μηδὲν παθούσας. παρδάλεως δέ ποτε ὀξυτάτῳ δρόμῳ τὸν ἐκκαλούμενον καταλαβούσης φθάσας τῷ ἀκοντίῳ μέλλουσαν δήξεσθαι, τὴν μὲν ἀπέκτεινε τὸν δὲ ἐρρύσατο, φθάσας τῇ τοῦ δόρατος αἰχμῇ τὴν τῶν ὀδόντων ἀκμήν. λεόντων δέ ποτε ἐξ ὑπογαίων ἑκατὸν ἅμα ἀφεθέντων ἰσαρίθμοις ἀκοντίοις πάντας ἀπέκτεινεν, ὡς ἐπὶ πολὺ κειμένων τῶν πτωμάτων δι᾽ αὐτὸ τοῦτο ἐπὶ σχολῆς πάντας ἀριθμῆσαι καὶ μηδ᾽ ἓν ἰδεῖν περιττὸν ἀκόντιον. μέχρι μὲν οὖν τούτων, εἰ καὶ βασιλείας τὰ πραττόμενα ἦν ἀλλότρια, πλὴν ἀνδρείας καὶ εὐστοχίας παρὰ τοῖς δημώδεσιν εἶχέ τινα χάριν. ἐπεὶ δὲ καὶ γυμνὸς ἐς τὸ ἀμφιθέατρον εἰσῆλθεν ὅπλα τε ἀναλαβὼν ἐμονομάχει, τότε σκυθρωπὸν εἶδεν ὁ δῆμος θέαμα, τὸν εὐγενῆ Ῥωμαίων βασιλέα μετὰ τοσαῦτα τρόπαια πατρός τε καὶ προγόνων οὐκ ἐπὶ βαρβάρους ὅπλα λαμβάνοντα στρατιωτικὰ ἢ Ῥωμαίων ἀρχῇ πρέποντα, καθυβρίζοντα δὲ τὸ ἀξίωμα αἰσχίστῳ καὶ μεμιασμένῳ σχήματι. ὃ μὲν οὖν μονομαχῶν ῥᾳδίως τῶν ἀνταγωνιστῶν περιεγίνετο καὶ μέχρι τραυμάτων προεχώρει ὑπεικόντων ἁπάντων καὶ τὸν βασιλέα οὐ τὸν μονομάχον ἐννοούντων, ἐς τοσοῦτον δὲ προεχώρησε μανίας, ὡς μηκέτι βούλεσθαι μηδὲ τὴν βασίλειον οἰκεῖν ἑστίαν· ἀλλὰ γὰρ μετοικισθῆναι ἐβούλετο ἐς τὸ τῶν μονομάχων καταγώγιον. ἑαυτὸν δὲ οὐκέτι Ἡρακλέα, ἀλλὰ τῶν μονομαχούντων ἐνδόξου τινὸς προτετελευτηκότος ὀνόματι καλεῖσθαι προσέταξε. τοῦ δὲ μεγίστου ἀγάλματος κολοσσιαίου, ὅπερ σέβουσι Ῥωμαῖοι εἰκόνα φέρον ἡλίου, τὴν κεφαλὴν ἀποτεμὼν ἱδρύσατο <τὴν> ἑαυτοῦ, ὑπογράψας τῇ βάσει [οὐχ] ἃς εἰώθασι βασιλικὰς καὶ πατρῴας προσηγορίας, ἀντὶ δὲ Γερμανικοῦ "μονομάχους χιλίους νικήσαντος".

ʿThe senate removed this statue of Commodus after his death and replaced it with a statue of Freedom. Now the emperor, casting aside all restraint, took part in the public shows, promising to kill with his own hands wild animals of all kinds and to fight in gladiatorial combat against the bravest of the youths. When this news became known, people hastened to Rome from all over Italy and from the neighboring provinces to see what they had neither seen nor even heard of before. Special mention was made of the skill of his hands and the fact that he never missed when hurling javelins or shooting arrows. His instructors were the most skillful of the Parthian bowmen and the most accurate of the Moroccan javelin men, but he surpassed them all in marksmanship. When the days for the show arrived, the amphitheater was completely filled. A terrace encircling the arena had been constructed for Commodus, enabling him to avoid risking his life by fighting the animals at close quarters; rather, by hurling his javelins down from a safe place, he offered a display of skill rather than of courage. Deer, roebuck, and horned animals of all kinds, except bulls, he struck down, running with them in pursuit, anticipating their dashes, and killing them with deadly blows. Lions, leopards, and other animals of the nobler sort he killed from above, running around on his terrace. And on no occasion did anyone see a second javelin used, nor any wound except the death wound. For at the very moment the animal started up, it received the blow on its forehead or in its heart, and it bore no other wound, nor did the javelin pierce any other part of its body: the beast was wounded and killed in the same instant. Animals were collected for him from all over the world. Then we saw in the flesh animals that we had previously marveled at in paintings. From India and Ethiopia, from lands to the north and to the south, any animals hitherto unknown he displayed to the Romans and then dispatched them. On one occasion he shot arrows with crescent-shaped heads at Moroccan ostriches, birds that move with great speed, both because of their swiftness afoot and the sail-like nature of their wings. He cut off their heads at the very top of the neck; so, after their heads had been severed by the edge of the arrow, they continued to run around as if they had not been injured. Once when a leopard, with a lightning dash, seized a condemned criminal, he thwarted the leopard with his javelin as it was about to close its jaws; he killed the beast and rescued the man, the point of the javelin anticipating the points of the leopard's teeth. Again, when a hundred lions appeared in one group as if from beneath the earth, he killed the entire hundred with exactly one hundred javelins, and all the bodies lay stretched out in a straight line for some distance; they could thus be counted with no difficulty, and no one saw a single extra javelin. As far as these activities are concerned, however, even if his conduct was hardly becoming for an emperor, he did win the approval of the mob for his courage and his marksmanship. But when he came into the amphitheater naked, took up arms, and fought as a gladiator, the people saw a disgraceful spectacle, a nobly born emperor of the Romans, whose fathers and forebears had won many victories, not taking the field against barbarians or opponents worthy of the Romans, but disgracing his high position by degrading and disgusting exhibitions. In his gladiatorial combats, he defeated his opponents with ease, and he did no more than wound them, since they all submitted to him, but only because they knew he was the emperor, not because he was truly a gladiator. At last he became so demented that he was unwilling to live in the imperial palace, but wished to change his residence to the gladiatorial barracks. He gave orders that he was no longer to be called Hercules, but by the name of a famous gladiator then dead. He removed the head of a huge Colossus, which the Romans worship and which bears the likeness of the Sun, replacing it with his own head, and inscribed on the base not the usual imperial and family titles; instead of "Germanicus" he wrote: "Conqueror of a Thousand Gladiators."' (Herodian 1.15.1-9)

This passage highlights the prevailing senatorial disgust that would have been prevalent throughout the reign of Commodus.[451] In this instance the primary focus was upon his excesses – such as the large expenditure of public resources that he seemingly wasted upon gaining the adoration of the lower classes. This corruption was of course confirmed by his ultimate identification with Heracles, but this has been discussed further in Chapter Six.[452] In this instance, however, it is important to note the large amount of detail provided by Herodian about the corruption of Commodus – this is in sharp contrast to the levels of authorial emphasis placed upon his actual administration. As far as Herodian was concerned the reign of Commodus was one of vice and corruption, a fact that made any of his other policies or actions almost entirely irrelevant. A similar trend and literary theme can also be viewed in the writings of Cassius Dio (73.10.2-3):

ὅτι ὁ Κόμμοδος εὐθυμίαις τε πάνυ προσέκειτο καὶ ἁρματηλασίᾳ προσεῖχε, καὶ οὔτ' ἀρχὴν τῶν τοιούτων τι αὐτῷ ἔμελεν, οὔτ' εἰ καὶ σφόδρα ἐπεφρόντικει, διαθέσθαι γε αὐτὰ ὑπὸ τῆς ἁβρότητος καὶ τῆς ἀπειρίας ἐδύνατο. καὶ οἱ Καισάρειοι τούτου ἀπαλλαγέντες (ἦν δὲ αὐτῶν κορυφαῖος ὁ Κλέανδρος) οὐδὲν ὅ τι κακὸν οὐκ ἔδρων, πωλοῦντες πάντα, ὑβρίζοντες, ἀσελγαίνοντες. Κόμμοδος δὲ τὸ πλεῖστον τοῦ βίου περί τε τὰς ῥαστώνας καὶ τοὺς ἵππους περί τε τὰς μάχας τῶν τε θηρίων καὶ τῶν ἀνδρῶν εἶχεν. ἄνευ γὰρ ὧν οἴκοι ἔδρα, πολλοὺς μὲν ἄνδρας ἐν τῷ δημοσίῳ πολλὰ δὲ καὶ θηρία πολλάκις ἔφθειρε· καὶ πέντε γοῦν ἵππους ποταμίους ἅμα καὶ δύο ἐλέφαντας ἄλλῃ καὶ ἄλλῃ ἡμέρᾳ χωρὶς αὐτὸς ταῖς ἑαυτοῦ χερσὶ κατεχρήσατο, καὶ προσέτι καὶ ῥινοκέρωτας ἀπέκτεινε καὶ καμηλοπάρδαλιν. ταῦτα μέν μοι κατὰ παντὸς τοῦ περὶ αὐτὸν λόγου γέγραπται.

'Commodus was wholly devoted to pleasure and gave himself up to chariot-racing, caring nothing for anything of that nature; and, indeed, if he had been deeply concerned, he would not have been able to administer them by reason of his indolence and his inexperience. And the imperial freedmen, with Cleander at their head, after getting rid of this man (Perennis), refrained from no form of mischief, selling all privileges, and indulging in wantonness and debauchery. Commodus devoted most of his life to ease and to horses and to combats of wild beasts and of men. In fact, besides all that he did in private, he often slew in public large numbers of men and beasts as well. For example, all alone with his own hands, he dispatched five hippopotami together with two elephants on two successive days; and he also killed rhinoceroses and a camelopard. This is what I have to say with reference to his career as a whole.' (Dio 73.10.2-3)

---

[451] See Traupman 1956, op.cit., p. 85.
[452] Grosso 1964, op.cit.

As can be seen in this passage, Commodus Antoninus was similarly characterised as being almost entirely corrupt and a definitively inappropriate emperor. This is a similar theme to the aforementioned extract by Herodian – that of his indulgence and weakness for personal pleasure. The emphasis by Cassius Dio though is more upon his almost complete lack of administrative responsibility, which is verified through reference to the powers used by Commodus' freedmen and his Praetorian Prefect, Cleander. The emperor was being shown as entirely carefree and open to the influence of his subordinates – not his senatorial peer group. Cassius Dio, unlike Herodian, pays minimal attention towards detail, but instead aims to present a succinct (but powerful) statement about the extent of Commodus' corruption. This was a central theme for his writings about him, epitomising the prominence of the anti-Commodus sentiment among these early authors. All the same, the prominence of Commodus' corruption within these accounts is most notable within the works of the *HA* biographer (3.5-9; 9.1-3; 10.3-9):

bellum etiam quod pater paene confecerat legibus hostium addictus remisit ac Romam reversus est. Romam ut rediit, subactore suo Saotero post se in curro locato ita triumphavit ut eum saepius cervice reflexa publice oscularetur. etiam in orchestra hoc idem fecit. et cum potaret in lucem helluareturque viribus Romani imperii, vespera etiam per tabernas ac lupanaria volitavit. misit homines ad provincias regendas vel criminum socios vel a criminosis commendatos. in senatus odium ita venit ut et ipse crudeliter in tanti ordinis perniciem saeviret fieretque e contempto crudelis.

He abandoned the war which his father had almost finished and submitted to the enemy's terms, and then he returned to Rome. After he had come back to Rome he led the triumphal procession with Saoterus, his partner in depravity, seated in his chariot, and from time to time he would turn around and kiss him openly, repeating this same performance even in the orchestra. And not only was he wont to drink until dawn and squander the resources of the Roman Empire, but in the evening he would ramble through taverns and brothels. He sent out to rule the provinces men who were either his companions in crime or were recommended to him by criminals. He became so detested by the senate that he in his turn was moved with cruel passion for the destruction of that great order, and from having been despised he became bloodthirsty.' (*Commodus* 3.5-9)

Simulavit se et in Africam iturum, ut sumptum itinerarium exigeret, et exegit eumque in convivia et aleam convertit. Motilenum, praefectum praetorii, per ficus veneno interemit. accepit statuas in Herculis habitu, eique immolatum est ut deo. multos praeterea paraverat interimere. quod per parvulum quendam proditum est, qui tabulam e cubiculo eiecit, in qua occidendorum erant nomina scripta.

'He pretended once that he was going to Africa, so that he could get funds for the journey, then got them and spent them on banquets and gaming instead. He murdered Motilenus, the prefect of the guard, by means of poisoned figs. He allowed statues of himself to be erected with the accoutrements of Hercules; and sacrifices were performed to him as to a god. He had planned to execute many more men besides, but his plan was betrayed by a certain young servant, who threw out of his bedroom a tablet on which were written the names of those who were to be killed.' (*Commodus* 9.1-3)

si quis sane se mori velle praedixisset, hunc invitum praecipitari iubebat. In iocis quoque pernicio- sus. nam eum, quem vidisset albescentes inter nigros capillos quasi vermiculos habere, sturno adposi- to, qui se vermes sectari crederet, capite suppuratum reddebat obtunsione oris. pinguem hominem medio ventre dissicuit, ut eius intestina subito funderentur. monopodios et luscinios eos, quibus aut singulos tulisset oculos aut singulos pedes fregisset, appellabat. multos praeterea passim exstinxit alios, quia barbarico habitu occurrerant, alios, quia nobiles et speciosi erant. habuit in deliciis homines appellatos nominibus verendorum utriusque sexus, quos libentius suis osculis ap- plicabat. habuit et hominem pene prominente ultra modum animalium, quem Onon appellabat, sibi carissimum. quem et ditavit et sacerdotio Herculis rustici praeposuit.

'And if any one, indeed, expressed a desire to die, he had him hurried to death, however really reluctant. In his humorous moments, too, he was destructive. For example, he put a starling on the head of one man who, as he noticed, had a few white hairs, resembling worms, among the black, and caused his head to fester through the continual pecking of the bird's beak — the bird, of course, imagining that it was pursuing worms. One corpulent person he cut open down the middle of his belly, so that his intestines gushed forth. Other men he dubbed one-eyed or one-footed, after he himself had plucked out one of their eyes or cut off one of their feet. In addition to all this, he murdered many others in many places, some because they came of his presence in the costume of barbarians, others because they were noble and handsome. He kept among his minions certain men named after the private parts of both sexes, and on these he liked to bestow kisses. He also had in his company a man with a male member larger than that of most animals, whom he called Onos. This man he treated with great affection, and even made him rich and appointed him to the priesthood of the Rural Hercules.' (*Commodus* 10.3-9)

The first passage (*Commodus* 3.5-9) was intended to provide largely anecdotal evidence of his corruption, exhibiting not only his misrule and lavish expenditure of public funds, but also his sexual depravity as well. It is notable that the *HA* biographer does not represent him as steadily declining into vice, but instead Commodus is depicted here as being corrupt from the outset of his sole reign. The second extract (*Commodus* 9.1-3) further establishes the characterisation of Commodus as being entirely vile and devoted to corruption accord- ing to the biographer. Again, owing to the largely anecdotal nature of this passage, it is difficult to entirely verify its context historically. Section 10.3-9 was primarily intended to exhibit the innate cruelty of Commodus – even his sense of humour was depicted as being de- voted to nastiness and the derision of others. The use of sexual in- vective was returned to by the *HA* biographer (*Commodus* 11.1-7;

14.4-8), which was a common literary form of establishing the base nature of an 'evil' *princeps*.

dicitur saepe pretiosissimis cibis humana stercora miscuisse nec abstinuisse gustum aliis, ut putabat, inrisis. duos gibbos retortos in lance argentea sibi sinapi perfusos exhibuit eosdemque statim promovit ac ditavit. praefectum praetorii suum Iulianum togatum praesente officio suo in piscinam detrusit. quem saltare etiam nudum ante concubinas suas iussit quatientem cymbala deformato vultu. genera leguminum coctorum ad convivium propter luxuriae continuationem raro vocavit. lavabat per diem septies atque octies et in ipsis balneis edebat. adibat deorum templa pollutus stupris et humano sanguine. imitatus est et medicum, ut sanguinem hominibus emitteret scalpris feralibus.

'It is claimed that he often mixed human excrement with the most expensive foods, and he did not refrain from tasting them, mocking the rest of the company, as he thought. He displayed two misshapen hunchbacks on a silver platter after smearing them with mustard, and then straightway advanced and enriched them. He pushed into a swimming-pool his praetor prefect Julianus, although he was clad in his toga and accompanied by his staff; and he even ordered this same Julianus to dance naked before his concubines, clashing cymbals and making grimaces. The various kinds of cooked vegetables he rarely admitted to his banquets, his purpose being to preserve unbroken the succession of dainties. He used to bathe seven and eight times a day, and was in the habit of eating while in the baths. He would enter the temples of the gods defiled with adulteries and human blood. He even aped a surgeon, going so far as to bleed men to death with scalpels.' (*Commodus* 11.1-7)

Multi sub eo et alienam poenam et salutem suam pecunia redemerunt. vendidit etiam suppliciorum diversitates et sepulturas et inminutiones malorum et alios pro aliis occidit. vendidit etiam provincias et administrationes, cum ii per quos venderet partem acciperent, partem vero Commodus. vendidit nonnullis et inimicorum suorum caedes. vendiderunt sub eo etiam eventus litium liberti. praefectos Paternum et Perennium non diu tulit, ita tamen ut etiam de iis praefectis quos ipse fecerat triennium nullus impleret, quorum plurimos interfecit vel veneno vel gladio. et praefectos urbi eadem facilitate mutavit.

'In his reign many a man secured punishment for another or immunity for himself by bribery. Indeed, in return for money Commodus would grant a change of punishment, the right of burial, the alleviation of wrongs, and the substitution of another for one condemned to be put to death. He sold provinces and administrative posts, part of the proceeds accruing to those through whom he made the sale and part to Commodus himself. To some he sold even the lives of their enemies. Under him the imperial freedmen sold even the results of law-suits. He did not long put up with Paternus and Perennis as prefects; indeed, not one of the prefects whom he himself had appointed remained in office as long as three years. Most of them he killed, some with poison, some with the sword.' (*Commodus* 14.4-8)

Section 11.1-7 continues this prevailing theme explicitly. According to the author the corruption of Commodus Antoninus almost knew no limitations. He was the embodiment of vice and depravity in this representation.[453] All the same, this clearly establishes the literary intentions of the author – the focus was upon his corruption in order to emphasise the unsuitability of Commodus as having attained the role of *princeps*. The *HA* biographer is unwavering in his approach – this is the unquestionable characterisation of Commodus. The corruption of the young emperor is further demonstrated in Section 14.4-8, but it was instead intended to be embodied in his lax administration in this instance. This is important to note because it shows how the author of the *Historia Augusta* sought to connect the personal vice of Commodus within his public official capacity. It is also apparent to again view the limited amount of detail provided by the *HA* biographer – thus making it extremely difficult to verify its accuracy.

So when considering the ancient literary representation of Commodus' corruption it is important to acknowledge the effect that these damning characterisations have had upon the appraisal of his principate. Unfortunately most of the ancient evidence provided by all of these authors is anecdotal, which makes them problematic. All the same, the corruption of Commodus Antoninus was continually emphasised by them. The focus upon his vice and depravity of course was not only appealing to them on an entertainment level, but it also allowed each author the opportunity to clearly establish how Commodus was not suitable for the position of *princeps*. Yet he reigned for over a decade. Nevertheless, the details surrounding his principate are not given prominence because of their prevailing anti-Commodus partiality. Therefore, it is the aim of the next section to try and gain some insight into the administration from AD 180-192 in order to determine its efficacy.

Commodus as an Administrator

The actual nature of Commodus' administration is difficult to determine, owing to the limited nature of the ancient evidence. The early literary sources present only brief descriptions of his involvement and these representations are of course focused upon the harm that he brought to the Roman Empire. The irony of these statements is that Commodus Antoninus is largely shown as being negligent and leaving the majority of decisions of State to others, which makes the accusation of such a lack of responsibility much more complex. This is not to absolve Commodus of all responsibility for the creation of

---

[453] Grosso 1964, *op.cit.*

such a characterisation, but it is intended to simply point out that the ancient literary sources often abridged the details to suit their portrayals of him (as discussed further below). So the remainder of this chapter has been intended to analyse and discuss the various early sources of evidence in order to gain a more holistic impression of his reign. All the same, one of the most prominent topics that must first be discussed is the role of the various Praetorian Prefects during this period from AD 180-192.

The importance of the Praetorian Prefects within the functioning of the Roman principate is self-evident. Be they 'king-makers' or 'autocrats' in their own right, their role was vital, not only for either the security (or albeit insecurity) of the *princeps*, or simply the basic running of the imperial household on numerous occasions over time. Examples such as Lucius Aurelius Sejanus (under the Emperor Tiberius) and Sutorius Macro (under both Tiberius and Caligula) are cases in point. These pivotal figures (as Praetorian Prefects) definitely had a severe impact upon the development of the principate. This is important to note because the early literary sources frequently depict Commodus as being entirely dependent (if not controlled) upon them, which led to their exploitation of the position. Essentially the portrayals infer that Commodus was not present, or in any type of control of the matters of State. So with this in mind, it is important to examine the careers of the two most pivotal (if not infamous) Praetorian Prefects from the reign of Commodus: Sextus Tigidius Perennis and Marcus Aurelius Cleander.

Sextus Tigidius Perennis is somewhat of a mystery as a character, in that he has a definitive style of portrayal in the ancient texts, but little else is known of him. Prior to his appointment as a member of the Praetorian *corps* during the joint principate of Marcus Aurelius and Commodus Antoninus his earlier career is largely unknown (and seemingly undistinguished). All the same, as of AD 180, the ancient literary sources continually emphasise his prominence:

Post haec Commodus numquam facile in publicum processit neque quicquam sibi nuntiari passus est nisi quod Perennis ante tractasset. Perennis autem Commodi persciens invenit quem ad modum ipse potens esset. nam persuasit Commodo, ut ipse deliciis vacaret, idem vero Perennis curis incumberet. quod Commodus laetanter accepit. hac igitur lege vivens ipse cum trecentis concubinis, quas ex matronarum meretricumque dilectu ad formae speciem concivit, trecentisque aliis puberibus exoletis, quos aeque ex plebe ac nobilitate vi pretiisque forma disceptatrice collegerat, in Palatio per convivia et balneas bacchabatur. inter haec habitu victimarii victimas immolavit. in harena rudibus, inter cubicularios gladiatores pugnavit lucentibus aliquando mucronibus. tunc tamen Perennis cuncta sibimet vindicavit. quos voluit interemit, spoliavit plurimos, omnia iura subvertit, praedam omnem in sinum contulit. ipse autem Commodus Lucillam sororem, cum Capreas misisset, occidit. sorori-

bus dein suis ceteris, ut dicitur, constupratis, consobrina patris complexibus suis iniuncta uni etiam ex concubinis matris nomen imposuit. uxorem, quam deprehensam in adulterio exegit, exactam relegavit et postea occidit. ipsas concubinas suas sub oculis suis stuprari iubebat. nec inruentium in se iuvenum carebat infamia, omni parte corporis atque ore in sexum utrumque pollutes.

'After this Commodus never appeared in public readily, and would never receive messages unless they had previously passed through the hands of Perennis. For Perennis, being well acquainted with Commodus' character, discovered the way to make himself powerful, namely, by persuading Commodus to devote himself to pleasure while he, Perennis, assumed all the burdens of the government — an arrangement which Commodus joyfully accepted. Under this agreement, then, Commodus lived, rioting in the Palace amid banquets and in baths along with 300 concubines, gathered together for their beauty and chosen from both matrons and harlots, and with minions, also 300 in number, whom he had collected by force and by purchase indiscriminately from the common people and the nobles solely on the basis of bodily beauty. Meanwhile, dressed in the garb of an attendant at the sacrifice, he slaughtered the sacrificial victims. He fought in the arena with foils, but sometimes, with his chamberlains acting as gladiators, with sharpened swords. By this time Perennis had secured all the power for himself. He slew whomsoever he wished to slay, plundered a great number, violated every law, and put all the booty into his own pocket. Commodus, for his part, killed his sister Lucilla, after banishing her to Capri. After debauching his other sisters, as it is said, he formed an amour with a cousin of his father, and even gave the name of his mother to one of his concubines. His wife, whom he caught in adultery, he drove from his house, then banished her, and later put her to death. By his orders his concubines were debauched before his own eyes, and he was not free from the disgrace of intimacy with young men, defiling every part of his body in dealings with persons of either sex.' (*HA Commodus* 5.1-11)

Such depictions clearly establish the perceived dominance of Commodus at the time. Both of these ancient authors emphasise how it was Perennis who made all of the decisions of State.[454] Of course he is not depicted as being honourable – he is shown as undeservedly exploiting his Praetorian role for the detriment of the Roman Empire.[455] All the same, these passages were also intended to be an even clearer damnation of Commodus' behaviour as *princeps* – he was young, inexperienced,[456] malleable, and was corrupted in all manner of fashions if the views of Herodian and Cassius Dio are to be believed. So, in many ways, the question remains as to whether this criticism was really directed towards Perennis, or his employer, Commodus. The theme is difficult to avoid in these texts. Neverthe-

---

[454] Traupman 1956, *op.cit.*, p. 55.

[455] Grosso 1964, *op.cit.*

[456] J.H. Oliver, "The Sacred Gerousia and the Emperor's Consilium", *Hesperia* 36.3, 1967, p. 334.

less, it would appear that Perennis was quite influential – at least up until AD 185.[457]

Eo tempore in Sarmatia res bene gestas per alios duces in filium suum Perennis referebat. hic tamen Perennis, qui tantum potuit, subito, quod bello Britannico militibus equestris loci viros praefecerat amotis senatoribus, prodita re per legatos exercitus hostis appellatus lacerandusque militibus est deditus. in cuius potentiae locum Cleandrum ex cubiculariis subrogavit.

'About this time the victories in Sarmatia won by other generals were attributed by Perennis to his own son. Yet in spite of his great power, suddenly, because in the war in Britain he had dismissed certain senators and had put men of the equestrian order in command of the soldiers, this same Perennis was declared an enemy to the state, when the matter was reported by the legates in command of the army, and was thereupon delivered up to the soldiers to be torn to pieces. In his place of power Commodus put Cleander, one of his chamberlains.' (*HA Commodus* 6.1-3)

Such passages illustrate a combination of themes. Initially there is the prominence and influence of Perennis. As mentioned previously, the Practorian Prefects were often highly influential – as he was as well seemingly, but as with the characterisations of Sejanus under the Emperor Tiberius there was a sudden (and drastic) fall from grace. All the same, this is notable – even if the ancient literary sources were correct about the dominance of Sextus Tigidius Perennis, his position was ultimately somewhat tenuous. The same could be said about both Sejanus and Macro seemingly. But secondly, the other vital theme established here by the ancient literature is the cruelty of Commodus. He sought to punish not only Perennis, but also his family. So Commodus is essentially the prime target of authorial ire in this regard – he allowed Perennis to gain power (through his own personal negligence) and then in turn punished him severely. Yet of course the details provided are seriously scant. They could be called 'thin' at best. So these ancient authors next focus upon the successor of Perennis (Cleander), namely for two reasons: firstly to exhibit his corruption (and in turn to display Commodus' neglect towards his duty), and secondly, to highlight the corruption of Commodus even more.[458]

Marcus Aurelius Cleander was seemingly just as notorious.[459] This is highlighted by the references to his promotion by Commodus Antoninus:

---

[457] A. Muller, "Zur Geschichte des Commodus", *Hermes* 18.4, 1883, p. 625.

[458] Grosso 1964, *op.cit.*

[459] Traupman 1956, *op.cit.*, p. 56.

τοιοῦτος μέν τις ὁ Οὐικτωρῖνος ἦν, ὁ δὲ δὴ Κλέανδρος ὁ μετὰ τὸν Περέννιον μέγιστον δυνηθεὶς καὶ ἐπράθη μετὰ τῶν ὁμοδούλων, μεθ᾽ ὧν καὶ ἀχθοφορήσων ἐς τὴν Ῥώμην ἐκεκόμιστο, χρόνου δὲ προϊόντος οὕτως ηὐξήθη ὥστε καὶ τοῦ Κομμόδου προκοιτῆσαι, τήν τε παλλακίδα αὐτοῦ Δαμοστρατίαν γῆμαι, καὶ τὸν Σαώτερον τὸν Νικομηδέα τὸν πρὸ αὐτοῦ τὴν τιμὴν ἔχοντα ταύτην ἀποκτεῖναι πρὸς πολλοῖς καὶ ἄλλοις· καίτοι καὶ ἐκεῖνος μέγιστον ἠδυνήθη, καὶ διὰ τοῦτο καὶ οἱ Νικομηδεῖς καὶ ἀγῶνα ἄγειν καὶ νεὼν τοῦ Κομμόδου ποιήσασθαι παρὰ τῆς βουλῆς ἔλαβον. ὁ δ᾽ οὖν Κλέανδρος μέγας ὑπὸ τῆς τύχης ἀρθεὶς καὶ ἐχαρίσατο καὶ ἐπώλησε βουλείας στρατείας ἐπιτροπείας ἡγεμονίας, πάντα πράγματα. καὶ ἤδη τινὲς πάντα τὰ ὑπάρχοντά σφισιν ἀναλώσαντες βουλευταὶ ἐγένοντο, ὥστε καὶ λεχθῆναι ἐπὶ Ἰουλίου Σόλωνος ἀνδρὸς ἀφανεστάτου ὅτι ἐς τὸ συνέδριον τῆς οὐσίας στερηθεὶς ἐξωρίσθη. ταῦτά τε ὁ Κλέανδρος ἐποίει, καὶ ὑπάτους ἐς <ἕνα> ἐνιαυτὸν πέντε καὶ εἴκοσιν ἀπέδειξεν· ὃ μήτε πρότερόν ποτε μήθ᾽ ὕστερον ἐγένετο· καὶ ἐν αὐτοῖς καὶ Σεουῆρος ὁ μετὰ ταῦτα αὐταρχήσας ὑπάτευσεν. ἠργυρολόγει μὲν οὖν πανταχόθεν, καὶ ἐκτήσατο πλεῖστα τῶν πώποτε ὀνομασθέντων προκοίτων, καὶ ἀπ᾽ αὐτῶν πολλὰ μὲν τῷ Κομμόδῳ ταῖς τε παλλακαῖς αὐτοῦ ἐδίδου, πολλὰ δὲ καὶ ἐς οἰκίας καὶ ἐς βαλανεῖα ἄλλα τέ τινα χρήσιμα καὶ ἰδιώταις καὶ πόλεσιν ἐδαπάνα. οὗτος οὖν ὁ Κλέανδρος ἐς τοσοῦτον ὄγκον ἀρθεὶς ἔπεσε καὶ αὐτὸς ἐξαίφνης καὶ ἀπώλετο μετὰ ἀτιμίας. ἀπέκτειναν δὲ αὐτὸν οὐχ οἱ στρατιῶται ὥσπερ τὸν Περέννιον, ἀλλ᾽ ὁ δῆμος. ἐγένετο μὲν γὰρ καὶ ἄλλως ἰσχυρὰ σιτοδεία, ἐπὶ πλεῖστον δ᾽ αὐτὴν Παπίριος Διονύσιος ἐπὶ τοῦ σίτου τεταγμένος ἐπηύξησεν, ἵν᾽ ὡς αἰτιώτατον αὐτῆς τὸν Κλέανδρον ἀπὸ τῶν κλεμμάτων ὄντα καὶ μισήσωσιν οἱ Ῥωμαῖοι καὶ διαφθείρωσι. καὶ ἔσχεν οὕτως. ἱπποδρομία τις ἦν, μελλόντων δὲ τὸ ἕβδομον τῶν ἵππων ἀγωνιεῖσθαι πλῆθός τι παιδίων ἐς τὸν ἱππόδρομον ἐσέδραμε, καὶ αὐτῶν παρθένος τις μεγάλη καὶ βλοσυρὰ ἡγεῖτο, ἣν δαίμονα ἐκ τῶν μετὰ ταῦτα συμβάντων ἐνόμισαν γεγονέναι.

'As for Cleander, who possessed the greatest influence after Perennis, he had formerly been sold as one of a group of slaves and had been brought to Rome with the others to be a pack-carrier; but in the course of time he advanced to such a point that he actually became Commodus' cubicularius, married the emperor's concubine Damostratia, and put to death Saoterus of Nicomedeia, his predecessor in this office, together with many others. Yet Saoterus, too, had possible very great influence, so great, in fact, that thanks to it the privilege of celebrating some games and of erecting a temple to Commodus. So Cleander, raised to greatness by the favour of Fortune, bestowed and sold senatorships, military commands, procuratorships, governorships, and, in a word, everything. In fact, some men became senators only after spending all they possessed, so that it was said of Julius Solon, a very obscure man, that he had been stripped of all his property and banished to — the senate. Besides all this, Cleander appointed twenty-five consuls for one year, a thing that never happened before or since; one of these consuls was Severus, who later became emperor. Cleander, accordingly, was obtaining money from every source, and he amassed more wealth than any who had ever been named *cubicularii*. A great deal it he gave to Commodus and his concubines, and he spent a great deal on houses, baths, and other works of benefit either to individuals or to cities. So this Cleander, too, who had been raised to so exalted a station, fell suddenly and perished in dishonour. It was not the soldiers, however, that killed him, as in the case of Perennis, but the populace. A famine occurred, sufficiently grievous in itself; but its severity was vastly increased by Papirius Dionysius, the grain commissioner, in order that Cleander, whose thefts would seem chiefly responsible for it, might incur the hatred of the Romans and be destroyed by them. And so it came to pass. There was a horse-race on, and as the horses were about to contend for the seventh time, a crowd of children ran into the Circus, led by a tall maiden of grim aspect, who, because of what afterwards happened, was thought to have been a divinity.' (Dio 73.12.1-13.3)

Multa sane post interfectum Perennem eiusque filium quasi a se non gesta rescidit, velut in integrum restituens. et hanc quidem paenitentiam scelerum ultra triginta dies tenere non potuit, graviora per Cleandrum faciens quam fecerat per supradictum Perennem. et in potentia quidem Cleander Perenni successerat, in praefectura vero Niger, qui sex tantum horis praefectus praetorio fuisse perhibetur. mutabantur enim praefecti praetorio per horas ac dies, Commodo peiora omnia, quam fecerat ante, faciente. fuit Marcius Quartus praefectus praetorio diebus quinque. horum successores ad arbitrium Cleandri aut retenti sunt aut occisi. ad cuius nutum etiam libertini in senatum atque in patricios lecti sunt, tuncque primum viginti quinque consules in unum annum, venditaeque omnes provinciae. omnia Cleander pecunia venditabat; revocatos de exsilio dignitatibus ornabat, res iudicatas rescindebat. qui tantum per stultitiam Commodi potuit, ut Burrum, sororis Commodi virum, reprehendentem nuntiantemque Commodo quae fiebant in suspicionem regni adfectati traheret et occideret, multis aliis, qui Burrum defendebant, pariter interemptis. praefectus etiam Aebutianus inter hos est interemptus; in cuius locum ipse Cleander cum aliis duobus, quos ipse delegerat, praefectus est factus. tuncque primum tres praefecti praetorio fuere, inter quos libertinus, qui a pugione appellatus est. Sed et Cleandro dignus tandem vitae finis impositus. nam cum insidiis illius Arrius Antoninus fictis criminibus in Attali gratiam, quem in proconsulatu Asiae damnaverat, esset occisus, nec eam tum invidiam populo saeviente Commodus ferre potuisset, plebi ad poenam donatus est, cum etiam Apolaustus aliique liberti aulici pariter interempti sunt. Cleander inter cetera etiam concubinas eius construpravit, de quibus filios suscepit, qui post eius interitum cum matribus interempti sunt.

'After Perennis and his son were executed, Commodus rescinded a number of measures on the ground that they had been carried out without his authority, pretending that he was merely re-establishing previous conditions. However, he could not maintain this penitence for his misdeeds longer than thirty days, and he actually committed more atrocious crimes through Cleander than he had done through the aforesaid Perennis. Although Perennis was succeeded in general influence by Cleander, his successor in the prefecture was Niger, who held this position as prefect of the guard, it is said, for just six hours. In fact, prefects of the guard were changed hourly and daily, Commodus meanwhile committing all kinds of evil deeds, worse even than he had committed before. Marcius Quartus was prefect of the guard for five days. Thereafter, the successors of these men were either retained in office or executed, according to the whim of Cleander. At his nod even freedmen were enrolled in the senate and among the patricians, and now for the first time there were twenty-five consuls in a single year. Appointments to the provinces were uniformly sold; in fact, Cleander sold everything for money. He loaded with honours men who were recalled from exile; he rescinded decisions of the courts. Indeed, because of Commodus' utter degeneracy, his power was so great that he brought Burrus, the husband of Commodus' sister, who was denouncing and reporting to Commodus all that was being done, under the suspicion of pretending to the throne, and had him put to death; and at the same time he slew many others who defended Burrus. Among these Aebutianus was slain, the prefect of the guard; in his place Cleander himself was made prefect, together with two others whom he himself chose. Then for the first time were there three prefects of the guard, among whom was a freedman, called the "Bearer of the Dagger". However, a full worthy death was at last meted out to Cleander also. For when, through his intrigues, Arrius Antoninus was put to death on false charges as a favour to Attalus, whom Arrius had condemned during his proconsulship in Asia, Commodus could not endure the hatred of the enraged people and gave Cleander over to the populace for punishment. At the same time Apolaustus and several other freedmen of the court were put to death. Among other outrages Cleander had debauched certain of Commodus' concubines, and from them had begotten sons, who, together with their mothers, were put to death after his downfall.' (*HA Commodus* 6.4-7.3)

As with the career of Perennis there was a sudden rise to prominence in the imperial court, which was in turn exploited by Cleander.[460] As can be seen from the aforementioned extracts, he seemingly possessed a great deal of influence within the imperial court. This is to be expected in view of his role. All the same, it is noteworthy that his is commonly portrayed by these ancient authors in a similar fashion to that of Perennis. This is also reminiscent of Sejanus and Macro under Tiberius as well[461] – all of these exhibitions of such notorious Praetorian Prefects are equally ambitious while serving under variously 'distracted' *principes*. Nevertheless, this was also indicative of how such early writers sought to represent Commodus – as the malleable, and irresponsible young emperor who possessed little (if any) honour or sense of duty towards the running of the State. Cleander is shown as manipulating the affairs of the Roman Empire and its various positions to suit his own selfish desires. This of course was not only intended to damn him, but also Commodus Antoninus.

καὶ ἔσχεν οὕτως. ἱπποδρομία τις ἦν, μελλόντων δὲ τὸ ἕβδομον τῶν ἵππων ἀγωνιεῖσθαι πλῆθός τι παιδίων ἐς τὸν ἱππόδρομον ἐσέδραμε, καὶ αὐτῶν παρθένος τις μεγάλη καὶ βλοσυρὰ ἡγεῖτο, ἣν δαίμονα ἐκ τῶν μετὰ ταῦτα συμβάντων ἐνόμισαν γεγονέναι. τά τε γὰρ παιδία συνεβόησαν πολλὰ καὶ δεινά, καὶ ὁ δῆμος παραλαβὼν αὐτὰ οὐδὲν ὅ τι οὐκ ἐξέκραγε, καὶ τέλος καταπηδήσας ὥρμησε πρὸς τὸν Κόμμοδον ἐν τῷ Κυιντιλίῳ προαστείῳ ὄντα, πολλὰ μὲν ἐκείνῳ κἀγαθὰ ἐπευχόμενος, πολλὰ δὲ καὶ κατὰ τοῦ Κλεάνδρου καταρώμενος. καὶ ὃς στρατιώτας τινὰς ἐπ' αὐτοὺς ἔπεμψε, καὶ ἔτρωσάν τινας καὶ ἀπέκτειναν· οὐ μέντοι καὶ ἀνείρχθη διὰ τοῦτο ὁ δῆμος, ἀλλὰ τῷ τε πλήθει σφῶν καὶ τῇ τῶν δορυφόρων ἰσχύι θαρρήσας ἐπὶ μᾶλλον ἠπείχθη. πλησιαζόντων δὲ αὐτῶν τῷ Κομμόδῳ, καὶ μηδενός οἱ μηνύοντος τὸ γινόμενον, Μαρκία ἐκείνη ἡ τοῦ Κουαδράτου ἐσήγγειλε τὸ πραττόμενον· καὶ ὁ Κόμμοδος οὕτως ἔδεισεν, ἄλλως τε καὶ δειλότατος ὤν, ὥστε αὐτίκα καὶ τὸν Κλέανδρον καὶ τὸ παιδίον αὐτοῦ, ὃ καὶ ἐν ταῖς

---

[460] Grosso 1964, *op.cit.*
[461] Adams 2007, *op.cit.*

τοῦ Κομμόδου χερσὶν ἐτρέφετο, σφαγῆναι κελεῦσαι. καὶ τὸ μὲν παιδίον προσουδίσθη καὶ διεφθάρη, τὸ δὲ τοῦ Κλεάνδρου σῶμα παραλαβόντες οἱ Ῥωμαῖοι ἔσυραν καὶ ἠκίσαντο, καὶ τὴν κεφαλὴν αὐτοῦ διὰ πάσης τῆς πόλεως ἐπὶ [τοῦ] κοντοῦ περιήνεγκαν, καὶ τινας καὶ ἄλλους τῶν μέγα ἐπ᾽ αὐτοῦ δυναμένων ἐφόνευσαν.

'And so it came to pass. There was a horse-race on, and as the horses were about to contend for the seventh time, a crowd of children ran into the Circus, led by a tall maiden of grim aspect, who, because of what afterwards happened, was thought to have been a divinity. The children shouted in concert many bitter words, which the people took up and then began to bawl out every conceivable insult; and finally the throng leaped down and set out to find Commodus (who was then in the Quintilian suburb), invoking many blessings on him and many curses upon Cleander. The latter sent some soldiers against them, who wounded and killed a few; but, instead of being deterred by this, the crowd, encouraged by its own numbers and by the strength of the Pretorians, pressed on with all the greater determination. They were already drawing near to Commodus, whom no one had kept informed of what was going on, when Marcia, the notorious wife of Quadratus, reported the matter to him. And Commodus was so terrified (he was ever the greatest coward) that he at once ordered Cleander to be slain, and likewise his son, who was being reared in the emperor's charge. The boy was dashed to the earth and so perished; and the Romans, taking the body of Cleander, dragged it away and abused it and carried his head all about the city on a pole. They also slew some other men who had enjoyed great power under him.' (Dio 73.13.3-6)

As can be viewed in this passage by this historian, the downfall of Marcus Aurelius Commodus was swift and telling. While Cassius Dio shows this as being entirely deserving, the onus was still focused upon the cruelty of the young emperor, Commodus. All the same, the death of Cleander occurred in an entirely different context to that of Sextus Tigidius Perennis – this was not a controlled execution, but one of desperation (as has been discussed further in Chapter Eight).[462] The primary reasoning for this literary characterisation by Cassius Dio was that of establishing exactly how far Roman society had fallen from grace throughout the influence of this 'despicable' *princeps*. Nevertheless, while the death of Cleander was used by the early literary sources as another example of the cruelty (and irresponsibility) of Commodus, it would also appear that the Praetorian Prefect had pushed the extent of his influence too far – perhaps his personal ambition got the better of him. These authors, however, could not really have it both ways – the result is somewhat contradictory. Therefore, it is necessary to consider how they depicted his role in all of this.

---

[462] Grosso 1964, *op.cit.*

αὐτὸς μὲν γὰρ κράτιστα ἵππευε, τὸ δὲ μειράκιον καμὸν οὐχ ὑπέμεινε καταλιπεῖν, ἀλλ᾽ ὡς κατελαμβάνετο, ἀπέκτεινε καὶ ἐκεῖνον καὶ ἑαυτόν. ἀνῃρέθη δὲ καὶ Διονύσιος πρὸς τοῦ Κομμόδου, ὁ ἐπὶ τοῦ σίτου ταχθείς. γέγονε δὲ καὶ νόσος μεγίστη ὧν ἐγὼ οἶδα· δισχίλιοι γοῦν πολλάκις ἡμέρας μιᾶς ἐν τῇ Ῥώμῃ ἐτελεύτησαν. πολλοὶ δὲ καὶ ἄλλως οὐκ ἐν τῷ ἄστει μόνον ἀλλὰ καὶ ἐν ὅλῃ ὡς εἰπεῖν τῇ ἀρχῇ ὑπ᾽ ἀνδρῶν κακούργων ἀπέθανον· βελόνας γὰρ μικρὰς δηλητηρίοις τισὶ φαρμάκοις ἐγχρίοντες ἐνίεσαν δι᾽ αὐτῶν ἐς ἑτέρους ἐπὶ μισθῷ τὸ δεινόν· ὅπερ που καὶ ἐπὶ τοῦ Δομιτιανοῦ ἐγεγόνει.

'But he could not bring himself to desert the lad, who had become wearied, and so, when he was being overtaken, he killed both the boy and himself. Dionysius, the grain commissioner, also met his death by the orders of Commodus. Moreover, a pestilence occurred, the greatest of any of which I have knowledge; for two thousand persons often died in Rome in a single day. Then, too, many others, not alone in the City, but throughout almost the entire empire, perished at the hands of criminals who smeared some deadly drugs on tiny needles and for pay infected people with the poison by means of these instruments. The same thing had happened before in the reign of Domitian.' (Dio 73.14.3-4)

ipse Commodus in subscribendo tardus et neglegens, ita ut libellis una forma multis subscriberet, in epistulis autem plurimis 'Vale' tantum scriberet. agebanturque omnia per alios, qui etiam condemnationes in sinum vertisse dicuntur. per hanc autem neglegentiam, cum et annonam vastarent ii qui tunc rem publicam gerebant, etiam inopia ingens Romae exorta est, cum fruges non deessent. et eos quidem qui omnia vastabant postea Commodus occidit atque proscripsit. ipse vero saeculum aureum Commodianum nomina adsimulans vilitatem proposuit, ex qua maiorem penuriam fecit.

'Commodus himself was so lazy and careless in signing documents that he answered many petitions with the same formula, while in very many letters he merely wrote the word "Farewell". All official business was carried on by others, who, it is said, even used condemnations to swell their purses. And because he was so careless, moreover, a great famine arose in Rome, not because there was any real shortage of crops, but merely because those who then ruled the state were plundering the food supply. As for those who plundered on every hand, Commodus afterwards put them to death and confiscated their property; but for the time he pretended that a golden age had come, "Commodian" by name, and ordered a general reduction of prices, the result of which was an even greater scarcity.' (*HA Commodus* 13.7-14.3)

In general terms, the ancient literary evidence (as seen above) provides few details about the role of Commodus Antoninus as an administrator of the Roman State. His corruption is instead passed onto that of his subordinates (such as Perennis and Cleander in this regard), but it still remains his corruption ultimately. So the question remains about the administration of Commodus. As mentioned previously, this was not an important factor within his characterisation by these ancient authors. All of these representations are brief in the extreme. The maladministration of Commodus was the primary focus here, rather than that of what he achieved during his principate. If he did anything at all of course. The portrayal by the *HA* biographer (*Commodus* 13.7-14.3) provides the most explicit representation of those passages quoted above, but again there was no detail provided about his policies. It would be expected that after such a long reign he would have been involved in at least some capacity (or otherwise his principate would have been much sorter in all likelihood). So therefore the other sources of ancient evidence must be consulted.

At first glance the ancient epigraphic evidence comes across as being quite slim. All the same, the prevalence of honorific statue bases throughout the Roman Empire surely should represent some kind of acceptance for Commodus' principate.[463] This is associated with the question about who the young emperor deemed to be a threat to his position – the senatorial aristocracy (the only real group that could have replaced him within the confines of the Roman political situation.[464] Whether this was justified or unjustified is a matter of contention – the important aspect to recognise, however, is that this was the way in which he seemingly perceived them. Traupman,[465] and Hekster,[466] have provided quite dissimilar interpretations of this, but these separate views are largely owing to their different *foci* and personal perspectives. The irony is that he prosopographical tradition illustrates a much more consistent approach towards the running of the Roman Empire during this period.[467] Commodus, in many ways, continued the policies of his father and his earlier predecessors. Some elements of the Roman aristocracy were suppressed, but not all of them – unlike what the ancient literary sources would have us believe.[468]

This is also suggested when the consulships from AD 181-192 are examined. The distribution of Rome's most important magistracy provides an excellent insight into Commodus' relations with his senatorial peers (or at least those that he favoured). He only held the position four times during this period (AD 181, 183, 186, 192), which suggests that he did not want to personally dominate the role to the exclusion of others. In addition to this there were only three known

[463] Hojte 2005, *op.cit.*, pp. 571-89.
[464] Traupman 1956, *op.cit.*
[465] Traupman 1956, *op.cit.*
[466] Hekster 2002, *op.cit.*
[467] Leunissen 1989, *op.cit.*
[468] Grosso 1964, *op.cit.*

relatives of his who held the position, all being his brothers-in-law: Lucius Antistius Burrus (AD 181), Marcus Petronius Sura Mamertinus (AD 182) and Lucius Bruttius Quintius Crispinus (AD 187) – which further highlights the minimal dominance of the consulship by the imperial *familia* during this twelve year period. This is a clear contrast, for example, to the Flavian policy under the Emperor Vespasian that sought to actively promote its various family members.

The interpretation of this process could be viewed as Commodus' sense of security in his role (or perhaps his arrogance), but this does not correlate with his exhibited preference for sense of self promotion as exhibited in the ancient literary sources. Similarly it would be expected that the establishment of the Antonine 'next generation' would have also been a priority for him, but it is evident that it was not. Therefore, this could be indicative of how equitable Commodus Antoninus may have been in this regard, through the sharing of this prominent position to non-imperial candidates that he deemed 'worthy' of the honour. This is also indicated by the number of suffect consulships from AD 181-192, which shows a marked contrast (be it higher) to the number provided in the previous periods to his sole principate. The advancement of leading figures beyond the imperial *familia* is exhibited for example by the consulships of Cassius Apronianus (AD 184), Atticus Bradua (AD 185), Lucius Septimius Severus (AD 190), and Quintus Tineius Sacerdos (AD 192). Each of these figures were either members of leading, well established families, or individuals who were clearly influential in their own right from other avenues (such as the military). This general process clearly indicates a well considered policy on the part of the *princeps*, which is more indicative of stability rather than corruption.

Therefore, the administration of Commodus Antoninus and its assessment largely depends on what the modern (or ancient?) interpreter wants to believe.[469] This is largely owing to the paucity of ancient literary references in this regard, which is often the easiest medium to interpret. All the same, if one only considered these textual sources in an entirely unquestioning fashion this book would not have been written.[470] But they are, nevertheless, of great use for the present study. One of the most important aspects to note is the ap-

---

[469] See W. Williams, "Individuality in the Imperial Constitutions: Hadrian and the Antonines", *JRS* 66, 1976, p. 82.

[470] Grosso 1964, *op.cit.*

parent prominence of the Praetorian Prefect throughout the period from AD 180-192. If the ancient literary sources are to be followed, Commodus made very few decisions throughout his reign – except those inclined towards his corruption and personal cruelty of course. This appears highly unlikely in reality – the known consular appointments seem well considered. It is probably more indicative of the predisposition of the ancient literary sources towards a negative portrayal of him. In turn, it appears logical that the primary antagonism between the emperor and his élite peers should be examined. The main point of concern was in the execution of senators without notice (or their approval). This had always been an issue since the establishment of the Roman principate, and remained as a serious concern between any *princeps* and his aristocratic peers.

Political Executions

As would be expected, the executions proscribed by Commodus Antoninus of his aristocratic peers came under serious scrutiny by the subsequent ancient literary sources. As far as these early authors were concerned this was one of the most damning attributes of an 'evil' Roman Emperor.[471] This theme was definitively exploited by all of them – and in this fashion the characterisation of Commodus came into being. Whether these executions ordered by the young emperor were justifiable is a matter of some questioning for modern scholars – all the same the important aspect is to note how poorly such decisions by him were received by his social peers. This in basic terms added to the pre-existing antagonism between both *princeps* and the senatorial aristocracy. The amount of detail provided by the ancient literary sources is, however, pivotal. The question surrounding who was executed and why such a drastic punishment was levelled against them seems to have been a second thought to these authors in most cases. Their primary focus was upon his corruption and his lack of respect towards his social peers at the time.

ἀπέκτεινε δὲ καὶ τὴν Κρισπῖναν ὁ Κόμμοδος, ἐπὶ μοιχείᾳ δή τινι ὀργισθεὶς αὐτῇ. πρὸ δὲ τοῦ ἀναιρεθῆναι καὶ ἀμφότεραι ἐς τὴν νῆσον τὴν Καπρίαν ὑπερωρίσθησαν. Μαρκία δέ τις Κουαδράτου τῶν τότε φονευθέντων ἑνὸς παλλακή, καὶ Ἔκλεκτος πρόκοιτος, ὁ μὲν καὶ τοῦ Κομμόδου πρόκοιτος ἡ δὲ παλλακὴ ἐγένετο, καὶ τοῦ Ἐκλέκτου μετὰ ταῦτα γυνή· καὶ ἐπεῖδε καὶ ἐκείνους βιαίως ἀποθνῄσκοντας. ἱστορεῖται δὲ αὕτη πολλά τε ὑπὲρ τῶν Χριστιανῶν σπουδάσαι καὶ πολλὰ αὐτοὺς εὐηργετηκέναι, ἅτε καὶ παρὰ τῷ Κομμόδῳ πᾶν δυναμένη. ὅτι ὁ Κόμμοδος καὶ Ἰουλιανὸν τὸν Σάλουιον καὶ Πάτερνον

---

[471] Traupman 1956, *op.cit.*

Ταρρουτήνιον ἐς τοὺς ὑπατευκότας κατειλεγμένον, ἄλλους τε μετ' αὐτῶν καί τινα καὶ γυναῖκα εὐπατρίδα ἀπέσφαξεν. καίτοι καὶ Ἰουλιανὸς δυνηθεὶς ἂν μετὰ τὴν Μάρκου τελευτὴν πᾶν εὐθὺς κατ' αὐτοῦ ὅ τι καὶ ἐβούλετο, ἅτε καὶ ἐλλογιμώτατος ὢν καὶ στρατιὰν μεγάλην ἐπιτετραμμένος τούς τε στρατιώτας ἀνηρτημένος, πρᾶξαι, οὐδὲν ἠθέλησε διά τε τὴν ἑαυτοῦ ἐπιείκειαν καὶ διὰ τὴν ἐκείνου καὶ τεθνηκότος εὔνοιαν νεοχμῶσαι· καὶ ὁ Πάτερνος ῥᾳδίως ἂν αὐτόν, εἴπερ ἐπεβεβουλεύκει οἱ, ὥσπερ ᾐτιάθη, φονεύσας ἕως ἔτι τῶν δορυφόρων ἦρχεν, οὐκ ἐποίησεν. ἐφόνευσε δὲ καὶ τοὺς Κυιντιλίους, τόν τε Κονδιανὸν καὶ τὸν Μάξιμον· μεγάλην γὰρ εἶχον δόξαν ἐπὶ παιδείᾳ καὶ ἐπὶ στρατηγίᾳ καὶ ὁμοφροσύνῃ καὶ πλούτῳ. ἐκ γὰρ δὴ τῶν προσόντων σφίσιν ὑπωπτεύοντο καλῶν, εἰ καὶ μηδὲν νεώτερον ἐνενόουν, ἄχθεσθαι τοῖς παροῦσι. καὶ οὕτως αὐτοί, ὥσπερ ἔζησαν ἅμα, οὕτω καὶ ἀπέθανον μεθ' ἑνὸς τέκνου· διαπρεπέστατα γὰρ τῶν πώποτε ἐφίλησαν ἀλλήλους, καὶ οὐκ ἔστιν ὅτε οὐδὲ ἐν ταῖς ἀρχαῖς διεχωρίσθησαν. ἐγένοντο δὲ καὶ πολυκτήμονες καὶ παμπλούσιοι, καὶ ἦρχον ὁμοῦ καὶ παρήδρευον ἀλλήλοις. Κονδιανὸς δὲ Σέξτος ὁ τοῦ Μαξίμου υἱός, φύσει τε καὶ παιδείᾳ τῶν ἄλλων διαφέρων, ἐπειδὴ ᾔσθετο καὶ τῆς ἐς αὐτὸν φερούσης θανατηφόρου ψήφου (διέτριβε δὲ ἐν Συρίᾳ), αἷμα λαγὼ ἔπιε, καὶ μετὰ τοῦτ' ἐπί τε ἵππον ἀνέβη καὶ κατέπεσεν ἀπ' αὐτοῦ ἐπίτηδες, τό τε αἷμα ἤμεσεν ὡς ἴδιον, καὶ ἀρθεὶς ὡς καὶ παραχρῆμα τελευτήσων ἐς οἴκημα ἐκομίσθη, καὶ αὐτὸς μὲν ἀφανὴς ἐγένετο, κριοῦ δὲ σῶμα ἐς λάρνακα ἀντ' αὐτοῦ ἐμβληθὲν ἐκαύθη. καὶ ἐκ τούτου ὁ μὲν ἀμείβων ἀεὶ τὸ σχῆμα καὶ τὴν ἐσθῆτα ἄλλοτε ἄλλῃ ἐπλανᾶτο, διαδοθέντος δὲ τοῦ λόγου τούτου (οὐ γὰρ οἷόν τ' ἐστὶ τὰ τηλικαῦτα ἐπὶ πολὺν χρόνον λανθάνειν) ζήτησις αὐτοῦ μεγάλη πανταχοῦ ὁμοίως ἐγένετο, καὶ πολλοὶ μὲν ἀντ' αὐτοῦ δι' ὁμοιότητα πολλοὶ δὲ ὡς καὶ συνεγνωκότες τι αὐτῷ ἢ καὶ ὑποδεδεγμένοι πῃ αὐτὸν ἐκολάσθησαν, ἔτι δὲ πλείους οὐδὲ ἑορακότες ποτὲ ἴσως αὐτὸν τῶν οὐσιῶν ἐστερήθησαν. καὶ ὁ μὲν εἴτε ὄντως ἐσφάγη (πλεῖσται γὰρ κεφαλαὶ ὡς ἐκείνου οὖσαι ἐς τὴν Ῥώμην ἐκομίσθησαν) εἴτε καὶ ἀπέφυγεν, οὐδεὶς οἶδεν· ἕτερος δέ τις ἐτόλμησε μετὰ τὸν τοῦ Κομμόδου θάνατον Σέξτος τε εἶναι φῆσαι καὶ πρὸς ἀνάληψιν τοῦ τε πλούτου καὶ τοῦ ἀξιώματος αὐτοῦ ὁρμῆσαι. καὶ πολλά γε ὑπὸ πολλῶν ἀνακριθεὶς ἐκομψεύσατο, ὡς μέντοι καὶ τῶν Ἑλληνικῶν τι αὐτὸν ὁ Περτίναξ, ὢν ἐκεῖνος διεπεφύκει, ἀνήρετο, πλεῖστον ἐσφάλη, μηδὲ συνεῖναι τὸ λεγόμενον δυνηθείς. οὕτω που τὸ μὲν εἶδος ἐκ φύσεως καὶ τἆλλα ἐξ ἐπιτηδεύσεως αὐτῷ ἕφκει, τῆς δὲ δὴ παιδείας αὐτοῦ οὐ μετεσχήκει. τοῦτό τε οὖν αὐτὸς ἤκουσα παρών, καὶ ἕτερον τοιόνδε εἶδον. ἔστιν ἐν Μαλλῷ πόλει τῆς Κιλικίας Ἀμφιλόχου χρηστήριον, καὶ χρᾷ δι' ὀνειράτων. ἔχρησεν οὖν καὶ τῷ Σέξτῳ, ὃ διὰ γραφῆς ἐκεῖνος ἐδήλωσε· παιδίον γὰρ τῷ πίνακι ἐνεγέγραπτο δύο δράκοντας ἀποπνίγον καὶ λέων νεβρὸν διώκων. οὐδὲ ἔσχον αὐτὰς συμβαλεῖν, τῷ πατρὶ συνὼν ἄρχοντι τῆς Κιλικίας, πρὶν πυθέσθαι τούς τε ἀδελφοὺς ὑπὸ τοῦ Κομμόδου, ὃς μετὰ ταῦτα τὸν Ἡρακλέα ἐζήλωσε, τρόπον τινὰ πνιγέντας, ὥσπερ καὶ ὁ Ἡρακλῆς ἔτι νήπιος ὢν ἱστόρηται τοὺς ὑπὸ τῆς Ἥρας ἐπιπεμφθέντας αὐτῷ δράκοντας ἀποπνῖξαι (καὶ γὰρ καὶ οἱ Κυιντίλιοι ἀπηγχονήθησαν), καὶ τὸν Σέξτον φεύγοντα καὶ διωκόμενον ὑπὸ τοῦ κρείττονος.

'Commodus also put Crispina to death, having become angry with her for some act of adultery. But before their execution both women were banished to the island of Capreae. There was a certain Marcia, the mistress of Quadratus (one of the men slain at this time), and Eclectus, his cubicularius; the latter became the cubicularius of Commodus also, and the former, first the emperor's mistress and later the wife of Eclectus, and she saw them also perish by violence. The tradition is that she greatly favoured the Christians and rendered them many kindnesses, inasmuch as she could do anything with Commodus. Commodus also killed Salvius Julianus and Tarrutenius Paternus, who was enrolled among the ex-consuls, and others with them, including even a woman of the nobility. And yet Julianus, after the death of Marcus, could have done at once anything whatever that he wished against Commodus, since he was a man of great renown, was in command of a large army, and enjoyed the devotion of his soldiers; but he had refused to make any rebellious move, both because of his own probity and because of the good will that he bore to Marcus even after that emperor's death. And Paternus, if he had plotted against Commodus, as he was accused of doing, could easily have killed him while he himself was still in command of the Pretorians; but he had not done so. Commodus likewise killed the two Quintilii, Condianus and Maximus; for they had a great reputation for learning, military skill, brotherly accord, and wealth, and their notable talents led to the suspicion that, even if they were not planning any rebellion, they were nevertheless displeased with existing conditions. And thus, even as they had lived together, so they died together, along with the son of one of them. They had offered to most striking example ever seen of mutual affection; and at no time had they ever been separated, even in the offices they held. They had grown prosperous and exceedingly wealthy, and were wont to hold office together and to act as assistants to each other. Sextus Condianus, the son of Maximus, who surpassed all others by reason both of his native ability and his training, when he heard that sentence of death had been pronounced against him, too, drank the blood of a hare (he was living in Syria at the time), after which he mounted a horse and purposely fell from it; then, as he vomited the blood, which was supposed to be his own, he was taken up, apparently on the point of death, and was carried to his room. 2 He himself now disappeared, while a ram's body was placed in a coffin in his stead and burned. After this, constantly changing his appearance and clothing, he wandered about here and there. And when this story got out (for it is impossible that such matters should remain hidden very long), diligent search was made for him high and low. Many were punished in his stead on account of their resemblance to him, and many, too, who were alleged to have shared his confidence or to have sheltered him somewhere; and still more persons who had perhaps never even seen him were deprived of their property. But no one knows whether he was really slain, — though a great number of heads purporting to be his were brought to Rome, — or whether he made good his escape. Some other man, however, after the death of Commodus boldly claimed to be Sextus and undertook to recover his wealth and rank. And he played the part bravely, though questioned much by many persons; yet when Pertinax asked him something about Grecian affairs, with which the real Sextus had been well acquainted, he showed the greatest embarrassment, being unable even to understand the question. Thus, though nature had made him like Condianus in appearance and practice had made him similar in other respects, yet he did not share in his learning. As for this matter, now, that I have just related, I myself was present and heard it; and I will mention another thing, that I saw. There is in the city of Mallus, in Cilicia, an oracle of Amphilochus that gives responses by means of dreams. Now it had given a response also to Sextus that he had indicated by means of a drawing; the picture which he had put on the tablet represented a boy strangling two serpents and a lion pursuing a fawn. I was with my father, who was governor of Cilicia at the time, and could not comprehend what the figures meant, until I learned that the brothers had been strangled, so to speak, by Commodus (who later emulated Hercules), just as Hercules, when an infant, is related to have strangled the serpents sent against him by Juno (for the Quintilii, too, had been strangled), and until I learned also that Sextus was a fugitive and was being pursued by a more powerful adversary.' (Dio 73.4.6-7.2)

Cassius Dio goes into great detail in this instance.[472] As mentioned previously, he identified with the Senate – not only as a member, but also with this group as his intended audience.[473] This is self-evident simply by considering the above extract (Dio 73.4.6-7.2). This passage exhibits how Cassius Dio sought to emphasise the depravity of Commodus Antoninus. Initially it is noteworthy to recognise the lack of detail provided by the author. As mentioned previously, the objections (or resistance) of Tiberius Claudius Pompeianus is also emphasised in order to exhibit the senatorial disgust (or perhaps insecurity?) surrounding the actions of the *princeps*.[474] The mention of Salvius Julianus and Tarruntenius Paternus was intended to further stress the importance of this resistance. This was further given emphasis to by Cassius Dio in the anecdote about Sextus Cordianus, which was meant to accentuate how depraved Commodus was and the lengths that some *nobiles* had to go to in order to survive. All of this was intended to emphasise the depravity of the young emperor, while similarly distancing him the Senate of course.

A passage highlights by Cassius Dio (Dio 73.7.3) epitomises the overall nature of the representation of Commodus here. It provides not only an excuse for why he has not gone into greater detail (of course for the benefit of his audience), but this attempts to reinforce the primary focus of his narrative – the depravity of Commodus Antoninus. This calls attention to the way in which the *princeps* was intended to be portrayed by all of the ancient literary sources.[475] The focus was upon his corruption rather than his actual role as Roman Emperor – but this is hardly surprising in view of their description of his entirely irresponsible attitude towards the running of the State. The same style of depiction is exhibited by Herodian, which in many ways represents the strength of the anti-Commodus sentiment that existed within the early scholarship surrounding his reign.

αὕτη μὲν δὴ πρώτη καὶ μεγίστη αἰτία τῷ μειρακίῳ μίσους ἐγένετο πρὸς τὴν σύγκλητον βουλήν· ἔτρωσέ τε αὐτοῦ τὴν ψυχὴν τὰ λεχθέντα, καὶ κοινοὺς ἐχθροὺς πάντας ἡγεῖτο,

---

[472] Grosso 1964, *op.cit.*
[473] See P.J. Sijpesteijn, "Commodus' Titulature in Cassius Dio", *Mnemosyne* 41, 1988, pp. 123-4.
[474] Grosso 1964, *op.cit.*
[475] Traupman 1956, *op.cit.*

μεμνημένος ἀεὶ τῆς τοῦ ἐπιδραμόντος φωνῆς. ὑπῆρξε δὲ καὶ τῷ Περεννίῳ πρόφασίς τε καὶ ὑπόθεσις αὐτάρκης· ἐκκόπτειν γὰρ ἀεὶ καὶ κολούειν αὐτῷ συνεβούλευε τοὺς ὑπερέχοντας, ὧν ἁρπάζων τὰς οὐσίας ῥᾷστα πλουσιώτατος ἐγένετο τῶν καθ' αὐτὸν ἀνθρώπων. γενομένης δ' ἐξετάσεως διὰ τοῦ Περεννίου ἀκριβεστέρας τήν τε ἀδελφὴν ὁ Κόμοδος διεχρήσατο καὶ πάντας ἀφειδῶς τούς τε ὄντας ἐν τῇ συνωμοσίᾳ καὶ τοὺς ἐφ' οἱαισδήποτε διαβληθέντας ὑποψίαις.

'This was the initial reason for the young emperor's hatred of the senate. He took Quintianus' words to heart and, ever mindful of what his attacker had said, now considered the entire senate his collective enemy. This incident also gave Perennis sufficient excuse for taking action, for he was always advising the emperor to eliminate and destroy the prominent men. By confiscating their property, Perennis easily made himself the richest man of his time. After the attempt at assassination had been thoroughly investigated by the prefect, Commodus without mercy put to death his sister, all those actually involved in the plot, and any who were under the slightest suspicion as well.' (Herodian 1.8.7-8)

ὁ δὲ Κόμοδος δεδιὼς μὲν τὴν τοῦ δήμου κίνησιν, μή τι καὶ περὶ αὐτὸν νεωτερίσειεν, ὅμως δὲ παρορμησάντων αὐτὸν τῶν οἰκείων κατελθὼν ἐς τὸ ἄστυ μετὰ πάσης εὐφημίας τε καὶ παραπομπῆς τοῦ δήμου ὑποδεχθεὶς ἐς τὴν βασίλειον ἐπανῆλθεν αὐλήν. πειραθεὶς δὲ τοιούτων κινδύνων ἀπίστως προσεφέρετο πᾶσιν ἀφειδῶς τε φονεύων καὶ πάσαις διαβολαῖς ῥᾳδίως πιστεύων μηδέ τινα προσιέμενος τῶν λόγου ἀξίων· ἀλλὰ τῆς μὲν περὶ τὰ καλὰ σπουδῆς ἀπῆγεν ἑαυτόν, δεδούλωτο δὲ πᾶσαν αὐτοῦ τὴν ψυχὴν νύκτωρ τε καὶ μεθ' ἡμέραν ἐπάλληλοι καὶ ἀκόλαστοι σώματος ἡδοναί. καὶ σώφρων μὲν πᾶς καὶ παιδείας κἂν ἔτι μετρίως μεμνημένος τῆς αὐλῆς ὡς ἐπίβουλος ἐδιώκετο, γελωτοποιοὶ δὲ καὶ τῶν αἰσχίστων ὑποκριταὶ εἶχον αὐτὸν ὑποχείριον. ἁρμάτων τε ἡνιοχείας καὶ θηρίων ἐξ ἀντιστάσεως μάχας ἐπαιδεύετο, τῶν μὲν κολάκων ἐς ἀνδρείας δόξαν αὐτὰ ὑμνούντων, τοῦ δὲ ἀπρεπέστερον μετιόντος ἢ βασιλεῖ σώφρονι ἥρμοζε.

'Although he feared a popular uprising and a new attempt upon his life, Commodus nevertheless, at the urging of his advisers, entered the city. Received there with great enthusiasm, he went to the imperial palace, escorted by the people. After undergoing such risks, the emperor trusted no one; he killed now without warning, listening to all accusations without question and paying no heed to those worthy of a hearing. He no longer had any regard for the "good life"; night and day, without interruption, licentious pleasures of the flesh made him a slave, body and soul. Men of intelligence and those who had even a smattering of learning were driven from the palace as conspirators, but the emperor gave enthralled attention to the filthy skits of comedians and actors. He took lessons in driving the chariot and trained to take part in the wild-animal fights; his flatterers praised these activities as proof of his manliness, but he indulged in them more often than befitted an intelligent emperor.' (Herodian 1.13.7-8)

As can viewed through these passages, Herodian definitely continued the same theme that was presented by Cassius Dio. The first extract (1.8.7-8) clearly establishes the animosity that seemingly existed between the *princeps* and the Senate, although of course the ire was more on Commodus' part, thus making him appear entirely unreasonable.[476] He is shown as being completely uncompromising and calculating. The second passage (1.13.7-8) exhibits a different theme, but one that worked well with the first. Commodus, owing to his corruption, was under the threat of a popular uprising, which in turn led to further executions and depravity on his part. So the theme is continued, and the amount of detail provided by Herodian is also somewhat lacking. The theme of Commodus' characterisation is much important to the author. The realm of the vice and depravity of Commodus Antoninus of course took different forms in this passage, but that underlines the sentiments that Herodian sought to accentuate.

domus praeterea Quintiliorum omnis exstincta, quod Sextus Condiani filius specie mortis ad defectionem diceretur evasisse. interfecta et Vitrasia Faustina et Velius Rufus et Egnatius Capito consularis. in exsilium autem acti sunt Aemilius Iuncus et Atilius Severus consules. et in multos alios varie saevitum est.

'Besides this, he exterminated the whole house of the Quintilii, because Sextus, the son of Condianus, by pretending death, it was said, had made his escape in order to raise a revolt. Vitrasia Faustina, Velius Rufus, and Egnatius Capito, a man of consular rank, were all slain. Aemilius Iuncus and Atilius Severus, the consuls, were driven into exile. And against many others he vented his rage in various ways.' (*HA Commodus* 4.9-11)

Occisus est eo tempore etiam Claudius quasi a latronibus, cuius filius cum pugione quondam ad Commodum ingressus est, multique alii senatores sine iudicio interempti, feminae quoque divites. et nonnulli per provincias a Perenni ob divitias insimulati spoliati sunt vel etiam interempti. iis autem quibus deerat ficti criminis adpositio obiciebatur, quod scribere noluissent Commodum heredem.

'At this time Claudius also, whose son had previously come into Commodus' presence with a dagger, was slain, ostensibly by bandits, and many other senators were put to death, and also certain women of wealth. And not a few provincials, for the sake of their riches, were charged with crimes by Perennis and then plundered or even slain; some, against whom there was not even the imputation of a fictitious crime, were accused of having been unwilling to name Commodus as their heir.' (*HA Commodus* 5.12-14)

In the first passage (*Commodus* 4.9-11), the *HA* biographer has clearly exhibited the unpopularity of the young emperor and his fatal response to these perceived threats (thus possibly implying that he was responsible for his own death by ignoring them). In this sense we can also see the continuation of the negative literary tradition sur-

---

[476] Grosso 1964, *op.cit.*

rounding him. All the same, one of the most notable aspects here is that his victims are overtly referred to, which was intended to add weight to this anti-Commodus sentiment. Nevertheless, while the use of such direct references to particular aristocrats was intended to give a greater impact and sense of accuracy for the audience, it is evident that the *HA* biographer often got rather confused by such details, such as in relation to the reference to Sextus, who was actually the son of Quintilius Valerius Maximus. The second extract (*Commodus* 5.12-14) was more representative of the general tradition in relation to Commodus, preferring to avoid specific details about those persons sentenced to execution by the young emperor. Instead the *HA* biographer sought to continue their primary theme – the cruelty and corruption of the *princeps*.

In cuius locum Iulianus et Regillus subrogati sunt, quos et ipsos postea poenis adfecit. his occisis interemit Servilium et Dulium Silanos cum suis, mox Antium Lupum et Petronios Mamertinum et Suram filiumque Mamertini Antoninum ex sorore sua genitum. et post eos sex simul ex consulibus Allium Fuscum, Caelium Felicem, Lucceium Torquatum, Larcium Eurupianum, Valerium Bassianum, Pactumeium Magnum cum suis, atque in Asia Sulpicium Crassum pro consule et Iulium Proculum cum suis Claudiumque Lucanum consularem et consobrinam patris sui Faustinam Anniam in Achaia et alios infinitos. destinaverat et alios quattuordecim occidere, cum sumptus eius vires Romani imperii sustinere non possent.

'As successors to Cleander Commodus appointed Julianus and Regillus, both of whom he afterwards condemned. After these men had been put to death he slew the two Silani, Servilius and Dulius, together with their kin, then Antius Lupus and the two Petronii, Mamertinus and Sura, and also Mamertinus' son Antoninus, whose mother was his own sister; after these, six former consuls at one time, Allius Fuscus, Caelius Felix, Lucceius Torquatus, Larcius Eurupianus, Valerius Bassianus and Pactumeius Magnus, all with their kin; in Asia Sulpicius Crassus, the proconsul, Julius Proculus, together with their kin, and Claudius Lucanus, a man of consular rank; and in Achaia his father's cousin, Annia Faustina, and innumerable others. He had intended to kill fourteen others also, since the revenues of the Roman Empire were insufficient to meet his expenditures.' (*HA Commodus* 7.4-8)

This passage again presents a large number of names of the *nobiles* executed by Commodus Antoninus. The primary objective by the author for their mention is self evident. All of these characters were seemingly notable figures within Roman society at the time, and the *HA* biographer went to great lengths to mention each of them at this point in order to create the most vivid representation of Commodus' cruelty. This explains the emphasis upon their previous consular roles and also how Commodus was essentially executing them in order to acquire their personal wealth. Such were the depths of his characterised depravity. Of course this was further emphasised by the author in their reference towards how he killed many more people than this who remain unnamed and had planned even more executions. All of this is impossible to substantiate, but of course it produced the desired effect for his characterisation of such a sinister Commodus.

Therefore, when considering the political executions ordered by Commodus Antoninus there are a few points that must be recognised. Firstly, the consistency of these descriptions is notable – while each extract is largely different, the theme presented barely wavers in their focus. Such was the effect of the anti-Commodus literary tradition. Secondly, the references to this aspect of his reign were clearly intended to correspond with the general characterisation of not only his principate, but also his personality. Corrupt, depraved and cruel. Finally, at least with the *HA* biographer more detail of these executions is provided when compared to his actual administration of the Roman State. It is for this reason that other sources of ancient evidence have now become the primary focus of this analysis. The anti-Commodus perspective of the ancient literary sources has been firmly established, but there is more to this story. So, therefore, the public structures constructed by order of Commodus have now been analysed for a clearer perspective of his principate.

Public Architecture

The analysis of public structures, particularly in Rome, provides a good source of information about not only what types of infrastructure were seemingly needed during the reign of Commodus Antoninus, but also about how he sought to establish (if not glorify) his principate.[477] The decision making processes behind these public works were often clear and calculating – seeking to make the greatest possible impact within the wider community. The symbolism of these public structures was highly significant and provides a good source of information about the social priorities of Commodus Antoninus – as well as personal preferences for wider propaganda. After all, were any of the imperial *fora* really constructed with pure altruism on the part of the various *principes* to provide communal space for the people? It is highly unlikely that the motives were so pure. Aside from their intended, literal function, each structure created had another purpose – to promote, establish and symbolise the reign of

---

[477] cf. D.M. Robathan, "Domitian's Midas-Touch", *TAPA* 73, 1942, p. 130.

the Roman Emperor. This is clearly evident in the projects initiated by Commodus Antoninus.

Figure 2 – Column of Marcus Aurelius (author's photograph)

Figure 3 – Column of Marcus Aurelius (author's photograph)

The most prominent existing monument constructed by Commodus was the Column of Marcus Aurelius (Fig. 2), which was of course a commemoration of his father (and possibly his mother).[478] While officially the column was conferred by the Senate to celebrate the success of Marcus Aurelius over the Marcomanni and Sarmatians between AD 172-5 (*Epitomator* 16) (Fig. 3), it is evident that it was highly influenced by Commodus in its construction – it being completed in AD 193.[479] It is almost impossible to believe that such an iconic celebration of Commodus' father (and his previous joint *princeps*) would not have greatly interested him (after all he had success-

---

[478] Lanciani 1967, *op.cit.*, p. 505.
[479] Platner 1926, *op.cit.*, p. 597.

fully concluded the war in AD 180). The Antonine tradition that existed within its design is also notable, being quite similar to Trajan's Column.[480] Although it still appears quite evident that the Column of Marcus Aurelius still possessed innovations in relation to symbolism, frontality and its reading.[481] All the same, the monumentality and overt propaganda of this structure cannot be ignored, linking Commodus to a gradually growing and evolving symbol of success and his ancestry on several different levels.

There were other imperial public structures that have been attributed to Commodus, but unfortunately they have not survived to the same extent as the previous monumental structure. Most have simply survived as references to their construction. One of the most notable of course was the Temple of *Divus Marcus Aurelius*. This structure was also conferred by the Senate (*HA Marcus* 18.8) and was built close to his column.[482] Unfortunately there is little else known about this monument – but it is clear that this would have been of great importance to Commodus. Another significant structure that has been referred to was the *Themae Commodianae* (the 'Baths of Commodus').[483] These baths are largely attributed to the Praetorian Prefect Cleander, despite them having been built in AD 183 (according to Jerome), which would place them prior to his period of prominence.[484] Their attribution to Cleander is based upon the themes within the ancient literary sources,[485] which seem less than reliable. Cleander did not rise to power until AD 185 – this conferral of responsibility appears to fit more with the anti-Commodus literary sentiment rather than historical fact. Unfortunately there is almost no other ancient evidence to either prove or disprove this temporal inconsistency.[486]

When considering the involvement of Commodus Antoninus and his influence over the development of Rome in the late Second Century, there is one further aspect that needs to be discussed: the great fire of AD 191. This episode has been fully described by Cassius Dio (72.24.1-2). This saw the destruction of several notable

---

[480] Richardson 1992, *op.cit.*, p. 95.

[481] See Scheid and Huet, 2000, *op.cit.*

[482] Richardson 1992, *op.cit.*, p. 244.

[483] Platner 1926, *op.cit.*, p. 525.

[484] See Richardson 1992, *op.cit.*, p. 390.

[485] Herodian 1.12.4; *HA* Commodus 17.5.

[486] Traupman 1956, *op.cit.*

structures, such as the Temple of Peace, the *Horrea Piperataria* and the Temple of Vesta.[487] Of course, while the occurrence of such dramatic fires within the city of Rome was previously occurred during the previous centuries (largely owing to over-crowding and poor design) it is of no great surprise that Commodus was directly associated (and blamed by some) for the disaster. It is important to compare how this was intended to reflect upon the 'evil' Commodus when the Emperor Titus suffered an equally calamitous conflagration in AD 80, and yet he is lauded for his effective response. But this further establishes how influential the ancient literary sources have been in creating a negative persona or characterisation of this *princeps*. This is not a defence of Commodus – simply a recognition that we need to take a step back in order to consider his reign hopefully in a more equitable fashion.

So judging from this aspect of Commodus Antoninus' principate there are several aspects that can be taken from his reign. Firstly, it is quite evident that Commodus made extended and concerted efforts to advertise both his lineage and in turn his legitimacy in his role as head of the Roman State. This is easily viewed through both the Column and Temple of Marcus Aurelius. Secondly, while few remains are still archaeologically extant, there are several projects that he actively promoted, one of which must be the *Thermae Commodianae*. While this has been attributed to the Praetorian Prefect Cleander, this was seemingly more in accordance with the anti-Commodus literary sentiment. It is also important to note the impact the process of *damnatio memoriae*. It is unlikely that Commodus was not impressed with the prospect of large scale monuments for his own promotion. One form was through immense public buildings (which were usually advisable), but another was through the construction of dominating private residences, which could have an equally disseminating effect of power and personal importance.

Private Architecture

The private architecture of Commodus Antoninus can also provide a good insight into our understanding of his principate. In order to gain the optimal perspective of this archaeological aspect, two types of residence have been considered: the palace on the Palatine Hill and the imperial suburban villas. Both of these contexts provide the optimal context in which to understand how a *princeps* (or any

---

[487] Richardson 1992, *op.cit.*, p. 455.

wealthy aristocrat for that matter) sought to display their prominence and social dominance. So, in order to discuss this aspect effectively the primary palace (either called the *Domus Palatina* or *Domus Severiana*) has been initially analyzed. Following from this several imperial villas from the Antonine period have also been discussed. These structures have been included in order to allow for a greater understanding of Commodus' extra urban residence. In order to gain a better perspective of his inclinations, the villa that he acquired (that of the Quintili brothers) has been evaluated in both prior and post acquisition contexts in order to establish the general effect of the emperor's alterations.[488]

When examining Roman villas and palaces in general terms there are some pertinent points that should be noted before examining the archaeological evidence from the suburbs of Rome. Firstly, one of the most important aspects to remember is that the buildings under discussion here are, for the most part, residences of the wealthy. In many ways, the ownership of a suburban villa was a status symbol in itself. These residences were then further enhanced with well-appointed décor and architecture, which was intended to further the social standing of the *dominus*.[489] This has been meticulously analyzed by Wallace-Hadrill (1988), which sought to clearly establish the link between the Roman house and the owners' social standing. This is an important feature to remember within this study because the décor and facilities at a residence should provide a good understanding of the aspirations of an owner and the resources available to them.[490] Naturally, the presence of any ostentatious display of wealth in private residences was not always the case. But the need for authors such as Cato and Columella to make remarks concerning lavish décor in their works suggests that it was a common feature of wealthy Roman residences during the period. Cicero (*De Legibus*, 3.30) freely admitted the presence of social pressures among the senatorial order to possess a magnificent villa. Columella (1.6.2) also advised the addi-

---

[488] Traupman 1956, *op.cit.*

[489] George, M., 1997b, "Servus and domus: the slave in the Roman house", in Laurence, R. and Wallace-Hadrill, A. (eds.), *Domestic Space in the Roman World: Pompeii and Beyond*, JRA Supp 22: Portsmouth, p. 16; Bergmann, B., 1994, "Painted Perspectives of a villa visit: landscape as status and metaphor", in Gazda, E.K. (ed.), *Roman Art in the Private Sphere*, University of Michigan Press: Ann Arbor, p. 65.

[490] Laurence, R., 1994, *Roman Pompeii: space and society*, Routledge: London, p. 127

tion of an appropriate *pars urbana* in the early Augustan period for the socially conscious villa owner. It was clearly an essential aspect of Roman public life, with a residence not only being a private sanctuary for the owner, but also a public display of their success, dignity and prestige. There seems to have been a consistent desire to stay abreast of the latest tastes in décor,[491] which is a consistent feature of the renovations that occurred in many residences and explains the consistent outflow of wealth on private buildings.[492]

Naturally, this is clearly going to be limited by the concept of public and private space within these residences, which has been discussed at length previously, but is important to note within the context of this study. It should also be mentioned that the possession of property, particularly agricultural estates, was of prime importance for determining the social position of a family within the hierarchy of the community.[493] This has been shown to be of particular significance in regard to those properties located close to the city, especially around Rome. Purcell has suggested a vivid description of the suburban landscape,[494] which illustrates the monumental characteristics of the wealthy residences beyond the city limits. Duncan-Jones has postulated what the average cost of land would cost in both urban and rural contexts,[495] and judging from this it would have been considerable in the *suburbium* of Rome. There seems to have been a strong sense of urbanism in the surrounding regions of Rome as well, with towns such as Falerii Novi, Orriculum and Forum Novum having clear associations with the capital.[496] The importance

---

[491] Gabriel, M.M., 1952, *Masters of Campanian Painting*, H. Bittner: New York, p. 60.

[492] Wallace-Hadrill, A., 1988, "The Social Structure of the Roman House", *PBSR* 56, p. 47.

[493] Saller, R.P., 1994, *Patriarchy, property and death in the Roman Family*, Cambridge University Press: Cambridge, p. 3.

[494] Purcell, N., 1987, "Town in Country and Country in Town", in MacDougall, E.B. (ed.), *Ancient Roman Villa Gardens*, Dumbarton Oaks Colloquium on the History of Landscape Architecture 10: Washington, pp. 188-9.

[495] Duncan-Jones, R., 1965, "An Epigraphic Survey of Costs in Roman Italy", *PBSR* 33, pp. 224-6.

[496] Patterson, H. and Millett, M., 1998, "The Tiber valley Project", *PBSR* 66, pp. 11-14; Potter, T.W., 1991, "Towns and territories in southern Etruria", in Rich, J. and Wallace-Hadrill, A. (eds.), *City and Country in the Ancient World*, Routledge: London, pp. 191-209; Gaffney, V., Patterson, H. and Roberts,

laid upon the possession of domestic property would have also placed a great deal of importance upon the family unit, with each member finding their place within the fundamental hierarchy of the household. The Roman residence for wealthy members of each community was closely tied in with friendship and patron-client relationships, which made the presentation of each opulent abode even more significant for social advancement and prestige.

By the end of the Republic, the Palatine had become one of the most aristocratic regions of Rome because of its intimate connection with the Curia, the Rostra and the Forum.[497] There were several impressive residences built in this region during the Republican era from around 150 BC,[498] such as the Houses of Q. Lutatius Catulus, M. Livius Drusus, Clodius and M. Aemilius Scaurus.[499] The house of Cicero on the Palatine was located on the south-west corner of the hill, overlooking the *Forum Romanum*, which would have been a prime location. It seems clear that by the end of the Republic, the Palatine had become one of the most important centres for Roman political and commercial life, which continued during the Roman Empire. During the Imperial period, the Palatine region was almost entirely occupied by the residences of the Emperors,[500] except for a region of roughly one hundred and seventy metres by one hundred metres.[501] The choice of this area was made by Augustus, who built his residence there: the House of Augustus. The Emperor Tiberius constructed a new wing of this structure, the *Domus Tiberiana*, which was connected to the House of Augustus by a series of underground corridors.

Domus Palatina

The Palace of the Emperors was probably one of the most impressive examples of an Imperial residence that remains (Fig. 4). The Imperial estate was reduced by Vespasian upon his accession in AD 69, limiting it to the previous limits of the Palatine. Vespasian began

---

P., 2001, "Forum Novum-Vescovio: studying urbanism in the Tiber valley", *JRA* 14, pp. 59-79.

[497] Lanciani 1967, *op.cit.*, p. 117.

[498] Dudley, D.R., 1967, *Urbs Roma*, Phaidon Press: London, pp. 162-3.

[499] Lanciani 1967, *op.cit.*, pp. 117-18.

[500] Cerutti 1997, *op.cit.*, p. 424.

[501] Lanciani 1967, *op.cit.*, p. 107.

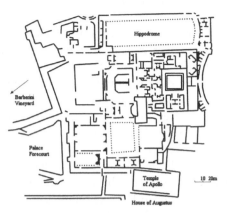

Figure 4 – *Domus Palatina*

the construction of the *Domus Palatina*, but it came to its true realization under Domitian.[502] This Imperial residence was located between the *Domus Tiberiana* and *Gaiana* on one side, with the House of Augustus on the other. The structure was placed in line with the valley that ran between the Arch of Titus towards the Circus. This valley was occupied by private houses and a couple of shrines at this time, which were not demolished but used to support the platform of the palace. The *Domus Palatina* was planned along the lines of a traditional Roman *domus*, but on a grander scale.[503] It is unknown as to whether the Emperors actually resided at the *Domus Palatina* frequently, but instead it may have been used for political and administrative purposes, such as holding assemblies, delivering judgments, presiding over councils of state and for official banquets.[504]

The layout of the Palace had impressive dimensions. There were three halls that opened to the front of the palace: the throne room (*aula regia*) in the centre, a *lararium* on the left and the *basilica* on the right.[505] The *aula regia* was constructed in brick and had impressive dimensions, measuring roughly forty-nine by thirty-seven metres.[506] This room was decorated with sixteen columns with bases and capi-

---

[502] Richardson 1992, *op.cit.*, p. 115.
[503] Giuliani, C.F., 1977, "Domus Flavia: una nuova lettura", *MDAIR(A)* 84, pp. 91-106.
[504] Lanciani 1967, *op.cit.*, p. 156.
[505] Giuliani 1977, *op.cit.*, p. 94.
[506] Lanciani 1967, *op.cit.*, p. 158.

tals cut in ivory-coloured marble. On either side of this room there were three niches for statues, flanked by small columns of porphyry. The throne itself (Room c), or *augustale solium*, was placed on the same axis as the entrance in the apse towards the rear. The *lararium* included a large altar at the far wall from the entrance. Behind this room was a small staircase, which led to an upper level of the residence. This level of rooms included areas for the conducting of state ceremonies for invited guests. Both the staircase (Room d) and the adjacent room (Room e) were adorned with fine frescoes that have not survived. The *basilica* was located on the other side of the *aula regia*, still possessing traces of the podium upon which the Emperor would have passed judgment.

Behind these three halls was an open *peristyle*, measuring roughly 3600 square metres. Suetonius (*Dom.* 14.4) refers to this area as being a favourite place for Domitian to walk under the colonnades away from the crowds and also danger. Two sides of the *peristyle* were bordered by a series of nine rooms, all of which served an unknown function, except the central vestibule that served as a reception room. It is probable that the other rooms served as the main residential rooms within the complex.[507] There was a *triclinium* located on the eastern side of the *peristyle*, which may have been the *Iovis Centaio*. None of the wall decorations have survived from this room, but the pavement of the apse was produced from pieces of porphyry, serpentine, giallo and pavonazzetto in geometric patterns. The remains of Neronian structures have been discovered under the foundations of this room,[508] which is indicative of the rebuilding by the Flavian Emperors to disassociate themselves from this predecessor. There was also a *nymphaeum* located to the right of the *triclinium* (Fig. 4), which seems to have several water features and good light and ventilation.[509] The central fountain was elliptical with niches and recesses, probably for plants and statues.

It must be noted that below these rooms and the *peristyle* there were more rooms, including fine apartments, galleries and a *cryptoporticus*. One of these rooms included a 'bathroom', which measured

---

[507] Richardson 1992, *op.cit.*, p. 116.
[508] Cassatella, A., 1990, "Un disegno di pirro Ligorio ed I resti sotto il Triclinio della Domus Flavia", in *Gli Orti Farnesiani sul Palatino*, Ècole Francaise de Rome: Rome, pp. 155-66.
[509] Gibson, S., DeLaine, J. and Claridge, A., 1994, "The Triclinium of the Domus Flavia: a new reconstruction", *PBSR* 62, p. 70.

over twenty metres in length, with walls encrusted with Florentine mosaic, a marble basin, porphyry columns and marble bas-reliefs of the highest quality. There is no evidence of rooms of lodging within the *Domus Palatina*, but it would be unrealistic to accept that none existed, in view of the complex's long period of use. In all likelihood these rooms would have probably been located on the upper levels of the residence, which have not survived. In this area of the *domus* there would have been greater opportunity for privacy, whereas the ground floor served a more public role. As with all of the large Imperial residences, the high platform upon which this palace was constructed would have created an impressive panorama, allowing for a dramatic view of the entire city. This would have been of some attraction to the emperors, providing them with a view of what they would have considered *their* city. It was also desirable because the elevated position added to the prominence of these residences in the eyes of the public, emphasising the importance of the *princeps*.

This representation of dominance would have been important to Commodus, but it is also essential to note that he seemingly preferred to reside in the suburbs. It is clear that the Palatine was a symbol of imperial dominance (which he would have sought to naturally maintain), but it is evident that the *principes* of the 2nd Century AD sought to create residences that suited their own tastes in the *suburbium* of Rome – close enough to maintain their political responsibilities and yet slightly removed enough to allow more freedom and relaxation. Therefore, this section has also evaluated and considered the villas of Trajan, Hadrian and Antoninus Pius, as well as the villa of Commodus and its previous owners (the Villa of the Quintili).

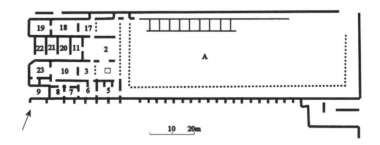

Figure 5 – Villa of Trajan

The Villa of Trajan

The Villa of Trajan at Arcinazzo (Fig. 5) was located approximately thirty-nine kilometres from Rome, which places it conceivably within the *suburbium* of the capital. The site has been investigated through both archaeological excavation and geophysical surveying to date, which has shown that it was a large, well-appointed structure with *otium* and *luxuria* being prime elements in its intended function. It seems pertinent to initially classify this imperial residence as an elite *villa suburbana*.

This complex (Fig. 5) comprised a large, open *peristyle* with several residential areas on the western perimeter of the establishment.[510] However, the use of geophysical surveying techniques has shown the existence of additional structures beyond the main residence as well.[511] The *peristyle* (Area A) was monumental in its design, being clearly intended more for *otium* rather than a utilitarian function. The walls were made of either *opus reticulatum* or *opus mixtum*.[512] While this villa was not as extensive as other imperial residences in the Roman *suburbium*, such as the Villas of Domitian and Hadrian, it was still a large and impressive *villa suburbana*.

The luxurious facilities present in the Villa of Trajan at Arcinazzo are not only shown in its general design (Fig. 5), but also in its decorative features. For example, the *peristyle* was adorned with plaster columns, which added to its well-appointed demeanour. The walls of the *pars urbana* were also decorated with either marble panels or notable wall-paintings.[513] In this regard, Room 10 was a fine example, with a diverse array of marbles and plasters being used to create a well-appointed dining area. This area was so beautifully adorned that Tomei has compared its decorative program with that of the Palace on the Palatine Hill.[514]

---

[510] Mari, Z., 2004, "La villa di Triano ad Arcinazzo Romano", *Journal of Fasti Online*. www.fastionline.org/docs/2004-1.pdf, p. 1.

[511] Piro, S., Goodman, D. and Nishimura, Y., 2003, "The Study and Characterization of Emperor Traiano's Villa", *Archaeological Prospection* 10, pp. 1-25; Goodman, D., Piro, S. and Nishimura, Y., 2002, "GPR Time Slice Images of the Villa of Emperor Trajanus, Arcinazzo, Italy (A.D. 52-117)", *Proceedings of SPIE* 4758, pp. 268-70.

[512] Tomei, M.A., 1985, "La Villa detta di Triano ad Arcinazzo", *ArchLaz* 7, pp. 180.

[513] Mari 2004, *op.cit.*, p. 4.

[514] Tomei 1985, *op.cit.*, p. 181.

The use of marble decorative features was also implemented for some of the floorings, which were also included in Room 10. In this regard, Mari has also compared it use of geometric marble pavements with the décor of the *Domus Palatina*.[515] The presence of these expensive decorative features not only exhibits the wealth of Trajan, but also the intended artistic pretensions that he sought for this imperial residence. While there are no direct literary references to his use of this villa,[516] the Villa at Arcinazzo would have suited his appreciation for mountainous woodlands (Pliny *Pan.*, 81.1-3): *Quodsi quando cum influentibus negotiis paria fecisti, instar refectionis existimas mutationem laboris. Quae enim remissio tibi, nisi lustrare saltus, excutere cubilibus feras, superare immensa montium iuga, et horrentibus scopulis gradum inferre, nullius manu, nullius vestigio adiutum; atque inter haec pia mente adire lucos, et occursare numinibus?* ['But when you have successfully curtailed the rush of your activities, the manner of leisure you favour is only this – a conversion of work. Your only relaxation is to wander the woods, to force the wild animals from their dens, to climb vast mountain heights, and set foot on rocky peaks, with no one to give assistance or to show the way; and among all this to stop at the sacred groves in a mood of piety, and offer yourself to the gods there'].

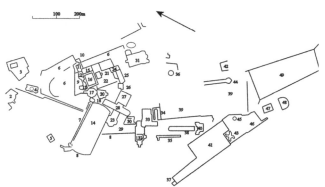

Figure 6 – Villa of Hadrian

Hadrian's Villa
The Villa of Hadrian at Tivoli was an estate that was the most extensive and elaborate complex discovered in the suburbs of Rome,

---

[515] Mari 2004, *op.cit.*, p. 5.
[516] Tomei 1985, *op.cit.*, p. 183.

roughly twenty-eight kilometres from the capital,[517] covering roughly three hundred acres (Fig. 6). The Imperial residence itself, including the Piazza d'Oro, Hall with Doric Pillars, Great *Peristyle* and the library courtyards still covered an area well over 50,000 square metres,[518] illustrating its grand dimensions. Originally there was a late Republican villa on the site previous to the construction of Hadrian's villa, some of its walls being incorporated into the palace *peristyle*. The general layout appears to have been planned in a coherent style,[519] but it is still difficult to understand as a whole. The position of each building was intended to take advantage of the topography, which added to the entire effect. The plan was aligned upon a series of different axes, but it suited the undulating nature of its position. Of the structures included within the villa complex, there were several designed for specific purposes, such as the libraries and sculpture galleries. The entire complex was a reflection of the emperor's tastes and cultural appreciation. Hadrian was initiated into the rites of the Eleusinian mysteries,[520] reflecting his appreciation for Hellenistic culture. In several of the structures, this understanding was displayed in his architectural tastes. This complex has been the topic of much discussion and for the purposes of this study, owing to its immense size, only certain aspects will be discussed. The particular rooms to be considered are the *triclinia*, such as the Arcaded and Scenic *triclinia* with their associated structures. Within the villa, Hadrian had provided enough space for banquets that almost a countless number of people could have been entertained. All of these reception rooms had been intended for summer dining, which appears to have been the time of year when the Emperor anticipated to be staying at this *villa suburbana*.[521]

The room called the Imperial *triclinium* was the first dining room to be constructed at the villa, probably completed by AD 125, but it has been questioned as to whether this room served as a dining room, or possibly as an *atrium*, which seems more likely. The most

---

[517] Packer, J.E., 1998, "Mire exaedificavit: three recent books on Hadrian's Tiburtine villa", *JRA* 11, p. 583.

[518] Aurigemma, S., 1964, *Villa Adriana near Tivoli*, trans. A.W. Van Buren, Arti Grafiche A. Chicca: Tivoli, p. 48.

[519] Adembri, B., 2000, *Hadrian's Villa*, Electa: Milan, p. 24.

[520] Clinton, K., 1989, "Hadrian's contribution to the Renaissance of Elusis", in Walker, S. and Cameron, A. (eds.), *The Greek Renaissance in the Roman Empire*, Institute of Classical Studies: London, pp. 56-68.

[521] Birley 1997, *op.cit.*, p. 199.

significant dining rooms at Hadrian's villa for this discussion are the Arcaded and Scenic *triclinia*, which were part of a *stibadium* under a vaulted canopy that was open to the view.[522] The Arcaded *triclinium* was originally designed on a north-south axis with three main quarters: an open columned portico, central hall and a southern semi-circular *exedra*. This region was later converted into a less conventional layout, eventually having only one solid wall, with an impressive spatial orientation allowing for an unimpeded view on most major axes. A major feature intended for viewing was a pool placed alongside the building. This region of the villa would have served as both dining area and reception room, having a large amount of spatial freedom. The large *stibadium* of the Scenic *triclinium*, which has been referred to as a *Serapeum*, was located beneath the half-dome of the Scenic *triclinium*, which was roughly thirteen metres in diameter. This was planned to view the Canopus, which served in a similar fashion to a *euripus*, as at many wealthy villas, but on a monumental scale with strong Egyptian influences.[523] The design was intended to join nature, art and architecture in a dynamic spatial concept.[524] There were also small pavilions located on either side, which served as *diaetae*, being open to the breeze and the Canopus. This Scenic *triclinium* was used for a relatively small number of people, designed as a two-part *grotto* with the Canopus serving as its ornamental water feature. The view of the Canopus would have been extremely impressive, especially with its associated sculptures.

The statues discovered around the end of the Canopus were influenced by Greek culture, but may have symbolised a return to the Augustan Golden Age.[525] However, it is interesting to note the use of different types of marble and the poor state of visibility for viewing these statues from the *grotto-triclinium*.[526] But it has generally been accepted that the vast array of statuary discovered at the site is indicative not only of the emperor's cultural influences during his trav-

---

[522] MacDonald, W.L. and Pinto, J.A., 1995, *Hadrian's Villa*, Yale University Press: New Haven, 1995, pp. 102-3.

[523] Ortolani, G., 1998, *Il Padiglione di Afrodite Cnida a Villa Adriana: progetto e significato*, Librerie Maze: Rome, p. 21.

[524] MacDonald and Pinto 1995, *op.cit.*, p. 112.

[525] Raeder, J., 1983, *Die Statuarische Ausstattung der Villa Hadriana bei Tivoli*, P. Lang: Frankfurt, pp. 304-14.

[526] Bellingham, D.C., 1985, "Die Statuarische ausstattung der Villa Hadriana bei Tivoli (review)", *JRS* 75, p. 275.

els,[527] but also that each piece was carefully considered in order to complement the architecture of its surroundings.[528] The Canopus region had a series of terraced gardens on the western side, with a series of *amphorae* that were cut in half used as planting pots.[529]

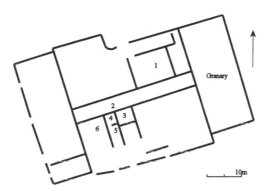

Figure 7 – Villa of Antoninus Pius

Antoninus Pius' Villa

The Villa of Antoninus Pius at Villa Magna (Fig. 7) was located approximately thirty-nine kilometres from Rome, which was within the outer limits of the perceived *suburbium* of the capital. As with the Villa of Trajan at Arcinazzo this site has been investigated using both archaeological excavation and geophysical surveying. This imperial villa was later covered by a monastery, which has limited its results, but this site was clearly an unusual villa in the hinterland of Rome.

While the entire structure of this imperial residence has not yet been fully excavated, the geophysical surveys have shown the limits of this complex (Fig. 7).[530] Judging from these results it is initially clear that this was the smallest imperial villa within the Roman *suburbium* that has been examined in this study. This villa was larger than

---

[527] Jashemski, W.F. and Salza Prina Ricotti, E., 1992, "Preliminary Excavations in the Gardens of Hadrian's Villa: the Canopus Area and the Piazza d'Oro", *AJA* 96, p. 580.

[528] Fullerton, M.D., 1986, "Die Statuarische Ausstattung der Villa Hadriana bei Tivoli (review)", *AJA* 90, p. 251.

[529] Jashemski and Salza Prina Ricotti 1992, *op.cit.*, pp. 579-97.

[530] Fentress, E., Goodson, C., Hay, S., Kuttner, A. and Maiuro, M., 2006, *Excavations at Villa Magna 2006*, pp. 2-4.

Tiberius' villa at Sperlonga, but this residence was not located in the Roman suburbs. The attribution of imperial ownership has largely been based upon the correlation between the highly decorated *cella vinaria* at this site[531] and a description of the site in a letter from Marcus Aurelius to Cornelius Fronto (4.6): *loti igitur in torculari cenavimus: non loti in torculari, sed ioti cenavimus; et rusticos cavillantes audivimus libenter* ['So we had dinner after we had bathed in the oil-press room; I do not mean bathed in the oil-press room, but when we had bathed, we had dinner there, and we took pleasure in listening to the country folk chatting to one another']. There is also an inscription from the local area that mentions the construction of a road from Anagni to the villa (*CIL* 10.5909), which supports its imperial ownership as well. The letter of Marcus Aurelius to Fronto refers to Antoninus Pius' presence at this occasion, and so this complex, with its opulent décor, has been attributed to him. This is also likely in view of how much time Antoninus spent in Italy during his principate when compared to Marcus Aurelius.

The most notable area that has been investigated at this site is Room 1, which primarily functioned as a *cella vinaria* (Fig. 7). However, this room was decorated with an *opus spicatum* pavement that included yellow marble beside the raised cistern (Fentress, Goodson *et al.* 2006, 5). This kind of décor for a seemingly utilitarian space is previously unheralded and corresponds nicely to the aforementioned letter from Marcus Aurelius to Fronto (4.6). All the same, this room also correlates well with the overall Roman conception of the use of domestic space: rooms within these residences were potentially used for a wide variety of functions. Nevertheless, such elaborate décor is highly unusual for such a primarily functional area, but this also epitomises the expendable capital of the imperial household. Therefore, this *cella vinaria* has been included within the areas of potential entertainment space for this complex at Villa Magna. No open areas have as of yet been uncovered, which makes the statistical data quite different to the other imperial villas as well. Room 6 was paved in white marble[532] and owing to its size and position within the complex (Fig. 7) seems to have also been used as a dining area.

---

[531] Fentress, E., Gatti, S., Goodson, C., Hay, S., Kuttner, A. and Maiuro, M., 2006, "Excavations at Villa Magna 2006", *Journal of Fasti Online.* www.fastionline.org/docs/2006-68.pdf, p. 5.

[532] Fentress, Goodson *et al.* 2006, *op.cit.*, p. 6.

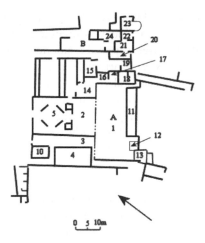

Figure 8 – Villa of the Quintili

Quintili Villa

The Villa of the Quintili (Fig. 8) is the latest structure included within the study, being dated to the late Hadrianic era or early Antonine period (AD 138-140).[533] The extant remains and its palatial facilities make it a fine example of a well-appointed aristocratic *villa suburbana*.[534] It was located eight kilometres from the city, clearly within the inner suburban regions of Rome, with a character that was luxurious enough to cause the demise of its owners, Quintilius Condianus and Quintilius Maximus,[535] at the hands of the Emperor Commodus (Dio 72.5).

It is for this reason that this villa provides another important feature that is unavailable in most suburban villas. The archaeological record illustrates that after the complex became an imperial residence there were significant additions to its structure and character. Comparing these changes illustrates the different facilities that existed at imperial suburban villas and other well-appointed *villae suburbanae*. Judging from the decorative additions, as well as the increased number of large structures for entertainment at this establishment, the difference in expendable capital gave the various *princeps* a significant advantage in the number of alterations that could be undertaken. In all likelihood it would have also increased the need for such recep-

---

[533] Paris 2000, *op.cit.*, p. 29.

[534] Annibaldi 1935, *op.cit.*, pp. 76-104.

[535] Lanciani 1967, *op.cit.*, p. 264.

tion/entertainment areas. However, for the purposes of the present discussion it is the structure that was owned by the Quintili that has been analysed, with the later imperial residence being discussed next.

This complex (Fig. 8) was originally constructed in the early-mid 2nd Century AD, having several distinct regions, which all served a separate function. For the purposes of this study the most important division was between the public (A) and private (B) areas of the residence, which provides the best indication of how this *villa suburbana* was used by its owners. They were both closely connected to each other, but there was a clear division in function between each region.

The private section (B) of this residence (Fig. 8) was located in the eastern quarters of the main complex. The first stage of the main structure was indicative of the pre-imperial ownership, which principally included a scenic wing that viewed the countryside towards the *Via Latina*. This was surrounded by a private garden that would have added to pleasant demeanour of the structure. This was later replaced a series of brick walls and the addition of small adjoining rooms, latrines, baths and servile rooms during the early phases of its imperial ownership. However, this area was accessed from the large courtyard (A 1) via a small hall (A 16), which led directly into two *cubicula* (B 17, 18) that also faced onto the courtyard (Fig. 8). Both of these rooms were heated, as was another impressive and well-appointed room (B 19), which also possessed marble pavement. It is likely that this room would have been the master bedroom for the residents.[536]

The public regions (A) of the Villa of the Quintili were located near the entrance. Upon entering the complex, the first area to be encountered was a large courtyard (A 1), which had white marble steps, marble pavement and a portico on one of the long sides (Fig. 8). It is likely that this area was used as a gathering/entertainment space. On one side of this area was a small cult building (A 12), which included a small fountain (A 13). In view of the presence of a larger example (H), this smaller example probably served a private role for the household. To the north of the courtyard there was a raised platform, which had three well-appointed rooms (A 2-4). The central room of this group (A 2) functioned as a vestibule for the large Octagonal Hall (A 5). This hall has only limited remains of its décor, but owing to its size and location it is more than likely to have

---

[536] Coarelli 1981, *op.cit.*, pp. 55-7.

been an important reception room. It possessed four entrances and the walls comprised of large pillars with triangular bases. All of these rooms on this level (A2-5) had hypocaust heating, which would have added to their comfort when being used for entertainment or reception.

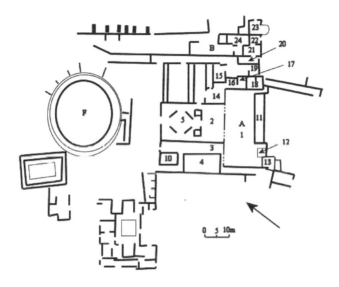

Figure 9 – Villa of Commodus

Villa of Commodus

The imperial form of this complex provides a unique opportunity to assess the impact of imperial ownership on an aristocratic residence in the Roman *suburbium*. As mentioned previously, it was a fine example of a well-appointed aristocratic *villa suburbana*.[537] It was located eight kilometres from the city, clearly within the inner suburban regions of Rome, with a character that was luxurious enough to cause the demise of its owners, Quintilius Condianus and Quintilius Maximus at the hands of the Emperor Commodus (Dio 73.5.3-4).[538] This in itself highlights how attractive suburban villas were to the Roman elite, especially in view of the emperor's urban residence that stood on the Palatine until the fire of AD 192.[539] Following this the

---

[537] Annibaldi 1935, *op.cit.*, pp. 76-104.

[538] Lanciani 1967, *op.cit.*, p. 264.

[539] Hekster 2002, *op.cit.*, pp. 78-9.

Emperor moved to another villa on the Caelian Hill, the Villa Vectiliana (*HA Commodus*, 16.3), although Herodian (1.15.8) included more suspicious motives:

de Palatio ipse ad Caelium montem in Vectilianas aedes migravit negans se in Palatio posse dormire (*HA Commodus*, 16.3)

'Commodus moved his abode from the Palace to the Vectilian Villa on the Caelian Hill, stating that he could not sleep in the Palace.'

τον δὲ προεχώρησε μανίας, ὡς μηκέτι βούλεσθαι μηδὲ τὴν βασίλειον οἰκεῖν ἑστίαν· ἀλλὰ γὰρ μετοικισθῆναι ἐβούλετο ἐς τὸ τῶν μονομάχων καταγώγιον. (Herodian 1.15.8)

'But his insanity had got hold of him to such an extent that he even refused to reside in the palace any longer and was aiming to go and live with the gladiators in their quarters.'

Considering that the pre-imperial complex has been already discussed, only a brief overview has been included at this point. This complex (Fig. 9) was originally constructed in the early-mid 2nd Century AD, having several distinct regions, which all served a separate function. For the purposes of this study the most important division was between the public (A) and private (B) areas of the residence, which provides the best indication of how this *villa suburbana* was used by its owners. They were both closely connected to each other, but there was a clear division in function between each region.

The private section (B) of this residence (Fig. 9) was located in the eastern quarters of the main complex. The first stage of the main structure was indicative of the pre-imperial ownership, which principally included a scenic wing that viewed the countryside towards the Via Latina. This was surrounded by a private garden that would have added to pleasant demeanour of the structure. This was replaced a series of brick walls and the addition of small adjoining rooms, latrines, baths and servile rooms during its imperial ownership. The well-appointed nature of this *villa suburbana* at this point is exhibited in that even the corridor (B 20) was decorated with marble wall panels, as well as the extremely elaborate décor in the large baths within this section of the residence (B 21-24) (Fig. 9). Baths were apparently quite important to the Emperor Commodus (*HA Commodus*, 11.5), which may explain the magnificent character of these rooms: *lavabat per diem septies atque octies et in ipsis balneis edebat* ['He used to bathe seven or eight times each day, and was in the practice of dining while in the baths'].

The public regions (A) of the Villa of the Quintili were located near the entrance. Upon entering the complex, the first area to be encountered was a large courtyard (A 1), which had white marble steps, marble pavement and a portico on one of the long sides. It is likely that this area was used as a gathering/entertainment space. On one side of this area was a small cult building (A 12), which included a small fountain (A 13). In view of the presence of a larger example (H), this smaller example probably served a private role for the household. To the north of the courtyard there was a raised platform, which had three well-appointed rooms (A 2-4). The central room of this group (A 2) functioned as a vestibule for the large Octagonal Hall (A 5). Behind this hall was Room A10, which would have been used as an entertainment area for viewing the landscape beyond. Further out from this was the so-called Maritime Theatre (F), which has been so named because of its similarity to the Theatre at Hadrian's Villa. The interior of this structure was paved and probably lined with a colonnade. It is more than likely that it also possessed a small ornamental garden in the middle.

As mentioned previously, this villa provides another important feature that is unavailable in most suburban villas. The archaeological record illustrates that after the complex became an imperial residence there were significant additions to its structure and character. Comparing these changes illustrates the different facilities that existed at imperial suburban villas and other well appointed *villae suburbanae*. Judging from the decorative additions, as well as the increased number of large structures for entertainment at this establishment, the difference in expendable capital gave the various *princeps* a significant advantage in the number of alterations that could be undertaken. In all likelihood it would have also increased the need for such reception/entertainment areas.

There is no evidence of agricultural productivity at this residence, but the Quintili family probably used other estates such as the property at Tusculum for this, being only eleven kilometres further from the capital. In the imperial phase it was for its residential facilities that Commodus valued this *villa suburbana*, not its productivity. Following from Commodus' additions to the Villa of the Quintili, it created a residence that was more indicative of his own personal tastes and social intentions. Each additional structure was purely for his personal use and for those who he wanted to entertain. It is for this reason that this *villa suburbana* on the Via Appia is useful: it highlights how the differences in personal taste affected the facilities at these aristocratic residences, especially when the expendable capital of the imperial *familia* was available for such additions and alterations.

Initially it must be noted that these imperial structures are hardly indicative of the majority of the populace – virtually unlimited power and similarly unlimited funds made such buildings highly exceptional. The analysis of these imperial villas has shown not only the variation in taste for each *princeps*, but also their desire to create their *own* domain, regardless of the existence of other imperial structures that would have come into their possession upon their accession. Consider the difference between the villas of Hadrian and Antoninus Pius. All the same, it is pertinent to note how the villa of Commodus had changed after its ownership by the Quintili brothers – agriculture was not added to the precinct, only luxury. The large bathing complex also seems to correspond with the references of some ancient literary sources. Nevertheless, none of the imperial villas from this period were seemingly interested in being agriculturally productive – almost all of them were devoted to *otium*. These structures provide a good insight into how these respective *principes* wanted to live – and in this regard Commodus Antoninus was relatively restrained. He reigned for a significant period of time, and yet he did not aim at building a huge palatial structure either in town or in the *suburbium*. Another source of ancient evidence in this regard is the sculpture from his reign – which while being largely used for propaganda or promotional material still provides an important source of information for the present study.

Sculptural Evidence

The primary aim of this section is to examine the sculptural propaganda produced by Commodus Antoninus to promote his principate.[540] These pieces would have seemingly been crafted in order to advertise the ideals of the young *princeps* in accordance with what he saw as being politically (or perhaps socially? personally?) important. This ties in well with the analysis of both his public and private architecture – all three elements were physical manifestations of Commodus Antoninus and his principate. As far as the sculptures are concerned it is important to point out that the study of Hekster (2002) is

---

[540] See R. Hannah, "The Emperor's Stars", *AJA* 90.3, 1986, pp. 337-42.

far more comprehensive than the present study. All the same, the current work has taken a broader approach to the available ancient evidence. For present purposes there are only three sculptures dealt with here specifically, but each has been chosen because they epitomise the principate of Commodus. All the same, initially some consideration has been given towards a wider perspective of the sculptural evidence of the *princeps*, but this has focused more upon the locations in which such representations have been discovered throughout the Mediterranean.

When considering this form of ancient evidence the style of representation is of course a vital point of consideration, but the location of these pieces is also of great importance as a point of consideration. In this regard the study of Hojte (2005) is of some assistance – it provides details about numerous statues dedicated to Commodus throughout the Empire over an extended period of time. Unfortunately, however, much of the archaeological evidence from Rome relating to Commodus has been lost, but this is largely owing to the process of *damnatio memoriae* following the reign of Commodus Antoninus. All the same, judging from the examples provided by Hojte (2005) it is evident that this was not a universally applied policy (considering there were many erected after his death up until AD 211).[541] This may have of course been a result of time in which it took to construct such monuments,[542] but it appears unlikely that this would have been a serious factor if the number of years is considered – sometimes being almost two decades in some instances.[543] Nevertheless, it is simply important to note that the sculptural commemorations of Commodus were distributed throughout the Roman Empire, and this exhibits how well received he was in the provinces over an extended period of time. It is at this point that the style of representation needs to be considered in this regard.

---

[541] Hojte 2005, *op.cit.*

[542] See Adams 2011, *op.cit.* for discussion of how this could impact upon modern readings of sculptures.

[543] Hojte 2005, *op.cit.*

Figure 10 – Commodus Antoninus (author's photograph)

This sculpture represents several aspects of Commodus' reign. Firstly, it is important to note the traditional nature of this sculpture. While some more 'extreme' or at least unique representations of him have been focused upon (and interpreted) by Hekster (2002), it is also vital to note the existence of such traditional portraiture. Secondly, it is also essential to note his portrayal in military garb. This was of course not an uncommon imperial representation, with similar approaches being applied to other *principes*, such as Augustus, Tiberius, and Hadrian to name a few. All the same, whether this was meant to be a symbolic representation of his power and leadership or a presentation of his capacity as a general remains a point of discussion and probable argument. This question has been dealt with in more detail in Chapter Seven.

Figure 11 – Commodus Antoninus (author's photograph)

Figure 12 – Antoninus Pius
(Palazzo Massimo Museum, author's photograph)

**Figure 13 – Marcus Aurelius
(Palazzo Altemps Museum, author's photograph)**

With Figure 10, which is located in the Vatican Museum, it is also possible to examine the portrayal of Commodus Antoninus within a stereotypical imperial context. This style of depiction clearly links him within the overall style of Second Century AD aristocratic portraiture. This form of representation was, in all likelihood, intended to present an image of power and dominance within the Roman State.[544] This was clearly constantly in keeping with the propagandistic tendencies of most Roman *principes*. All the same, both Figures 10 and 11 overtly place Commodus stylistically within the preexisting Antonine traditional form of imperial representation.[545] The presentation of a *princeps* with short, curled hair and a beard had been fashionable for a *princeps* (and probably most other of their social peers) since the time of the Emperor Hadrian. The continuation of

---

[544] Kleiner 1992, *op.cit.*; Strong 1961, *op.cit.*
[545] See A. Kalinowski, "The Vedii Antonini", *Phoenix* 56, 2002, p. 144.

this can be seen in the above sculptures of Antoninus Pius and Marcus Aurelius (Figs. 12, 13). Commodus is shown here (Fig. 11) as both a continuation from these previous *principes*, but also as an extension of their success.

**Figure 14 – Commodus Antoninus as Hercules
(Capitoline Museum, author's photograph)**

The above sculpture (Fig. 14) is easily one of the most famous sculptural portraits of Commodus Antoninus. This is a magnificent piece, which was clearly both a very expensive item and one that was also closely considered in its iconography. One of the most notable aspects is the separation of the lion's head from that of Commodus' head. This was seemingly in order to maintain little question about not only who was being represented, but also the stylistic Antonine heritage of the *princeps*. This piece was clearly one of great significance – the religious iconography is the most apparent, but this has been dealt with in Chapter Six. All the same, for the purposes of the present discussion it is important to note that this sculpture is also representative of Commodus' personal (religious? iconographic?) tastes and yet also his social (or economic) dominance. In this regard it is evidently in line with the previous examples of his sculptural iconography in their propagandistic function.

Judging from these examples it is obvious to see three general trends. Firstly, it is important to note just how iconic these representations were. Each of them are rife with symbolic iconography that would have been easily understood by the general Roman audience. Secondly, all of these sculptures are clearly indicative of what propagandistic value was important to the young *princeps* – political and social dominance. Finally, with particular emphasis upon the comparison of all three examples used here it is possible to view the dualism of Commodus Antoninus' iconography – traditionalism within the Antonine style of portraiture (Figs. 12, 13) and yet a degree of innovation (or perhaps personality) at the same time (Fig. 14). This seems to epitomise his principate in many ways – variation to the known establishment, but only when it suited him. This is also visible when examining the numismatic iconography of his reign as well.

Numismatic Iconography

The analysis of any numismatic iconography can always be a rather fruitful realm of exploration by a modern scholar for an understanding of the Roman Empire. The distribution of State produced coinage enabled a *princeps* to clearly disseminate the key ideals or themes that were their priority at a particular point in time (assuming though that they sought such communication, which seems more than likely). While it has already been recognised that there was a great deal of repetition (or more likely traditionalism) in theme over the decades, as noted previously in Chapter Two, there were still different interpretations about what each *princeps* sought to accentuate. In addition to this it must also be acknowledged that the entire Roman Empire did not use exactly the same currency – there were different denominations (eastern, western) as well as different mints throughout the principate – thus communicating with different audiences. It was not a simple (or neglected) mode of imperial communication. Therefore, in order to keep this analysis relatively concise, several issues from both the Roman and Alexandrian mints have been discussed here in order to gain some understanding of a few of the numerous messages that Commodus sought to emphasise. While this is a selective approach, they have been chosen in order to give some insight into a general approach. It should be added that the primary focus here has been upon the imagery of the reverses (although the obverse sides are also occasionally discussed, but only to add to the interpretation of the reverses).

When considering the imagery of Commodus' imagery taken from the Roman mint from the issues under question there are several interesting points. One of the most telling aspects to be examined is how Commodus Antoninus continued to follow many of the numismatic traditions that had been established since the creation of the principate under Augustus (as previously discussed in Chapter Two).[546] As with his imperial predecessors he continued several of the dominant numismatic themes by associating himself with various deities (or concepts) such as *Roma*, *Liberalitas*, and *Pietas*.[547] In many regards this reflects the elements of how Commodus Antoninus sought to align himself with the recognised (and lauded) traditions of the Roman principate[548] – in this respect he was an imperial conformist.[549] All the same, he also sought to promote himself, sometimes by depicting himself on both sides of an issue (mind you this was not previously unheard of). In addition to this he also sought to promote the imperial *familia*, such as with the issue representing Crispina (his wife) and the god of abundance, Ceres. The primary aim, however, still seems to have been largely focused upon conformity through self promotion.[550]

The coins distributed from (and produced in) the Alexandrian mint present similar and yet dissimilar types of imagery. The style in which Commodus Antoninus is represented upon the obverse is largely reminiscent to that of the Roman issues, and as with these Alexandrian productions there are also various issues where Commodus is depicted upon both the obverse and the reverse. The most obvious difference, however, is how the legend is presented in Greek (as compared to Latin), but this is to be expected owing to the intended audience within their predominant distribution patterns – namely the Greek speaking eastern provinces in this regard. The

---

[546] See C.H.V. Sutherland, "Roman Coinage from Antoninus to Commodus [Review]", *CR* 55.2, 1941, p. 95.

[547] See C. Howgego, "The Supply and Use of Money in the Roman World", *JRS* 82, 1992, pp. 29-30.

[548] See H. Elton, "Commodus: an Emperor at the Crossroads [Review]", *JRS* 93, 2003, p. 397.

[549] See A. Meadows and J. Williams, "Moneta and the Monuments", *JRS* 91, 2001, p. 49.

[550] See A. Wallace-Hadrill, "The Emperor and his Virtues", *Historia* 30.3, 1981, p. 311.

placement of his mint should also be of little great surprise – as *princeps* Commodus theoretically maintained direct control over Egypt as a province, thus making it a secure region for grain production (as well as an easy and protected distribution point for the minting of coins in the eastern provinces). The iconography should also come as of little surprise in its Greek (or at least eastern) orientation, such as in the depiction of the Nile, Zeus Ammon, Selene, and Tyche. All the same, this simply shows how considered such imagery was – the intended audience was the primary factor behind such propagandistic pieces – or at least as long as they conformed with the views of the issuer, or in this instance Commodus Antoninus.

So, therefore, it is evident that this form of ancient evidence needs to be considered along a few different lines within themselves, but also in conjunction with the literary tradition. Firstly, it is evident that there were a variety of media and denominations produced by the various mints of Commodus. This illustrates how each issue was intended to communicate to a different range of the Roman populations within both Rome and in the provinces. Secondly, while there was some consistency in these numismatic representations there also seems to have been some flexibility in the choice of imperial iconography. This would suggest that some thought was given to its production within the majority of these divergent issues (in all likelihood there were numerous 'stock standard' productions as well). This naturally adds to the importance of their propaganda value for Commodus Antoninus (and their subsequent modern interpretation).[551] All the same, while the iconography is essential to note for the present study, the state of the economy under Commodus is another vital aspect that requires further consideration.

The Economy

The numismatic evidence provides an important source of information for not only an understanding of the financial management of the Roman State during Commodus Antoninus' reign (or mismanagement according to the ancient literary sources). Nevertheless, it is evident that the numismatic evidence also provides a good source of information about the financial circumstances during his reign.

---

[551] See D.C.A. Shotter, "The Principate of Nerva", *Historia* 32.2, 1983, p.226.

According to the *HA* biographer, Commodus inherited a large financial surplus from Marcus Aurelius, but that through his financial mismanagement this did not last long into his reign:

ipse Commodus in subscribendo tardus et neglegens, ita ut libellis una forma multis subscriberet, in epistulis autem plurimis 'Vale' tantum scriberet. agebanturque omnia per alios, qui etiam condemnationes in sinum vertisse dicuntur. per hanc autem neglegentiam, cum et annonam vastarent ii qui tunc rem publicam gerebant, etiam inopia ingens Romae exorta est, cum fruges non deessent. et eos quidem qui omnia vastabant postea Commodus occidit atque proscripsit. ipse vero saeculum aureum Commodianum nomina adsimulans vilitatem proposuit, ex qua maiorem penuriam fecit.

'Commodus himself was so lazy and careless in signing documents that he answered many petitions with the same formula, while in very many letters he merely wrote the word "Farewell". All official business was carried on by others, who, it is said, even used condemnations to swell their purses. And because he was so careless, moreover, a great famine arose in Rome, not because there was any real shortage of crops, but merely because those who then ruled the state were plundering the food supply. As for those who plundered on every hand, Commodus afterwards put them to death and confiscated their property; but for the time he pretended that a golden age had come, "Commodian" by name, and ordered a general reduction of prices, the result of which was an even greater scarcity.' (*HA Commodus* 13.7-14.3)

Congiarium dedit populo singulis denarios septingenos vicenos quinos. circa alios omnes parcissimus fuit, quod luxuriae sumptibus aerarium minuerat. circenses multos addidit ex libidine potius quam religione et ut dominos factionum ditaret.

'He gave largess to the people, 725 denarii to each man. Toward all others he was close-fisted to a degree, since the expense of his luxurious living had drained the treasury. He held many races in the Circus, but rather as the result of a whim than as an act of religion, and also in order to enrich the leaders of the factions.' (*HA Commodus* 16.8-9)

This emphasis upon Commodus' financial irresponsibility is a consistent theme within the ancient sources, with the young emperor's financial needs usually being used to explain his inappropriate actions and numerous unjustified executions. All the same, judging from the numismatic evidence,[552] this does not appear to have been representative of the monetary system under Commodus Antoninus'. In order to establish this, the various weights of several issues (*aurei, denarii*, and *sestertii*) of his coinage have been calculated in order to establish if there was any depreciation in their values during his reign. These particular issues have been chosen because of either their inherent value (*aurei, denarii*) or because of their standardised use

---

[552] See A. Wilson, "Machines, Power and the Ancient Economy", *JRS* 92, 2002, p. 28.

within Roman commerce (*denarii, sestertii*). This has been calculated to establish the continuity (or discontinuity) of the inherent quality (i.e. the content of precious metals) of his coinage. In turn these results have also been compared with the same issues of Marcus Aurelius (AD 169-175) and the joint principate in order to establish the continuity of numismatic quality across these periods. The various weights have been taken from those issues mentioned in *Coins of the Roman Empire in the British Museum* Volume IV by Harold Mattingly, which provides not only a large corpus of material but also a thorough account of the particular details for each issue. These weights under discussion are measured in grams, which has been applied to all coins under discussion. These results have been exhibited in a number of scatter charts (Charts 1-15) that clearly exhibit the trends exhibited by each denomination.

All the same, it must first be recognised that one of Commodus' most important fiscal innovations was the expansion of the *pomerium* ('city limits') of Rome.[553] It has been argued that this was ordered by Commodus in order to increase the taxable regions of the capital.[554] While the ancient literary sources have interpreted this action in a critical light (accusing Commodus of corruption and fiscal irresponsibility), it must also be noted that the general *pomerium* of the city had gradually expanded over the previous centuries, such as by Caesar,[555] Claudius,[556] and Vespasian[557] previously. So, therefore, the expansion of these symbolic (or in this instance taxable) urban limits seems to be more indicative of social and fiscal responsibility in fact – representing the recognition of the ever increasing pressures and requirements of the growing *urbs*. This not only draws into question the highly critical nature of the ancient literary sources, but it also emphasises the necessity of examining the consistency of the various coin weights between the periods from AD 169-192.

---

[553] See Richardson 1992, *op.cit.*
[554] See Platner 1926, *op.cit.*
[555] Dio 43.50.
[556] Tacitus *Annals* 12.23-24.
[557] *ILS* 248.

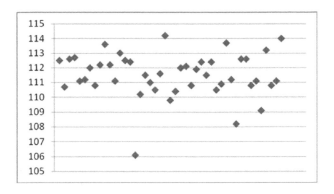

Chart 1 – Weights of the *Aureus* Issues under Commodus

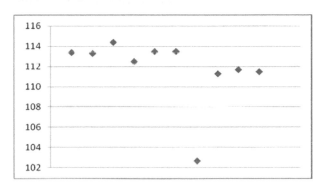

Chart 2 – Weights of the *Aureus* Issues under Marcus Aurelius

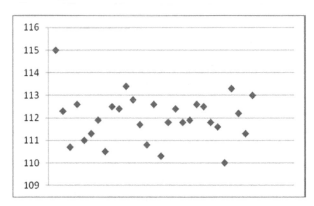

Chart 3 – Weights of the *Aureus* Issues under the Joint Principate

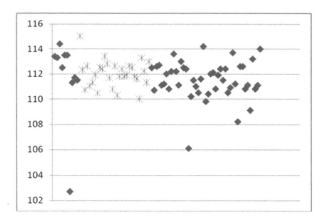

Chart 4 – Weights of All *Aureus* Issues under Question

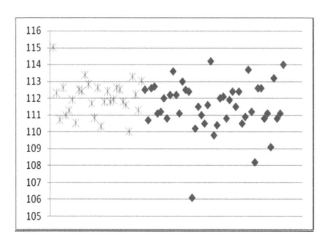

Chart 5 – Weights of All *Aureus* Issues under the Joint Principate and Commodus' Sole Reign

When the results are taken from Commodus' *aurei* and they are examined (Chart 1), it initially seems that the weights, and therefore the quality as well, of his issues are quite erratic. There is a large amount of variation between approximately 106 to over 144 grams, which may suggest a degree of instability in the production of this issue. Nevertheless, these results do not correspond with the general theme of the literary sources because there is no indication of severe depreciation. The average weight for these issues is 111.53, which is highlighted by the majority of these issues being placed within the 111 to 113 gram range. The consistency of Commodus' *aurei* is also highlighted by the comparative variation in Marcus Aurelius' issues of the same denomination (Chart 2), which largely ranged from 111 to 114 grams. All the same, Marcus' average weight for his *aurei* was 111.78, being slightly higher than Commodus' average of 111.53. Yet the average result for the *aurei* from the joint principate (Chart 3) has been calculated at 112 grams, which suggests that there had already been some inconsistency in the weight for the *aureus* across all three periods (Chart 4).[558] These results clearly suggest that the financial mismanagement that is associated with Caligula's reign did not result in the depreciation of his coinage, highlighting that his administration may not have been as incompetent as the sources would have us believe. Chart 5 illustrates how although the weights of *aurei* under Commodus Antoninus were more erratic, the majority of issues remained quite consistent in general, having most results continuing a general (albeit slight) trend of depreciation since AD 169.

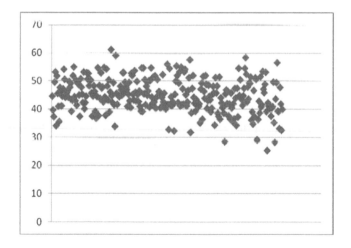

Chart 6 – Weights of the *Denarius* Issues under Commodus

---

[558] The *aureus* issues of the joint principate are denoted by 'X' marks in Charts 4, 5, 9, 10, 14 and 15 whereas those of Marcus Aurelius and Commodus are shown as diamonds.

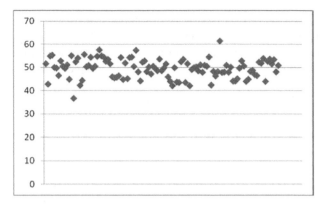

Chart 7 – Weights of the *Denarius* Issues under Marcus Aurelius

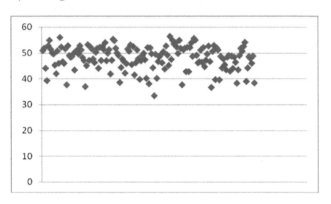

Chart 8 – Weights of the *Denarius* Issues under the Joint Principate

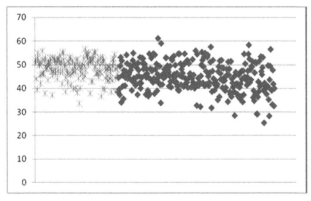

Chart 9 – Weights of the *Denarius* Issues under the Joint Principate and Commodus' Sole Reign

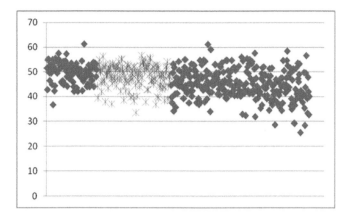

Chart 10 – Weights of All *Denarius* Issues under Question

The *denarii* issued by Commodus Antoninus exhibit a strong sense of consistency (and yet some depreciation over time) in their weights (Chart 6). They mostly range within the 30-60 gram range. When this is compared with the *denarii* issues of Marcus Aurelius (Chart 7) and the joint principate (Chart 8), there is a similar level of consistency throughout all three periods, with all of them gradually depreciating to a slightly lower weight (Charts 9 and 10). The vast majority of all of these *denarii* issues have ranged between the 35-55 gram ranges, which clearly exhibits the consistency in these issues across the time period (Chart 10). So while Commodus has been attributed with large scale fiscal irresponsibility by the ancient literary sources it is also evident that this trend of economic depreciation had existed long before AD 180 and his sole principate.

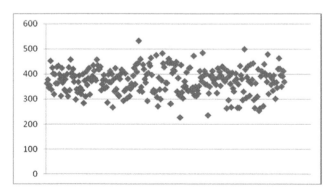

Chart 11 – Weights of the *Sestertius* Issues under Commodus

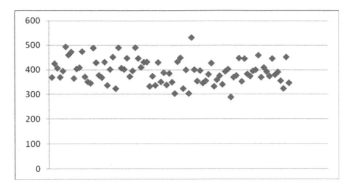

Chart 12 – Weights of the *Sestertius* Issues under Marcus Aurelius

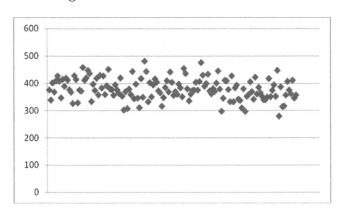

Chart 13 – Weights of the *Sestertius* Issues under the Joint Principate

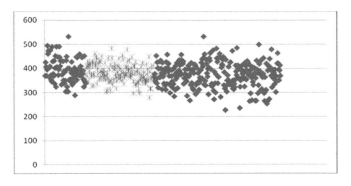

Chart 14 – Weights of All *Sestertius* Issues under Question

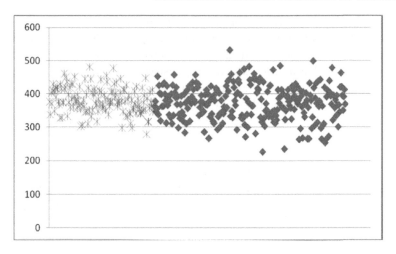

Chart 15 – Weights of *Sestertius* Issues under the Joint Principate and Commodus' Sole Reign

These consistent results are comparable with the weights of the *sestertii*, which are varied but relatively stable. The *sestertius* was a common and standardised commercial device, which justifies its inclusion within this form of analysis. The *sestertii* weights of Commodus Antoninus largely range from 350 to 500 grams (Chart 11), having an average weight of 373.2 grams. This average result is comparable to the issues of Marcus Aurelius, which had an average of 393.59 grams and ranged from 300 to 500 grams (Chart 12). Commodus' *sestertii* had a lower overall average, suggesting that he had a greater use for these issues than his predecessor, which is also suggested by the high number that he struck during his reign. This was probably owing to the necessity to strike such issues for the payment of the military (including the Praetorians). The *sestertii* issues of the joint principate had a consistent (and yet gradually declining) range of weights than those of Marcus Aurelius (Chart 13), and had an average weight of 380.23 grams. When compared with the issues of Marcus Aurelius and Commodus, it is quite clear that the *sestertius* denomination of the son was noticeably consistent in its weight (Chart 14) and conformed to the evident standard depreciation that had existed since AD 169. This would further the suggestion that the *sestertius* was particularly important to Commodus, probably because of its use for military pay (which necessitated a stable currency) as well as its high circulation rate, thus allowing him to spread his imperial propaganda to a wider audience. Chart 15 illustrates how while the majority of issues remained relatively consistent in their weights over time, there was a clear gradual decline from AD 169-192. The Roman economy appears to have been in decline long before the sole principate of Commodus Antoninus, which emphasises the extreme (and unjustified) negativity of the ancient literary sources towards him in this regard. Whether he could have prevented such fiscal decline is of course an entirely hypothetical discussion that is beyond the scope of the present discussion.

Overall, both the numismatic evidence and sculptural imagery give a clear indication of Commodus' priorities in regard to his official public image. The fiscal stability that he clearly sought to maintain was intended to secure the allegiances of his prime support base: the military. If the monetary system was destabilised, it had the potential to cause disruption among *his* military forces, which could have made his position untenable (particularly owing to the disintegration of his relationship with the Senate). All the same, the present analysis has shown that while these issues depreciated during the reign of Commodus, this had been a general trend since AD 169 (and had also occurring since the early First Century AD).[559] This also clearly depicts how the ancient literary sources cannot be taken at face value. Therefore, in general terms this overtly correlates with the overall theme of the present study – while Commodus was not an ideal *princeps* for a variety of reasons, he was also not as bad as how the ancient literary sources would have us believe.

Conclusions

One of the primary themes that have been focused upon throughout this chapter is that of Commodus Antoninus' corruption. This textual characterisation of him was a central element of the ancient literary sources, epitomising their highly negative appraisal of him. The accusations levelled against him were both numerous and varied in nature. Financial, judicial, administrative and personal details (or general policies) were all provided as prime examples of his corruption. The primary reason for such anecdotes and literary references was to discredit Commodus' legitimacy (or at least suitability) for the principate. Whether these accusations are entirely reliable is certainly questionable once the general theme of the authors is considered, but conversely they also cannot be completely ignored. Undoubtedly

---

[559] See P. Temin, "A Market Economy in the Early Roman Empire", *JRS* 91, 2001, p. 180.

these indictments have subsequently raised serious concerns about his principate, which has ultimately coloured the following perceptions of him. Altogether this emphasises the necessity of examining other sources of ancient evidence in conjunction with the extant textual descriptions in order to evaluate this period as effectively as possible.

The physical (or archaeological) evidence considered here has examined both architectural (in public and domestic contexts) and sculptural forms of remains. When examining the public structures of Commodus Antoninus it is evident that he undertook several efforts (that we know of) to promote not only himself, but also his Antonine lineage (or even his legitimacy?) through such media. It is also clear, however, that these efforts on his part have subsequently suffered from the significant process of *damnatio memoriae* against him. The Villa of the Quintili (and subsequently that of Commodus) has also exhibited the personal tastes of the young emperor. While this is important, the manner of the acquisition of this valuable extra urban precinct also raises questions about his possible corruption. The statues discovered of him, especially the statue bases from throughout the Roman Empire, have exhibited not only the promotion of Commodus' principate (sometimes by people other than himself), but also the possible longevity of his popularity throughout the provinces. While it could be argued that this differentiates between those exposed (or removed) from his innate cruelty, it does also suggest that perhaps he was not as universally hated (or feared) at the time as the ancient literary sources would have us believe.[560]

The remaining evidence from the numismatic corpus has exhibited further information about not only the wider promotion of Commodus' principate throughout the Roman Empire, but also the nature of its economic standing from AD 180-192. The imagery used by Commodus Antoninus was clearly intended to communicate with the widest possible audience. It is also evident that the young emperor had a mutual interest in continuing both some Antonine traditions about numismatic imagery and yet he also sought to provide his own style of representation on his issues. All the same, the fiscal strength of his issues (within a difficult economic context) is even more telling. The analysis of the coin weights for the *aurei*, *denarii*, and *sestertii*

---

[560] For an opposing view see B.M. Levick, "Konsuln un Konsulare in der Zeit von Commodus bis Severus Alexander [Review]", *CR* 42.1, 1992, p. 117; Leunissen 1989, *op.cit.*

illustrate that over time there was clearly a sense of economic depreciation. Nevertheless, this process of fiscal decline had originated long before AD 180 (also continuing with various attempts to stabilise it after Commodus' principate) and the results from AD 180-192 do not exhibit anything other than the trend that had existed since AD 169. This questions the presented views of both financial indifference and excess on his part that is a fundamental feature of the ancient texts.

The question remains as to whether it is possible to gain a clear perspective about the reign of Commodus Antoninus. Well, it is certainly difficult, but there are several possible insights available to the modern interpreter. Firstly, it is important to note that this period (AD 180-192) was much more complex than the ancient literary sources would have us believe – Commodus was not just an 'evil' *princeps* who sought personal indulgence and cruelty – there were numerous challenging features within the Roman Empire that made the administration difficult. Secondly, owing to the economic findings from this period it is evident that Commodus was not solely responsible for the economic downturn that existed during the late Second/early Third Centuries AD. There had clearly been a gradual decline in fiscal stability (for a variety of reasons) long before AD 180, which simply continued under his reign. Finally, while he clearly behaved in a more autocratic fashion than suited the sensibilities of his social peers, it appears to be somewhat of a stretch to place him with the sole responsibility for Rome's decline at this point in time. It is therefore pertinent to now examine the prime reasons for why he was painted in such an autocratic fashion – namely his interests in religion (namely his devotion to Hercules and his own self promotion) and his gladiatorial interests.

CHAPTER 6

THE RELIGIOUS POLICIES AND GLADIATORIAL ACTIVITIES OF COMMODUS

Introduction

There are two primary intentions behind the inclusion of this chap
ter: firstly, to consider the importance of Hercules as a 'divine
influence' upon Commodus Antoninus and their resulting impact
upon his religious policies; and secondly, to examine his pronounced
interest and enthusiasm for spectacles and games with particular
emphasis being placed upon gladiatorial combat. It has been deemed
that these two aspects of Commodus' characterisation require
specific attention owing to their anecdotal prominence within the
ancient evidence, specially the early textual accounts. Thus these
three elements (Heracles, his divinity, games and spectacles), particularly in relation to Commodus' portrayed obsession with them have
been here as being representative of his depicted mania – in the case
of Heracles it is of course associated with his supposed aspirations
for personal deification. Whether such views are accurate or not has
been discussed further below, but it is certainly clear that there was
an exhibitionist element within the public persona of the young emperor at the very least. According to the ancient literary sources, this
seemingly progressed towards his personal excesses (rightly or
wrongly) and has been subsequently linked with not only his ultimate
demise but the final decline of the Roman State in general. Hence
why it was determined that such a discussion of these 'insane' aspects
required their own analysis for the purposes of the present study.[561]

The religious aspects of Commodus Antoninus' principate provide an excellent insight into the general social priorities of this
young Roman Emperor. It was common for most previous *principes*
to publically identify themselves with particular deities in order to
promote specific aspects of both themselves as leaders and the suc-

---

[561] Grosso 1964, *op.cit.*

cess of their reigns. It is of no great surprise that Jupiter was commonly represented (as the chief, leading imperial deity), but some Roman emperors actively promoted other (possible more personal) gods and goddesses, such as Augustus' connection with Apollo and Venus, whereas the Emperor Domitian had a particular preference for Minerva and Isis in addition to Jupiter.[562] For Commodus his favourite was seemingly Heracles. It is evident that he directly associated himself with this god, which has led to postulations about the possible godly aspirations on the part of Commodus. In turn this has resulted in subsequent accusations of both his insanity and megalomania by some writers – both ancient and modern alike. Therefore, it is pertinent to critically evaluate all of the available ancient evidence in order to determine whether this view has any viability. This is also vital to consider because of the insanity or megalomaniac question. It has already been established that the prevalence of the anti-Commodus literary tradition has had a significant impact upon his ensuing perception. This has in turn affected the way in which his general principate has been judged – so by analysing this question it should ultimately assist in developing the best perspective possible.

As with the devotion of Commodus Antoninus towards Heracles the young emperor has also been exhibited as being thoroughly addicted to the presentation (and participation within) various spectacles and games in Rome. The presentation of such events had of course been a common feature within Roman social and political life for centuries – it was a means of gaining for Roman leaders popularity within the guise of a religious celebration – but in this instance the ancient literary accounts make it clear that Commodus went to even greater lengths than his predecessors – he became actively involved as frequently as possible. This was naturally linked by them with accusations of fiscal and social irresponsibility on his part. The accentuation of him offering of such lavish spectacles by these authors emphasised his preference for gladiatorial shows, even suggesting that he himself was involved in some carefully staged bouts. The reliability of such accounts is of course highly questionable, and they must be carefully considered in turn. All the same, even the provision of such large scale and regular events still presents him as a character with definite tendencies towards a degree of exhibitionism. This of course would not have been welcomed by the more conservative elements within his social peer group.

---

[562] Adams 2005, *op.cit.*

Despite the present chapter being focused upon these relatively distinct features of Commodus Antoninus' reign these concepts are still intrinsically focused to the remainder of this analysis. Even aside from the religious associations between the topics under question, the primary focus here has been upon the way in such events and associations were displayed by Commodus,[563] which ties in intrinsically with their seemingly ostentatious character for such public declarations. So while the previous chapters have examined the logistical and functional nature of his principate in association with his rise in social and political prominence, this section has been focused more directly upon his public persona within the capital itself – particularly in association with such critical elements of his characterisation (Hercules, his divinity, and the games). These connections (especially with Hercules and gladiators) seemingly presented such a distraction for him that he completely ignored his imperial responsibilities and in turn this resulted in the decline of Roman supremacy on many levels (of course if the ancient authors are to be believed). This view is clearly somewhat simplistic. The complexity of Commodus' association cannot be underestimated, let alone connected to the general decline and fall of the Roman Empire. So, therefore, in order to gain a better understanding of the general religious circumstances at the time, Hercules as a deity (and his important to the *princeps*) have now been analysed – this will add to our understanding of this very public association.

The Importance of Heracles and his Significance to Commodus

As can be seen from the images of this deity (Figs. 15-18) the sculptural representations of Hercules were highly varied in their theme,[564] largely in accordance to which of the many myths that he was associated with in the Greco-Roman world. Typically the club (and sometimes the lion skin) was the primary identifying features (see Figs. 15, 16), but it is also clear that this was not always the case (see Figs. 17, 18). So it is initially notable to recognise the different aspects being represented in these examples (parental, respectable, drunken) – but

---

[563] Traupman 1956, *op.cit.*
[564] See C. Vermeule, "The Weary Herakles of Lysippos", *AJA* 79.4, 1975, p. 329.

Figure 15– Hercules (author's photograph)

Figure 16 – Hercules (Louvre, author's photograph)

Figure 17 – Hercules (Capitoline Museum, author's photograph)

this typifies how he was viewed as a character from the outset – a hero/deity of a wide range of aspects. It is evident that Hercules was a popular deity for the reason that he exhibited both strength and weakness at the same time – he provided lessons of actions to both follow and avoid. Hercules was of course most famous for his 'Twelve Tasks', but the mythology surrounding him went even further. His famous strength from an early age (Fig. 17) and his subsequent trials were built upon with a very complex array of various myths that sounded him – thus epitomising his popularity. All the same, this was balanced by various less reputable depictions of his rage, wantonness and drunkenness (see the *Alcestis* by Euripides) (Fig. 18), which provided a serious counterweight to the other side of his characterisations – and yet makes the figure of him in such tales even more compelling.

**Figure 18 – The Drunken Hercules
(Herculaneum, author's photograph)**

The popularity of Hercules as a mythological figure did not diminish at all during the Roman period. This is epitomised by the previous Figures (17, 18), which exhibit a clear appreciation for this divinity. As a mythological figure during this time he was clearly venerated in Rome, as mentioned by Dionysius of Halicarnassus (7.72.13-14). There were several sacred sites dedicated to him throughout the capital, with one of the most prominent being the Temple of Hercules Victor (Fig. 19), which clearly embodies his veneration throughout the community. He was also a prominent figure with the cults that dealt with the afterlife, which largely resulted from his mythological transition from being a mortal to an immortal. This is most effectively represented on several Roman sarcophagi, such as Figure 20, which is a Third Century AD example of the glorification of his famous twelve labours.

Figure 19 – Temple of Hercules Victor (Rome, author's photograph)

Figure 20 – Sarcophagus Frieze of Hercules
(Palazzo Altemps Museum, author's photograph)

The ancient literary sources provide an almost manic devotion by Commodus Antoninus towards Hercules. Many of these accounts not only focus upon his identification with Hercules but also the question of his personal aspirations towards divinity,[565] which have dealt with in the next section. All the same, for the purposes of the present discussion two passages from the *Historia Augusta* have been included for analysis (*HA Commodus* 8.5; 10.9):

appellatus est etiam Romanus Hercules, quod feras Lanuvii in amphitheatro occidisset. erat enim haec illi consuetudo, ut domi bestias interficeret.

---

[565] Traupman 1956, *op.cit.*, p. 54.

'He was called also the Roman Hercules, on the ground that he had killed wild beasts in the amphitheatre the Lanuvium; and, indeed, it was his custom to kill wild beasts on his own estate.' (*HA Commodus* 8.5)

habuit et hominem pene prominente ultra modum animalium, quem Onon appellabat, sibi carissimum. quem et ditavit et sacerdotio Herculis rustici praeposuit.

'He also had in his company a man with a male member larger than that of most animals, whom he called Onos. This man he treated with great affection, and even made him rich and appointed him to the priesthood of the Rural Hercules.' (*HA Commodus* 10.9)

These two extracts clearly exhibit different themes in this regard. Section 8.5 presents Commodus Antoninus in the guise of a Roman Hercules, possessing an almost fanatical appreciation of the deity. His identification with Hercules is a common theme in the ancient literary corpus and is typically presented in a negative guise. The second passage (*HA Commodus* 10.9) shows this perfectly, presenting Commodus as being entirely disrespectable through the appointment of 'Onus' as a priest of the Rural Hercules. These extracts are only two of many references towards Commodus' fascination (or his possible identification) with Hercules, which have been analysed in the next section of this chapter that deals with the divinity question. All the same, this connection between Commodus and Hercules is also represented in the sculptural evidence as well, as noted previously.

This image is the most famous sculptural representation of Commodus in the guise of Hercules, currently in the Capitoline Museum in Rome. This fine piece evidently confirms the devotion of Commodus Antoninus towards Hercules as described by the ancient authors, but this does not confirm his divine aspirations. While this could be interpreted as being suggestive of his desire to be viewed as a god (see the further discussion below), it could also be interpreted as simply a singular devotion to a particular deity. As mentioned previously, it was not unusual for a Roman *principes* to have a 'favourite' deity that they revered in particular, and it must be noted that Commodus did not promote Hercules to the exclusion of all other gods or goddesses – this can be seen in his chosen numismatic iconography. So while Figure 14 does epitomise a very strong devotion on the part of Commodus towards Hercules, the extreme characterisations of the ancient literary sources (with their inherent anti-Commodus biases having already been recognised) should not be allowed to significantly colour our interpretation of this level of religious respect. All the same, it is also evident that he did not only represent himself in the guise of a deity – the portrayal of Faustina II (his mother) with Marcus Aurelius (his father) as Venus and Mars respectively (Fig. 21),[566] which is currently in the Vatican Museum, provides an excellent example. This sculpture has to be dated to the period of Commodus' sole principate and exhibits the identification of the imperial *familia* in such religious fashions. He was descended from deities, so perhaps his identification with a hero who became an immortal was something that he viewed as being entirely appropriate (and within his prestigious birthright). Commodus was clearly a figure of extremes, but this does not necessarily equal religious mania.[567] All the same, the other sources of ancient media need to be considered for a fuller examination of this topic.

Figure 21 – Faustina II and Marcus Aurelius as Venus and Mars (author's photograph)

---

[566] See K. Scott, "The Significance of Statues in Precious Metals in Emperor Worship", *TAPA* 62, 1931, p. 120.
[567] Grosso 1964, *op.cit.*

In this sense, the contemporaneous numismatic evidence is a useful source of comparative information. If Commodus Antoninus had a singular (or possibly manic?) obsession with the god Hercules it would have certainly been evident within his coinage – a medium by which he could have promoted such a personal devotion. There are several representations of Heracles on the coinage of Commodus (*RIC Commodus* 259, 365, 399b, 641 for example) and each of these represents him in a variety of forms and associations. It is, however, initially important to note that the numismatic portrayal of Hercules extends throughout the reign of Commodus, which establishes his continued promotion.[568] All the same, towards the latter stages of his principate Commodus was often associated with the inscription of the 'Roman Hercules' (*RIC Commodus* 221, 253, 254b, 637, 639, 640, 643, 644 for example). While this could be connected with a direct Commodus and Hercules identification (as the early literature would have us believe), it should still be treated with caution. It is evident that Hercules was used as a symbol on his coinage by Commodus more than his Antonine predecessors, but, as previously stated, this exhibits a personal preference at the very least.[569] It cannot be construed to his divine aspirations. In this regard it should be noted that both the Emperors Trajan (*RIC Trajan* 37, 45, 50, and 689) and Hadrian (*RIC Hadrian* 56, 148d, 149c, 156) also frequently represented Hercules on their coinage. In many ways it was the public way in which Commodus directly associated himself with Hercules that caused comment at the time, which was naturally accentuated by the anti-Commodus disposed perspectives of the ancient literary sources.

The association between Commodus Antoninus and the god Heracles is truly fascinating. The dedication of this Roman emperor towards the deity is indisputable, a fact which is exhibited in the literary, sculptural and numismatic sources of ancient evidence. All the same, the question remains about whether this devotion should be viewed in as such a negative fashion as the ancient authors would have us believe. As mentioned previously, it was not unusual for Roman individuals to have a particular preference for specific deities (Apollo with both Apollo and Venus; Domitian with Minerva and Isis as clear examples), so in this regard Commodus Antoninus was hardly a singular case. It was the extreme fashion in which he expressed his devotion that seemingly became more of an issue, which

---

[568] Traupman 1956, *op.cit.*
[569] Grosso 1964, *op.cit.*

was willingly accentuated by his detractors. If Commodus had publically pretended to be Hercules it would have clearly been a remarkable occurrence. All the same, we only have literary anecdotes for this having occurred – thus, being naturally suspicious is to be warranted. It is important to not simply take such descriptions at face value, especially in view of the dominant anti-Commodus textual tradition. The extremity of these descriptions makes them notable and accessible, but a critical reading of them is essential. This is particularly important because the Hercules references made in relation to Commodus are often connected to accusations of his aspirations for divinity at the same time, which must also be considered at this point of the study.

The Question of Commodus and his Divinity

As discussed in the previous section, some of Commodus Antoninus' behaviour has clearly shown an extreme interpretation of religious devotion (whether through sculptural representation or through the literary accounts), which was viewed in a dismissive fashion by the ancient authors. The association between Commodus and Hercules in turn was augmented by textual allegations that he sought to be viewed as a god in his own right. This is a common accusation by the ancient historians and biographers against those *principes* who were judged to be somewhat autocratic. If the ancient literary accounts are to be believed, another possible interpretation could simply be that his desire to 'play' at being Hercules may have been more about an attention seeking impulse on the part of the emperor. All the same, it is more important to view this in a critical light. Caligula,[570] Nero,[571] and Domitian[572] were all criticised for their divine aspirations.[573] If Commodus Antoninus did possess such sentiments his identification with Hercules would have been a natural fit (a mortal who became immortal).[574] Nevertheless, the ancient literary evidence must first be considered prior to any conclusions being drawn.

---

[570] Dio 59.26.7.
[571] Dio 63.20.5.
[572] Martial *Epigrams*, 9.64.
[573] Grosso 1964, *op.cit.*
[574] Traupman 1956, *op.cit.*, p. 54.

ἐς τοσοῦτόν τε μανίας καὶ παροινίας προὐχώρησεν, ὡς πρῶτον μὲν τὴν πατρῴαν προσηγορίαν παραιτήσασθαι, ἀντὶ δὲ Κομόδου καὶ Μάρκου υἱοῦ Ἡρακλέα τε καὶ Διὸς υἱὸν αὐτὸν κελεύσας καλεῖσθαι ἀποδυσάμενός τε τὸ Ῥωμαίων καὶ βασίλειον σχῆμα λεοντῆν ἐπεστρώννυτο καὶ ῥόπαλον μετὰ χεῖρας ἔφερεν· ἀμφιέννυτό τε ἁλουργεῖς καὶ χρυσουφεῖς ἐσθῆτας, ὡς εἶναι καταγέλαστον αὐτὸν ὑφ᾿ ἑνὶ σχήματι καὶ θηλειῶν πολυτέλειαν καὶ ἡρώων ἰσχὺν μιμούμενον. τοιοῦτος μὲν δὴ προιὼν ἐφαίνετο, ἤλλαξε δὲ καὶ τῶν ἐνιαυσίων μηνῶν τὰ ὀνόματα, ὅσα μὲν ἀρχαῖα καταλύσας, πάντας δὲ ταῖς ἑαυτοῦ προσηγορίαις ὀνομάσας, ὧν αἱ πλεῖσται ἐς Ἡρακλέα δῆθεν ὡς ἀνδρειότατον ἀνεφέροντο. ἔστησε δὲ καὶ ἀνδριάντας αὐτοῦ κατὰ πᾶσαν τὴν πόλιν, ἀλλὰ μὴν καὶ ἀντικρὺ τοῦ τῆς συγκλήτου συνεδρίου τόξον διηγκυλημένον· ἐβούλετο γὰρ δὴ καὶ τὰς εἰκόνας αὐτῷ φόβον ἀπειλεῖν.

'First he discarded his family name and issued orders that he was to be called not Commodus, son of Marcus, but Hercules, son of Zeus. Abandoning the Roman and imperial mode of dress, he donned the lion skin, and carried the club of Hercules. He wore purple robes embroidered with gold, making himself an object of ridicule by combining in one set of garments the frailty of a woman and the might of a superman. This was the way he looked in his public appearances. He assigned new names to the months of the year; abolishing the old ones, he called the months after his own list of names and titles, most of which actually referred to Hercules as the manliest of men. He erected statues of himself throughout the city, but opposite the senate house he set up a special statue representing the emperor as an archer poised to shoot, for he wished even his statues to inspire fear of him.' (Herodian 1.14.8-9)

ἔδει δὲ ἄρα ποτὲ κἀκεῖνον παύσασθαι μεμηνότα καὶ τὴν Ῥωμαίων ἀρχὴν τυραννουμένην. νέου μὲν γὰρ ἔτους τῆς εἰσιούσης ἔμελλεν ἡμέρας <.... ἐκείνης γὰρ τῆς ἡμέρας> σέβουσι [τε] τὴν ἑορτὴν Ῥωμαῖοι ἐς θεὸν ἀρχαιότατον τῆς Ἰταλίας ἐπιχώριον ἀναφέροντες. φασὶ γὰρ αὐτοῦ καὶ Κρόνον ὑπὸ Διὸς ἐκβληθέντα τῆς ἀρχῆς κατελθόντα ἐς γῆν γενέσθαι ξένον, δεδιότα δὲ τὴν τοῦ παιδὸς δυναστείαν παρ᾿ αὐτῷ κρυπτόμενον λαθεῖν· ὅθεν καὶ τὸ ὄνομα δοθῆναι τῷ χώρῳ τῆς Ἰταλίας Λάτιόν τε κληθῆναι, ἀπὸ τῆς Ἑλλάδος φωνῆς ἐς τὴν ἐπιχώριον παραχθέν. διὰ ταῦτά τοι καὶ μέχρι νῦν Ἰταλιῶται τὰ μὲν Κρόνια προεορτάζουσι θεῷ τῷ λαθόντι, τὴν δὲ τοῦ ἔτους ἀρχὴν ἱερομηνίαν ἄγουσι τῷ τῆς Ἰταλίας θεῷ. διπρόσωπον δὲ αὐτοῦ τὸ ἄγαλμα ἵδρυται, ἐπειδὴ ἐς αὐτὸν ὁ ἐνιαυτὸς ἄρχεταί τε καὶ παύεται. ταύτης δὲ τῆς ἑορτῆς προσιούσης, ἐν ᾗ μάλιστα Ῥωμαῖοι δεξιοῦνταί τε ἀλλήλους καὶ προσαγορεύουσι νομισμάτων τε ἀντιδόσεσι καὶ κοινωνίᾳ τῶν γῆς καὶ θαλάσσης καλῶν εὐφραίνουσιν αὐτούς· ἀρχαί τε ἐπώνυμοι τότε πρῶτον τὴν ἔνδοξον καὶ ἐνιαύσιον πορφύραν περιτίθενται, πάντων ἑορταζόντων ὁ Κόμοδος ἐβούλετο οὐκ ἐκ τῆς βασιλείου, ὡς ἔθος, προελθεῖν οἰκίας, ἀλλ᾿ ἐκ τοῦ τῶν μονομάχων καταγωγίου, ἀντὶ δὲ τῆς εὐπαρύφου καὶ βασιλικῆς πορφύρας ὅπλα τε αὐτὸς φέρων καὶ συμπροιόντων τῶν λοιπῶν μονομάχων ὀφθῆναι τοῖς Ῥωμαίοις. ἐπεὶ δὲ τὴν γνώμην αὐτοῦ ταύτην ἀνήνεγκε πρὸς Μαρκίαν, ἣν εἶχε τῶν παλλακίδων τιμιωτάτην, καὶ οὐδέν τι ἀπεῖχε γαμετῆς γυναικός, ἀλλὰ πάντα ὑπῆρχεν ὅσα Σεβαστῇ πλὴν τοῦ πυρός, [ἣ] μαθοῦσα τὴν παράλογον οὕτω καὶ ἀπρεπῆ βούλησιν αὐτοῦ τὰ πρῶτα ἐλιπάρει καὶ προσπίπτουσα μετὰ δακρύων ἐδεῖτο μήτε τὴν Ῥωμαίων ἀρχὴν καθυβρίσαι μηθ᾿ ἑαυτὸν ἐπιδόντα μονομάχοις καὶ ἀπεγνωσμένοις ἀνθρώποις κινδυνεῦσαι. ἐπεὶ δὲ πολλὰ ἱκετεύουσα οὐκ ἐτύγχανεν αὐτοῦ, ἡ μὲν δακρύουσα ἀπέστη, ὁ δὲ Κόμοδος μεταπεμψάμενος Λαῖτόν τε τὸν ἔπαρχον τῶν στρατοπέδων

Ἐκλεκτόν τε τὸν τοῦ θαλάμου προεστῶτα ἐκέλευεν αὐτῷ <πάντα> παρασκευασθῆναι ὡς διανυκτερεύσων ἐν τῷ τῶν μονομάχων καταγωγίῳ κἀκεῖθεν προελευσόμενος ἐπὶ τὰς θυσίας τῆς ἱερομηνίας, ὡς Ῥωμαίοις ἔνοπλος ὀφθείη. οἱ δὲ ἱκέτευον καὶ πείθειν ἐπειρῶντο μηδὲν ἀνάξιον τῆς βασιλείας ποιεῖν.

'But the time had finally come for Commodus to cease his mad antics and for the Roman empire to be rid of this tyrant. This occurred on the first day of the New Year, when the Romans celebrate the festival which they trace back to the most ancient of the Italic native gods. They believe that Saturn, ousted from his realm by Jupiter, came down to earth and was the guest of Janus. Fearful of his son's power, he escaped when Janus hid him. This episode gave the region of Latium its name, which is derived from the Greek word *lathein*, "to escape notice." For this reason the Italians continue to celebrate the Saturnalia down to the present time, to commemorate the sheltering of the god, and they observe at the beginning of the year the festival of the Italic god Janus. The statues of Janus have two faces because the year begins and ends with him. On the day of this festival the Romans go out of their way to greet each other and exchange gifts. On this day, too, they dine together gaily on the delicacies of land and sea. This is also the day on which the consuls who give their names to the year first don the purple robes of office for their one-year term. When all were occupied in the celebration, Commodus had it in mind to appear not from the imperial palace, in the customary fashion, but from the gladiatorial barracks, clad in armor instead of in the splendid imperial purple, and accompanied by the rest of the gladiators. He announced his intentions to Marcia, whom, of all his mistresses, he held in highest esteem; he kept nothing from this woman, as if she were his legal wife, even allowing her the imperial honors except for the sacred fire. When she learned of his plan, so unreasonable and unbecoming an Emperor, she threw herself at his feet, entreating him, with tears, not to bring disgrace upon the Roman empire and not to endanger his life by entrusting it to gladiators and desperate men. After much pleading, unable to persuade the emperor to abandon his plan, she left him, still weeping. Commodus then summoned Laetus, the praetorian prefect, and Eclectus, his bedroom steward, and ordered them to make arrangements for him to spend the night in the gladiatorial barracks, telling them that he would leave for the festival sacrifices from there, and show himself to the Romans under arms. And these men, too, pleaded with the emperor not to do anything unworthy of his imperial position.' (Herodian 1.16.1-4)

The textual references by Herodian epitomise the prevalent anti-Commodus sentiment that surrounds him. The author presents a variety of themes and the initial passage (1.14.8-9) makes the insanity of Commodus Antoninus the primary theme from the very outset. This extract also directly associates this mental derangement with his almost megalomaniac desire for self promotion. All the same, this ties in well with the overall anti-Commodus literary sentiment. This is also exhibited through the emphasis upon extravagance and self indulgence – a recurring theme in the textual representation of Commodus. The second passage (1.16.1-5) also emphasises his insanity from the very outset – there is little doubt about what Herodian was trying to characterise at this point. While the author provides an excursus on religious festivals, it is evident that the primary focus is upon the mania of the young emperor. This of course is directly connected with his apparent obsession with gladiators, but this has been discussed further below. All the same, for the purposes of the present analysis, it is especially important to note the emphasis upon Commodus' mania by Herodian. Cassius Dio is the next ancient author to be examined in this regard:

Κομμοδιανὴν γοῦν τήν τε Ῥώμην αὐτὴν καὶ τὰ στρατόπεδα Κομμοδιανά, τήν τε ἡμέραν ἐν ᾗ ταῦτα ἐψηφίζετο Κομμοδιανὰ καλεῖσθαι προσέταξεν. ἑαυτῷ δὲ ἄλλας τε παμπόλλους ἐπωνυμίας καὶ τὴν Ἡρακλέους ἀπήνεγκε. τὴν δὲ Ῥώμην ἀθάνατον εὐτυχῆ κολωνίαν οἰκουμένην τῆς γῆς (καὶ γὰρ ἄποικον αὐτὴν ἑαυτοῦ δοκεῖν ἐβούλετο) ἐπωνόμασεν. καὶ ἀνδριάς τε αὐτῷ χρυσοῦς χιλίων λιτρῶν μετά τε ταύρου καὶ βοὸς θηλείας ἐγένετο, καὶ τέλος καὶ οἱ μῆνες ἀπ' αὐτοῦ πάντες ἐπεκλήθησαν, ὥστε καταριθμεῖσθαι αὐτοὺς οὕτως, Ἀμαζόνιος Ἀνίκητος Εὐτυχὴς Εὐσεβὴς Λούκιος Αἴλιος Αὐρήλιος Κόμμοδος Αὔγουστος Ἡράκλειος Ῥωμαῖος Ὑπεραίρων. αὐτὸς μὲν γὰρ ἄλλοτε ἄλλα μετελάμβανε τῶν ὀνομάτων, τὸν δ' Ἀμαζόνιον καὶ τὸν Ὑπεραίροντα παγίως ἑαυτῷ ἔθετο ὡς καὶ ἐν πᾶσιν ἁπλῶς πάντας ἀνθρώπους καθ' ὑπερβολὴν νικῶν· οὕτω καθ' ὑπερβολὴν ἐμεμήνει τὸ κάθαρμα. καὶ τῇ βουλῇ οὕτως ἐπέστελλεν "αὐτοκράτωρ Καῖσαρ Λούκιος Αἴλιος Αὐρήλιος. Κόμμοδος Αὔγουστος εὐσεβὴς εὐτυχής, Σαρματικὸς Γερμανικὸς μέγιστος Βρεττανικός, εἰρηνοποιὸς τῆς οἰκουμένης [εὐτυχής] ἀνίκητος, Ῥωμαῖος Ἡρακλῆς, ἀρχιερεύς, δημαρχικῆς ἐξουσίας τὸ ὀκτωκαιδέκατον, αὐτοκράτωρ τὸ ὄγδοον, ὕπατος τὸ ἕβδομον, πατὴρ πατρίδος, ὑπάτοις στρατηγοῖς δημάρχοις, γερουσίᾳ Κομμοδιανῇ εὐτυχεῖ χαίρειν". καὶ ἀνδριάντες αὐτοῦ παμπληθεῖς ἐν Ἡρακλέους σχήματι ἔστησαν. καὶ τὸν αἰῶνα τὸν ἐπ' αὐτοῦ χρυσοῦν τε ὀνομάζεσθαι καὶ ἐς τὰ γράμματα πάντα ὁμοίως ἐσγράφεσθαι ἐψηφίσθη. οὗτος οὖν ὁ χρυσοῦς, οὗτος ὁ Ἡρακλῆς, οὗτος ὁ θεός (καὶ γὰρ <καὶ> τοῦτ' ἤκουεν) ἐξαίφνης ποτὲ μετὰ μεσημβρίαν ἐκ τοῦ προαστείου σπουδῇ ἐς τὴν Ῥώμην ἐλάσας τριάκοντα ἵππων ἁμίλλας ἐν δυσὶν ὥραις ἐποίησεν. ὅθεν οὐχ ἥκιστα καὶ τὰ χρήματα αὐτὸν ἐπέλιπεν.

'He actually ordered that Rome itself should be called Commodiana, the legions Commodian, and the day on which these measures were voted Commodiana. Upon himself he bestowed, in addition to a great many other names, that of Hercules. Rome he styled the "Immortal, Fortunate Colony of the Whole Earth"; for he wished it to be regarded as a settlement of his own. In his honour a gold statue was erected of a thousand pounds weight, representing him together with a bull and a cow. Finally, all the months were named after him, so that they were enumerated as follows: Amazonius, Invictus, Felix, Pius, Lucius, Aelius, Aurelius, Commodus, Augustus, Herculeus, Romanus, Exsuperatorius. For he himself assumed these several titles at different times, but "Amazonius" and "Exsuperatorius" he applied constantly to himself, to indicate that in every respect he surpassed absolutely all mankind superlatively; so superlatively mad had the abandoned wretch become. And to the senate he would send messages couched in these terms: "The Emperor Caesar Lucius Aelius Aurelius Commodus Augustus Pius Felix Sarmaticus Germanicus

Maximus Britannicus, Pacifier of the Whole Earth, Invincible, the Roman Hercules, Pontifex Maximus, Holder of the Tribunician Authority for the eighteenth time, Imperator for the eighth time, Consul for the seventh time, Father of his Country, to consuls, praetors, tribunes, 6 and the fortunate Commodian senate, Greeting." Vast numbers of statues were erected representing him in the garb of Hercules. And it was voted that his age should be named the "Golden Age," and that this should be recorded in all the records without exception. Now this "Golden One," this "Hercules," (this 'god' (for he was even given this name, too) suddenly drove into Rome one afternoon from his suburb and conducted thirty horse-races in the space of two hours. These proceedings had much to do with his running short of funds.' (Dio 73.15.2-16.1)

Cassius Dio also persists with the anti-Commodus theme, emphasising the aspects of his divine aspirations throughout his reign.[575] The first passage (73.15.2-16.1) presents a different slant to that which has been presented by Herodian, stressing how he wanted to change the name of Rome to *Commodiana*, as well as the renaming of the various legions. This was also connected to the renaming of the calendar months (with their important religious connotations) – which was intended to further characterise the megalomania and divine aspirations of the emperor.[576] Whether this change actually occurred is open as a moot point for the various modern scholars, but the purposes of the present discussion it is simply vital to note how Cassius Dio exhibits the autocratic tendencies and the insanity of Commodus Antoninus. Another passage (73.17.4) continues the theme presented by Herodian in the desire of the *princeps* to dress up as a deity.[577] The association with the god Hercules here is clearly evident, but in this instance it is not purely restricted to him.[578] The primary element to note here is how extreme the devotion of Commodus towards deities that were relevant to him was expressed – he may have even dressed up at them.[579] This of course would have been entirely inappropriate for a Roman *princeps* according to the more conservative elements among his social peers. Nevertheless, the question remains as to whether this was really indicative of insanity, or over exuberance on the part of the young emperor. Ultimately it

---

[575] See W.J. Moulton, "Gleanings in Archaeology and Epigraphy", *Annual of the American School of Oriental Research in Jerusalem* 1, 1919-20, p. 88.

[576] Traupman 1956, *op.cit.*

[577] cf. M. Rostovtseff and H. Mattingly, "Commodus-Hercules in Britain", *JRS* 13, 1923, p. 105.

[578] Traupman 1956, *op.cit.*

[579] Grosso 1964, *op.cit.*

would have been viewed as highly unusual[580] – but it is important to also note that Commodus was the *princeps* after all, which meant he could do this if he so desired. The biographer of the *Historia Augusta* assists in this regard:

fuit praeterea ea dementia, ut urbem Romanam coloniam Commodianam vocari voluerit. qui furor dicitur ei inter delenimenta Marciae iniectus. voluit etiam in Circo quadrigas agitare. dalmaticatus in publico processit atque ita signum quadrigis emittendis dedit. et eo quidem tempore quo ad senatum rettulit de Commodiana facienda Roma, non solum senatus hoc libenter accepit per inrisionem, quantum intellegitur, sed etiam se ipsum Commodianum vocavit, Commodum Herculem et deum appellans. Simulavit se et in Africam iturum, ut sumptum itinerarium exigeret, et exegit eumque in convivia et aleam convertit. Motilenum, praefectum praetorii, per ficus veneno interemit. accepit statuas in Herculis habitu, eique immolatum est ut deo. multos praeterea paraverat interimere. quod per parvulum quendam proditum est, qui tabulam e cubiculo eiecit, in qua occidendorum erant nomina scripta. Sacra Isidis coluit, ut et caput raderet et Anubim portaret. Bellonae servientes vere exsecare bracchium praecepit studio crudelitatis. Isiacos vere pineis usque ad perniciem pectus tundere cogebat. cum Anubim portaret, capita Isiacorum graviter obtundebat ore simulacri. clava non solum leones in veste muliebri et pelle leonina sed etiam homines multos adflixit. debiles pedibus et eos, qui ambulare non possent, in gigantum modum formavit, ita ut a genibus de pannis et linteis quasi dracones tegerentur, eosdemque sagittis confecit. sacra Mithriaca homicidio vero polluit, cum illic aliquid ad speciem timoris vel dici vel fingi soleat.

'He had, besides, an insane desire that the city of Rome should be renamed Colonia Commodiana. This mad idea, it is said, was inspired in him while listening to the blandishments of Marcia. He had also a desire to drive chariots in the Circus, and he went out in public clad in the Dalmatian tunic and thus clothed gave the signal for the charioteers to start. And in truth, on the occasion when he laid before the senate his proposal to call Rome Commodiana, not only did the senate gleefully pass this resolution, but also took the name "Commodian" to itself, at the same time giving Commodus the name Hercules, and calling him a god. He pretended once that he was going to Africa, so that he could get funds for the journey, then got them and spent them on banquets and gaming instead. He murdered Motilenus, the prefect of the guard, by means of poisoned figs. He allowed statues of himself to be erected with the accoutrements of Hercules; and sacrifices were performed to him as to a god. He had planned to execute many more men besides, but his plan was betrayed by a certain young servant, who threw out of his bedroom a tablet on which were written the names of those who were to be killed. He practiced the worship of Isis and even went so far as to shave his head and carry a statue of Anubis. In his passion for cruelty he actually ordered the votaries of Bellona to cut off one of their arms, and as for the devotees of Isis, he forced them to beat their breasts with pinecones even to the point of death. While he was carrying about the statue of Anubis, he used to smite the heads of the devotees of Isis with the face of the statue. He struck with his club, while clad in a woman's garment or a lion's skin, not lions only, but many men as well. Certain men who were lame in their feet and others who could not walk, he dressed up as giants, encasing their legs from the knee down in

---

[580] For another example of this interpretation, see K.A. Esdaile, "The Commodus-Mithras of the Salting Collection", *JRS* 7, 1917, pp. 71-3.

wrappings and bandages to make them look like serpents, and then despatched them with his arrows. He desecrated the rites of Mithra with actual murder, although it was customary in them merely to say or pretend something that would produce an impression of terror.' (*HA Commodus* 8.6-9.6)[581]

adibat deorum templa pollutus stupris et humano sanguine. imitatus est et medicum, ut sanguinem hominibus emitteret scalpris feralibus. Menses quoque in honorem eius pro Augusto Commodum, pro Septembri Herculem, pro Octobri Invictum, pro Novembri Exsuperatorium, pro Decembri Amazonium ex signo ipsius adulatores vocabant. Amazonius autem vocatus est ex amore concubinae suae Marciae, quam pictam in Amazone diligebat, propter quam et ipse Amazonico habitu in arenam Romanam procedere voluit.

'He would enter the temples of the gods defiled with adulteries and human blood. He even aped a surgeon, going so far as to bleed men to death with scalpels. Certain months were renamed in his honour by his flatterers; for August they substituted Commodus, for September Hercules, for October Invictus, for November Exsuperatorius, and for December Amazonius, after his own surname. He had been called Amazonius, moreover, because of his passion for his concubine Marcia, whom he loved to have portrayed as an Amazon, and for whose sake he even wished to enter the arena of Rome dressed as an Amazon.' (*HA Commodus* 11.6-9)

adsumptus est in omnia collegia sacerdotalia sacerdos XIII kal. Invictas Pisone Iuliano consulibus. profectus in Germaniam XIIII Kal. Aelias, ut postea nominavit. iisdem consulibus togam virilem accepit. cum patre appellatus imperator V kal. Exsuperatorias Pollione et Apro iterum consulibus. triumphavit X kal. Ian iisdem consulibus. iterum profectus III nonas Commodias Orfito et Rufo consulibus.

'He was received into all the sacred colleges as a priest on the thirteenth day before the Kalends of "Invictus", in the consulship of Piso and Julianus. He set out for Germany on the fourteenth day before the Kalends of the month which he later named Aelius, and assumed the toga in the same year. Together with his father he was acclaimed Imperator on the fifth day before the Kalends of "Exsuperatorius", in the year when Pollio and Aper served their second consulships, and he celebrated a triumph on the tenth day before the Kalends of January in this same year. He set out on his second expedition on the third day before the Nones of "Commodus" in the consulship of Orfitus and Rufus.' (*HA Commodus* 12.1-6)

The first extract by the *HA* biographer (*Commodus* 8.6-9.6) makes another clear reference to his direct association with the god Hercules, as well as his intention to rename the capital as *Colonia Commodiana*.[582] It also continues the prevalent theme of accentuating both his mania as well as his desire to be the popular centre of attention. All the same, it is notable that he is also shown as being equally fer-

---

[581] See R.J. Penella, "S.H.A. Commodus 9.2-3", *AJPh* 97.1, 1976, p. 39.
[582] Traupman 1956, *op.cit.*, p. 86.

vent in his devotion to Isis in this instance – an often questioned deity by some of the ancient literary sources. The second passage (*Commodus* 11.6-9) also mentions Commodus' intention to rename of months of the calendar as mentioned by Cassius Dio, but with a different interpretation.[583] Nevertheless, neither account is positive towards the *princeps*, which in turn epitomised the prevailing literary tradition among the ancient authors. This is also continued in Section 12.1-6 of the *Commodus*. While this provides an account of Commodus Antoninus' military undertakings in a highly critical fashion, it was also clearly making a mockery of him in reference to the names of the months by suggesting that he had already renamed them. The whole point of these passages by the *HA* biographer was to demonstrate how ridiculous the young emperor was – regardless of his actual achievements and their benefit for the Roman State in general. These aspects would have not conformed to the literary intentions of the author – essentially a highly negative characterisation of the *princeps*.

In general terms, the various references towards the renaming of Rome and of the months sought to emphasise one aspect in particular: the autocratic tactics (or sentiments) of Commodus Antoninus. This is both impossible to either refute categorically or to prove definitively because there is no evidence beyond the scope of the ancient literary accounts. So while the extremity of his devotion towards the god Hercules is manifest by using a variety of ancient sources, this accusation of his divine aspirations may have simply been a result of a personal desire on his part to further establish his connection with these deities, which in turn has been used by the authors as a means of further establishing his characterisation of being manic and autocratic. But this is impossible to tell with any certainty. What becomes clearly evident is the existence of an early literary tradition that sought to discredit almost every aspect of his reign regardless of whether it was justifiable or not. It appears likely that Commodus Antoninus chose some poorly devised means by which he could express his devotion to particular gods, which clearly underestimated the conservatism of some parts of Roman society at the very least. A more extreme interpretation would be that he saw himself (or at least aspired) to be a divinity in his own right. But as mentioned previously – it is difficult to tell.

---

[583] Grosso 1964, *op.cit.*

When the question of the divine aspirations of a *princeps* is raised by the ancient literary sources it is always difficult for the modern interpreter. The reliability of such accounts (which are almost always within the context of a critical analysis by the ancient authors) is almost impossible to quantify with any certainty. For example, it was also a common accusation against other unpopular (or possibly despotic) Roman *principes*, such as Caligula, Nero and Domitian. Whether or not such allegations were justifiable is a matter of some consideration – but the consistency of the ancient literary tradition is undeniable. One good example of this was the reference to Commodus reworking the Colossus (the immense state of Nero erected by himself,[584] which was later dedicated to Sol by Vespasian[585], and later moved by Hadrian to the north of the Colosseum[586]) to depict the young *princeps* in the guise of Hercules.[587] This accusation is entirely based on the ancient literary descriptions, which are highly dubious – none of them can really agree about the details of it (such as Dio 72.22.3; Herodian 1.15.9; *HA Commodus* 15.8). Therefore, it is questionable as to whether Colossus would have even still been standing at this point in time during the late Second Century AD. So the question remains as to whether this immense piece of Neronian sculpture would have survived the *Domus Aurea* and other unpopular public monuments of that time into the reign of Commodus Antoninus.[588] This appears to be somewhat unlikely. It appears much more probable that this was a symbolic literary device that was used as a means of connecting two 'unpopular' *principes* (Nero and Commodus) in order to establish the despotism of both. Therefore, judging from all of the ancient evidence it is at least clear that the connection between Commodus and Hercules existed (as was the extremity of his devotion),[589] but the divine aspirations of the emperor is an entirely different matter.

So, in general terms, the question surrounding Commodus Antoninus and his divine aspirations remains – the ancient evidence can be interpreted in a variety of ways. The early literary tradition is

---

[584] Suetonius *Nero*, 31.1.
[585] Suetonius *Vespasian* 18.
[586] *HA Hadrian*, 19.
[587] Richardson 1992, *op.cit.*; Platner 1926, *op.cit.*
[588] Grosso 1964, *op.cit.*
[589] See O. Hekster, "Of Mice and Emperors: a Note on Aelian 'De Natura animalium' 6.40", *CPh* 97.4, 2002, p. 370.

compelling, but it must also be viewed in a critical fashion. The devotion of Commodus towards Hercules is self evident and it also appears that he sought to have shown himself as a Roman Hercules,[590] but this does not necessarily mean that he saw himself as a god during his lifetime though. These are two entirely distinct aspects to consider, which would have also been easily misunderstood (or perhaps manipulated) at the time. One clear aspect to note is that Commodus wanted to be involved in such celebrations – if not to be centre of attention. This ties in perfectly with the ancient accounts about his appreciation for games and spectacles, regardless of his divine aspirations. He seemingly wanted to be the central focus of the people – either as a presenter of such large scale popular occasions, or as a key participant within them. His primary role as Roman *princeps* (and its social expectations of respectability) did not appear to have been a significant concern for him.

Games and Spectacles under Commodus

While the attachment of Commodus Antoninus towards the god Hercules can be interpreted as being representative of his personal divine aspirations by some, his rigorous appreciation for games and spectacles cannot be similarly attributed or explained.[591] All the same, they do tie in well with his general attention seeking demeanour.[592] According to the ancient literary sources, such as Cassius Dio and the *HA* biographer Commodus produced numerous games and spectacles, thus indicating not only his personal appreciation for them, but also his strong desire for wider popularity among the 'regular' (or perhaps non-élite) people. Of course these textual descriptions were deliberately associated with the excessive expense of the *princeps* entailed by the ancient authors, thus continuing and conforming to their themes of his fiscal maladministration and the general anti-Commodus sentiment in this sector. However, while such public occasions were expensive, Commodus was hardly alone in his presentation of these events with many aspiring Roman leaders having acted similarly over the previous centuries. The other primary accusation levelled against the emperor is that these spectacles were so important to him that he neglected the running of the Roman

---

[590] Traupman 1956, *op.cit.*

[591] See K.M. Coleman, "Fatal Charades: Roman Executions Staged as Mythological Enactments", *JRS* 80, 1990, p. 73.

[592] Grosso 1964, *op.cit.*

State – but this is an allegation that is both impossible to either confirm or deny. Therefore, it is essential to examine the various early textual accounts of his games and spectacles in turn.[593]

All the same, the way in which such occasions are referred to by the ancient literary sources must first be considered. The presentation of such grand events could have been cast in a variety of ways by these early authors. If the intended theme was constructed in a positive light then the sponsor of the spectacle would be shown as undertaking significant personal financial loss for the benefit of the wider Roman community. In this regard the literary theme would of general munificence and altruism at a significant expense to the benefactor. It is also notable that the similar presentation of games and spectacles could also be represented as being indicative of fiscal irresponsibility by exactly the same authors – as entirely unnecessary financial burdens upon the resources of the Roman State.[594] The distinction between these two literary constructions was entirely subjective during the Imperial period, entirely being reliant upon the purposes of the author's intentions. On a practical level, it is also important to note that a question would have existed about the existing distinction that was drawn between the finances of the State and the resources of the *princeps*. Regardless of this inherently subjective interpretation (and representation) in these texts, however, it is evident that Commodus Antoninus was shown here in a highly negative light – but these accounts require close scrutiny in turn, beginning with the references presented by Cassius Dio (73.17.1):

καὶ ἐν μὲν τῷ δημοσίῳ οὐδαμόθεν ἅρματα ἤλασε, πλὴν εἰ μή που ἐν ἀσελήνῳ νυκτί, ἐπιθυμήσας μὲν καὶ δημοσίᾳ ἁρματηλατῆσαι, αἰσχυνθεὶς δὲ καὶ ὀφθῆναι τοῦτο ποιῶν· οἴκοι δὲ συνεχῶς τοῦτ' ἔπραττε, τῇ πρασίνῳ σκευῇ χρώμενος.

'In public he nowhere drove chariots except sometimes on a moonless night, for, though he was eager to play the charioteer in public, too, he was ashamed to be seen doing so; but in private he was constantly doing it, adopting the Green uniform.' (Dio 73.17.1)

Cassius Dio has exhibited a definitive characterisation in the first passage (73.17.1) – illustrating how his interest in playing the character in front of an audience (and yet his inability to do so), but this was used by this ancient author to clearly show the personal inclina-

---

[593] Traupman 1956, *op.cit.*
[594] Grosso 1964, *op.cit.*

tions of Commodus Antoninus and in turn his individual shame. This was intended to portray his mental instability and corruption. All the same, another extract (73.18.1-20.3) overtly contradicts this though by representing him with his personal involvement in gladiatorial combat publically at large scale spectacles. This showed a different side – his irresponsibility and desire for self promotion. All the same, this was also intended to exhibit his shamefulness, just in a different light. These accounts by Cassius Dio sought to completely discredit his character and definitively maintained the anti-Commodus tradition. It is important to note the laboured emphasis upon his own interest in these public events, which corresponds with his lack of attention towards the administration of the Roman State by Commodus in these characterisations. Tiberius Claudius Pompeianus was clearly used here as the standard of morality by the author, which sought to accentuate the depravity of the *princeps*.

Spectator gladiatoria sumpsit arma, panno purpureo nudos umeros advelans. habuit praeterea morem, ut omnia quae turpiter, quae impure, quae crudeliter, quae gladiatorie, quae lenonie faceret, actis urbis indi iuberet, ut Marii Maximi scripta testantur. Commodianum etiam populum Romanum dixit, quo saepissime praesente gladiator pugnavit. sane cum illi saepe pugnanti ut deo populus favisset, inrisum se credens populum Romanum a militibus classiariis, qui vela ducebant, in amphitheatro interimi praeceperat. urbem incendi iusserat, utpote coloniam suam. quod factum esset, nisi Laetus praefectus praetorii Commodum deterruisset. appellatus est sane inter cetera triumphalia nomina etiam sescenties vicies Palus Primus Secutorum.

'At gladiatorial shows he would come to watch and stay to fight, covering his bare shoulders with a purple cloth. And it was his custom, moreover, to order the insertion in the city-gazette of everything he did that was base or foul or cruel, or typical of a gladiator or a procurer — at least, the writings of Marius Maximus so testify. He entitled the Roman people the "People of Commodus," since he had very often fought as a gladiator in their presence. And although the people regularly applauded him in his frequent combats as though he were a god, he became convinced that he was being laughed at, and gave orders that the Roman people should be slain in the Amphitheatre by the marines who spread the awnings. He gave an order, also, for the burning of the city, as though it were his private colony, and this order would have been executed had not Laetus, the prefect of the guard, deterred him. Among other triumphal titles, he was also given the name "Captain of the Secutores" six hundred and twenty times.' (*HA Commodus* 15.3-8)

As with the accounts of Cassius Dio, the *HA* biographer also emphasises the devotion of Commodus Antoninus towards such entertainment. In a similar fashion, this author has also stressed the focus of his appreciation for the most vile and violent events as well. It is also notable that this was also directly connected with his own involvement as a gladiator (as well as his role as an aspiring god), but this is discussed further below. Another remarkable aspect here is the reference to his desire to punish the common people by burning down the city. The authorial connection of all of these quite extreme themes by the *HA* biographer was clearly thematically intentional – they unquestionably characterised Commodus as being an unstable megalomaniac. All the same, this early textual depiction cannot be taken at face value – there was probably a degree of factual basis for this type of representation, but it also seems that the *HA* biographer was exaggerating the point in order to present the emperor in the most extreme light possible.

Therefore, it is important to consider the style of textual representation used here more critically. Commodus Antoninus was clearly behaving in a fashion that was viewed as being not appropriate for a stereotypical Roman *princeps* – a point that was not lost upon (and greatly accentuated) by the extant ancient literary sources. As mentioned previously, the provision of games and spectacles by a leading Roman citizen (let alone a *princeps*) was not unusual if not a prevalent occurrence. This had been a prevalent method for the social élites to engage with the wider community in the capital for centuries. So in this regard Commodus was following a well established Roman tradition, but with this matter he was subsequently overtly criticised as being too extreme. This thematic criticism will become even more apparent in the next section of the present study. All the same, it is evident that the ancient literary sources wanted to exhibit his presentation of spectacles and games in a direct connection with his divine aspirations and his public devotion to Hercules. The literary tradition shows these poorly accepted aspects in the most comprehensive and extensive fashion of course.[595]

All of these literary accounts clearly accentuate the ancient literary tradition surrounding Commodus Antoninus. He is shown as not only presenting these large scale games and spectacles, but also as being directly involved in them. While this was intended to emphasise the inappropriate nature of his behaviour, it also continued the sense that the emperor had tendencies towards attention seeking. These events are also connected by the authors to the massive expense incurred by such public occasions, but as mentioned previously this was hardly atypical for more Roman *principes*. All the same, this was characterised in a highly critical light by the ancient literary sources (whereas there was an equal opportunity for them to depict

---

[595] Grosso 1964, *op.cit.*

this as a laudable feature if they sought to cast him as a 'good' emperor). Therefore, at this point it is important to consider the role of Commodus as a participant in gladiatorial contests in greater detail, especially because it was a fundamental feature of the anti-Commodus tradition in the ancient literary sources.

Commodus as a Gladiator

The representation of Commodus acting as a gladiator is a pivotal aspect to consider for the purposes of this study. This feature of his reign has been used by ancient and modern scholars alike as an indicator of his mental instability and the inappropriate nature of his principate. There are numerous references to this role playing by the ancient literary sources, but of course such anecdotal evidence provided excellent material for the perpetuation of the anti-Commodus tradition. The most obvious attribution by these early authors was simply that Commodus Antoninus was mentally unstable, thus exhibiting their negative characterisations against him. All the same, as referred to previously, this could have also simply been indicative of his evident attention seeking inclinations as well, which appears more likely. However, the negative and critical intentions of the authors are undeniable. This is clearly shown by the *Epitomator* (17.4), which exhibits the prominence of this personality feature in the literary tradition. While there is a definite lack of detail in this account, the fact that this aspect was included in such a generally brief description symbolises how frequently this feature was referred to by the ancient literary sources. Another excellent example of this is provided by the late Second Century historian, Herodian (1.15.1-9):

τὸν μὲν οὖν ἀνδριάντα μετὰ τὴν ἐκείνου τελευτὴν καθελοῦσα ἡ σύγκλητος Ἐλευθερίας εἰκόνα ἵδρυσεν· ὁ δὲ Κόμοδος μηκέτι κατέχων ἑαυτοῦ δημοσίᾳ θέας ἐπετέλεσεν, ὑποσχόμενος τά τε θηρία πάντα ἰδίᾳ χειρὶ κατακτενεῖν καὶ τοῖς ἀνδρειοτάτοις τῶν νεανιῶν μονομαχήσειν. διαδραμούσης δὲ τῆς φήμης ἔκ τε τῆς Ἰταλίας πάσης καὶ τῶν ὁμόρων ἐθνῶν, θεασόμενοι ἃ μὴ πρότερον μήτε ἑωράκεσαν μήτε ἠκηκόεσαν. καὶ γὰρ διηγγέλλετο αὐτοῦ τῆς χειρὸς τὸ εὔστοχον, καὶ ὅτι ἔμελεν αὐτῷ ἀκοντίζοντι καὶ τοξεύοντι μὴ πταίειν. συνῆσαν δὲ παιδεύοντες αὐτὸν Παρθυαίων οἱ τοξικὴν ἀκριβοῦντες καὶ Μαυρουσίων οἱ ἀκοντίζειν ἄριστοι, οὓς πάντας εὐχειρίᾳ ὑπερέβαλλεν. ἐπεὶ δὲ κατέλαβον αἱ τῆς θέας ἡμέραι, τὸ μὲν ἀμφιθέατρον πεπλήρωτο, τῷ δὲ Κομόδῳ περίδρομος κύκλῳ κατεσκεύαστο, ὡς μὴ συστάδην τοῖς θηρίοις μαχόμενος κινδυνεύοι, ἄνωθεν δὲ καὶ ἐξ ἀσφαλοῦς ἀκοντίζων εὐστοχίας μᾶλλον ἢ ἀνδρείας παρέχοιτο δεῖξιν. ἐλάφους μὲν οὖν καὶ δορκάδας ὅσα τε κερασφόρα πλὴν ταύρων, συνθέων αὐτοῖς καὶ καταδιώκων ἔβαλλε φθάνων τε αὐτῶν τὸν δρόμον καὶ πληγαῖς καιρίοις ἀναιρῶν· λέοντας δὲ καὶ παρδάλεις ὅσα τε ζῷα γενναῖα περιθέων ἄνωθεν κατηκόντιζεν. οὐδέ τις εἶδεν ἀκόντιον δεύτερον οὐδὲ τραῦμα ἄλλο πλὴν τοῦ θανατηφόρου· ἅμα γὰρ τῇ τοῦ ζῴου ὁρμῇ κατὰ τοῦ μετώπου ἢ κατὰ καρδίας ἔφερε τὴν πληγήν, καὶ οὐδέποτε σκοπὸν ἄλλον ἔσχεν οὐδὲ ἐπ' ἄλλο μέρος ἦλθε τὸ ἀκόντιον τοῦ σώματος, ὡς μὴ ἅμα τε τρῶσαι καὶ φονεῦσαι. τὰ δὲ πανταχόθεν ζῷα ἠθροίζετο αὐτῷ. τότε γοῦν εἴδομεν ὅσα ἐν γραφαῖς ἐθαυμάζομεν· ἀπό τε γὰρ Ἰνδῶν καὶ Αἰθιόπων, εἴ τι πρότερον ἄγνωστον ἦν, μεσημβρίας τε καὶ τῆς ἀρκτῴας γῆς ζῷα πάντα φονεύων Ῥωμαίοις ἔδειξε. τὸ δ' εὔστοχον τῆς χειρὸς αὐτοῦ πάντες ἐξεπλήττοντο. λαβὼν οὖν ποτὲ βέλη ὧν αἱ ἀκμαὶ ἦσαν μηνοειδεῖς, ταῖς Μαυρουσίαις στρουθοῖς ὀξύτατα φερομέναις καὶ ποδῶν τάχει καὶ κολπώσει πτερῶν ἐπαφιεὶς τὰ βέλη κατ' ἄκρου τοῦ τραχήλου ἐκαρατόμει, ὡς καὶ τῶν κεφαλῶν ἀφῃρημένας ὁρμῇ τοῦ βέλους ἔτι περιθεῖν αὐτὰς ὡς μηδὲν παθούσας. παρδάλεως δὲ ποτε ὀξυτάτῳ δρόμῳ τὸν ἐκκαλούμενον καταλαβούσης φθάσας τῷ ἀκοντίῳ μέλλουσαν δήξεσθαι, τὴν μὲν ἀπέκτεινε τὸν δὲ ἐρρύσατο, φθάσας τῇ τοῦ δόρατος αἰχμῇ τὴν τῶν ὀδόντων ἀκμήν. λεόντων δέ ποτε ἐξ ὑπογαίων ἑκατὸν ἅμα ἀφεθέντων ἰσαρίθμοις ἀκοντίοις πάντας ἀπέκτεινεν, ὡς ἐπὶ πολὺ κειμένων τῶν πτωμάτων δι' αὐτὸ τοῦτο ἐπὶ σχολῆς πάντας ἀριθμῆσαι καὶ μηδ' ἓν ἰδεῖν περιττὸν ἀκόντιον. μέχρι μὲν οὖν τούτων, εἰ καὶ βασιλείας τὰ πραττόμενα ἦν ἀλλότρια, πλὴν ἀνδρείας καὶ εὐστοχίας παρὰ τοῖς δημώδεσιν εἶχέ τινα χάριν. ἐπεὶ δὲ καὶ γυμνὸς ἐς τὸ ἀμφιθέατρον εἰσῆλθεν ὅπλα τε ἀναλαβὼν ἐμονομάχει, τότε σκυθρωπὸν εἶδεν ὁ δῆμος θέαμα, τὸν εὐγενῆ Ῥωμαίων βασιλέα μετὰ τοσαῦτα τρόπαια πατρός τε καὶ προγόνων οὐκ ἐπὶ βαρβάρους ὅπλα λαμβάνοντα στρατιωτικὰ ἢ Ῥωμαίων ἀρχῇ πρέποντα, καθυβρίζοντα δὲ τὸ ἀξίωμα αἰσχίστῳ καὶ μεμιασμένῳ σχήματι. ὁ μὲν οὖν μονομαχῶν ῥᾳδίως τῶν ἀνταγωνιστῶν περιεγίνετο καὶ μέχρι τραυμάτων προεχώρει ὑπεικόντων ἁπάντων καὶ τὸν βασιλέα οὐ τὸν μονομάχον ἐννοούντων, ἐς τοσοῦτον δὲ προεχώρησε μανίας, ὡς μηκέτι βούλεσθαι μηδὲ τὴν βασίλειον οἰκεῖν ἑστίαν· ἀλλὰ γὰρ μετοικισθῆναι ἐβούλετο ἐς τὸ τῶν μονομάχων καταγώγιον. ἑαυτὸν δὲ οὐκέτι Ἡρακλέα, ἀλλὰ τῶν μονομαχούντων ἐνδόξου τινὸς προτετελευτηκότος ὀνόματι καλεῖσθαι προσέταξε. τοῦ δὲ μεγίστου ἀγάλματος κολοσσιαίου, ὅπερ σέβουσι Ῥωμαῖοι εἰκόνα φέρον ἡλίου, τὴν κεφαλὴν ἀποτεμὼν ἱδρύσατο <τὴν> ἑαυτοῦ, ὑπογράψας τῇ βάσει [οὐχ] ἃς εἰώθασι βασιλικὰς καὶ πατρῴας προσηγορίας, ἀντὶ δὲ Γερμανικοῦ "μονομάχους χιλίους νικήσαντος".

The senate removed this statue of Commodus after his death and replaced it with a statue of Freedom. Now the emperor, casting aside all restraint, took part in the public shows, promising to kill with his own hands wild animals of all kinds and to fight in gladiatorial combat against the bravest of the youths. When this news became known, people hastened to Rome from all over Italy and from the neighboring provinces to see what they had neither seen nor even heard of before. Special mention was made of the skill of his hands and the fact that he never missed when hurling javelins or shooting arrows. His instructors were the most skillful of the Parthian bowmen and the most accurate of the Moroccan javelin men, but he surpassed them all in marksmanship. When the days for the show arrived, the amphitheater was completely filled. A terrace encircling the arena had been constructed for Commodus, enabling him to avoid risking his life by fighting the animals at close quarters; rather, by hurling his javelins down from a safe place, he offered a display of skill rather than of courage. Deer, roebuck, and horned animals of all kinds, except bulls, he struck down, running with them in pursuit, anticipating their dashes, and killing them with deadly blows. Lions, leopards, and other animals of the nobler sort he killed from above, running around on his terrace. And on no occasion did anyone see a second javelin used, nor any wound except the death wound. For at the very moment the animal started up, it received the blow on its forehead or in its heart, and it bore no other wound, nor did the javelin pierce any other part of its body: the beast was wounded and killed in the same instant. Animals were collected for him from all over the world. Then we saw in the flesh animals that we had previously marveled at in paintings. From India and Ethiopia, from lands to the north and to the south, any animals hitherto unknown he displayed to the Romans and then dispatched them. On one occasion he shot arrows with crescent-shaped heads at Moroccan ostriches, birds that move with great speed, both because of their swiftness afoot and the sail-like nature of their wings. He cut off their heads at the very top of the neck; so, after their heads had been severed by the edge of the arrow, they continued to run around as if they had not been injured. Once when a leopard, with a lightning dash, seized a condemned criminal, he thwarted the leopard with his javelin as it was about to close its jaws; he killed the beast and rescued the man, the point of the javelin anticipating the points of the leopard's teeth. Again, when a hundred lions appeared in one group as if from beneath the earth, he killed the entire hundred with exactly one hundred javelins, and all the bodies lay stretched out in a straight line for some distance; they could thus be counted with no difficulty, and no one saw a single extra javelin. As far as these activities are concerned, however, even if his conduct was hardly becoming for an emperor, he did win the approval of the mob for his courage and his marksmanship. But when he came into the amphitheater naked, took up arms, and fought as a gladiator, the people saw a disgraceful spectacle, a nobly born emperor of the Romans, whose fathers and forebears had won many victories, not taking the field against barbarians or opponents worthy of the Romans, but disgracing his high position by degrading and disgusting exhibitions. In his gladiatorial combats, he defeated his opponents with ease, and he did no more than wound them, since they all submitted to him, but only because they knew he was the emperor, not because he was truly a gladiator. At last he became so demented that he was unwilling to live in the imperial palace, but wished to change his residence to the gladiatorial barracks. He gave orders that he was no longer to be called Hercules, but by the name of a famous gladiator then dead. He removed the head of a huge Colossus which the Romans worship and which bears the likeness of the Sun, replacing it with his own head, and inscribed on the base not the usual imperial and family titles; instead of "Germanicus" he wrote: "Conqueror of a Thousand Gladiators."' (Herodian 1.15.1-9)

The initial sentence within the above passage is absolutely fantastic – it sets up the overt negativity that was ingrained in these accounts against Commodus Antoninus – he was the opposite of Roman freedom according to Herodian. The author has then progressed into a series of textual episodes that establish not only his martial skill, but primarily his innate cowardice (which is accentuated through his removal of himself from danger). Whether the emperor actually did this is of course highly questionable. In connection to this, it is also important to recognise how much emphasis is placed by Herodian upon this feature of his character – it was clearly an important authorial theme that he sought to not only stress, but also unequivocally dramatise. All the same, this author does recognise (1.15.7) that this did result in wider popularity for the emperor among the common people, which is accentuated by his depiction of this in a definitively 'base' fashion (thus also showing Herodian's own sense of social elitism). The primary emphasis of this early author was upon the shameless actions of Commodus Antoninus – which in turn were attributed to his perceived mania. It is important to note how Herodian connects all of these negative aspects so effectively – a compelling literary account in its own right, and yet entirely questionable on a historical level. Therefore, it is vital to consider the characterisation produced by Cassius Dio in this regard of the young *princeps* – another essential and influential source.

θηρία μέντοι πολλὰ μὲν οἴκοι ἀπέσφαξε, πολλὰ δὲ καὶ ἐν τῷ δημοσίῳ. καὶ μέντοι καὶ ἐμονομάχει, οἴκοι μὲν ὥστε καὶ φονεύειν τινά (ἐν ξυρῷ τε ἑτέρων, ὡς καὶ τὰς τρίχας ἀφαιρῶν, παρέτεμνε τῶν μὲν ῥῖνα τῶν δὲ οὖς τῶν δὲ ἄλλο τι), ἐν δὲ τῷ κοινῷ ἄνευ σιδήρου καὶ ἄνευ αἵματος ἀνθρωπείου. ἐνέδυνε δέ, πρὶν μὲν ἐς τὸ θέατρον ἐσιέναι, χιτῶνα χειριδωτὸν σηρικὸν λευκὸν διάχρυσον (καὶ ἐν τούτῳ γε αὐτὸν τῷ σχήματι ὄντα ἠσπαζόμεθα), ἐσιὼν δὲ ὁλοπόρφυρον χρυσῷ κατάπαστον, χλαμύδα τε ὁμοίαν τὸν Ἑλληνικὸν τρόπον λαμβάνων, καὶ στέφανον ἔκ τε λίθων Ἰνδικῶν καὶ ἐκ χρυσοῦ πεποιημένον, κηρύκειόν τε τοιοῦτον φέρων ὁποῖον ὁ Ἑρμῆς.

'As for wild beasts, however, he slew many both in private and in public. Moreover, he used to contend as a gladiator; in doing this at home he managed to kill a man now and then, and in making close passes with others, as if trying to clip off a bit of their hair, he sliced off the noses of some, the ears of others, and sundry features of still others; but in public he refrained from using steel and shedding human blood. Before entering the amphitheatre he would put on a long-sleeved tunic of silk, white interwoven with gold, and thus arrayed he would receive our greetings; but when he was about to go inside, he put on a robe of pure purple with gold spangles, donning also after the Greek fashion a chlamys of the same colour, and a crown made of gems from India and of gold, and he carried a herald's staff like that of Mercury.' (Dio 73.17.2-3)

Cassius Dio presents a similar theme, but it is unfortunate that he has an equal disregard for verifying such a portrayal. While it is not expected for the ancient literary sources to *prove* their accounts definitively all the time, the prominent vagueness of all these accounts does raise some alarm bells – one does have to question their intent. All the same, the reference by Cassius Dio to Commodus participating as a gladiator (73.19.3-20.3) has already been noted previously in this study, which in turn illustrates the prevalent theme presented by the author – every one of the disreputable topics were presented in an entirely connected and quite convincing fashion. A great deal of detail is delivered by Cassius Dio in this instance in order to accentuate the complete irresponsibility of the young *princeps* and was also intended to simultaneously stress his mania. Judging from such passages it is evident that Commodus was clearly 'insane' (or at the very least irresponsible) – but there is little verifiable data to support this. The question, however, remains about whether these textual descriptions should be taken at face value by the modern scholar. The key issue here is about authorial intent. While not seeking to defend Commodus in this regard (which is impossible because he needed to be much more aware of his social and political circumstances before even remotely behaving in such a fashion), a cautious approach towards the reading of such portrayals is essential. This also becomes quite noticeable when examining the descriptions provided by the *HA* biographer (*Commodus* 5.5; 11.10-12; 12.10-12):

inter haec habitu victimarii victimas immolavit. in harena rudibus, inter cubicularios gladiatores pugnavit lucentibus aliquando mucronibus.

'Meanwhile, dressed in the garb of an attendant at the sacrifice, he slaughtered the sacrificial victims. He fought in the arena with foils, but sometimes, with his chamberlains acting as gladiators, with sharpened swords. By this time Perennis had secured all the power for himself.' (*HA Commodus* 5.5)

Gladiatorium etiam certamen subiit et nomina gladiatorum recepit eo gaudio quasi acciperet triumphalia. ludum semper ingressus est et, quotiens ingrederetur, publicis monumentis indi iussit. pugnasse autem dicitur septingenties tricies quinquies.

'He engaged in gladiatorial combats, and accepted the names usually given to gladiators with as much pleasure as if he had been granted triumphal decorations. He regularly took part in the spectacles, and as often as he did so, ordered the fact to be inscribed in the public records. It is said that he engaged in gladiatorial bouts seven hundred and thirty-five times.' (*HA Commodus* 11.10-12)

inter haec refertur in litteras pugnasse illum sub patre trecenties sexagies quinquies. item postea tantum palmarum gladiatoriarum confecisse vel victis retiariis vel occisis, ut mille contingeret. ferarum autem diversarum manu sua occidit, ita ut elephantos occideret, multa milia. et haec fecit spectante saepe populo Romano.

'Besides these facts, it is related in records that he fought 365 gladiatorial combats in his father's reign. Afterwards, by vanquishing or slaying *retiarii*, he won enough gladiatorial crowns to bring the number up to a thousand. He also killed with his own hand thousands of wild beasts of all kinds, even elephants. And he frequently did these things before the eyes of the Roman people.' (*HA Commodus* 12.10-12)

As shown previously with Herodian and Cassius Dio, the strength of the anti-Commodus tradition by the biographer of the *Historia Augus-*

ta is impossible to disregard. The first excerpt (*Commodus* 5.5) provides little detail about the events, but the sense of the allegation is clear – the *princeps* was both corrupt and unstable in his desires (and behaviour). This is also shown in the second passage (*Commodus* 11.10-12) – the continuation of the authorial theme is impossible to resist. However, as with the previous example, one must acknowledge the lack of detail presented here by the *HA* biographer (which is indicative of the work in general). The third extract quoted above (*Commodus* 12.10-12) also continues this theme of depravity, corruption and mental instability. So, therefore, it is important to note for present purposes how all three of these accounts not only sought to present a continuous thematic representation of Commodus' perceived depravity and mania, but they were also directly associated with other 'instances' of his megalomania. All the same, the question surrounding how these allegations are established by each respective author still remains. The simple fact is that they are not. As texts they are very convincing, which is a credit to the authors – but this does not equate with definitive evidence once their inherent perspective and intended audiences are considered in order to contextualise them effectively. Nevertheless, this does not presume that these accounts were entirely false – only that their perspectives (or, in some cases, the lack thereof) must be taken into consideration.

So, therefore, the accuracy and impartiality of these early accounts must be drawn into serious doubt. As shown previously, the strength of the anti-Commodus tradition and its impact upon the emperor's historical representation is unquestionable.[596] Whether these literary descriptions were accurate of course remains in doubt, which primarily ties in with the topic of their reception. It is pertinent to ask at this point – as audience members do *we* want Commodus Antoninus to be entirely reproachable? He becomes a much more interesting and compelling character when he is depicted in such a bad light. He is shown as being completely underhanded and cruel – almost without any redeeming features. This could have also seemingly made him infinitely more interesting to write about as an early author – hence the great amount of detail provided by them. The whole point behind this was to represent him as being an entirely inappropriate person to attain the position of Roman *princeps* – this was another central aspect of consideration for the ancient literary sources. All the same, this question can be taken back to the question

---

[596] Traupman 1956, *op.cit.*

of Commodus' actual legitimacy by birth. The biographer of the *Historia Augusta* presents an ideal example of the primacy of this tradition (see below), which is taken from the *Vita Marci Antonini Philosophi* (19.1-9). In this section the legitimacy of Commodus Antoninus as the sole remaining son and heir of Marcus Aurelius is overtly drawn into question:

Aiunt quidam, quod et veri simile videtur, Commodum Antoninum, successorem illius ac filium, non esse de eo natum sed de adulterio, ac talem fabellam vulgari sermone contexunt: Faustinam quondam, Pii filiam, Marci uxorem, cum gladiatores transire vidisset, unius ex his amore succensam, cum longa aegritudine laboraret, viro de amore confessam. quod cum ad Chaldaeos Marcus rettulisset, illorum fuisse consilium, ut occiso gladiatore sanguine illius sese Faustina sublavaret atque ita cum viro concumberet. quod cum esset factum, solutum quidem amorem, natum vero Commodum gladiatorem esse, non principem, qui mille prope pugnas publice populo inspectante gladiatorias imperator exhibuit, ut in vita eius docebitur. quod quidem veri simile ex eo habetur quod tam sancti principis filius iis moribus fuit quibus nullus lanista, nullus scaenicus, nullus arenarius, nullus postremo ex omnium dedecorum ac scelerum conluvione concretus. multi autem ferunt Commodum omnino ex adulterio natum, si quidem Faustinam satis constet apud Caietam condiciones sibi et nauticas et gladiatorias elegisse. de qua cum diceretur Antonino Marco, ut eam repudiaret, si non occideret, dixisse fertur "si uxorem dimittimus, reddamus et dotem". dos autem quid habebatur? imperium, quod ille ab socero volente Hadriano adoptatus acceperat.

'Some say, and it seems plausible, that Commodus Antoninus, his son and successor, was not begotten by him, but in adultery; they embroider this assertion, moreover, with a story current among the people. On a certain occasion, it was said, Faustina, the daughter of Pius and wife of Marcus, saw some gladiators pass by, and was inflamed for love of one of them; and afterwards, when suffering from a long illness, she confessed the passion to her husband. And when Marcus reported this to the Chaldeans, it was their advice that Faustina should bathe in his blood and thus couch with her husband. When this was done, the passion was indeed allayed, but their son Commodus was born a gladiator, not really a prince; for afterwards as emperor he fought almost a thousand gladiatorial bouts before the eyes of the people, as shall be related in his life. This story is considered plausible, as a matter of fact, for the reason that the son of so virtuous a prince had habits worse than any trainer of gladiators, any play-actor, any fighter in the arena, anything brought into existence from the offscourings of all dishonour and crime. Many writers, however, state that Commodus was really begotten in adultery, since it is generally known that Faustina, while at Caieta, used to choose out lovers from among the sailors and gladiators. When Marcus Antoninus was told about this, that he might divorce, if not kill her, he is reported to have said "If we send our wife away, we must also return her dowry." And what was her dowry? The Empire, which, after he had been adopted at the wish of Hadrian, he had inherited from his father-in-law Pius.' (*HA Marcus* 19.1-9)

The above passage clearly demonstrates the extent of the anti-Commodus tradition within the ancient literary sources – even the reputations of his parents, Marcus Aurelius and Faustina the Younger, were called into question as a means of discrediting him.[597] All the same, the reasoning behind the extremity of such an anecdote must be considered. Of course, the most prevalent reasoning provided by the ancient authors was that of insanity as a result of being of low birth – this was the most logical reason (to their minds) for such behaviour.[598] Nevertheless, this is impossible to prove and raises serious questions about his parents in turn. However, it is also not possible to disprove either. Despite all of the anti-Commodus rhetoric that was displayed by these ancient texts, through a critical reading it could remain possible to understand them. There are two elements that come become increasingly apparent: his lack of conformity with élite social expectations, and his inclinations towards seeking personal attention from the wider population. Both of these elements of his character did not seemingly sit well with his senatorial peers, which is overtly exhibited in the ancient literary sources. Nevertheless, this is also a damning criticism of him – he should have responded to this response (through curtailing his overt behaviour) in order to be perceived as an effective Roman *princeps*.

Overall Conclusions

Judging from the general discussion provided here by the present analysis there are several themes that clearly become apparent. Commodus Antoninus was, firstly, seemingly a complex character and it is evident that the ancient literary tradition surrounding him did not fully present this. Secondly, this complexity (his attention seeking, his overt devotion to a single deity for example) was used (and possibly accentuated) by the early textual sources in order to present the most negative portrayal of him possible. This may have been justified in some sense, but their absolutist interpretation makes one sceptical. In the ancient texts, there is little 'grey area', which indicates a holistic (or even biased) interpretation of the emperor – thus inclining the modern interpreter to disbelieve the more extreme aspects. All the same, there is clearly one theme (or aspect) that comes through these early literary characterisations – Commodus Antoninus was an attention seeker. Regardless of his possible mania or instability, even a critical reading of the ancient literary sources present this feature of his character. It may not have necessarily been a truly negative aspect for his administrative duties (he did after all

---

[597] Adams 2013, *op.cit.*
[598] Grosso 1964, *op.cit.*

maintain a healthy level of support among the military and the non-élite members of the capital), but it was evidently seen as such by his social peers – another highly influential group within the Roman community.

It is evident that both the god Hercules and the spectacles of gladiatorial combat were key elements of Roman society over the centuries. All the same, Commodus Antoninus was not alone in his appreciation of them – as stated before numerous *principes* expressed a singular appreciation for particular deities. Commodus seems to have simply taken his personal interests one step further (or perhaps one too far). This is shown not only by the ancient literary sources, but also in the sculptural evidence – being identified in connection to a deity was one thing (for example, see the Pima Porta sculpture of Augustus), but being shown *as* them was an entirely different matter. Nevertheless, this does not necessarily prove that all of the early literary references were entirely accurate in this regard either. As mentioned previously, Commodus Antoninus sought to be the centre of attention – this manifested itself in a variety of ways, and in turn it seems to have been generally misunderstood (or at least misinterpreted) by a range of people. Commodus did not behave like his social peers would have expected him to as a Roman *princeps*. This could also possibly be connected to his own perceived sense of entitlement. There may have also been another reason for it. It is impossible to tell with any certainty, which is the perennial difficulty with the nature of the ancient evidence in general.

All the same, the devotion of Commodus Antoninus towards the god Hercules is clearly evident and this has been used by the ancient literary sources as a means of discrediting him to the point of accentuating the divine aspirations of the young *princeps*. However, it must be reiterated that this was not an uncommon form of criticism levelled against seemingly 'bad' Roman emperors. Two other perfect examples of this style of treatment by the ancient literary sources is exhibited in the Emperors Gaius Caligula and Domitian. There was no better way to condemn the memory of a despotic or overly autocratic *princeps* than to accuse them of wanting to be treated as a deity (compare this of course with the final comments of Vespasian described by Suetonius. Naturally this is impossible to prove (or disprove mind you) with any certainty, as with so many of these extreme character traits attributed to Commodus Antoninus. Nevertheless, this could have been attributed to his innate attention seeking tendencies, particularly *if* he did enjoy dressing up as both particular deities and participating as a gladiator. All the same, this would have been viewed as being entirely inappropriate by the more conservative elements of Roman society, particularly his élite social peers.

So in conclusion, while the nature of the ancient evidence discussed in this chapter has been shown to be largely problematic and often inherently subjective in its interpretation, some findings are possible. The characterisation of Commodus Antoninus in this regard clearly places emphasis upon his personal instability and his over blown view of his own self importance. All the same, the primary element that has become starkly noticeable has been his attention seeking tendencies. The relative stability (or instability) of the young emperor is clearly a point of some consideration – it is largely dependent upon how the ancient evidence is interpreted by modern writers. Therefore, it is important to consider a different aspect of Commodus' reign in order to gain a more comprehensive view of his principate in the late Second Century AD – his foreign policies and its administration. This course of action under the young emperor presents a different perspective and another avenue of analysis – one focused upon the administration of Commodus rather than his public persona within the capital.

CHAPTER 7

COMMODUS AND HIS FOREIGN AND PROVINCIAL POLICIES

Introduction

The present discussion has focused upon both the foreign policies and the provincial administrative affairs of Commodus' principate. The aim of this is to provide a more comprehensive modern perspective about the nature of his reign. It is of no great surprise that the ancient literary sources were primarily focused upon the negative aspects of his principate in this regard. This chapter has aimed to view Commodus Antoninus as a leader for the most part. This has been achieved through a holistic approach to the extant ancient evidence – the early literary authors are often compelling, there are other remaining sources of evidence of course. If only the ancient texts were used then this project would be much simpler – Commodus would be viewed as entirely inept. The reality, as noted previously was much more complex. Therefore, in order to gauge the intricacy of these sources of evidence and the general affairs at the time both militaristic policy and internal provincial affairs have been largely dealt with in unison – after all they were intrinsically connected for the most part. All the same, the militaristic focus has been previously more topical for modern observers.

The question surrounding Commodus Antoninus' capacity as a military leader arises in the ancient literature as soon as he becomes sole Roman *princeps* in AD 180. This 'negative' aspect is a key feature of his early discreditation. In this regard, the military insurgencies that occurred against the emperor from AD 180-192 were of course a key feature – the difficulties that he had in *Germania* and northern *Britannia* have of course provided the greatest source of discussion. In this regard the primary discussion has been upon how Commodus dealt with such instances of insurrection. All the same, this focus has also been connected implicitly with the general frontier policy of the young emperor as well. If the Roman State was to survive and prosper it required a clear and cogent frontier policy in order for it to do so. It should, however, be pointed out that even the 'good' Roman *principes* sometimes failed in this regard – Trajan could be used as an example with his over extension of the military resources which ultimately led to a lack of attention to internal security in north Africa. For a Roman emperor the most important centre of attention needed to be upon the security of the internal Roman State initially – the question of expansionism was a secondary concern. So another vital aspect of this chapter for consideration was the administration of the existing Roman provinces – after all they were the front line of the Empire.

The analysis of these provinces under Commodus Antoninus is of great significance for this overall analysis. The evaluation of these various regions provides an important insight into the administration and productivity of the Roman Empire from AD 180-192 in general terms, which in turn casts further insight upon the principate of the young emperor. These provinces have been dealt with on a regional (or perhaps collective) basis in this study in order to consider both the fiscal productivity of each area and its levels of martial security. By considering these aspects in conjunction they ultimately tie in with the question of the occasions of insurgency against Commodus as well, thus reflecting the levels of accountability that this Roman emperor had for dealing with such rebellions. While resistance towards a particular *princeps* has been detailed on many occasions by the ancient literary sources as an indicator of popular dissatisfaction for an emperor (such as in relation to the revolt of Saturninus against the Emperor Domitian),[599] the real provocation of these affairs was often a much more complicated affair. All the same, the primary aim of the present analysis is to examine the general state of affairs that existed in the provinces from AD 180-192, which provides a much greater insight into the nature (and possible success or failure) of Commodus' principate.

Judging from the nature of the extant ancient evidence considered in Chapter Six (albeit being of a primarily literary nature) the general viewpoint that was produced exhibits a stance that Commodus' principate was largely unsuccessful.[600] All the same, this perspective does not really represent all of the available ancient sources of information – only those that were available for that particular topic.

---

[599] Suetonius *Domitian* 6.
[600] Grosso 1964, *op.cit.*

The analysis of both Commodus' foreign policy and provincial circumstances certainly does provide much greater insight into his role as Roman *princeps* through the use of a wide corpus of evidence. In turn this should assist in developing a much more coherent image of the state of play within the empire during the late Second Century AD. Therefore, in turn the questions raised by the ancient literary sources surrounding the efficiency of Commodus Antoninus' role as Roman *princeps* can now be cast in a clearer light. Through this analysis it is also possible to consider the attention seeking feature of his characterisation, which has been made quite apparent in the previous chapter. All the same, initially it is vital to consider the general nature of Commodus' provincial administration and its overall representation in the ancient record in order to ascertain how it has been portrayed prior to more in depth analyses within this study.

The Administration of the Provinces

The provincial management of Commodus Antoninus was not overtly represented by the ancient literary sources, largely for two reasons: firstly, it was not their intended focus area; secondly, the actual nature of his reign (and the matters of the Roman State) was not their primary focus. For the purposes of the present discussion it is, however, vital to consider how Commodus was represented by each type of extant ancient source of information (be it literary, archaeological, numismatic for example) in order to provide the most accurate portrayal of the sources and their interpretation possible. In view of the last chapter and the unfortunate modern dependence on the ancient literary sources, the primary focus here has been upon the contrasting views provided by both the ancient literature and other forms of evidence (such as sculpture for example). This is not intended to discredit the ancient literature entirely, but rather to place it in a broader historical context, which adds to greater interpretative perspective. As mentioned previously, a holistic approach is clearly advisable in this regard. It is only though this methodology that the administration of provincial and foreign concerns under Commodus can be understood with any kind of efficacy. In addition to this, it is via this avenue that the modern scholar can understand the competence of the young emperor's principate and his role as an administrator. All the same, beginning with the textual evidence, one of the best examples of the difficulties with the representations provided by the ancient authors is exhibited in the account of the *HA* biographer (*Commodus* 14.1-3):

per hanc autem neglegentiam, cum et annonam vastarent ii qui tunc rem publicam gerebant, etiam inopia ingens Romae exorta est, cum fruges non deessent. et eos quidem qui omnia vastabant postea Commodus occidit atque proscripsit. ipse vero saeculum aureum Commodianum nomina adsimulans vilitatem proposuit, ex qua maiorem penuriam fecit.

'And because he was so careless, moreover, a great famine arose in Rome, not because there was any real shortage of crops, but merely because those who then ruled the state were plundering the food supply. As for those who plundered on every hand, Commodus afterwards put them to death and confiscated their property; but for the time he pretended that a golden age had come, "Commodian" by name, and ordered a general reduction of prices, the result of which was an even greater scarcity.' (*HA Commodus* 14.1-3)

There are numerous references in the ancient literary sources towards the inept administration of Commodus Antoninus, but most have been discussed (and critically analysed) previously. Yet there is of course little reference by such authors towards his provincial administration, which of course would have been a vital aspect of his general role as Roman emperor (but seemingly of little interest to these authors). The previous passage (*HA Commodus* 14.1-3) is one of the few extracts that provides any reference to what seemingly occurred during his reign in the provinces, but of course it placed a very strong emphasis upon how poorly the Roman State was being run in general – in order to discredit the *princeps* of course. The stress upon his corruption is, however, entirely in keeping with the overall ancient literary tradition. Another feature here that is consistent with the general character of such literary representations is also the almost complete lack of specific detail provided by the biographer of the *Historia Augusta*. All the same, this again epitomises how this author was more focused upon creating a negative characterisation of Commodus rather than providing and specific (or really historical) detail.[601]

The poor nature of Commodus Antoninus' provincial administration was indeed the overall basis of the accounts provided by the ancient authors when writing about this Roman *princeps*. Nevertheless, it must be recognised that such textual representations were entirely focused upon Commodus as an individual, thus producing a perspective that he was completely responsible for the entire Roman State on his own. Theoretically as *princeps* this was true, but in reality this was certainly not the case. So while such judgements by the ancient literary sources were nominally true (and they, of course, also

---

[601] Grosso 1964, *op.cit.*

worked well within the creation of their literary constructions), it is also important to note that the running of such a large empire was a much more complicated series of interworking factors that just the *princeps* himself. This must also be considered in connection with the general economic state of the Roman principate at the time as well. As noted in Chapter Five the economic policies of Commodus (as reflected in the respective coin weights of himself and his predecessor) exhibit the consistency of the Roman economy from AD 169-192. All the same, it is also evident that the currency was by no means as strong as the early imperial period. Yet this was not the fault of Commodus, there being numerous extenuating factors involved in this. The charges of fiscal 'maladministration' by the ancient sources seem to be more indicative of such factors and that Commodus became a rather easy scapegoat for this economic downturn (after a period of such economic 'success' under all of the previous 'good' Antonine *principes* – a difficult hypothesis to argue really).

So, with this in mind, the question remains about how Commodus Antoninus was viewed in the Roman provinces as an administrator. If the ancient literary sources are to be believed his inept (if not corrupt) behaviour would certainly have reduced his popularity. All the same, when the extant evidence of statue bases dedicated to him are considered this definitely does not appear to have been the case. Out of one hundred and eleven known statue bases,[602] of which only four have been discovered in the capital,[603] a total of twenty were erected after his death.[604] This is a telling point. Statues glorifying him during his life and sole principate throughout the Roman Empire could be viewed as being inspired by a desire to express fealty towards him as the *princeps*, but this should have certainly have ended if the *damnatio memoriae* against him was as effective as indicated by the ancient authors. This corpus of post mortem statue bases represents eighteen per cent of the entire extant collection,[605] indicating that the administration of the provinces by Commodus may not have been as ineffective as previously suggested.

---

[602] Hojte 2005, *op.cit.*, pp. 571-89.

[603] Hojte 2005, *ibid.*, *Commodus* nos. 1-4.

[604] Grosso 1964, *op.cit.*

[605] Hojte 2005, *ibid.*, *Commodus* nos. 3, 4, 5, 16, 21, 31, 32, 35, 36, 37, 38, 42, 45, 51, 59, 60, 94, 101, 108.

Therefore, the impression provided by the ancient evidence (be it either literary or epigraphic sources) is a rather mixed view in its presentation of Commodus Antoninus' provincial administration. Clearly the ancient authors maintained the primary focus upon his negative characterisation by accusing him of corruption and poor administration. This view, however, is not supported by the ancient epigraphic evidence dedicated to him after his assassination. While these erections cannot definitively prove that he was an excellent administrator, at the very least they certainly do raise questions about his perceived (or represented) inefficacy. One other aspect that now requires discussion is the military insurgencies that occurred throughout the reign of Commodus because they have been often used as indicators of the unpopularity of his principate by the ancient literary sources. All the same, this was not as simple as it appears at first. The representation of the revolt of Avidius Cassius against Marcus Aurelius in AD 175 was downplayed in the ancient texts, despite it being a very serious affair at the time. However, Marcus Aurelius was characterised as a 'good' *princeps* unlike his son, so therefore it was not depicted as a serious affair. Conversely, the insurgencies against Commodus were naturally *very* serious because he was seemingly highly unpopular.

The Insurgency against Commodus

As mentioned previously, the mention of such insurgencies were used by the ancient literary sources as indicators of the unpopularity of 'bad' emperors – such as Tiberius, Nero, Otho, Vitellius and Domitian – each of them provide perfect comparisons. All the same, this cannot be taken as a definitive interpretation of all these rebellions. The military insurgencies under Commodus Antoninus occurred in Dacia and northern Britain, which were clearly indicative of much more complicated demographic factors rather than the unpopularity and irresponsibility of Commodus himself.[606] They were important to note, however, because of the relationship between the *princeps* and the military forces – a vital source of imperial support that had been well established since before the time of the Emperor Augustus. It is also essential to recognise how Commodus was overtly shown as not being directly involved in suppressing either of these revolts as well, which seemingly sought to emphasise his ineptitude

---

[606] Grosso 1964, *op.cit.*

as a leader. Therefore, it is pertinent at this point to view the revolt that occurred against him in Dacia during AD 183.

Victi sunt sub eo tamen, cum ille sic viveret, per legatos Mauri, victi Daci, Pannoniae quoque compositae, in Britannia, in Germania et in Dacia imperium eius recusantibus provincialibus. quae omnia ista per duces sedata sunt. ipse Commodus in subscribendo tardus et neglegens, ita ut libellis una forma multis subscriberet, in epistulis autem plurimis 'Vale' tantum scriberet. agebanturque omnia per alios, qui etiam condemnationes in sinum vertisse dicuntur.

'The Moors and the Dacians were conquered during his reign, and peace was established in the Pannonias, but all by his legates, since such was the manner of his life. The provincials in Britain, Dacia, and Germany attempted to cast off his yoke, but all these attempts were put down by his generals. Commodus himself was so lazy and careless in signing documents that he answered many petitions with the same formula, while in very many letters he merely wrote the word "Farewell." All official business was carried on by others, who, it is said, even used condemnations to swell their purses.' (*HA Commodus* 13.5-8)

dein per Commodum ad Galliam translatus, in qua fusis gentibus Transrhenanis celebre nomen suum et apud Romanos et apud barbaros fecit.

'Next, Commodus transferred him to Gaul; and here he routed the tribes from over the Rhine and made his name illustrious among both Romans and barbarians.' (*HA Clodius Albinus* 6.3)

As can be seen from the previous passages there is not a vast amount of detail provided about these insurgencies by the ancient literary sources. The *vita Clodius Albinus* by the biographer of the *Historia Augusta* is the most speculative, indicating that he may have been one of the generals involved in the conflict.[607] The account of Cassius Dio (73.3.1-3) provides by contrast much more information outlining the nature of the agreement between Commodus Antoninus and the Dacian tribe, the Buri. This literary description was almost complimentary of Commodus' policy (an unusual occurrence), but of course the authorial praise was directed towards the abilities and diplomacy of Sabinus rather than the *princeps* himself. The biographer of the *Historia Augusta* presents some further insight in the *Commodus* (13.5-8),[608] which not only sought to emphasise the wide spread nature of insurrection during Commodus' principate, but also his lack of personal involvement in its suppression. All of this evidence exhibits not only Commodus' reliance upon his military leaders for the security of the realm, but also his great dependence upon their loyal-

---

[607] See also Dio 73.8.1.
[608] Grosso 1964, *op.cit.*

ty as well. In addition to this it also exemplifies the great pressures that existed upon the northern frontiers at the time, but this has been discussed in greater detail below.

ἐγένοντο δὲ καὶ πόλεμοί τινες αὐτῷ πρὸς τοὺς ὑπὲρ τὴν Δακίαν βαρβάρους, ἐν οἷς ὅ τε Ἀλβῖνος καὶ ὁ Νίγρος οἱ τῷ αὐτοκράτορι Σεουήρῳ μετὰ ταῦτα ἀντιπολεμήσαντες εὐδοκίμησαν, μέγιστος δὲ ὁ Βρεττανικός. τῶν γὰρ ἐν τῇ νήσῳ ἐθνῶν ὑπερβεβηκότων τὸ τεῖχος τὸ διορίζον αὐτούς τε καὶ τὰ <τῶν> Ῥωμαίων στρατόπεδα, καὶ πολλὰ κακουργούντων, στρατηγόν τέ τινα μετὰ τῶν στρατιωτῶν οὓς εἶχε κατακοψάντων, φοβηθεὶς ὁ Κόμμοδος Μάρκελλον Οὔλπιον ἐπ' αὐτοὺς ἔπεμψεν. οὑτοσὶ δὲ ὁ ἀνὴρ μέτριος καὶ εὐτελὴς ὤν, στρατιωτικῶς τε ἀεὶ καὶ περὶ τὴν τροφὴν καὶ περὶ πάντα τἆλλα ζῶν, ὅτε ἐπολέμει, ὑψηλόφρων καὶ φρονηματώδης ἐγίγνετο, χρημάτων τε διαφανῶς ἀδωρότατος ἦν, οὐ μὴν καὶ ἡδὺς τὸ ἦθος ἢ φιλάνθρωπος. ἀυπνότατος δὲ τῶν στρατηγῶν γενόμενος, καὶ τοὺς ἄλλους τοὺς συνόντας αὐτῷ ἐγρηγορέναι βουλόμενος, δώδεκα γραμματεῖα, οἷά γε ἐκ φιλύρας ποιεῖται, καθ' ἑκάστην ἑσπέραν ὡς εἰπεῖν συνέγραφε, καὶ προσέταττέ τινι ἄλλο ἄλλῃ ὥρᾳ κομίζειν τισίν, ἵν' ἐγρηγορέναι τὸν στρατηγὸν ἀεὶ νομίζοντες μηδὲ αὐτοὶ ἄδην καθεύδοιεν. ἦν μὲν γὰρ καὶ ἄλλως ὑπνομαχεῖν πεφυκώς, ἐπὶ πλέον δὲ τοῦτο ἐκ τῆς ἀσιτίας ἤσκηκει. τά τε γὰρ ἄλλα ἥκιστα ἄδην ἐσιτεῖτο, καὶ ὅπως μηδὲ τῶν ἄρτων διαπιμπλᾶται, ἐκ τῆς Ῥώμης αὐτοὺς μετεπέμπετο, οὐχ ὡς οὐ δυνάμενος τῶν ἐπιχωρίων ἐσθίειν, ἀλλ' ἵν' ὑπὸ τῆς παλαιότητος αὐτῶν μὴ δύνηται μηδὲ σμικρῷ πλέον τοῦ πάνυ ἀναγκαίου φαγεῖν· τὰ γὰρ οὖλα αὐτοῦ κακῶς ἔχοντα ῥᾳδίως ὑπὸ τῆς τῶν ἄρτων ξηρότητος ἡμάσσετο. ἐπετήδευε δ' οὖν ἐπὶ μεῖζον αὐτὸ πλάττεσθαι, ἵν' ὡς μάλιστα διαγρυπνεῖν δοκῇ. Μάρκελλος μὲν δὴ τοιοῦτος ὢν τούς τε βαρβάρους τοὺς ἐν Βρεττανίᾳ δεινῶς ἐκάκωσε, καὶ μικροῦ δεῖν ὑπὸ τοῦ Κομμόδου μετὰ ταῦτα διὰ τὴν ἰδίαν ἀρετὴν ἀποθανεῖν μελλήσας ὅμως ἀφείθη.

'He also had some wars with the barbarians beyond Dacia, in which Albinus and Niger, who later fought against the emperor Severus, won fame; but the greatest struggle was the one with the Britons. When the tribes in that island, crossing the wall that separated them from the Roman legions, proceeded to do much mischief and cut down a general together with his troops, Commodus became alarmed but sent Ulpius Marcellus against them. This man, who was temperate and frugal and always lived like a soldier in the matter of his food as well as in everything else when he was at war, was becoming haughty and arrogant; he was most conspicuously incorruptible, and yet was not of a pleasant or kindly nature. He showed himself more wakeful than any other general, and as he wished the others who were associated with him to be alert also, he used to write orders on twelve tablets, such as are made out of linden wood, almost every evening, and bid an aide to deliver them to such-and-such persons at various hours, so that these officers, believing the general the always awake, might not themselves take their fill of sleep. For nature in the first place had made him able to resist sleep, and he had developed this faculty by the discipline of fasting. For in general he would never eat to satiety, and in order that he might not take his fill even of bread, he used to send to Rome for it. This was not because he could not eat the bread of the country, but in order that his bread might be so stale that he should be unable to eat even a small portion more than was absolutely necessary; for his gums were tender and, if the bread was very dry, would soon begin to bleed. However, he purposely exaggerated his natural tendency by

simulating, in order that he might have the greatest possible reputation for wakeful-
ness. Such a man was Marcellus; and he ruthlessly put down the barbarians of Britain, and later, when, thanks to his peculiar excellence, he was all but on the point of
being put to death by Commodus, he was nevertheless pardoned.' (Dio 73.8.1-6)

*hic tamen Perennis, qui tantum potuit, subito, quod bello Britannico militibus equestris loci viros
praefecerat amotis senatoribus, prodita re per legatos exercitus hostis appellatus lacerandusque
militibus est deditus.*

'Yet in spite of his great power, suddenly, because in the war in Britain he had dismissed certain senators and had put men of the equestrian order in command of the
soldiers, this same Perennis was declared an enemy to the state, when the matter was
reported by the legates in command of the army, and was thereupon delivered up to
the soldiers to be torn to pieces.' (*HA Commodus* 6.2)

The problems in northern Britain appear to have occurred on the
island during the following year, AD 184. Cassius Dio (73.8.1-6)
provides the most information about this particular conflict, al-
hough the author ultimately emphasises how Commodus was so
ineffective as a leader at the end of the account. Little detail is provided by Cassius Dio except about the personality and strict discipline of Ulpius Marcellus, which seemingly resulted in the suppression of a revolt located north of the Antonine Wall, which appears to
have been quite significant.[609] The reference in the *Commodus* (6.2) by
the *HA* biographer adds little to the account of Cassius Dio, except
to tie in the revolt of the Praetorian Prefect Perennis against Commodus (see Chapter Eight).[610] Although, as a result of this incursion,
Commodus accepted the title of *Britannicus*, which was celebrated on
numerous coin issues (*RIC Commodus* 110, 128, 155, 174, 198, 221 for
example). Such a title for the war conducted by an imperial legate
was of course critically viewed by the ancient literary sources, but
such titles were hardly unknown in previous imperial contexts.[611] All
the same, the primary focus here still further exemplifies the dependence of the young emperor upon his leading generals in dealing with
such insurgencies.

These insurgencies against Commodus Antoninus were hardly
the treats to the emperor throughout his reign (see Chapter Eight),
but they do highlight the potential threats that existed in the provincial regions of the Roman Empire. They are also indicative of how

---

[609] See C.J. Simpson, "Ulpius Marcellus Again", *Britannia* 11, 1980, pp. 338-
9.
[610] Traupman 1956, *op.cit.*
[611] Grosso 1964, *op.cit.*

reliant he was upon maintaining a close relationship with the Roman military, who sought to secure up these often hostile frontier regions. Owing to his frequent presence in the capital Commodus also became increasingly dependent upon the leadership of his generals as well – characters who seemingly often had more dubious senses of imperial allegiance than would have been ideally preferred. So while the ancient literary sources clearly sought to emphasise the occurrence of such rebellions during the reign of Commodus it has also become evident that they were not really directed against him (as a rejection of the *princeps*, as compared to that against the Roman State) – so it seems that they were more directed against the idea of subservience to the Empire – but ultimately this highlights the often tenuous nature of the frontiers during the late Second Century AD. The most insecure region at this time of course was the northern frontier, which now requires a more specific level of consideration. This area was often shown by the ancient literary sources as being the greatest failure of Commodus Antoninus, which in turn ended up with the general decline and fall of the Roman Empire – a clearly simplistic and ill-judged hypothesis.

Northern Frontier

The analysis of Commodus' northern frontier policy is of the utmost importance for any analysis of the border security issues that existed for any Roman *principes* during the Second Century AD. The significance of his area during the First and Second Centuries AD can simply be judged by the number of legions stationed in this region over time – there were many located there because the area was not only militarily important (and volatile), but also financially/strategically essential to control. In relation to Commodus Antoninus himself (and his representation) this region was also highly significant because it was deemed to have been a major failure of his principate, primarily because of his 'withdrawal' (or otherwise known as 'peace terms') from the Germanic campaign in AD 180. This 'peace settlement' has led some authors to target Commodus as being responsible for the subsequent loss of Roman domination throughout these northern precincts. It is evident, however, that the state of affairs in this region was much more complicated than the ancient literary sources would have us believe, but this is best shown though an analysis of the previous decade of campaigning, such as since AD 169. But for an initial insight into the literary tradition, Commodus is clearly blamed for this downturn, as shown by both

Eutropius (15.1) and Aurelius Victor (17.3). These passages epitomise the dominance of the anti-Commodus sentiment in the ancient literary sources – albeit in a rather brief (or succinct) fashion. Nevertheless, whether such an appraisal was fitting is of course highly questionable. All the same, for the purposes of the present study the province of *Germania* has been the primary focus of this analysis, but its impact, such as upon Dacia and the Danubian provinces has also been considered here.[612]

The German provinces never seem to have been an easy region for the Roman State, going all the way back to the time of the Emperor Augustus.[613] During the reign of Commodus Antoninus the state of play was no different. The Germanic provinces were more than troublesome,[614] which bought about the inclusion of an extra Roman legion in the region.[615] Clearly the northern frontier was of great concern (and instability) throughout this period, not only through the control of the provinces themselves but also because of the tribal dynamics and social (geographic) pressures that existed beyond the Roman *limes*. This of course resulted in an imperial process of strengthening the fortifications of both Upper and Lower German forts in stone after AD 180.[616] This represents an important boost (and in turn an imperial interest) for the maintaining of the provincial defences, even though it has been suggested previously that governors were responsible for such decisions rather than the *princeps* himself.[617] His epitomises the significance of the northern frontier, especially in relation to the dealings with *Germania*. The accounts of Cassius Dio (73.2.1-4) and Herodian (1.6.1-7.4) are as follows:

ὅτι οἱ Μαρκομάνοι οὔτε τροφὴν οὔτ' ἄνδρας συχνοὺς ὑπό τε τοῦ πλήθους τῶν ἀπολλυμένων καὶ ὑπὸ τῆς ἀεὶ τῶν χωρίων κακώσεως ἔτι εἶχον· δύο γοῦν μόνους τῶν πρώτων καὶ δύο ἄλλους τῶν καταδεεστέρων πρέσβεις πρὸς αὐτὸν ὑπὲρ τῆς εἰρήνης ἔπεμψαν. καὶ ἐξεργάσασθαι αὐτοὺς δυνάμενος ῥᾳδίως, μισόπονος δὲ δὴ ὢν καὶ πρὸς τὰς ἀστικὰς ῥᾳστώνας ἐπειγόμενος ἐσπείσατο αὐτοῖς ἐπί τε τοῖς ἄλλοις ἐφ' οἷς ὁ πατὴρ αὐτοῦ συνετέθειτο, καὶ ἵνα τούς τε αὐτομόλους καὶ τοὺς αἰχμαλώτους, οὓς μετὰ ταῦτα ἔλαβον, ἀποδῶσιν αὐτῷ, καὶ σῖτόν τινα κατ' ἔτος τακτὸν τελῶσιν, ὃν ὕστερον

[612] Grosso 1964, *op.cit.*
[613] Ruger 2000, *op.cit.*, p. 496.
[614] Weber 1965, *op.cit.*, p. 384.
[615] *CIL* 11.6057.
[616] Ruger 2000, *op.cit.*, p. 03.
[617] Weber 1965, *op.cit.*, n. 385.

αὐτοῖς ἀφῆκεν. ὅπλα τέ τινα παρ' αὐτῶν ἔλαβε, καὶ στρατιώτας παρὰ μὲν τῶν Κουάδων μυρίους καὶ τρισχιλίους, παρὰ δὲ τῶν Μαρκομάνων ἐλάττους· ἀνθ' ὧν ἀνῆκεν αὐτοῖς τῶν κατ' ἔτος διδόναι τινὰς προσεπέταξε μέντοι σφίσιν ἵνα μήτε πολλάκις μήτε πολλαχοῦ τῆς χώρας ἀθροίζωνται, ἀλλ' ἅπαξ ἐν ἑκάστῳ μηνὶ καὶ ἐς τόπον ἕνα ἑκατοντάρχου τινὸς Ῥωμαίου παρόντος, πρὸς δὲ καὶ ἵνα μήτε τοῖς Ἰάζυξι μήτε τοῖς Βούροις μήτε τοῖς Οὐανδίλοις πολεμῶσιν. ἐπὶ μὲν τούτοις συνηλλάγη, καὶ τά τε φρούρια πάντα τὰ ἐν τῇ χώρᾳ αὐτῶν ὑπὲρ τὴν μεθορίαν τὴν ἀποτετμημένην ὄντα ἐξέλιπεν.

'The Marcomani by reason of the multitude of their people that were perishing and the constant ravishing of their lands no longer had an abundance of either food or men. At any rate they sent only two of their chief men and two others of inferior rank as envoys to sue for peace. And, although Commodus might easily have destroyed them, yet he made terms with them; for he hated all exertion and was eager for the comforts of the city. In addition to the conditions that his father had imposed upon them he also demanded that they restore to him the deserters and the captives that they had taken in the meantime, and that they furnish annually a stipulated amount of grain — a demand from which he subsequently released them. Moreover, he obtained some arms from them and soldiers as well, thirteen thousand from the Quadi and a smaller number from the Marcomani; and in return for these he relieved them of the requirement of an annual levy. However, he further commanded that they should not assemble often nor in many parts of the country, but only once each month and in one place, and in the presence of a Roman centurion; and, furthermore, that they should not make war upon the Iazyges, the Buri, or the Vandili. On these terms, then, he made peace and abandoned all the outposts in their country beyond the strip along the frontier that had been neutralized.' (Dio 73.2.1-4)

ὀλίγου μὲν οὖν τινὸς χρόνου πάντα ἐπράττετο τῇ γνώμῃ τῶν πατρῴων φίλων, οἳ πανημέριοι συνῆσαν αὐτῷ τὰ βέλτιστα συμβουλεύοντες, καὶ τοσοῦτον ἐνδιδόντες χρόνον, ὅσον ἐνόμιζον αὐτάρκη πρὸς σώφρονα τοῦ σώματος ἐπιμέλειαν. παρεισδύντες δέ τινες τῶν ἐπὶ τῆς αὐλῆς οἰκετῶν διαφθείρειν ἐπειρῶντο νέον ἦθος βασιλέως, ὅσοι τε κόλακες τραπέζης [καὶ] τὸ εὔδαιμον γαστρὶ καὶ τοῖς αἰσχίστοις μετροῦσιν, ὑπεμίμνησκον αὐτὸν τῆς ἐν Ῥώμῃ τρυφῆς, θεάματά τε καὶ ἀκούσματα τερπνὰ διηγούμενοι τήν τε τῶν ἐπιτηδείων δαψίλειαν καταριθμοῦντες διαβάλλοντές τε πᾶσαν τὴν ἐπὶ ταῖς ὄχθαις τοῦ Ἴστρου ὥραν, μήτε ὀπώρας εὔφορον κρυεράν τε ἀεὶ καὶ συννεφῆ. "οὐ παύσῃ" δὲ ἔλεγον "ὦ δέσποτα, πηγνύμενόν τε καὶ ὀρυττόμενον πίνων ὕδωρ; ἄλλοι δὲ ἀπολαύσουσι πηγῶν τε θερμῶν καὶ ψυχροῦ νάματος ἀτμίδων τε καὶ ἀέρων, ὧν Ἰταλία μόνη εὔφορος." τοιαῦτα δή τινα τῷ μειρακίῳ ὑποτυπούμενοι ἤγειρον αὐτοῦ τὰς ὀρέξεις ἐς τὴν ἡδονῶν ἐπιθυμίαν. αἰφνιδίως δὲ καλέσας τοὺς φίλους ποθεῖν ἔλεγε τὴν πατρίδα· ὁμολογεῖν δὲ τὰς αἰτίας τῆς αἰφνιδίου ὁρμῆς αἰδούμενος, δεδιέναι προσεποιεῖτο, μή τις ἐκεῖσε προκαταλάβοι τὴν βασίλειον ἑστίαν τῶν εὐπατριδῶν πλουσίων, εἶθ' ὥσπερ ἐξ ὀχυρᾶς ἀκροπόλεως δύναμιν καὶ περιβολὴν συγκροτήσας ἐπιθῆται τῇ ἀρχῇ. αὐτάρκης δὲ ὁ δῆμος χορηγῆσαι πλῆθος ἐπιλέκτων νεανιῶν. τοιαῦτά τινα προφασιζομένου τοῦ μειρακίου οἱ μὲν ἄλλοι συνεστάλησάν τε τὴν ψυχήν, καὶ σκυθρωπαῖς ταῖς ὄψεσιν ἐς γῆν ἔνευσαν. Πομπηιανὸς δέ, ὃς πρεσβύτατός τε ἦν ἁπάντων καὶ κατ' ἐπιγαμίαν προσήκων αὐτῷ (συνῴκει γὰρ τῇ πρεσβυτάτῃ τῶν ἀδελφῶν τοῦ Κομόδου), "ποθεῖν μέν σε", ἔφη, "τέκνον καὶ δέσποτα,

τὴν πατρίδα εἰκός· καὶ γὰρ αὐτοὶ τῶν οἴκοι ὁμοίᾳ ἐπιθυμίᾳ ἑαλώκαμεν. ἀλλὰ τὰ
ἐνταῦθα προυργιαίτερα ὄντα καὶ μᾶλλον ἐπείγοντα ἐπέχει τὴν ἐπιθυμίαν. τῶν μὲν γὰρ
ἐκεῖσε καὶ ὕστερον ἐπὶ πλεῖστον αἰῶνα ἀπολαύσεις, ἐκεῖ τε ἡ Ῥώμη, ὅπου ποτ' ἂν ὁ
βασιλεὺς ᾖ. τὸν δὲ πόλεμον ἀτελῆ καταλιπεῖν μετὰ τοῦ ἀπρεποῦς καὶ ἐπισφαλές.
θάρσος γὰρ ἐμβαλοῦμεν τοῖς βαρβάροις, οὐκ ἐπανόδου πόθῳ ἀλλὰ φυγὴν καὶ δέος
ἡμῶν καταγνοῦσι. καλὸν δέ σοι χειρωσαμένῳ πάντας αὐτοὺς καὶ τῷ ὑπὸ τὴν ἄρκτον
ὠκεανῷ τὴν ἀρχὴν ὁρίσαντι ἐπανελθεῖν οἴκαδε θριαμβεύοντί τε καὶ δεσμίους ἀπάγοντι
καὶ αἰχμαλώτους βασιλεῖς τε καὶ σατράπας βαρβάρους. τούτοις γὰρ οἱ πρὸ σοῦ
Ῥωμαῖοι μεγάλοι τε καὶ ἔνδοξοι γεγόνασι. δεδιέναι δέ σε οὐ χρή, μή τις ἐκεῖ τοῖς
πράγμασιν ἐπιθῆται. οἵ τε γὰρ ἄριστοι τῆς βουλῆς ἐνταῦθα σὺν σοί, ἥ τε στρατιωτικὴ
δύναμις παροῦσα πᾶσα τῆς σῆς ἀρχῆς προασπίζει· ταμιεῖά τε χρημάτων βασιλικῶν
ἐνταῦθα πάντα· ἥ τε τοῦ πατρὸς μνήμη αἰώνιόν σοι πίστιν καὶ εὔνοιαν παρὰ τῶν
ἀρχομένων ἐβεβαίωσεν." τοιαῦτά τινα ἐς προτροπὴν καὶ τὴν πρὸς τὰ κρείττονα ὁρμὴν
ὁ Πομπηιανὸς εἰπὼν διέτρεψε πρὸς ὀλίγον τὸ μειράκιον. αἰδεσθεὶς γὰρ ὁ Κόμοδος τὰ
λεχθέντα, οὐδέν τε οἷός τε ὢν εὐλόγως ἀποκρίνασθαι, τοὺς φίλους ἀπεπέμψατο, φήσας
ἀκριβέστερον καθ' αὑτὸν ἐπισκέψεσθαι τὸ πρακτέον. ἐγκειμένων δὲ τῶν περὶ αὐτὸν
θεραπόντων οὐκέτι μὲν τοῖς φίλοις οὐδὲν ἐκοινώσατο, ἐκπέμψας δὲ γράμματα, καὶ
διανείμας οἷς ἐδοκίμασε τῆς ὄχθης τοῦ Ἴστρου τὴν πρόνοιαν προστάξας τε αὐτοῖς
ἀνέχειν τὰς τῶν βαρβάρων ἐπιδρομάς, ἐπαγγέλλει τὴν ἔξοδον. οἱ μὲν οὖν διῴκουν τὰ
ἐγκεχειρισμένα· οἳ καὶ οὐ πολλῷ χρόνῳ πλείστους τῶν βαρβάρων ὅπλοις ἐχειρώσαντο,
τοὺς δὲ ἐπὶ μεγάλαις συντάξεσιν ἐς φιλίαν ἐπηγάγοντο ῥᾷστα πείσαντες. φύσει γὰρ τὸ
βάρβαρον φιλοχρήματον, καὶ κινδύνων καταφρονήσαντες ἢ δι' ἐπιδρομῆς καὶ ἐφόδου
τὸ χρειῶδες πρὸς τὸν βίον πορίζονται, ἢ μεγάλων μισθῶν τὴν εἰρήνην
ἀντικαταλλάσσονται. ἅπερ ὁ Κόμοδος εἰδὼς καὶ τὸ ἀμέριμνον ὠνούμενος ἀφειδῶς τε
ἔχων χρημάτων, πάντα ἐδίδου τὰ αἰτούμενα. τῆς δὲ ἐξόδου διαγγελθείσης κίνησις δὴ
μεγίστη καταλαμβάνει τὸ στρατόπεδον, καὶ πάντες αὐτῷ συναπελθεῖν ἤθελον, ὡς
‹ἂν› ἀπαλλαγεῖεν μὲν τῆς ἐν τῇ πολεμίᾳ διατριβῆς, ἀπολαύσειαν δὲ τῆς ἐν Ῥώμῃ
τρυφῆς. ἐπειδὴ δὲ διεφοίτησεν ἡ φήμη ἄγγελοί τε ἧκον κηρύττοντες τὴν τοῦ βασιλέως
ἄφιξιν, ὑπερήσθη τε ὁ Ῥωμαίων δῆμος καὶ χρηστὰς εἶχεν ἐλπίδας νέου αὐτοκράτορος
ἐπιθημίᾳ, πατρῴζειν τὸ μειράκιον ἡγούμενοι. ἀνύσας δὲ τὴν ὁδοιπορίαν ὁ Κόμοδος
μετὰ νεανικῆς σπουδῆς καὶ διαδραμὼν τὰς ἐν μέσῳ πόλεις, ὑποδεχθείς τε πανταχοῦ
βασιλικῶς καὶ δήμοις ἑορτάζουσιν ἐπιφανείς, ἀσπαστός τε καὶ ποθεινὸς πᾶσιν ὤφθη.
ὡς δὲ πλησίον ἐγένετο τῆς Ῥώμης, πᾶσά τε ἡ σύγκλητος βουλὴ καὶ πανδημεὶ ὅσοι τὴν
Ῥώμην κατῴκουν ἄνθρωποι, μὴ κατασχόντες αὑτῶν ἀλλ' ἕκαστος φθάσαι θέλων,
δαφνηφόροι τε καὶ πάντα ἐπιφερόμενοι ἄνθη τότε ἀκμάζοντα, ὡς ἕκαστος οἷός τε ἦν,
πόρρω τῆς πόλεως ὑπήντων, θεασόμενοι τὸν νέον καὶ εὐγενῆ βασιλέα. ἐπόθουν γὰρ
αὐτὸν ἀληθεῖ ψυχῆς διαθέσει ἅτε παρ' αὐτοῖς γεννηθέντα τε καὶ τραφέντα καὶ ἄνωθεν
ἐκ τριγονίας βασιλέα τε καὶ εὐπατρίδην ὄντα Ῥωμαίων. τὸ μὲν γὰρ πρὸς πατρὸς αὐτῷ
γένος ἐκ τῶν τῆς συγκλήτου βουλῆς ἐπισήμων ἦν· Φαυστῖνα δ' ἡ μήτηρ βασίλισσα
γεγένητο θυγάτηρ τε οὖσα Ἀντωνίνου τοῦ εὐσεβοῦς ἐπικληθέντος, καὶ Ἁδριανοῦ
ἔκγονος κατὰ θηλυγονίαν, ἀνήνεγκε δὲ τὸ γένος αὕτη ἐπὶ Τραϊανὸν πρόπαππον.

'Then, for a short time, the emperor did everything as the advisers appointed by his
father suggested. They were with him every day, giving him wise counsel; they allowed him only as much leisure as they thought necessary for the sensible care of his
body. But some of his court companions interfered and tried to corrupt the character of the naive emperor. All the sycophants at his table, men who gauge their pleas-

ure by their bellies and something a little lower, kept reminding him of the gay life at Rome, describing the delightful spectacles and musical shows and cataloguing the abundance of luxuries available there. They complained about wasting their time on the banks of the Danube, pointing out that the region was not productive in summer and that the fog and cold were unending. "Master," they said again and again, "when will you stop drinking this icy liquid mud? In the meantime, others will be enjoying warm streams and cool streams, mists and fine air too, all of which only Italy possesses in abundance." By merely suggesting such delights to the youth, they whetted his appetite for a taste of pleasures. And so he immediately summoned his advisers and informed them that he longed to see his native land. But, ashamed to admit the real reason for his sudden interest in returning, he pretended to be fearful that one of the wealthy aristocrats in Rome would seize the empire and, after raising an army and a rampart, take control of the empire, as if from an impregnable fortress. For the Roman populace was sufficiently large to supply numerous picked young men for such an army. While the youth was alleging such specious excuses, the rest, sick at heart, kept their eyes fixed on the ground in dismay. But Pompeianus, the oldest of his advisers and a relation of the emperor by marriage (his wife was Commodus' eldest sister), said to him: "Child and master too, it is entirely reasonable for you to long to see your native land; we too are gripped by hunger to see those we left at home. But more important and more urgent matters here put a curb on that yearning. For the rest of your life you will have the enjoyment of things at home; and for that matter, where the emperor is, Rome is. But to leave this war unfinished is both disgraceful and dangerous. That course would increase the barbarians' boldness; they will not believe that we long to return to our home, but will rather accuse us of a cowardly retreat. After you have conquered all these barbarians and extended the boundaries of the empire to the northern seas, it will be glorious for you to return home to celebrate your triumph, leading as fettered captives barbarian kings and governors. The Romans who preceded you became famous and gained renown in this way. There is no reason to fear that someone at home may seize control. The most distinguished senators are right here with you; the imperial troops are here to protect you; all the funds from the imperial depositories are here; and finally, the memory of your father has won for you the eternal loyalty and good will of your subjects." Eager to improve the situation, Pompeianus, by his exhortations, restrained the youth for a short time. Commodus, shamed by his words and unable to make a suitable reply, dismissed the group, saying that he would consider personally and at greater length what he should do. Then, yielding to his companions, he no longer consulted his advisers about anything. He sent off letters and, after assigning command of the Danube to men whom he considered capable, ordering them to block the barbarians' attacks, he announced his departure for Rome. Those left behind carried out their assignments; soon they subdued most of the barbarians by force of arms, and easily won the friendship of the rest by substantial bribes. The barbarians are by nature fond of money; contemptuous of danger, they obtain the necessities of life either by pillaging and plundering or by selling peace at a huge price. Commodus was aware of this practice; since he had plenty of money, he bargained for release from care and gave them everything they demanded. When the emperor's decision was announced, the army was in turmoil; all the soldiers wanted to leave with him, so that they might stop wasting their time in the war and enjoy the pleasures at Rome. When the news was circulated and messengers arrived to report the approach of the emperor, the Roman people were overjoyed; they had the highest hopes for the reign of the young emperor, believing that he would rule as his father had ruled. Speeding with the vigor of youth, Commodus passed quickly through the cities between Pannonia and Rome. Received everywhere with imperial pomp, he appeared in person before the celebrating crowds, a pleasing sight to all. As he drew near Rome, the entire senate and the people of the city cast aside all restraint. Bearing laurel branches and every kind of flower then in bloom, each man carrying as much as he could manage and eager to be first, they came out some distance from the city to welcome their young and nobly born emperor. For they did indeed give him all their affection, since he was born and reared among them and was of imperial ancestry through three generations of distinguished Romans. His father's family tree included a number of distinguished senators; his mother, the empress Faustina, was the daughter of Antoninus Pius; she was the granddaughter of Hadrian on her mother's side and traced her ancestry to Trajan, her great-grandfather.' (Herodian 1.6.1-7.4)

The account above by Cassius Dio is quite illuminating. It is evident that the primary focus of the author was upon illustrating just how unstable the region was under the leadership of Commodus Antoninus (especially as compared to that of his father, Marcus Aurelius).[618] The leading emphasis here was clearly upon how lax the peace terms were that he drew up with the Marcomanni and the Quadi. The textual accusation that the abandoned these northern regions appears somewhat vindictive on the author's part considering that Cassius Dio's mention of the Iazyges, Buri and Vandili illustrates the large number of tribal groups (and self interests) being dealt with in this encounter.[619] The question remains about whether Commodus Antoninus was wrong or not to put an end to the northern war after such a long period of time. By contrast, this passage by Herodian (1.6.1-7.4) evidently accentuates these elements even further.[620] The level of detail presented about the Germanic campaign (as showing a preference for the emperor being shown as an inappropriate *princeps*) is minimal in this instance, but this epitomises his authorial intent. Herodian emphasises the campaign between Commodus and his father, Marcus Aurelius, largely to accentuate the subsequent failure of the son. The length of this account exhibits how important the 'withdrawal' was for Herodian's characterisation of Commodus. All the same, it does not seem to reflect the seriousness of the situation at all.

---

[618] Traupman 1956, *op.cit.*

[619] cf. L.F. Pitts, "Relations between Rome and the German Kings on the Middle Danube in the First to Fourth Centuries A.D.", *JRS* 79, 1989, pp. 45-58.

[620] Grosso 1964, *op.cit.*

bellum etiam quod pater paene confecerat legibus hostium addictus remisit ac Romam reversus est. Romam ut rediit, subactore suo Saotero post se in curro locato ita triumphavit ut eum saepius cervice reflexa publice oscularetur. etiam in orchestra hoc idem fecit.

'He abandoned the war which his father had almost finished and submitted to the enemy's terms, and then he returned to Rome. After he had come back to Rome he led the triumphal procession with Saoterus, his partner in depravity, seated in his chariot, and from time to time he would turn around and kiss him openly, repeating this same performance even in the orchestra.' (*HA Commodus* 3.5-6)

profectus in Germaniam XIIII Kal. Aelias, ut postea nominavit. iisdem consulibus togam virilem accepit. cum patre appellatus imperator V kal. Exsuperatorias Pollione et Apro iterum consulibus. triumphavit X kal. Ian iisdem consulibus. iterum profectus III nonas Commodias Orfito et Rufo consulibus. datus in perpetuum ab exercitu et senatu in domo Palatina Commodiana conservandus XI kal. Romanas Praesente iterum consule. tertio meditans de profectione a senatu et populo suo retentus est. vota pro eo facta sunt nonis Piis Fusciano iterum consule. inter haec refertur in litteras pugnasse illum sub patre trecenties sexagies quinquies.

'He set out for Germany on the fourteenth day before the Kalends of the month which he later named Aelius, and assumed the toga in the same year. Together with his father he was acclaimed Imperator on the fifth day before the Kalends of "Exsuperatorius", in the year when Pollio and Aper served their second consulships, and he celebrated a triumph on the tenth day before the Kalends of January in this same year. He set out on his second expedition on the third day before the Nones of "Commodus" in the consulship of Orfitus and Rufus. He was officially presented by the army and the senate to be maintained in perpetuity in the Palatine mansion, henceforth called Commodiana, on the eleventh day before the Kalends of "Roma-nus", in the year that Praesens was consul for the second time. When he laid plans for a third expedition, he was persuaded by the senate and people to give it up. Vows were assumed in his behalf on the Nones of "Pius", when Fuscianus was consul for the second time. Besides these facts, it is related in records that he fought 365 gladiatorial combats in his father's reign.' (*HA Commodus* 12.2-10)

In the *Commodus* 3.5-6 the biographer of the *Historia Augusta* briefly outlines the peace terms in a rather negative light by emphasising the prior successes of Marcus Aurelius. Even the reference to the trium-phal procession is degraded by the author through the accentuation of the involvement of Saoterus, despite it being celebrated at the time with his fourth acclamation as *Imperator* and it being hailed as *triumphus felicissimus Germanicus secundus* (*CIL* 14.2922). The second passage *Commodus* 12.2-10) outlines Commodus' initial involvement in the Germanic campaign in AD 175 until AD 180.[621] As with the previously quoted section, this description is rife with rather derisive elements that epitomise the lack of subtlety possessed by the *HA*

---

[621] Traupman 1956, *op.cit.*

biographer.[622] The inclusion of Commodus' renaming of the calendar months by the author were intended to be overt criticisms of him and were also designed to distract the intended audience away from any possible positivity towards the subject at hand – the achievements of the Roman *princeps*. The literary intent was to show Commodus Antoninus as being ridiculous rather than to provide information about the northern frontier at the time.

Therefore, in general terms, the ancient literary sources provide little but criticism of Commodus' attitude and policies towards the northern frontier of the Roman Empire. All the same, the peace terms (or perhaps the 'withdrawal') created by the emperor must also be viewed within the context of over a decade of conflict, the circumstances beyond the Roman frontiers, and his position (or support) within Rome itself. The matter was much more complicated than a simple desire for him to indulge himself. The question remains about the viability of whether Rome would be able to maintain an entirely secure (or dominant) position in this region in view of the societal circumstances that existed both within and beyond the Roman *limes* at this time. It must also be stressed that such pressures existed long before the peace treaty of AD 180. All the same, in order to gain greater perspective in this regard other frontiers need to be assessed, of which the eastern frontier is quite useful in order to fully understand the general policies of Commodus Antoninus.

Eastern Frontier

The frontiers and provinces on the east perimeter of the Roman Empire (and their relative stability) were absolutely vital for the general economic and defensive prosperity of the principate in the late Second Century AD. Therefore, this region would have been absolutely essential for the overall success of Commodus' provincial administration. All the same, it must be noted that there is a general dearth of current information about his governance of these eastern provinces provided by the ancient literary sources. While such a paucity of discussion in this regard should not be stressed too much, it could indicate that the eastern provinces were relatively stable throughout the vast majority of Commodus' principate. After all, if there had been even the slightest indication of general insurgency or instability in the region during his reign it would have been exploited (or emphasised) by the ancient authors in accordance with the wider

---

[622] Grosso 1964, *op.cit.*

anti-Commodus literary tradition. Nevertheless, in order to gain a better perspective for this study the provinces of Syria, Asia, Cappadocia and Egypt have been considered in relation to the policies of the emperor in this region.

Syria as a province provides an interesting perspective about Roman domination from the First to Second Centuries AD. While there was a constant threat posed by the strength of the Parthian Empire to the east, there appears to have been a relatively strong process of Romanisation in the region.[623] One example of this process is exhibited in the clear process of producing socially élite clients in this region,[624] thus exhibiting a general acceptance of Roman social and political traditions. In the province of Asia, it was slightly more complicated (owing to its long history) and yet there was also a continued theme of general stability since the First Century AD. In this instance, the system continued to utilise a process of self governance, which was also reminiscent of its Greek heritage.[625] Cappadocia was of course a turbulent region during the early to mid Roman principate, it being a closely associated province to Armenia – the buffer zone between the Roman and Parthian Empires.[626] This region was exceedingly difficult to manage over time for a variety of reasons,[627] but it was also essential for the Roman military command. Under Emperors such as Trajan this region was relatively calm,[628] but that was largely because of their clear interest in the eastern states of the Empire.[629] Romanisation in this area seemed to be more sporadic than in others,[630] but this was probably owing to the highly Hellenised nature of the area at the time. Egypt of course was a pivotal region for the Roman principate – it was after all an imperial province and a highly controlled district. Egypt's security throughout the period epitomises not only its significance to each *princeps* over time, but also its general importance for the maintenance of the Roman State itself.[631]

---

[623] Cumont 1965, *op.cit.*, p. 624.

[624] Satre 2000, *op.cit.*, p. 640.

[625] Keil 1965, *op.cit.*, p. 587.

[626] Cumont 1965, *op.cit.*, pp. 608-9.

[627] Levick 2000, *op.cit.*, p. 605.

[628] Cumont 1965, *op.cit.*, p. 609.

[629] Grosso 1964, *op.cit.*

[630] Levick 2000, *op.cit.*, p. 630.

[631] See C. Bradford Welles, "A Yale Fragment of the Acts of Appian", *TA-PA* 67, 1936, pp. 7-23.

The analysis of the eastern frontier under Commodus Antoninus requires the examination of the extant epigraphic initially, which clearly illustrates how the emperor was honoured and commemorated in this region both during his lifetime and after his death.[632] Such examples of course have not only been discovered on the Greek peninsula, but also in the more turbulent eastern regions such as Cappadocia (see Hojte *Commodus* n. 102 for example). All the same, when considering each of these regions in isolation it has become increasingly evident that under Commodus the eastern frontier was relatively stable from AD 180-192.[633] Syria for example had not become destabilised following the revolt of Avidius Cassius in AD 175,[634] and the subsequent punishment of Antioch by Marcus Aurelius.[635] Cappadocia clearly had its problems over time from AD 180-192, but this was largely owing to its precarious position between the Roman and Parthian Empires. Nevertheless, it does appear to have been quite successful during this period. In addition to this the vital province of Egypt was also maintained in a safe and secure fashion, thus epitomising a degree of stability at this time.[636]

By comparison, the eastern frontier under Commodus Antoninus does receive somewhat of a mixed review in terms of a mixed review in terms of provincial policy, but this appears to have stemmed from regional issues that were often beyond the direct control of the *princeps*. For decades (if not centuries) this region had presented numerous problems for various Roman leaders that were in many ways more challenging because of the complexity of the cultural issues that were presented by such a diverse range of regional communities. Therefore, it would seem that in general terms there was a fair degree of stability on this frontier throughout the principate of Commodus Antoninus. This then presents the possibility that despite the plethora of long standing regional issues in the east, the emperor may have actually presented an effective frontier policy in this region. In this regard, however, it could also be argued against by stating that this success was really the responsibility (and ultimate accomplishment) of his appointed governors, but the question remains that even 'good' *principes* were given credit for such achieve-

---

[632] See Hojte 2005, *op.cit.*, nos. *Commodus* 79-111.

[633] Traupman 1956, *op.cit.*

[634] Satre 2000, *op.cit.*, p. 641.

[635] *HA Marcus* 25.8-12. See Adams 2013, *op.cit.*, pp. 118-19.

[636] Grosso 1964, *op.cit.*

ments by their legates. Therefore, it is important to also consider other frontier regions in order to gain more perspective – so now the western provinces have been dealt with in this regard.

Western Frontier

As mentioned previously, there were some instances of regional insurrection in the western frontier districts during the reign of Commodus Antoninus (such as in northern Britain), which suggests that his provincial administration presented issues that were quite challenging at times.[637] The western provinces had been a vital area for both social and military support for a Roman *princeps* since the time of the Emperor Augustus, which made their administration a key aspect for the security of each successive principate over time. Despite the occurrence of some difficulties on this frontier during the reign of Commodus, it appears that the emperor was able to maintain a relative degree of regional stability in the western provinces – the issues that presented themselves over time seem to have resulted from both external pressures and excessive Roman imperialism (or possibly expansionism). Therefore, in order to gain the optimal perspective about Commodus' provincial administration in the western regions the primary focuses here has been upon Spain, Gaul and Britain. Through an analysis of these regions the stability of his governance (or of his legates) has become apparent.[638]

The Spanish region was of great importance for the general stability of the Roman State, and had been at least since the Second Century BC. Following the onset of the Roman principate in the First Century AD this position had been clearly solidified.[639] The significance of this region can be most simply viewed through the prevalence and advancement of élite Spanish figures during the Flavian and Antonine periods (of course with the Emperors Trajan and Hadrian being Spanish themselves for example). Since the 'pacification' of the Mediterranean though during the Roman Republic, the Iberian Peninsula had been a largely stable region of Roman dominion for the benefit of both regions. Gaul was much more of a complicated matter. Since the time of the wars of Julius Caesar, Gaul had been a region of the Roman State,[640] but this did not preclude

---

[637] Traupman 1956, *op.cit.*

[638] Grosso 1964, *op.cit.*

[639] Alfoldy 2000, *op.cit.*, p. 444.

[640] Goudineau 2000, *op.cit.*

these western provinces from the realities of the external pressures (economic, military, and demographic for example) beyond the *limes*. Gaul was often impacted upon by the economic, military and demographic issues that were developing in Germany and in the Lowlands, which made them more vulnerable than Spain during this period in the First and Second Centuries AD. The same issues were presented in Britain – during the First Century to Second Century AD there were several difficulties in the south east (the rebellion of Boudicca for example), but it was largely stabilised. All the same, the ejection of Roman dominion in the western and northern regions of the island still required vigilance for both administrative and military reasons during this time period.[641]

Occiso sane Perenni Commodus Pertinaci satisfecit eumque petiit litteris, ut ad Britanniam proficisceretur. profectusque milites ab omni seditione deterruit, cum illi quemcumque imperatorem vellent habere et ipsum specialiter Pertinacem. tunc Pertinax malevolentiae notam subiit, quod dictus est insimulasse apud Commodum adfectati imperii Antistium Burrum et Arrium Antoninum. et seditiones quidem contra se ipse compescuit in Britannia, verum Ingens periculum adiit seditione legionis paene occisus, certe inter occisos relictus. quam quidem rem idem Pertinax acerrime vindicavit. denique postea veniam legationis petiit, dicens sibi ob defensam disciplinam infestas esse legiones. After Perennis had been put to death, Commodus made amends to Pertinax, and in a letter asked him to set out for Britain. After his arrival there he kept the soldiers from any revolt, for they wished to set up some other man as emperor, preferably Pertinax himself. And now Pertinax acquired an evil character for enviousness, for he was said to have laid before Commodus the charge that Antistius Burrus and Arrius Antoninus were aspiring to the throne. And certainly he did suppress a mutiny against himself in Britain, but in so doing he came into great danger; for in a mutiny of a legion he was almost killed, and indeed was left among the slain. This mutiny Pertinax punished very severely.' (*HA Pertinax* 3.5-10)

During the reign of Commodus Antoninus the Spanish provinces were well under control – largely on political, economic, military and demographic levels. All the same, there were developments in Gaul, requiring the returned introduction of troops in some of the regions. As with the eastern frontier this appears to have also been affected by circumstances beyond the confines of the Roman Empire – therefore, the question still remains about how the emperor was meant to directly 'control' this area. The demographic pressures beyond the confines of the *limes* (and how they affected the population pressures within the Empire) were increasingly problematic for Commodus, and would have been so for any incumbent *princeps*. As discussed previously, there were also issues in Britain as well, which were dealt

---

[641] Traupman 1956, *op.cit.*

with in a variety of fashions (as quoted above). So while these literary accounts provide some insight into how successful Rome was in general at this point, it does also raise questions about the validity (or practicality) of Roman imperialism. After all, the topic of whether the incursions in northern Britain were more about or anti-Commodus insurrection or anti-Roman imperialistic dominion remains as a matter of interpretation. All the same, it appears that the western frontiers provide a good representation of the provincial stability that existed in general terms throughout the reign of Commodus, while also noting the continuing elements of dissatisfaction against Roman dominion among some provincial elements.

When considering the western frontier there is a wide consideration of elements that impacted upon the region. These include political, economic, military and demographic concerns to name the least. While the general frontier issues of the eastern provinces were not present on the western border, the wider concerns (such as population pressures and external incursions) were still a common thread. All the same, it still seems that in general terms the western provinces were not really a large point of concern for Commodus Antoninus. The issues in *Germania* certainly provided population, militaristic and economic pressures upon the Roman State in the north, as did the tribal incursions in Britain, but while they have been used by the ancient literary sources in association with Commodus, these references also appear somewhat excessive in their vitriol against him. In general terms, the western regions were quite stable in relation to the overall steadiness of the principate from AD 180-192. The modern analysis of the western provinces provides little more than this perspective – so again, perhaps Commodus Antoninus was not as inept as some of the ancient authors would have us believe. All the same, the southern frontier of the emperor's principate also requires examination in this regard for a holistic view of his efficiency (or inefficiency of course).[642]

Southern Frontier

The southern frontier of the Roman Empire presented a different range of issues from AD 180-192, but in general terms this quite important region was also quite stable during the principate of Commodus Antoninus. Unfortunately the ancient literary sources provide few details about the specific circumstances in northern

---

[642] Grosso 1964, *op.cit.*

Africa during this period, with there really only being one specific reference o the district, which is made in the *Historia Augusta* (*Commodus* 13.5-8) (see below). This passage simply refers to the defeat of the Moors in Mauretania by the emperor, but this seems to have purely been included by the *HA* biographer to accentuate the 'general instability' of his reign rather than to present any precise details about the circumstances in northern Africa. All the same, at the outset of this section the economic importance of the region must be stressed – thus highlighting the necessity of maintaining its stability for every Roman *princeps*. In order to fully ascertain the general circumstances in these districts, the provinces of Africa, Cyrenaica and Mauretania have all been analysed. Each of these regions provides different perspectives and contexts for this examination of Commodus' southern frontier, thereby giving the optimal source of information for our understanding and examination.

In general terms, the regions of northern Africa were of great importance for the wider prosperity of the Roman State. The province of Africa had become a highly valued region since the period of the middle to late Republic, being a vital source of revenue for the Roman Empire overall. In order to maintain this economic viability, the province itself required stability and security.[643] The region of course had a very wide range of ethnic groups to consider for its administration,[644] which epitomised the important existing trade networks in the province. Cyrenaica was a much more turbulent region, experiencing a variety of cultural and social influences within the Empire on both their eastern and western boundaries.[645] There were a series of difficulties that occurred from the First into the Second Centuries AD throughout the province, which made a coherent policy quite problematic for the various Roman *principes*.[646] The history (and multiple population demographics) of this region of course made the formulation of a definitive security policy quite challenging over time. Mauretania was also equally difficult to manage, but it had also become an important source of military manpower by the time of Commodus Antoninus' principate.[647] Prior to this there had been

---

[643] Whittaker 2000, *op.cit.*, p. 514.

[644] Albertini 1965, *op.cit.*, p. 481.

[645] Idris Bell 1965, *op.cit.*, p. 667.

[646] Reynolds 2000, *op.cit.*, pp. 547-53.

[647] Albertini 1965, *op.cit.*, pp. 482-3.

a series of conflicts that had destabilised the region,[648] which extended as far as occasional attacks on Spanish territory. All the same, aside from the brief account provided by the biographer of the *Historia Augusta* (*Commodus* 13.5-8), few details have survived:

Victi sunt sub eo tamen, cum ille sic viveret, per legatos Mauri, victi Daci, Pannoniae quoque compositae, in Britannia, in Germania et in Dacia imperium eius recusantibus provincialibus. quae omnia ista per duces sedata sunt. ipse Commodus in subscribendo tardus et neglegens, ita ut libellis una forma multis subscriberet, in epistulis autem plurimis 'Vale' tantum scriberet. agebanturque omnia per alios, qui etiam condemnationes in sinum vertisse dicuntur.

'The Moors and the Dacians were conquered during his reign, and peace was established in the Pannonias, but all by his legates, since such was the manner of his life. The provincials in Britain, Dacia, and Germany attempted to cast off his yoke, but all these attempts were put down by his generals. Commodus himself was so lazy and careless in signing documents that he answered many petitions with the same formula, while in very many letters he merely wrote the word "Farewell." All official business was carried on by others, who, it is said, even used condemnations to swell their purses.' (*HA Commodus* 13.5-8)

As mentioned previously, the number of details provided by the ancient literary sources in this regard about the North African provinces is minimal to say the least. The previous passage presented by the biographer of the *Historia Augusta* provides an excellent example of the minimalist approach towards detail by the ancient authors in this regard. It simply outlines that Commodus (or more accurately – his legate) defeated the Moors,[649] which appears to have occurred in Mauretania after AD 184 if the epigraphic evidence is used as a corroborating tool.[650] As with the other frontier regions, the general impression provided by the statue bases also reflects the wider popularity of Commodus throughout the area.[651] In all likelihood this reflects how well secured the region was during the period and also how important it was generally for all Roman *principes* in the Second Century AD. Cyrenaica still provided some difficulties for most of the Antonine Emperors,[652] but most of these inter-state (or perhaps inter-community) rivalries appear to have become resolved by the period from AD 180-192. This suggests that perhaps Commodus as a provincial *princeps* may not have been such an incompetent adminis-

---

[648] Whittaker 2000, *op.cit.*, pp. 522-3.

[649] Traupman 1956, *op.cit.*

[650] Dessau 1916, *op.cit.*, no. 396.

[651] Hojte 2005, *op.cit.*, *Commodus* nos. 46-63.

[652] Reynolds 2000, *op.cit.*, pp. 553-8.

trator as the ancient literary sources would suggest – or at the very least he seems to have been good at appointing the right people to control, administer and secure these regions.[653]

When examining the southern frontier of the Roman State under the guidance of Commodus Antoninus there are two significant aspects that must be recognised: firstly, this region was vitally important for the economic stability of the Roman Empire in general. Secondly, it is also essential to emphasise the prominence of the various leaders derived from this provincial area at the time,[654] which of course becomes even more apparent with the ultimate rise and dominance of the Emperor Septimius Severus during the post-Commodus period. In general terms, however, it is also essential to note how stable (if not secure) these areas were from AD 180-192. While there may have been the occasional point of concern for Commodus Antoninus, in essence these provinces worked well and appear to have been well administered. As with the other frontiers previously discussed, there does not seem to have been an overall impression of incompetence on the part of the emperor. At the very least he seems to have appointed capable people for the various positions of governance and administration, even if he was not directly involved in each region personally.[655] Therefore, it appears that the provincial administration of the southern frontier worked well during the principate of Commodus. So at this point it seems appropriate to examine the provincial policies of the emperor in general terms in order to gain the optimal perspective of this aspect of his principate.

General Foreign Policy and its Administration

When considering the overall foreign policy position of Commodus Antoninus, the first point that must be stressed was the wide variety of issues that he had to face. There were highly duplicitous areas of concerns, factors and constraints involved when considering such a huge range of ethnic, cultural, geographic and topographical variations that made each region quite different – and in turn difficult to manage. Unfortunately, when analysing these aspects of his principate, there is also a severe lack of extant information provided that also needs to be recognised as well. Of the extant ancient literary

---

[653] Grosso 1964, *op.cit.*

[654] Champlin 1980, *op.cit.*

[655] See Traupman 1956, *op.cit.*

sources of information, as noted previously, there was also a prevalent anti-Commodus sentiment that has coloured the nature of our knowledge. If the ancient literary sources are to be believed, Commodus Antoninus was a hopeless provincial administrator – an untenable hypothesis. So despite this negativity, the general impression presents quite a different view. It would, therefore, appear that these ancient authors have suffered from the historiographical (and biographical) dilemmas of both hindsight and the predilections of their intended audience – the conservative, pro-senatorial aristocracy. So, therefore, the emperor had to be shown in the worst light possible, regardless of its accuracy. The literary style used in this regard was that of negative allusion rather than the provision of fact or detail.[656]

In relation to military affairs, it is initially quite apparent to note the negativity of the ancient literary sources towards the *princeps*. According to these accounts of Commodus Antoninus, he had either little or no experience in running military campaigns, and even less interest in conducting such warlike affairs. All the same, it must also be recognised that he did have *some* experience in the undertaking of a significant military operation – after all he had been mostly present on the German frontier from AD 175/6 until AD 180.[657] While the ancient literary sources downplay his role (in preference for accentuating the seniority and leadership of his father, Marcus Aurelius), at the very least he must have observed *some* of the ways in which such a campaign was conducted and also interacted with the other military leaders involved. In addition to this, it is evident that he clearly understood the importance of the Roman military as a support base for himself (and for the security of the Roman State),[658] which is overtly demonstrated through the numismatic evidence whereby he affiliated himself with them.[659] Therefore, while he is characterised as neglecting the Roman military it becomes increasingly evident that he did not underestimate their importance at all (and the vital support that they gave to him maintaining his position). So while he did not undertake any major campaigns himself after the 'peace treaty' of AD 180 in *Germania*, his seems to have been more indicative of a change

---

[656] Grosso 1964, *op.cit.*

[657] See Traupman 1956, *op.cit.*

[658] See M.P. Speidel, "Commodus the God-Emperor and the Army", *JRS* 83, 1993, pp. 109-14.

[659] *RIC Commodus* 9a, 46, 54, 128, 190, 249; Gnecchi 53/12.

in policy rather than the complete neglect of provincial frontier affairs from AD 180-192.[660]

The attitude of Commodus Antoninus towards the management of the Roman provinces has also been criticised by the ancient literary sources, but this similarly appears quite unjustified following further scrutiny. One of the clear features of his principate in this regard was his distance from the provinces – after the creation of the 'peace terms' with the various Germanic tribes (such as the Marcomanni, Quadi, and Buri for example) in AD 180, Commodus maintained some separation from direct involvement in provincial affairs.[661] Of course this was characterised by the ancient authors as being a reflection of his personal disinterest (and his preference for city-based corrupt indulgence). All the same, it appears that this perspective was unduly critical of the emperor – after all Antoninus Pius provides another excellent example of a Roman *princeps* who created provincial policy while being based solely in Italy rather than on the 'front line'.[662] The Emperor Augustus is another example of a leader who maintained provincial affairs from a distance as well. So, in many ways, while Commodus was viewed as being distant, he did also seemingly make good provincial appointments for the most part, which appears to have produced a quite stable provincial environment from AD 180-192.[663] With the benefit of hindsight (which must only be used on a cursory level), it is also important to note that the general instability of many provinces subsequently in the Third Century AD has in turn affected many of the ensuing views about Commodus' policy in this regard – in essence he has been blamed for causing the future frontier and security issues after his death. The attribution of such responsibility against the emperor is clearly unjustified and was really more symbolic of the general state of the Roman Empire throughout such a difficult period.[664]

One of the primary themes presented by the ancient literary sources about Commodus Antoninus' policy in this regard was fo-

---

[660] Grosso 1964, *op.cit.*

[661] See R. Scranton, "Two Temples of Commodus at Corinth", *Hesperia* 13.4, 1944, pp. 315-48.

[662] See J.H. Oliver, "Three Attic Inscriptions concerning the Emperor Commodus", *AJPh* 71.2, 1950, pp. 170-9.

[663] cf. Raubitschek, A.E., 1949, "Commodus and Athens", *Hesperia Supp.* 8, pp. 279-466.

[664] Traupman 1956, *op.cit.*

cused upon the general instability of the Roman Empire. As mentioned previously, he was characterised as being almost entirely disinterested in the management of the provinces, thus casting him as an entirely inappropriate *princeps*. Yet this impression has been contrasted by the view given by the statue bases discovered throughout the Roman State – this source of evidence suggests a popular and well respected emperor even after his death in Ad 192. Both types of ancient evidence have, of course, their respective limitations, but they are equally important because of this inherent contrast in perspective. In general terms, it does certainly become evident that the Roman provinces were not as insecure (or unstable) as the ancient texts would have us believe, but this does also appear to have been largely reliant upon the success of Commodus' regional appointments. In this regard, the selection of Ulpius Marcellus in northern Britain may have been less than successful.[665] All the same, it must be noted that this was always a complicated issue for a Roman *princeps* – in many ways it was more connected to the élite domestic politics of the capital rather than administrative proficiency. In addition to this it is also essential to recognise that even Commodus' highly experienced Antonine predecessors such as the Emperors Trajan and Hadrian also made mistakes in this regard, which resulted in periods of instability during their more 'successful' principates.[666]

So when considering the foreign policy and provincial administration of Commodus Antoninus in general terms there are two primary elements that become clearly apparent. Firstly, there are fundamental issues with all of the ancient sources of evidence, be they literary, epigraphic or numismatic. All of them have their limitations, but in turn this also exemplified the reason why they *must* all be used in conjunction. By examining such a diverse range of perspectives (and intentions) it is possible to gain the most holistic view possible by critically reading each extant source on its own merits. Therefore, having viewed the ancient evidence, in general terms it does appear that the overall frontier policy and provincial administration position of Commodus seems to have been sound for the most part. All the same, in this regard it is now possible to make an exploratory suggestion about the policies of Commodus Antoninus – it would seem that the emperor was more inclined towards diplomatic

---

[665] See M.G. Jarrett, "The Case of the Redundant Official", *Britannia* 9, 1978, p. 289.
[666] Grosso 1964, *op.cit.*

resolutions rather than military ones. This is of course impossible to determine in any kind of absolutist fashion, but it is a vital consideration. This has been discussed further in the next section of the study.[667]

Overall Conclusions

Overall, the analysis of Commodus' foreign policy and provincial administration has provided a great deal of insight into his principate in general terms. The accusations of his corruption and maladministration have clearly affected the subsequent interpretations of his reign, but this does not really seem to have been the case once the provinces and a wider range of ancient sources are considered specifically. The analysis of Commodus Antoninus' administration in this regard seemingly provides an important counterpoint to the more *personal* characterisations that have become so dominant in the historical interpretations of this particular *princeps*. Therefore, it is essential to examine the provincial matters as objectively as possible – a difficult task in view of the limited range of extant ancient evidence available. Firstly, it has been clearly shown that Commodus preferred to use legates in the provinces (nominally in the role of governor) rather than becoming directly involved himself. Nevertheless, this was not unusual for a Roman *princeps* and in many ways it epitomises the practicalities of running such a large (and culturally diverse) Empire. Yet Commodus is cast an inattentive and entirely irresponsible character. The decision to accept terms with the various Germanic tribes (while shown as a disaster) seems to have actually been a prudent decision after so many years of campaigning.[668] The possibility of his preference for diplomacy rather than overt conflict was of course not mentioned by the ancient literary sources, and yet it seems to have been quite a wise choice (with the benefit of hindsight naturally).

The ancient authors have clearly accentuated the occurrence of frontier insurgency during the reign of Commodus Antoninus rather than his ability to administer the Roman provinces themselves. This conforms to their literary intent and the views of their intended audience. The difficulties in Dacia and northern Britain were not complete catastrophes – yet they were accentuated in the ancient texts

---

[667] Grosso 1964, *op.cit.*

[668] See Alföldy, G., 1971, "Der Friedensschluss des Kaisers Commodus mit den Germanen", *Historia* 20.1.

unlike the actual state of affairs on the frontiers in general. This was of course to be expected from such authors – the administration of affairs was hardly compelling to describe, and unlikely to be included if the interest of an audience was to be maintained. As mentioned previously, Commodus was not directly involved in the provinces after AD 180 – a point used to exhibit his corruption and inattentive behaviour.[669] Yet this was not uncommon for a Roman emperor. The most important aspect that Commodus needed to maintain in this regard was his provincial military support – without the backing of the military, his imperial position would not have continued (in real terms). The necessity of the assistance of the Roman army is illustrated by the response of Pertinax after the death of Commodus – the army needed to receive their expected payment to ensure their services. Unfortunately for him he did not apply the same principle to the Praetorian Guard. However, for present purposes, the military were needed by every *princeps* to secure their position, which Commodus Antoninus clearly understood. All the same, if his general foreign and provincial policies are considered it is evident that he did not seek to undertake large scale campaigns – he accepted the name of *Britannicus* after a minor campaign, but this was early in his reign (essentially indicating that the desire for his legitimacy was the real motivator). All the same, it is evident that the emperor appreciated (and enjoyed) the support of the Roman army, and while the emphasis upon insurgency against him by the ancient literary sources sought to discredit this, the general impression provides an entirely different perspective.

As mentioned previously, the extant ancient evidence provided about his provincial administration was varied and somewhat contradictory. The early literary sources present an image of instability and insecurity while also providing very few details in their accounts – he negative inferences were largely mere suggestions. By contrast, the statue bases from the Roman provinces were laudatory towards him, which is to be expected in such an honorific context. This divergence in representation is important because it highlights the general complexity of the relationship between *princeps* and author/actor. It is notable that Commodus Antoninus had little direct contact with the provinces from AD 180-192, but this was not previously unheard of. In many ways, the use of provincial legates and governors was not only common if not essential in light of the prac-

---

[669] Traupman 1956, *op.cit.*

ticalities of running such a large (and culturally diverse) area. As would be expected, the anti-Commodus literary tradition has cast him as being reticent towards his duties in this regard, but this seems somewhat unfair. What has become evident is that Commodus did not favour an expansionist policy – diplomacy (as shown in *Germania* and the general dealings in the period) was seen as being the pre-ferred option for the most part. While the impression given by the ancient literary sources was one of indolence and disregard, their characterisations may not have necessarily been the entire story.[670]

The frontier policy of Commodus Antoninus appears to present a combination of sources of information (minimally) and misinfor-mation at the same time (through the accentuation of relatively mi-nor incursions). As mentioned previously, the ancient literary sources depict him as being not involved in any successes, and yet of course he was entirely responsible for any dissension. All the same, once these 'major' insurgencies are considered objectively (in Dacia and northern Britain), as well as the defeat of the Moors in Mauretania and the 'peace terms' in *Germania*, it seems that Commodus' reign was actually quite stable in relative terms. After all the suppression of revolts in Dacia and northern Britain can hardly be viewed either as major successes nor major concerns for that matter. In that sense, Commodus' adoption of the name *Britannicus* seems to be more in dicative of a desire for personal prestige early in his reign rather than the celebration of a momentous success – he was not even there. Unlike many of his predecessors it is evident that Commodus Anto-ninus did not seek any major campaigns in order to promote his principate he was clearly not a military animal (in the traditional sense). So while he has been characterised as inexperienced and less than interested in these affairs, another possibility – that of diploma-cy – is just as likely. This tactic seems somewhat reminiscent of An-toninus Pius – his grandfather. The cessation of the war in *Germania* after a decade should really come as little surprise (despite the ad-monition of the ancient literary sources). Perhaps it is more likely that Commodus had seen a stalemate coming (unlike the later an-cient authors) and also that he had more pressing concerns – the security of his own position in a highly volatile political system: the capital of ancient Rome.

Therefore, the analysis of Commodus' frontier policy and pro-vincial administration has clearly exhibited a diverse range of opin-

---

[670] Grosso 1964, *op.cit.*

ions, sources and general conclusions about the period. That is what makes such an examination fascinating. If priority is given to one over everything else, it becomes far too subjective. The irony that becomes most apparent at first glance is how although he was a 'bad' *princeps*, he also received a high degree of respect and honour in the provinces after his death (and not just in Africa to pay allegiance to his deifier – Septimius Severus). In general terms once all of these sources are compared, this does not really add up – with the numerous changes in Emperor after the death of Commodus (from AD 192-197), there was no dynastic succession and little but symbolic reason to still honour Commodus. This is particularly pertinent if he was such a widely unpopular, irresponsible and corrupt *princeps*, who ultimately suffered from *damnatio memoriae*. The simplicity (and weaknesses) of the ancient literary sources in this regard becomes all too apparent. The fact remains – Commodus Antoninus received twenty statue bases (out of one hundred and eleven extant examples) after his death in AD 192 – nineteen of these refer to him as being deified (even one of these nineteen was produced in Rome – see Hojte (2005), *Commodus* number 4). Would this have happened if he had been so vehemently hated?

So with all of this in mind, the question remains about how the material (and in turn Commodus' foreign/provincial policies) can be best examined. The only logical take would be to be critical of the authorial motives of the ancient literary sources, while also factoring in the promotional intentions of the epigraphic and numismatic evidence. Each source is vital four our knowledge, but each of them also pursued their own interests (and those of their intended audience) – otherwise they would not have been produced in the first place. All the same, the possibility of Commodus Antoninus not following an expansionist policy (in preference for a diplomatic one) was not conceivable for them. Marcus Aurelius had fought a German campaign from AD 169-180 to little avail. Lucius Verus had conducted a Parthian campaign that had success, but this joint-emperor seemingly never arrived. Since the time of Antoninus Pius the northern frontier of Britain had been a series of both successes and setbacks. Trajan had great success in Dacia and Parthia, and yet he suffered from rebellions in both Egypt and northern Africa at the end of his reign. So it would appear that with every success there was often a (less celebrated) difficulty over the generations. The reality was that such a large, diverse Roman Empire was exceedingly difficult to not only manage, but to also definitively secure. *Germania* had been challenging for centuries (and yet it was vital as well). So the possibility remains that Commodus Antoninus may have learnt from his time on the northern *limes* (AD 175-180), or perhaps from the actions of his ancestors – but it seems that he ultimately realised that it was best to consolidate the Roman frontier. In turn, he could have also tried to consolidate and secure a much more hazardous realm – the domain of Roman internal politics. This topic has been left for the final chapter of this study.

CHAPTER 8

CONSPIRACY DURING COMMODUS' REIGN, HIS ASSASSINATION AND AN OVERALL PERSPECTIVE OF HIS REIGN

Introduction

In general terms, the aim of this chapter is to primarily consider the threats that were aimed against Commodus and how this reflects upon his principate. The ultimate assassination of the emperor is of course a primary focus. All the same, this is not intended to either justify or vilify his reign, but instead it aims to understand Commodus' principate on a more holistic level – in order to understand him we must also consider the views of his opponents (and also examine why they opposed him). In order for this to occur there must be a critical interpretation of all the ancient sources of extant evidence, as has been applied in the previous chapters of this study. So while the ancient literary sources are the primary focus here in many ways, this is largely because of their dominant impact upon current (uncritical?) interpretations of the reign of Commodus. This study seeks to promote critical thought, especially about Commodus and the way in which ancient sources treat their respective subjects. The view provided here will never be definitive, but it is worthy of consideration. In this light, the present chapter culminates with a general analysis of Commodus and a consideration about whether he deserved such a gruesome end. If the ancient literary sources are to be believed unequivocally, then it was clearly justifiable – yet the resulting years were hardly ideal, and these authors have been shown to be lacking in objectivity as well. In addition to this, should we really examine historical figures in such a 'black and white' fashion? Life would be easier to understand if it was so clear cut.

When evaluating the conspiracies that occurred against the principate of Commodus the same method must be applied. So while the ancient literary sources provide their accounts of such dissension, they must also be read in a critical light. The primary emphasis by them is upon the general insecurity of Commodus' principate.[671] By accentuating such instability, as mentioned previously, it was a means of exhibiting Commodus as an entirely inappropriate *princeps* – a view that already seems questionable. All the same, when considering the conspiracies themselves there is more to the story rather than an amassed group that sought to liberate themselves from an oppressive dictator. The literary sources would have us believe this, but it is much more complex (especially on a literary, let alone historical, level). Nevertheless, for the purposes of the present discussion it is simply vital to note the diversity in range of conspirators that rose in prominence at various times during the reign of Commodus. They come from numerous 'walks of life' and are presented for acting as such for as many diverse reasons. The primary aim for the ancient authors was to show that the emperor was not suited for the principate. According to such textual accounts Commodus was illegitimate as *princeps*, and every literary avenue was followed in order to prove it – none was better than emphasising that people (regardless of their status) sought to have him deposed. This is best shown in the accounts of his assassination – a topic that received a great deal of attention by the ancient literary sources.

The assassination of Commodus is of course a key element of discussion for the present study. The most important aspect to note initially are the numerous and lengthy accounts dealing with this affair presented by the ancient literary sources. The death of Commodus provided an excellent opportunity for them to characterise him in the most negative light possible. All the same, it is also vital to recognise the lack of specific detail provided by many of these representations. This exhibits how the death (as gruesome as it was) was their primary focus point, rather than the details of what actually happened at the time. Therefore, this leads to the question about whether or not he was really deserving of such a death. While this is an inherently subjective point of consideration in which to consider, it is still a vital aspect to recognise. To my mind, the end of Commodus' life seems to have been more indicative of the state of affairs within the Roman principate at the time rather than his incapacity, but this has been discussed further below. Was the death of Commodus really indicative of his reign in general terms? It is for this reason that the most holistic approach possible must be taken (in

---

[671] Grosso 1964, *op.cit.*

relation to sources of ancient evidence), particularly by viewing most of them through a suitably critical lens.

While this chapter has attempted to judiciously consider the instability and ultimate demise of Commodus' principate, the primary focus here has really been upon the *princeps* and the nature of internal Roman politics. This is because when evaluating the dominance of the ancient literary sources it is essential to note the general impact of their anti-Commodus stance. It has already been established that such a position was not always sustainable in this regard – therefore, the analysis of Commodus' position within Roman politics is a vital consideration. He must be viewed within the overall scheme of social and political implications that existed within his reign. After all, if the ancient literary sources are to be trusted in an unquestioning fashion, was he really suitable to be *princeps* from the start? Why was he accepted as joint-emperor? Should Marcus Aurelius bear responsibility? If that is the case, why are these authors at pains to distance the father from the son? The number of questions that resonates highlights the discrepancy in such characterisations. So in essence, is this more indicative of Roman conservative bias, which has been readily accepted by both ancient and modern audiences? In many ways 'evil' characters are much more fascinating creatures for both author and audience alike. It is for this reason that the present chapter has focused upon both the successful and unsuccessful attempts to remove Commodus as *princeps*. Therefore, at this point the conspiracies against the emperor (or be they unsuccessful attempts) have been discussed in light of how they were intended to upon his principate. Following on from this the assassination of Commodus has been dealt with.

Conspiracies against Commodus

The analysis of the conspiracies against Commodus provides a valuable insight into the general perspective of his principate (or at least the extant recorded view). While it has already been acknowledged that the ancient literary sources followed a definitively anti-Commodus stance in their characterisations, this was not the entire story. All the same, such perspectives do provide an insight into how his principate was viewed in the Third Century AD and beyond. So while the presentation of these conspiracies against Commodus were intended to reflect poorly upon his reign, once this is recognised it is still possible to draw conclusions about the overall state of affairs within the Roman Empire at the time. The reference towards conspiracies against Commodus was intended to criticise (and delegitimize) his principate,[672] but it is noticeable that not every conspiracy was cast in such a light. When considering the ancient authors under question (such as Herodian, Cassius Dio and the *HA* biographer), the example of Avidius Cassius is a perfect example of such a contrast – there is no implied blame upon Marcus Aurelius at all for being deficient as an emperor. Therefore, it is quite clear that such a categorisation of 'good' or 'bad' is far too simplistic in this regard. All of this is important because the ancient literary sources are the primary foundations for this discussion, which makes the recognition of such inherent subjectivity a vital point of consideration.

So when evaluating these authors there are a variety of issues that must be recognised. The general perspectives of each writer have already been considered, but their intended audience is probably an even more important issue – the reception of each work would have been a focal consideration during the composition (or more importantly – publication: an expensive process at the time) of each text. So, who were these texts written for? The wealthy classes ('senatorial' is probably too politically and socially restrictive really). They would have not only been the intended audience, but may have also financially (or at least socially) supported the production of such texts. In this regard, there is also an ironic confusion in the ancient literary sources about the nature of these conspiracies.[673] This makes such representations appear even more dubious. Hence this is a significant dilemma. So according to the texts, Commodus appears to have been such a poor *princeps* that these conspiracies were somewhat justified – even this aspect varied in accordance with which conspirator is being discussed. In this regard it is also important to note the range of social and political backgrounds for each respective leading conspirator – they reflect a diverse set of personal circumstances, which was intended to accentuate the wide acceptance and recognition of Commodus' failings. Most notable of these was of course Claudius Pompeianus Quintianus, a well connected figure in Rome at the time.

The suggestion that Claudius Pompeianus Quintianus was a part of a conspiracy against Commodus is fascinating. As mentioned previously, he would have been a relative through marriage (he was

---

[672] Traupman 1956, *op.cit.*
[673] Grosso 1964, *op.cit.*

the son of Tiberius Claudius Pompeianus,[674] so hence the step-son of Lucilla), but he was also from a well known and highly influential family – descended from a well respected member of the Roman aristocracy beyond the imperial *familia*. So he was important. Nevertheless, prior to examining the conspiracy against Commodus, it is vital to consider the symbolic importance of his inclusion as such a dissident by the ancient literary sources. One of the primary concerns for such authors representing the unpopularity of 'evil' *principes* was to accentuate the breadth of acceptance (if not active involvement) of movements against these despots by their social (and influential) peers.[675] Pompeianus provides an excellent instance whereby Commodus could be rejected within these narratives owing to the individual's connections and ancestry, thereby exhibiting the dissatisfaction of the Roman élite establishment.[676] With this in mind, it must also be recognised that Claudius Pompeianus Quintianus could have been viewed as a potential replacement – presumably having a great deal of support among his peers. So it is quite likely that he could have been viewed as a potential threat by Commodus – an equally young and well connected suitor for the principate. The ancient literary sources detailing this conspiracy (and its precursors) are as follows:

μέχρι μὲν οὖν τινος ἐπεῖχε τὸν νεανίσκον ἥ τε τοῦ πατρὸς μνήμη καὶ ἡ πρὸς τοὺς φίλους αἰδώς. ἀλλὰ γάρ, ὥσπερ τινὸς πονηρᾶς καὶ βασκάνου τύχης ἀνατρεπούσης αὐτοῦ τὸ ἔτι σῶφρον καὶ κόσμιον, συνέβη τι τοιοῦτον. Λουκίλλα ἦν τῷ Κομόδῳ πρεσβυτάτη πάντων ἀδελφή. αὕτη πρότερον Λουκίῳ Βήρῳ αὐτοκράτορι συνῴκει, ὃν κοινωνὸν τῆς βασιλείας Μᾶρκος ποιησάμενος, ἐκδοὺς [τε] αὐτῷ τὴν θυγατέρα, δεσμὸν εὐνοίας ἐχυρώτατον τὴν πρὸς αὐτὸν ἐπιγαμίαν ἐποιήσατο. ἀλλ᾽ ἐπεὶ συνέβη τὸν Λούκιον τελευτῆσαι, μενόντων τῇ Λουκίλλῃ τῶν τῆς βασιλείας συμβόλων Πομπηιανῷ ὁ πατὴρ ἐξέδοτο αὐτήν. οὐδὲν ἧττον μέντοι καὶ ὁ Κόμοδος ἐφύλαττε τὰς τιμὰς τῇ ἀδελφῇ· καὶ γὰρ ἐπὶ τοῦ βασιλείου θρόνου καθῆστο ἐν τοῖς θεάτροις, καὶ τὸ πῦρ προεπόμπευεν αὐτῆς. ἐπεὶ δὲ ὁ Κόμοδος γυναῖκα ἠγάγετο, Κρισπῖναν ὄνομα, ἀνάγκη τε ἐγένετο τὴν προεδρίαν ἀπονέμεσθαι τῇ τοῦ βασιλεύοντος γυναικί, δυσφόρως τοῦτο φέρουσα ἡ Λουκίλλα, καὶ τὴν ἐκείνης τιμὴν ἑαυτῆς ὕβριν νομίζουσα, τὸν μὲν ἑαυτῆς ἄνδρα Πομπηιανὸν εἰδυῖα ἀγαπῶντα τὸν Κόμοδον, οὐδὲν αὐτῷ περὶ ἐπιθέσεως τῆς ἀρχῆς ἀνακοινοῦται, Κοδράτου δέ, νεανίσκου εὐγενοῦς τινος καὶ πλουσίου, ἐφ᾽ οὗ καὶ λανθανούσῃ συνουσίᾳ διεβάλλετο, πεῖραν τῆς γνώμης λαμβάνουσα, περί τε τῆς προεδρίας συνεχῶς ἀπωδύρετο, καὶ κατ᾽ ὀλίγον ἀνέπεισε τὸν νεανίσκον ὀλέθρια βουλεύσασθαι αὐτῷ τε καὶ πάσῃ τῇ συγκλήτῳ. συνωμότας γὰρ ἐκεῖνος τῆς βουλῆς

---

[674] *PIR²* C973.
[675] Traupman 1956, *op.cit.*
[676] Grosso 1964, *op.cit.*

λαβών τινας τῶν ἐξεχόντων ἀναπείθει νεανίσκον τινά, καὶ αὐτὸν ὄντα τῆς βουλῆς, Κυιντιανὸν ὄνομα, προπετῆ δὲ καὶ θρασύν, λαβόντα ἐγχειρίδιον ὑπὸ κόλπου, καιρὸν φυλάξαντα καὶ τόπον ἐπιτήδειον, ἐπιπεσεῖν τε τῷ Κομόδῳ καὶ φονεῦσαι, τὰ λοιπὰ φήσας αὐτὸς κατορθώσεσθαι χρημάτων ἐπιδόσει. ὃ δ' ὑποστὰς ἐν τῇ τοῦ ἀμφιθεάτρου εἰσόδῳ (ζοφώδης δὲ αὕτη, διὸ καὶ λήσεσθαι ἤλπισε), γυμνώσας τὸ ξιφίδιον, ἐπελθών τε αἰφνιδίως τῷ Κομόδῳ, καὶ μεγάλῃ φωνῇ προειπὼν ὑπὸ τῆς συγκλήτου αὐτῷ ἐπιπεπέμφθαι, τρῶσαι μὴ φθάσας, ἀλλ' ἐν ᾧ περὶ τὴν τῶν ῥημάτων προφορὰν ἠσχολεῖτο καὶ τὴν δεῖξιν τοῦ ξίφους, συλληφθεὶς ὑπὸ τῶν σωματοφυλάκων τοῦ βασιλέως δίκην ἀνοίας ὑπέσχεν, ὃς προεῖπε τὸ βεβουλευμένον μᾶλλον ἢ ἔδρασε, παρέσχε τε αὐτῷ μὲν προγνωσθέντι ἁλῶσαι, ἐκείνῳ δὲ προμαθόντι φυλάξασθαι.

'For the present, however, the memory of his father and his respect for his advisers held Commodus in check. But then a disastrous stroke of ill fortune completely altered his previously mild, moderate disposition. It happened this way. The oldest of the emperor's sisters was Lucilla. She had formerly been married to Lucius Verus Caesar, whom Marcus had made his associate in governing the empire; by marrying Lucilla to Lucius, Marcus had made her marriage to his Caesar the strongest bond of mutual good will. But after Lucius died, Lucilla, who retained all the privileges of her imperial position, was married by her father to Pompeianus. Commodus, too, allowed his sister to retain the imperial honors; she continued to occupy the imperial seat at the theaters, and the sacred fire was carried before her. But when Commodus married Crispina, custom demanded that the front seat at the theater be assigned to the empress. Lucilla found this difficult to endure, and felt that any honor paid to the empress was an insult to her; but since she was well aware that her husband Pompeianus was devoted to Commodus, she told him nothing about her plans to seize control of the empire. Instead, she tested the sentiments of a wealthy young nobleman, Quadratus, with whom she was rumored to be sleeping in secret. Complaining constantly about this matter of imperial precedence, she soon persuaded the young man to set in motion a plot which brought destruction upon himself and the entire senate. Quadratus, in selecting confederates among the prominent senators, prevailed upon Quintianus, a bold and reckless young senator, to conceal a dagger beneath his robe and, watching for a suitable time and place, to stab Commodus; as for the rest, he assured Quintianus that he would set matters straight by bribes. But the assassin, standing in the entrance to the amphitheater (it was dark there and he hoped to escape detection), drew his dagger and shouted at Commodus that he had been sent by the senate to kill him. Quintianus wasted time making his little speech and waving his dagger; as a result, he was seized by the emperor's bodyguards before he could strike, and died for his stupidity in revealing the plot prematurely. Thus found out beforehand, Quintianus brought about his own death, and Commodus was put on his guard by this forewarning.' (Herodian 1.8.3-6)

Vita Commodi Quadratum et Lucillam compulit ad eius interfectionem consilia inire, non sine praefecti praetorio Tarrutenii Paterni consilio. datum autem est negotium peragendae necis Claudio Pompeiano propinquo. qui ingressus ad Commodum destricto gladio, cum faciendi potestatem habuisset, in haec verba prorumpens 'Hunc tibi pugionem senatus mittit' detexit facinus fatuus nec implevit, multis cum eo participantibus causam. post haec interfecti sunt Pompeianus primo et Quadratus, dein Norbana atque Norbanus et Paralius; et mater eius et Lucilla in exsilium exacta.

'Finally the actions of Commodus drove Quadratus and Lucilla, with the support of Tarrutenius Paternus, the prefect of the guard, to form a plan for his assassination. The task of slaying him was assigned to Claudius Pompeianus, a kinsman. But he, as soon as he had an opportunity to fulfil his mission, strode up to Commodus with a drawn sword, and, bursting out with these words, "This dagger the senate sends thee", betrayed the plot like a fool, and failed to accomplish the design, in which many others along with himself were implicated. After this fiasco, first Pompeianus and Quadratus were executed, and then Norbana and Norbanus and Paralius; and the latter's mother and Lucilla were driven into exile.' (*HA Commodus* 4.1-4)

These accounts are vital for the present focus upon how conspiracies are characterised in antiquity. Lucilla is highly involved (largely because of her own 'illegitimate' aspirations)[677] and Claudius Pompeianus Quintianus is depicted as being just as too ambitious. It is important to firstly note how Tiberius Claudius Pompeianus is shown as being quite disconnected (or potentially even 'above') of such a conspiracy (perhaps being indicative of the positive Marcus Aurelius textual after-effect). Yet the ancient literary sources use such a conspiracy as a means of exhibiting the base nature of Commodus' principate. Whether such sedition was actually planned by Lucilla and Claudius Pompeianus Quintianus is highly debatable, but it certainly suited the purposes of the ancient authors. It is notable how Cassius Dio (73.4.1-6) in particular represents this conspiracy within a general view of the people's dissatisfaction with Commodus' early principate.[678] This time period makes the probability of such an account even less likely in reality. All the same, the potential for Lucilla and Claudius Pompeianus Quintianus being viewed as a threat by Commodus would have been all too real. Even if Tiberius Claudius Pompeianus was entirely uninvolved, the potential danger of his general influence (see Herodian 1.6.4-9) would have been enough of a threat (in combination with the emperor's sister and his son) for any recently installed *princeps*. So while this study does not either aim to confirm or deny such a conspiracy, at the very least the ancient literary sources aimed to accentuate the rejection of Commodus from the earliest stages of his reign. This was further accentuated by the references to the next perceived conspiracy – that of Maternus.

χρόνου δὲ οὐ πολλοῦ διαγενομένου ἑτέρα τις ἐπιβουλὴ τοιαύτη κατ᾽ αὐτοῦ συνεσκευάσθη. Μάτερνος ἦν τις στρατιώτης μὲν πρότερον, πολλὰ δὲ καὶ δεινὰ τολμήσας, τήν τε τάξιν λιπὼν καὶ πείσας ἑτέρους ἀπὸ τῶν αὐτῶν ἔργων συναποδρᾶναι,

---

[677] Traupman 1956, *op.cit.*, pp. 54-5.
[678] Grosso 1964, *op.cit.*

χεῖρα πολλὴν κακούργων ἐν ὀλίγῳ ἀθροίσας χρόνῳ, τὰ μὲν πρῶτα κώμαις τε καὶ ἀγροῖς ἐπιτρέχων ἐλήστευεν, ἐπεὶ δὲ πολλῶν χρημάτων ἐγκρατὴς ἐγένετο, μεῖζόν τι πλῆθος ἤθροισε κακούργων μεγάλαις τε δωρεῶν ὑποσχέσεσι καὶ τῶν ἁλισκομένων κοινωνίᾳ, ὡς μηκέτι λῃστῶν ἀλλὰ πολεμίων ἔχειν ἀξίωμα. πόλεσι γὰρ ἤδη μεγίσταις ἐπετίθεντο, καὶ τὰ ἐν αὐταῖς δεσμωτήρια βίᾳ ῥηγνύντες, τοὺς ἐφ᾽ οἱαισδὴ καθειρχθέντας αἰτίαις δεσμῶν ἐλευθέρους ἀφιέντες ἄδειάν τε ὑπισχνούμενοι, εὐεργεσίαις ἐς τὴν συμμαχίαν προσήγοντο· πᾶσάν τε κατατρέχοντες τὴν Κελτῶν καὶ Ἰβήρων χώραν, πόλεσί τε ταῖς μεγίσταις ἐπιόντες, καὶ μέρη μὲν ἐμπιπράντες, τὰ δὲ λοιπὰ <δι᾽> ἁρπαγῆς ποιούμενοι ἀνεχώρουν. ὡς δὲ ταῦτα ἐδηλώθη τῷ Κομόδῳ, μετὰ πάσης ὀργῆς τε καὶ ἀπειλῆς ἐπιστέλλει τοῖς τῶν ἐθνῶν ἡγουμένοις ῥαθυμίαν ἐγκαλῶν καὶ κελεύει στρατὸν ἐπ᾽ αὐτοὺς ἀθροισθῆναι. μαθόντες δὲ ἐκεῖνοι δύναμιν ἀγειρομένην ἐπ᾽ αὐτούς, τῶν μὲν χωρίων ἃ ἐπόρθουν ἀπέστησαν, λαθόντες δὲ διὰ ταχείας καὶ ἀβάτου ὁδοιπορίας κατ᾽ ὀλίγους ἐς τὴν Ἰταλίαν παρεδύοντο, καὶ περὶ βασιλείας ἤδη καὶ μειζόνων πραγμάτων ὁ Μάτερνος ἐβουλεύετο. ἐπεὶ γὰρ αὐτῷ τὰ προπεπραγμένα πάσης ἐλπίδος μειζόνως ἦν προχωρήσαντα, ᾠήθη δεῖν μέγα τι δράσας κατορθῶσαι, ἢ ἐπείπερ ἅπαξ ἐν κινδύνῳ καθειστήκει, μὴ ἀσήμως μηδ᾽ ἀδόξως τελευτῆσαι. ἐπεὶ δὲ αὐτῷ μὴ τοσαύτην ὑπάρχειν δύναμιν ἡγεῖτο ὡς ἐξ ἀντιστάσεως ἰσορρόπου καὶ φανερᾶς ἐφόδου συστῆναι πρὸς τὸν Κόμοδον (τό τε γὰρ πλῆθος τοῦ Ῥωμαίων δήμου ἐλογίζετο εὔνουν ἔτι τῷ Κομόδῳ ὑπάρχον, τήν τε περὶ αὐτὸν τῶν δορυφόρων εὔνοιαν), τέχνῃ καὶ σοφίᾳ ἤλπισε περιέσεσθαι. καὶ μηχανᾶται τοιόνδε τι· ἦρος ἀρχῇ ἑκάστου ἔτους ὡρισμένης ἡμέρας μητρὶ θεῶν πομπὴν τελοῦσι Ῥωμαῖοι· καὶ πάντα ὅσα παρ᾽ ἑκάστοις πλούτου σύμβολα κειμήλιά τε βασιλέων ὕλης τε ἢ τέχνης θαύματα, τῆς θεοῦ προπομπεύει. ἀνετός τε πᾶσι δέδοται ἐξουσία παντοδαπῆς παιδιᾶς, ἕκαστός τε ὃ βούλεται σχῆμα ὑποκρίνεται· οὐδ᾽ ἔστιν οὕτως μέγα ἢ ἐξαίρετον ἀξίωμα, ὃ μὴ παντὶ τῷ βουλομένῳ ἀμφιεσθέντι ὑπάρχει παῖξαί τε καὶ κρύψαι τὴν ἀλήθειαν, ὡς μὴ ῥᾳδίως διαγνῶναι τόν τε ὄντα καὶ τὸν μιμούμενον. ἔδοξε δὴ τῷ Ματέρνῳ καιρὸς ἐπιτήδειος εἶναι ἐς τὸ τὴν ἐπιβουλὴν λαθεῖν. ἤλπισε γὰρ αὐτός τε ἀναλαβὼν τὸ τῶν δορυφόρων σχῆμα καὶ τοὺς σὺν αὐτῷ ὁπλίσας ὁμοίως ἀναμίξας τε τῷ πλήθει τῶν αἰχμοφόρων καὶ τῆς πομπῆς νομισθεὶς μέρος, μηδενὸς [τε] προφυλαττομένου αἰφνιδίως ἐπιπεσὼν τὸν Κόμοδον διαχρήσεσθαι. ἀλλὰ προδοσίας γενομένης [καὶ] τινῶν τῶν σὺν αὐτῷ προκατελθόντων ἐς τὴν πόλιν καὶ τὴν ἐπιβουλὴν κατειπόντων (φθόνος γὰρ αὐτοὺς ἐς τοῦτο παρώξυνεν, εἰ δὴ ἔμελλον ἀντὶ <ἀρχι>λῃστοῦ δεσπότην ἕξειν βασιλέα), πρὶν ἐλθεῖν τὴν ἑορτὴν αὐτός τε ὁ Μάτερνος συλληφθεὶς τὴν κεφαλὴν ἀπετμήθη, καὶ οἱ συνωμόται ἀξίας ὑπέσχον δίκας. ὁ δὲ Κόμοδος θύσας τε τῇ θεῷ καὶ χαριστήρια ὁμολογήσας τὴν ἑορτὴν ἐπετέλει, παρέπεμπέ τε τὴν θεὸν χαίρων. καὶ σωτήρια τοῦ βασιλέως ὁ δῆμος μετὰ τῆς ἑορτῆς ἐπανηγύριζεν.

'But before long another plot was organized against Commodus. It involved a former soldier named Maternus, who had committed many frightful crimes. He deserted from the army, persuading others to flee with him, and soon collected a huge mob of desperadoes. At first they attacked and plundered villages and farms, but when Maternus had amassed a sizable sum of money, he gathered an even larger band of cutthroats by offering the prospect of generous booty and a fair share of the loot. As a result, his men no longer appeared to be brigands but rather enemy troops. They now attacked the largest cities and released all the prisoners, no matter what the reasons for their imprisonment. By promising these men their freedom, he persuaded them to join his band in gratitude for favors received. The bandits roamed over all Gaul and Spain, attacking the largest cities; a few of these they burned, but the rest they abandoned after sacking them. When he was informed of these developments, Commodus, in a towering rage, sent threatening dispatches to the governors of the provinces involved, charging them with negligence and ordering them to raise an army to oppose the bandits. When the brigands learned that an army was being raised against them, they left the regions which they had been ravaging and slipped unnoticed, a few at a time, into Italy, by a quick but difficult route. And now Maternus was plotting for the empire, for larger stakes indeed. Since everything he had attempted had succeeded beyond his fondest hopes, he concluded that if he were to undertake something really important it was bound to succeed; having committed himself to a hazard from which it was impossible to withdraw, he would, at least, not die obscure and unknown. But when he reflected that he did not have an army sufficiently powerful to resist Commodus on equal terms and in open opposition (for it was thought that the majority of the Roman people were still well disposed toward Commodus, and he also had the support of the Praetorian Guard), Maternus hoped to balance this inequality of forces by guile and cunning. This is the way he undertook to accomplish it. Every year, on a set day at the beginning of spring, the Romans celebrate a festival in honor of the mother of the gods. All the valuable trappings of each deity, the imperial treasures, and marvelous objects of all kinds, both natural and man-made, are carried in procession before this goddess. Free license for every kind of revelry is granted, and each man assumes the disguise of his choice. No office is so important or so sacrosanct that permission is refused anyone to put on its distinctive uniform and join in the revelry, concealing his true identity; consequently, it is not easy to distinguish the true from the false. This seemed to Maternus an ideal time to launch his plot undetected. By donning the uniform of a praetorian soldier and outfitting his companions in the same way, he hoped to mingle with the true praetorians and, after watching part of the parade, to attack Commodus and kill him while no one was on guard. But the plan was betrayed when some of those who had accompanied him into the city revealed the plot. (Jealousy led them to disclose it, since they preferred to be ruled by the emperor rather than by a bandit chief.) Before he arrived at the scene of the festivities, Maternus was seized and beheaded, and his companions suffered the punishment they deserved. After sacrificing to the goddess and making thank offerings, Commodus completed the festivities and did honor to the goddess, rejoicing at his escape. The people continued to celebrate their emperor's deliverance after the festival came to an end.' (Herodian 1.10.1-7)

Maternus was an otherwise unknown conspirator against Commodus except from the works of Herodian, and so there is almost nothing known about him (or even if he really existed for that matter). Regardless of this obvious difficulty, the account of Herodian in relation to Maternus highlights a vital aspect – he represents the military and the non-élites. Maternus epitomises the exact opposite of Claudius Pompeianus Quintianus – the 'everyday person' who hated Commodus and one who sought through dubious means to replace him.[679] The tale provided by Herodian is both compelling and yet

---

[679] Grosso 1964, *op.cit.*

also unconvincing. It is tempting to believe the story, and yet it is clearly authorial invention. While such a comment seems dismissive of Herodian (for which his is definitely not the case – his work is fascinating), the focus must be upon why the author created such an episode. Book One of Herodian's text sought to emphasise how bad Commodus was (especially in comparison with his father, Marcus Aurelius)[680] and the use of such anecdotes simply sought to make a point – Commodus was rejected by all. It was upon this precept that this text was based – the evaluation of leaders and their interpretation by Herodian. This was an important concept to the author – hence the long description of a non-existent occurrence. There is no other reference to Maternus in any ancient source aside from Herodian. So the literary emphasis for the author was paramount. Unlike Maternus, however, the next conspirator is well attested – Sextus Tigidius Perennis.

Περέννιον δὲ τῶν δορυφόρων μετὰ τὸν Πάτερνον ἄρχοντα συνέβη διὰ τοὺς στρατιώτας στασιάσαντας ἀναιρεθῆναι. τοῦ γὰρ Κομμόδου ἁρματηλασίαις καὶ ἀσελγείαις ἐκδεδωκότος ἑαυτόν, καὶ τῶν τῇ ἀρχῇ προσηκόντων οὐδὲν ὡς εἰπεῖν πράττοντος, ὁ Περέννιος ἠναγκάζετο οὐχ ὅτι τὰ στρατιωτικὰ ἀλλὰ καὶ τἆλλα διὰ χειρὸς ἔχειν καὶ τοῦ κοινοῦ προστατεῖν.

'Perennis, who commanded the Pretorians after Paternus, met his death as the result of a mutiny of the soldiers. For, inasmuch as Commodus had given himself up to chariot-racing and licentiousness and performed scarcely any of the duties pertaining to his office, Perennis was compelled to manage not only the military affairs, but everything else as well, and to stand at the head of the State. The soldiers, accordingly, whenever any matter did not turn out to their satisfaction, laid the blame upon Perennis and were angry with him.' (Dio 73.9.1)

ὁ δὲ Περέννιος ἀποσκευασάμενος πάντας, οὓς καὶ ὁ Κόμοδος ᾑδεῖτο καὶ ὅσοι πατρῴαν αὐτῷ εὔνοιαν ἐπεδείκνυντο τῆς τε ἐκείνου σωτηρίας προμήθειαν εἶχον, ποιησάμενός τε αὐτὸν ἐπ' ἐξουσίας, ἐπεβούλευε τῇ ἀρχῇ, καὶ τοῖς τε υἱοῖς αὐτοῦ νεανίαις οὖσιν ἐγχειρίσαι πείθει τὸν Κόμοδον <τὴν> πρόνοιαν τῶν Ἰλλυρικῶν στρατευμάτων, αὐτός τε πλεῖστα χρήματα ἤθροιζεν ἐς τὸ ἐπιδόσεσι λαμπραῖς ἀποστῆσαι τὸ στρατιωτικόν. οἱ δὲ παῖδες αὐτοῦ λανθάνοντες συνεκρότουν δύναμιν, ὡς ἂν τοῦ Περεννίου κατεργασαμένου τὸν Κόμοδον ἐπιθοῖντο τῇ ἀρχῇ. ἐγνώσθη δ' ἡ ἐπιβουλὴ παραδόξῳ τρόπῳ. ἱερὸν ἀγῶνα τελοῦσι Ῥωμαῖοι Διὶ Καπετωλίῳ, θεάματά τε <θυμέλης> καὶ ἰσχύος πάντα ἀθροίζεται ὡς ἐς βασιλίδα πόλιν πανηγυρίζουσαν. θεατὴς δὲ καὶ ἀθλοθέτης σὺν τοῖς λοιποῖς ἱερεῦσιν, οὓς ἐκ περιόδων χρόνων ἡ τάξις καλεῖ, ὁ βασιλεὺς γίγνεται. κατελθόντος δὴ τοῦ Κομόδου ἐπὶ τὴν ἀκρόασιν τῶν ἐνδόξων ἀγωνιστῶν, καὶ αὐτοῦ μὲν προκαθίσαντος ἐν τῇ βασιλείῳ ἕδρᾳ, πληρωθέντος

---

[680] See Adams 2013 for further discussion.

δὲ τοῦ θεάτρου μετὰ πάσης εὐκοσμίας, τῶν τε ἐν ἀξιώσεσιν <ἐν> ἐξαιρέτοις ἕδραις καὶ ὡς ἑκάστοις διετέτακτο ἱδρυμένων, πρίν τι λέγεσθαι ἢ πράττεσθαι ἐπὶ τῆς σκηνῆς ἀνὴρ φιλοσόφου φέρων σχῆμα (βάκτρον γὰρ ἦν αὐτοῦ μετὰ χεῖρας, ἡμιγύμνῳ τε αὐτῷ ἐκκρεμὴς πήρα) εἰςδραμὼν καὶ στὰς ἐν μέσῃ τῇ σκηνῇ τῷ τε χειρὸς νεύματι τὸν δῆμον κατασιγάσας "οὐ πανηγυρίζειν σοι καιρός" ἔφη "Κόμοδε, νῦν, οὐδὲ θέαις καὶ ἑορταῖς σχολάζειν. ἐπίκειται γάρ σου τοῖς αὐχέσι τὸ τοῦ Περεννίου ξίφος, καὶ εἰ μὴ φυλάξῃ κίνδυνον οὐκ ἐπαιωρούμενον ἀλλ᾽ ἤδη παρόντα, λήσεις ἀπολόμενος. αὐτός τε γὰρ ἐνταῦθα δύναμιν ἐπὶ σοὶ καὶ χρήματα ἀθροίζει, οἵ τε παῖδες αὐτῷ τὴν Ἰλλυρικὴν στρατιὰν ἀναπείθουσιν. εἰ δὲ μὴ φθάσεις, διαφθερῇ." ταῦτα εἰπόντος αὐτοῦ, εἴτε ὑπό τινος δαιμονίου τύχης ἐπειχθέντος, εἴτε καὶ τολμήσαντος ἵνα δόξαν ἄρηται πρότερον ἄγνωστος καὶ ἄσημος ὤν, εἴτε ἐλπίσαντος ἀμοιβῆς μεγαλοδώρου τεύξεσθαι παρὰ τοῦ βασιλέως, ἀφασία τὸν Κόμοδον καταλαμβάνει. καὶ πάντες ὑπώπτευον μὲν τὰ λεχθέντα, πιστεύειν δὲ οὐ προσεποιοῦντο. κελεύει δὲ αὐτὸν συλληφθῆναι ὁ Περέννιος, οἷά τε μεμηνότα καὶ ψευδῆ λέγοντα πυρὶ παραδοθῆναι. ὁ μὲν δὴ ἀκαίρου παρρησίας τοιαύτην ὑπέσχε δίκην· οἱ μέντοι περὶ τὸν Κόμοδον, ὅσοι τε εὐνοεῖν προσεποιοῦντο, καὶ πάλαι μὲν ἀπεχθῶς πρὸς τὸν Περέννιον διακείμενοι (βαρὺς γὰρ καὶ ἀφόρητος ἦν ὑπεροψίᾳ καὶ ὕβρει), τότε <δὲ> καιρὸν εὔκαιρον ἔχοντες, διαβάλλειν ἐπειρῶντο, ἐχρῆν τε ἄρα τὸν Κόμοδον τὴν ἐπιβουλὴν ἐκφυγεῖν καὶ τὸν Περέννιον σὺν τοῖς παισὶ διολέσθαι κακῶς. ἦλθον γὰρ μετ᾽ οὐ πολὺ στρατιῶταί τινες λαθόντες τὸν τοῦ Περεννίου παῖδα, καὶ νομίσματα ἐκόμισαν ἐκτετυπωμένα τὴν ἐκείνου εἰκόνα. λαθόντες δὲ καίτοι ἔπαρχον ὄντα τὸν Περέννιον καὶ δείξαντες τῷ Κομόδῳ τὰ νομίσματα διδάξαντές τε τῆς ἐπιβουλῆς τὰ λανθάνοντα αὐτοὶ μὲν ἔτυχον μεγάλων δωρεῶν· ἀγνοοῦντος δὲ ταῦτα τοῦ Περεννίου μηδέν τέ τι τοιοῦτον προσδεχομένου νύκτωρ ὁ Κόμοδος πέμψας ἀποτέμνει τὴν κεφαλήν· καὶ τὴν ταχίστην, ὅπως τὴν τῶν πραττομένων γνῶσιν φθάσωσιν, ἐκπέμπει τοὺς πορευσομένους φήμης ὀξυτέρῳ δρόμῳ ἐπιστῆναί τε δυνησομένους τῷ παιδὶ τοῦ Περεννίου τὰ ἐπὶ τῆς Ῥώμης ἀγνοοῦντι, γράμματά τε φιλικὰ ποιήσας καὶ <ἐπὶ> μείζοσι φήσας καλεῖν ἐλπίσιν αὐτὸν ἥκειν κελεύει. ὁ δὲ μήτε <τι> τῆς παρασκευῆς πω καὶ τῶν βεβουλευμένων μήτε τι τῶν κατὰ τὸν πατέρα εἰδώς, τῶν ἀγγέλων εἰπόντων ταῦτα καὶ τὸν πατέρα ἐντετάλθαι ῥήμασι, μηδὲν δὲ ἐπεσταλκέναι ταῖς βασιλείοις ἀρκούμενον γράμμασι, πιστεύσας ὁ νεανίας, ἀσχάλλων μὲν καὶ δυσφορῶν ὅτι δὴ ἀτελῆ κατέλιπε τὰ βεβουλευμένα, ὅμως δὲ θαρρῶν τῇ τοῦ πατρὸς ὡς ἔτι συνεστώσῃ δυνάμει, ποιεῖται τὴν ἔξοδον. γενόμενον δὲ αὐτὸν κατὰ τὴν Ἰταλίαν, οἷς τοῦτο ἐντέταλτο, διεχρήσαντο. τοιοῦτο μὲν δὴ τέλος ἐκείνους κατέλαβεν· ὁ δὲ Κόμοδος δύο τοὺς ἐπάρχους καταστήσας ἀσφαλέστερον ᾠήθη μὴ ἑνὶ πιστεύειν τοσαύτην ἐξουσίαν, μερισθεῖσαν δὲ αὐτὴν ἀσθενεστέραν ἔσεσθαι ἤλπισε πρὸς τὴν βασιλείας ἐπιθυμίαν.

'After he had removed the men whom Commodus had reason to fear, those who showed him good will for his father's sake, and those who were concerned for the emperor's safety, Perennis, now a powerful figure, began to plot for the empire. Commodus was persuaded to put the prefect's sons in command of the army of Illyricum, though they were still young men; the prefect himself amassed a huge sum of money for lavish gifts in order to incite the army to revolt. His sons quietly increased their forces, so that they might seize the empire after Perennis had disposed of Commodus. This plot came to light in a curious fashion. The Romans celebrate a sacred festival in honor of Jupiter Capitolinus, and all the stage shows and athletic exhibitions are sent to take part in this festival in the capital. The emperor is both spectator and judge, together with the rest of the priests, who are summoned in rotation for this duty. Upon his arrival for the performance of the famous actors, Commodus took his seat in the imperial chair; an orderly crowd filled the theater, quietly occupying the assigned seats. Before any action took place on the stage, however, a man dressed as a philosopher (half-naked, carrying a staff in his hand and a leather bag on his shoulder) ran out and took his stand in the center of the stage. Silencing the audience with a sweep of his hand, he said: "Commodus, this is no time to celebrate festivals and devote yourself to shows and entertainments. The sword of Perennis is at your throat. Unless you guard yourself from a danger not threatening but already upon you, you shall not escape death. Perennis himself is raising money and an army to oppose you, and his sons are winning over the army of Illyricum. Unless you act first, you shall die." Whether he said this by divine inspiration, or whether, obscure and unknown before, he was making an effort to gain fame, or hoped to receive a generous reward from the emperor — whatever the reason, Commodus was thunderstruck. Everyone was suspicious of the man's words, and no one believed him. Perennis ordered the philosopher to be seized and burned for making insane and lying accusations. Such was the penalty that the beggar paid for his ill-timed outspokenness. The emperor's intimate friends, however, who had long been secretly hostile to Perennis (for the prefect was harsh and unbearable in his insolence and arrogance), believed that the time had come and began to bring charges against him. As a result, Commodus escaped the plot, and Perennis and his sons perished miserably. For not much later, some soldiers visited Perennis' son in secret and carried off coins bearing the prefect's portrait. And, without the knowledge of Perennis, the praetorian prefect, they took the coins directly to Commodus and revealed to him the secret details of the plot. They were richly rewarded for their service. While Perennis was still ignorant of these developments and anticipated nothing of the sort, the emperor sent for him at night and had him beheaded. And he dispatched men to Perennis' son by the fastest route, so that they might reach him before he knew what had happened. These men were to take a route shorter than the one by which news was regularly carried; in this way they would be able to come to the youth before he was aware of events at Rome. Commodus wrote the youth a friendly letter, telling him that he was recalling him to greater expectations, and ordering him to come to Rome. Perennis' son knew nothing of the reception awaiting him and was unaware of his father's fate. When the messengers informed him that his father had given these same orders orally but, satisfied with the emperor's letter, had not written a separate note, the youth was convinced, although he was concerned about leaving the plot unfinished. Nevertheless, relying on his father's power as if that power still existed, he left Illyricum. On the way to Italy the youth was killed by the emperor's men. Such was the fate of Perennis and his son. Thereafter Commodus regularly appointed two praetorian prefects, believing that it was safer not to place too much authority in the hands of one man; he hoped that this division of authority would discourage any desire to seize the imperial power.' (Herodian 1.9.1-10)

Post haec Commodus numquam facile in publicum processit neque quicquam sibi nuntiari passus est nisi quod Perennis ante tractasset. Perennis autem Commodi persciens invenit quem ad modum ipse potens esset. nam persuasit Commodo, ut ipse deliciis vacaret, idem vero Perennis curis incumberet. quod Commodus laetanter accepit. hac igitur lege vivens ipse cum trecentis concubinis, quas ex matronarum meretricumque dilectu ad formae speciem concivit, trecentisque aliis puberibus exoletis, quos aeque ex plebe ac nobilitate vi pretiisque forma disceptatrice collegerat, in Palatio per convivia et balneas bacchabatur. inter haec habitu victimarii victimas immolavit. in harena rudibus, inter cubicularios gladiatores pugnavit lucentibus aliquando mucronibus. tunc tamen Perennis cuncta sibimet vindicavit. quos voluit interemit, spoliavit plurimos, omnia iura subvertit, praedam omnem in sinum contulit. ipse autem Commodus Lucillam sororem, cum Capreas misisset, occidit. sorori- bus dein suis ceteris, ut dicitur, constupratis, consobrina patris complexibus suis iniuncta uni etiam ex concubinis matris nomen imposuit. uxorem, quam deprehensam in adulterio exegit, exactam relegavit et postea occidit. ipsas concubinas suas sub oculis suis stuprari iubebat. nec inruentium in se iuvenum carebat infamia, omni parte corporis atque ore in sexum utrumque pollutus. Occisus est eo tempore etiam Claudius quasi a latronibus, cuius filius cum pugione quondam ad Commodum ingressus est, multique alii senatores sine iudicio interempti, feminae quoque divites. et nonnulli per provincias a Perenni ob divitias insimulati spoliati sunt vel etiam interempti. iis autem quibus deerat ficti criminis adpositio obiciebatur, quod scribere noluissent Commodum heredem. Eo tempo- re in Sarmatia res bene gestas per alios duces in filium suum Perennis referebat. hic tamen Perennis, qui tantum potuit, subito, quod bello Britannico militibus equestris loci viros praefecerat amotis senatoribus, prodita re per legatos exercitus hostis appellatus lacerandusque militibus est deditus.

'After this Commodus never appeared in public readily, and would never receive messages unless they had previously passed through the hands of Perennis. For Perennis, being well acquainted with Commodus' character, discovered the way to make himself powerful, namely, by persuading Commodus to devote himself to pleasure while he, Perennis, assumed all the burdens of the government — an ar- rangement which Commodus joyfully accepted. Under this agreement, then, Com- modus lived, rioting in the Palace amid banquets and in baths along with 300 concubines, gathered together for their beauty and chosen from both matrons and harlots, and with minions, also 300 in number, whom he had collected by force and by purchase indiscriminately from the common people and the nobles solely on the basis of bodily beauty. Meanwhile, dressed in the garb of an attendant at the sacrifice, he slaughtered the sacrificial victims. He fought in the arena with foils, but sometimes, with his chamberlains acting as gladiators, with sharpened swords. By this time Perennis had secured all the power for himself. He slew whomsoever he wished to slay, plundered a great number, violated every law, and put all the booty into his own pocket. Commodus, for his part, killed his sister Lucilla, after banishing her to Capri. After debauching his other sisters, as it is said, he formed an amour with a cousin of his father, and even gave the name of his mother to one of his concubines. His wife, whom he caught in adultery, he drove from his house, then banished her, and later put her to death. By his orders his concubines were de- bauched before his own eyes, and he was not free from the disgrace of intimacy with young men, defiling every part of his body in dealings with persons of either sex. At this time Claudius also, whose son had previously come into Commodus' presence with a dagger, was slain, ostensibly by bandits, and many other senators were put to death, and also certain women of wealth. And not a few provincials, for the sake of their riches, were charged with crimes by Perennis and then plundered or even slain; some, against whom there was not even the imputation of a fictitious crime, were accused of having been unwilling to name Commodus as their heir. About this time the victories in Sarmatia won by other generals were attributed by Perennis to his own son. Yet in spite of his great power, suddenly, because in the war in Britain he had dismissed certain senators and had put men of the equestrian order in command of the soldiers, this same Perennis was declared an enemy to the state, when the matter was reported by the legates in command of the army, and was thereupon delivered up to the soldiers to be torn to pieces.' (*HA Commodus* 5.1-6.2)

Perennis provides another useful insight into the conspiracies that arose against Commodus. As mentioned previously, it appears that in his role as Praetorian Prefect, Perennis gained a great deal of influence in the imperial court.[681] The ancient literary sources clearly exhibit him as having exploited his position, which ultimately led to his imperial aspirations in such textual characterisations. All the same, this representation was not just meant to be critical of Perennis – is also sought to denigrate the view of Commodus in that he was shown as being both inept and irresponsible. None of the characters involved in this affair are depicted as either honourable or legitimate. Nevertheless, the question as to whether Perennis actually symbolised an actual threat to Commodus must be addressed. In real terms any ambitious Praetorian Prefect was always a threat to any emperor, owing to their personal influence and their access to the *princeps*.[682] So the removal of Perennis may have been entirely justified, but this is impossible to tell with any certainty. In many ways, the 'idea' (or perception) of a conspiracy by Perennis would have been enough for Commodus' removal of him – a feature that was of course accentuated by the ancient literary sources. It was probably indicative of the tenuous position of any emperor at this point.[683] However, Perennis was executed ultimately and replaced by Marcus Aurelius Cleander – the next unsuccessful conspirator.

ἐπέσχε δὲ κατ' αὐτὸ καὶ λιμὸς τὴν πόλιν ἐξ αἰτίας τοιαύτης. Κλέανδρός τις ἦν, τὸ μὲν γένος Φρύξ, τῶν δημοσίᾳ εἰωθότων ὑπὸ κήρυκι πιπράσκεσθαι. οἰκέτης δὲ βασιλικὸς γενόμενος συναυξηθείς τε τῷ Κομόδῳ ἐς τοσοῦτον ὑπ' αὐτοῦ τιμῆς καὶ ἐξουσίας προήχθη, ὡς τήν τε τοῦ σώματος φρουρὰν καὶ τὴν τοῦ θαλάμου ἐξουσίαν τήν τε τῶν <βασιλικῶν> στρατιωτῶν ἀρχὴν ἐγχειρισθῆναι. ὑπὸ δὲ πλούτου καὶ τρυφῆς ἀνεπείσθη καὶ πρὸς βασιλείας ἐπιθυμίαν. ἀθροίζων δὲ χρήματα καὶ πλεῖστον σῖτον συνωνούμενος καὶ ἀποκλείων, ἤλπιζε<ν> ὑπάξεσθαι τόν τε δῆμον καὶ τὸ στρατόπεδον, εἰ πρῶτον ἐν σπάνει τῶν ἐπιτηδείων καταστήσας ἐπιδόσεσι λαμπραῖς ἁλόντας πόθῳ τοῦ χρειώδους προσαγάγοιτο. μέγιστον δὲ γυμνάσιον κατασκευάσας λουτρὸν δημόσιον ἀνῆκεν αὐτοῖς. ὁ μὲν οὖν οὕτως τὸν δῆμον ἐθελέαζεν. οἱ δὲ Ῥωμαῖοι ἀπεχθῶς ἔχοντες πρὸς αὐτὸν καὶ τῶν δεινῶν τὰς αἰτίας ἐς ἐκεῖνον ἀναφέροντες μισοῦντές τε αὐτοῦ τὸ ἀκόρεστον τῆς τοῦ πλούτου ἐπιθυμίας, τὰ μὲν πρῶτα ἐν τοῖς θεάτροις συνιστάμενοι κατὰ πλήθη κακῶς ἠγόρευον, καὶ τὸ τελευταῖον, διάγοντος ἐν προαστείῳ τοῦ Κομόδου, ἐπελθόντες πανδημεὶ ἐβόων καὶ τὸν Κλέανδρον ἐς θάνατον ᾔτουν. ταραχῆς δ' οὔσης περὶ τὸ προάστειον τοῦ τε Κομόδου ἐν τοῖς ἀνακεχωρηκόσι τόποις ἡδοναῖς

---

[681] Traupman 1956, *op.cit.*, p. 58.

[682] Grosso 1964, *op.cit.*

[683] See P.A. Brunt, "The Fall of Perennis: Dio-Xiphilinus 72.9.2", *CQ* 23.1, 1973, pp. 172-7.

σχολάζοντος ἀγνοοῦντός τε τὰ θρυλούμενα, ἐπείπερ ὁ Κλέανδρος ἀγγέλλεσθαί τι τῶν πραττομένων ἐκώλυεν αὐτῷ, αἰφνιδίως, οὐ προσδοκῶντος τοῦ δήμου, ἐπιφαίνονται ὡπλισμένοι κελεύσαντος τοῦ Κλεάνδρου πάντες οἱ βασίλειοι ἱππεῖς τούς τε ἐντυγχάνοντας ἔβαλλον καὶ ἐτίτρωσκον. ὁ δὲ δῆμος οὐδ' ἀντιστῆναι οἷός τε ἦν, ἄνοπλοι πρὸς ὡπλισμένους καὶ πεζοὶ πρὸς ἱππεῖς· τροπῆς δὲ γενομένης ἔφευγον ἐς τὴν πόλιν. ἐφθείρετο δὲ ὁ δῆμος οὐ μόνον βαλλόμενος ὑπὸ τῶν στρατιωτῶν οὐδὲ πατούμενος ὑπὸ τῶν ἵππων, ἀλλὰ καὶ ὑπὸ τοῦ πλήθους ὠθούμενοι καὶ [ὑπὸ τῶν ἱππέων] ἐπ' ἀλλήλους πίπτοντες πολλοὶ ἀπώλοντο. μέχρι μὲν οὖν τῶν τῆς Ῥώμης πυλῶν ἀκωλύτως οἱ ἱππεῖς διώκοντες τοὺς ἐμπίπτοντας ἀφειδῶς ἀνῄρουν. ἐπεὶ δὲ οἱ ἐν τῇ πόλει μείναντες αἰσθόμενοι τὸ κατειληφὸς πάθος, ἀποκλείσαντες τὰς τῶν οἰκιῶν εἰσόδους ἔς τε τὰ δωμάτια ἀναβάντες λίθοις καὶ κεράμοις ἔβαλλον τοὺς ἱππεῖς, οἱ δὲ ἔπασχον ἅπερ δεδράκεσαν, οὐδενὸς μὲν αὐτοῖς συστάδην μαχομένου, τοῦ δὲ πλήθους ἐξ ἀσφαλοῦς ἤδη βάλλοντος αὐτούς, τιτρωσκόμενοι τοίνυν καὶ μὴ φέροντες ἐς φυγὴν ἐτράπησαν, πολλοὶ δὲ αὐτῶν διεφθείροντο· ὑπό τε τῆς τῶν λίθων συνεχοῦς βολῆς οἱ ἵπποι κυλινδουμένοις τοῖς λίθοις ἐπιβαίνοντες ὠλίσθανον καὶ τοὺς ἐπιβάτας ἀπεωθοῦντο. πολλῶν δὲ ἑκατέρωθεν πιπτόντων ἐπεβοήθουν τῷ δήμῳ καὶ οἱ τῆς πόλεως πεζοὶ στρατιῶται μίσει τῶν ἱππέων. ὄντος δὲ πολέμου ἐμφυλίου ἄλλος μὲν οὐδεὶς ἀγγεῖλαι τὰ πραττόμενα τῷ Κομόδῳ ἐβούλετο δέει τῆς Κλεάνδρου ἐξουσίας, ἡ δὲ πρεσβυτάτη τῶν Κομόδου ἀδελφῶν (Φαδίλλα ἦν ὄνομα αὐτῇ) εἰσδραμοῦσα πρὸς τὸν βασιλέα (ῥαδία δὲ ἡ εἴσοδος αὐτῇ καὶ ἀκώλυτος ἅτε ἀδελφῇ) λυσαμένη τὰς τρίχας ῥίψασά τε ἐς τὴν γῆν ἑαυτήν, οὐδὲν ἀλλ' ἢ πένθους σχῆμα δείξασα "σὺ μὲν" ἔφη "ὦ βασιλεῦ, μένων ἐπὶ ἡσυχίᾳ τῶν πραττομένων ἀγνοίᾳ, <ἐν> ἐσχάτῳ καθέστηκας κινδύνῳ· ἡμεῖς δέ, τὸ σὸν γένος, ὅσον οὐδέπω ἀπολούμεθα. οἴχεται δέ σοι ὅ τε δῆμος Ῥωμαίων καὶ τὸ πλεῖστον τοῦ στρατιωτικοῦ. ἃ δὲ πρὸς μηδενὸς βαρβάρων πείσεσθαι προσεδοκῶμεν, ταῦτα δρῶσιν ἡμᾶς οἱ οἰκεῖοι, καὶ οὓς μάλιστα εὐηργέτησας, τούτους ἐχθροὺς ἔχεις. Κλέανδρος ἐπὶ σὲ τόν τε δῆμον καὶ τὸ στρατιωτικὸν ὥπλισεν· ἐκ δὲ διαφόρου καὶ ἐναντίας γνώμης οἱ μὲν μισοῦντες αὐτόν, [ὁ δῆμος,] οἱ δὲ στέργοντες, [πᾶν τὸ ἱππικὸν τάγμα,] ἐν ὅπλοις εἰσί, καὶ φθείροντες ἀλλήλους ἐμφυλίου αἵματος τὴν πόλιν ἐπλήρωσαν. τὰ δ' ἑκατέρου τοῦ πλήθους δεινὰ ἡμᾶς προσλήψεται, εἰ μὴ τὴν ταχίστην πρὸς τὸν θάνατον ἐκδώσεις <τὸν> πονηρὸν οἰκέτην, ὀλέθρου τοσούτου τοῖς μὲν αἴτιον ἤδη γεγονότα, ἡμῖν δὲ ἐσόμενον ὅσον οὐδέπω." τοιαῦτά τινα εἰποῦσα ῥηξαμένη τε τὴν ἐσθῆτα, καὶ τῶν παρόντων τινές (ἐθάρρησαν γὰρ τοῖς τῆς ἀδελφῆς τοῦ βασιλέως λόγοις) τὸν Κόμοδον ἐτάραξαν. ἐκπλαγεὶς δὲ ἐκεῖνος τόν τε ἐπικείμενον κίνδυνον οὐ μέλλοντα ἀλλὰ παρόντα ἤδη φοβηθεὶς μεταπέμπεται τὸν Κλέανδρον, οὐδὲν μέν τι εἰδότα τῶν ἀπηγγελμένων, οἰόμενον δέ. ἐλθόντα οὖν αὐτὸν συλληφθῆναι κελεύει καὶ τὴν κεφαλὴν ἀποτεμὼν δόρατί τε ἐπιμήκει ἐγκαταπήξας ἐκπέμπει τερπνὸν καὶ ποθεινὸν τῷ δήμῳ θέαμα. ἔστη γὰρ οὕτως τὸ δεινόν, καὶ ἑκάτεροι πολεμοῦντες ἐπαύσαντο, οἱ μὲν στρατιῶται ἀνῃρημένον ἰδόντες ὑπὲρ οὗ ἐμάχοντο, δέει τε τῆς τοῦ βασιλέως ὀργῆς (συνίεσαν γὰρ ἐξηπατῆσθαι καὶ τὰ δρασθέντα παρὰ γνώμην αὐτοῦ τετολμηκέναι), ὁ δὲ δῆμος κεκόρεστο τιμωρίαν παρὰ τοῦ τὰ δεινὰ δράσαντος εἰληφώς. προσανεῖλον δὲ καὶ τοὺς παῖδας τοῦ Κλεάνδρου (δύο δὲ ἦσαν ἄρρενες αὐτῷ), πάντας τε ὅσους ᾔδεσαν ἐκείνῳ φίλους διεχρήσαντο· σύροντές τε τὰ σώματα καὶ πᾶσαν ὕβριν ἐνυβρίσαντες, τέλος λελωβημένα ἐς τοὺς ὀχετοὺς φέροντες ἔρριψαν. τοιούτῳ μὲν δὴ τέλει Κλέανδρός τε καὶ οἱ περὶ αὐτὸν ἐχρήσαντο, φιλοτιμουμένης, ὡς ἄν τις εἴποι, τῆς φύσεως ἐν ἑνὶ δεῖξαι, ὅτι ἐκ τῆς ἐσχάτης εὐτελείας ἐς τὸ μέγιστον ὕψος ἆραι καὶ πάλιν τὸν ἀρθέντα ῥῖψαι ὀλίγη καὶ ἀνέλπιστος δύναται τύχης ῥοπή.

'Famine gripped the city at the same time. Responsible for it was a Phrygian named Cleander, one of the slaves offered for sale by the public auctioneer for the benefit of the state. As a slave in the imperial household, Cleander grew up with Commodus and eventually was raised to a position of honor and authority: the command of the bodyguard, the stewardship of the imperial bedroom, and the control of the imperial armies were all entrusted to him. Because of his wealth and wantonness, Cleander coveted the empire. He bought up most of the grain supply and put it in storage; he hoped in this way to get control of the people and the army by making a generous distribution of grain at the first sign of a food shortage, anticipating that he would win the support of the people when they were suffering from a scarcity of food. He also built a huge gymnasium and public bath and turned them over to the people. In this way he tried to curry favor with the mob. The Romans, however, hated the man and blamed him for all their difficulties; they especially despised him for his greed. At first they attacked him bitterly when they thronged the theaters; later, however, they went in a body to Commodus, who was passing the time on his estate near the city, and there, raising a fearful din, they demanded Cleander for execution. During this tumult on the grounds of his suburban estate, Commodus was loitering in the pleasant, secluded inner rooms, for Cleander had kept him in ignorance of what was happening. Suddenly, unlooked for by the assembled mob, the imperial cavalry appeared fully armed and, at the order of the prefect, butchered those in their path. The people were unable to withstand the assault, for they were unarmed men on foot fighting against armed men on horseback. And so they fell, not only because they were attacked by the cavalry and trampled by the horses, but also because they were overwhelmed by the sheer weight of their own numbers, and many died in the pile-ups. The horsemen pursued the fugitives right to the gates of Rome and slaughtered them without mercy as they attempted to force their way into the city. When those who had remained in Rome heard what had happened, they blocked the doors of their houses and went up on the roofs to throw down stones and roof tiles on the cavalry, who now suffered what they had inflicted, for no one opposed them in formal battle; most of the people were hurling missiles at them from safe positions. Finally, unable to endure the onslaught any longer, the wounded horsemen turned and fled, leaving many dead behind. In the steady hail of missiles, their horses stumbled and fell on the round stones, throwing their riders. After many had been killed on both sides, the infantry in the city, who despised the cavalry, came to the aid of the mob. Even though a civil war was raging, no one was willing to report to Commodus what was happening, for fear of Cleander. Finally the emperor's eldest sister (her name was Phadilla) rushed into the palace (as his sister, she had free and easy access to the emperor), and, loosing her hair, threw herself down and cried out in anguish: "Here you are, emperor, taking your leisure, ignorant of what is happening, when you are actually in the gravest danger. And we, your own flesh and blood, are at this very moment threatened with murder. Already the Roman people and most of the army are lost to you. What we would not think of enduring at the hands of barbarians, our own people are doing to us. And those people whom you have treated with special consideration, you now find to be your enemies. Cleander has armed the people and the soldiers against you. Those who hate him because they hold differing opinions, the mob, and the entire imperial cavalry, who support him, are up in arms, killing each other and choking the city with blood. The fury of both factions will fall upon us unless you immediately hand over to them for execution this scoundrelly servant of yours, who already has been the cause of so much destruction for the people and who threatens to be the cause of so much destruction for us." After she had made these statements, tearing her clothes in grief, others who were present (for they became bolder at the words of the emperor's sister) urged Commodus to take action. He was terrified by this pressing danger, which did not merely threaten but was already upon him. In his panic he sent for Cleander, who knew nothing of what had been reported to the emperor, but had his suspicions. When the prefect appeared, Commodus ordered him seized and beheaded, and, impaling his head on a long spear, sent it out to the mob, to whom it was a welcome and long-desired sight. In this way he terminated the danger, and both sides stopped fighting: the soldiers, because they saw that the man for whom they had been fighting had been killed and also because they feared the wrath of the emperor (for they realized that he had been deceived and that Cleander had done everything without imperial approval); the people, because their desire for vengeance was satisfied by the arrest of the man responsible for the appalling crimes. They put Cleander's children to death (for he had two sons), and killed all his known friends. They dragged their bodies through the streets, subjecting them to every indignity, and finally brought the mutilated corpses to the sewer and threw them in. Such was the fate of Cleander and his associates; it was as if Nature had undertaken to demonstrate that a small and unexpected twist of fate can raise a man from the lowest depths to the greatest heights and then plunge the man so exalted down to the depths again.' (Herodian 1.12.3-15.6)

τά τε γὰρ παιδία συνεβόησαν πολλὰ καὶ δεινά, καὶ ὁ δῆμος παραλαβὼν αὐτὰ οὐδὲν ὅ τι οὐκ ἐξέκραγε, καὶ τέλος καταπηδήσας ὥρμησε πρὸς τὸν Κόμμοδον ἐν τῷ Κυιντιλίῳ προαστείῳ ὄντα, πολλὰ μὲν ἐκείνῳ κάγαθὰ ἐπευχόμενος, πολλὰ δὲ καὶ κατὰ τοῦ Κλεάνδρου καταρώμενος. καὶ ὃς στρατιώτας τινὰς ἐπ' αὐτοὺς ἔπεμψε, καὶ ἔτρωσάν τινας καὶ ἀπέκτειναν· οὐ μέντοι καὶ ἀνείρχθη διὰ τοῦτο ὁ δῆμος, ἀλλὰ τῷ τε πλήθει σφῶν καὶ τῇ τῶν δορυφόρων ἰσχύι θαρρήσας ἐπὶ μᾶλλον ἠπείχθη. πλησιαζόντων δὲ αὐτῶν τῷ Κομμόδῳ, καὶ μηδενὸς οἱ μηνύοντος τὸ γινόμενον, Μαρκία ἐκείνη ἡ τοῦ Κουαδράτου ἐσήγγειλε τὸ πραττόμενον· καὶ ὁ Κόμμοδος οὕτως ἔδεισεν, ἄλλως τε καὶ δειλότατος ὤν, ὥστε αὐτίκα καὶ τὸν Κλέανδρον καὶ τὸ παιδίον αὐτοῦ, ὃ καὶ ἐν ταῖς τοῦ Κομμόδου χερσὶν ἐτρέφετο, σφαγῆναι κελεῦσαι. καὶ τὸ μὲν παιδίον προσουδίσθη καὶ διεφθάρη, τὸ δὲ τοῦ Κλεάνδρου σῶμα παραλαβόντες οἱ Ῥωμαῖοι ἔσυραν καὶ ἠκίσαντο, καὶ τὴν κεφαλὴν αὐτοῦ διὰ πάσης τῆς πόλεως ἐπὶ [τοῦ] κοντοῦ περιήνεγκαν, καί τινας καὶ ἄλλους τῶν μέγα ἐπ' αὐτοῦ δυναμένων ἐφόνευσαν.

'The children shouted in concert many bitter words, which the people took up and then began to bawl out every conceivable insult; and finally the throng leaped down and set out to find Commodus (who was then in the Quintilian suburb), invoking many blessings on him and many curses upon Cleander. The latter sent some soldiers against them, who wounded and killed a few; but, instead of being deterred by this, the crowd, encouraged by its own numbers and by the strength of the Pretorians, pressed on with all the greater determination. They were already drawing near to Commodus, whom no one had kept informed of what was going on, when Marcia, the notorious wife of Quadratus, reported the matter to him. And Commodus was so terrified (he was ever the greatest coward) that he at once ordered Cleander to be slain, and likewise his son, who was being reared in the emperor's charge. The boy was dashed to the earth and so perished; and the Romans, taking the body of Cleander, dragged it away and abused it and carried his head all about the city on a pole.

They also slew some other men who had enjoyed great power under him.' (Dio 73.13.4-6)

Just as with Perennis, Cleander was also an ambitious Praetorian Prefect according to the ancient literary sources.[684] It is of no great surprise that such a potential conspirator against Commodus would be emphasised in this way by the ancient authors[685] – just as with Perennis, the primary intention was to clearly establish the instability of the emperor's principate.[686] By accentuating such prominent and influential characters like Perennis and Cleander these texts continued their predominant anti-Commodus sentiment – not only were these Praetorian Prefects ambitious and seditious, but they also took over control of the Empire (owing to the 'dubious' behaviour of Commodus) and sought the principate for themselves (regardless of their social station – but again this was the fault of Commodus). Whether Cleander could have replaced the emperor is naturally a hypothetical moot point, but the most significant factor to bear in mind is how the representation of such a conspiracy was intended to reflect upon the wider acceptance of Commodus' principate. This conspiracy also clearly accentuates the presence of highly ambitious men within the *consilium* of the emperor, thus further demonstrating the overly insecure nature of Commodus' reign.

These conspiracies have demonstrated several key elements for the progression of this analysis. The actual seriousness of each case of sedition is unfortunately impossible to tell with any certainty. All the same, it is possible to note how despite not including any real details about the conspiracies, the narratives provided by the ancient literary sources sought to emphasise the significant threat that they posed and in turn the instability that resulted for Commodus' principate. They clearly sought to epitomise the validity of the prevailing anti-Commodus tradition. If these accounts were accurate it must be recognised that they did present a real possibility of danger to the *princeps*. This is particularly notable in the case of Claudius Pompeianus Quintianus, Sextus Tigidius Perennis and Marcus Aurelius Cleander – this is shown through their social positions and close proximity to the imperial household. Nevertheless, it is important that they were *shown* as being real by the authors – Commodus is not

---

[684] Traupman 1956, *op.cit.*
[685] Grosso 1964, *op.cit.*
[686] Traupman 1956, *op.cit.*, p. 62.

depicted as being paranoid – just unsuitable. These conspiracies were also intrinsically connected to the ultimate assassination of Commodus – typically as precursors to the event in the texts. Therefore, it is appropriate at this point to consider the death of Commodus and its wider implications.

Assassination

As far as the majority of ancient accounts are concerned Commodus deserved his end, which would have been entirely expected for someone who was characterised with such a negative representation. The primary aim of this section is to evaluate whether such a perspective was entirely deserved. Unfortunately, in this regard (as with the section about the conspiracies against him) the modern interpreter is completely reliant upon the accounts provided by the ancient literary sources. Nothing can be done to avoid this though. So all of these early accounts have been viewed in a critical fashion to begin with in order that each text (and author) can be examined in turn. This should provide the most hopeful outcome – an assessment that is as objective as possible. Not an easy task to say the least. This is largely owing to the dominance of the anti-Commodus tradition. This is a feature mentioned frequently throughout the present study, but also one that has to not only be recognised, but also ideally negated. This is only possible by viewing the principate of Commodus beyond the limitations presented by such accounts. Was he really responsible for all of the subsequent issues that arose during the Third Century AD?[687] No, he was not. However, nor was he an ideal emperor either. History is easily categorised and yet it is more easily manipulated.

When examining such accounts, there are several salient points that need to be initially noted. The first consideration is the length of the assassination narratives by each author – in view of the comparative details provided by the ancient literary sources about his corruption and excesses (as distinct from his 'good' administration), the death notices are extremely large. The assassination of Commodus demanded their attention because it epitomised their general historical/biographical point – he was a 'bad' emperor. The irony within this, however, is that the details provided are minimal (if not somewhat contradictory) – the key 'players' are largely mentioned, but the divergence in their actions illustrates the difficulty in determining

---

[687] See de Blois 1984, *op.cit.*

exactly what occurred.[688] With this in mind, no attempt has been made here to argue about the precise events – it would not only be erroneous, but also futile (by prioritising one text over another). Yet what can be noted is the general emphasis among them upon drama rather than cause (or their rationale) – all of the accounts provide fantastical episodes, which are ultimately successful as narratives (i.e. in their overall effect and influence). This leads to the final questions about the general principate of Commodus and about whether the circumstances at the time were as bad as have been narrated – the answer to this seems mixed, but largely owing to situations beyond the control of the emperor. So the accounts of Herodian (1.13.7-15.1; 1.17.1-12; 2.1.1-5) are most appropriate to begin with:

ὁ δὲ Κόμοδος δεδιὼς μὲν τὴν τοῦ δήμου κίνησιν, μή τι καὶ περὶ αὐτὸν νεωτερίσειεν, ὅμως δὲ παρορμησάντων αὐτὸν τῶν οἰκείων κατελθὼν ἐς τὸ ἄστυ μετὰ πάσης εὐφημίας τε καὶ παραπομπῆς τοῦ δήμου ὑποδεχθεὶς ἐς τὴν βασίλειον ἐπανῆλθεν αὐλήν. πειραθεὶς δὲ τοσούτων κινδύνων ἀπίστως προσεφέρετο πᾶσιν ἀφειδῶς τε φονεύων καὶ πάσαις διαβολαῖς ῥᾳδίως πιστεύων μηδέ τινα προσιέμενος τῶν λόγου ἀξίων· ἀλλὰ τῆς μὲν περὶ τὰ καλὰ σπουδῆς ἀπῆγεν ἑαυτόν, δεδούλωτο δὲ πᾶσαν αὐτοῦ τὴν ψυχὴν νύκτωρ τε καὶ μεθ᾽ ἡμέραν ἐπάλληλοι καὶ ἀκόλαστοι σώματος ἡδοναί. καὶ σώφρων μὲν πᾶς καὶ παιδείας κἂν ἔτι μετρίως μεμνημένος τῆς αὐλῆς ὡς ἐπίβουλος ἐδιώκετο, γελωτοποιοὶ δὲ καὶ τῶν αἰσχίστων ὑποκριταὶ εἶχον αὐτὸν ὑποχείριον. ἁρμάτων τε ἡνιοχείας καὶ θηρίων ἐξ ἀντιστάσεως μάχας ἐπαιδεύετο, τῶν μὲν κολάκων ἐς ἀνδρείας δόξαν αὐτὰ ὑμνούντων, τοῦ δὲ ἀπρεπέστερον μετιόντος ἢ βασιλεῖ σώφρονι ἥρμοζε. ἐγένοντο δέ τινες κατ᾽ ἐκεῖνο καιροῦ καὶ διοσημεῖαι. ἀστέρες γὰρ ἡμέριοι συνεχῶς ἐβλέποντο ἕτεροί τε ἐς μῆκος κεχαλασμένοι ὡς ἐν μέσῳ ἀέρι κρέμασθαι δοκεῖν· ζῷά τε παντοῖα καὶ τὴν ἑαυτῶν φύσιν μὴ τηροῦντα σχήμασί τε ἀλλοδαποῖς καὶ μέρεσι σώματος ἀναρμόστοις πολλάκις ἀπεκυήθη. τὸ μέγιστον δὲ δεινόν, ὃ καὶ τὸν παρόντα καιρὸν ἐλύπησε καὶ πρὸς τὸ μέλλον οἰωνίσματι καὶ φαύλῳ συμβόλῳ χρωμένους πάντας ἐτάραξεν· οὔτε γὰρ ὄμβρου προϋπάρξαντος οὔτε νεφῶν ἀθροισθέντων, σεισμοῦ δὲ ὀλίγου προγενομένου γῆς, εἴτε σκηπτοῦ νύκτωρ κατενεχθέντος, εἴτε καὶ πυρός ποθεν ἐκ τοῦ σεισμοῦ διαρρυέντος, πᾶν τὸ τῆς Εἰρήνης τέμενος κατεφλέχθη, μέγιστον καὶ κάλλιστον γενόμενον τῶν ἐν τῇ πόλει ἔργων. πλουσιώτατον δὲ ἦν πάντων ἱερῶν, δι᾽ ἀσφάλειαν ἀναθήμασι κεκοσμημένον χρυσοῦ τε καὶ ἀργύρου· ἕκαστος δέ, ἃ εἶχεν, ἐκεῖσε ἐθησαυρίζετο. ἀλλὰ τὸ πῦρ ἐκείνης νυκτὸς πολλοὺς ἐκ πλουσίων πένητας ἐποίησεν· ὅθεν ὠλοφύροντο κοινῇ μὲν πάντες τὰ δημόσια, ἕκαστος δὲ τὰ ἴδια αὐτοῦ. καταφλέξαν δὲ τὸ πῦρ τόν τε νεὼν καὶ πάντα τὸν περίβολον, ἐπενεμήθη καὶ τὰ πλεῖστα τῆς πόλεως καὶ κάλλιστα ἔργα· ὅτε καὶ τῆς Ἑστίας τοῦ νεὼ καταφλεχθέντος ὑπὸ τοῦ πυρὸς γυμνωθὲν ὤφθη τὸ τῆς Παλλάδος ἄγαλμα, ὃ σέβουσί τε καὶ κρύπτουσι Ῥωμαῖοι κομισθὲν ἀπὸ Τροίας, ὡς λόγος· ὃ τότε πρῶτον [καὶ] μετὰ τὴν ἀπ᾽ Ἰλίου ἐς Ἰταλίαν ἄφιξιν εἶδον οἱ καθ᾽ ἡμᾶς ἄνθρωποι. ἁρπάσασαι γὰρ τὸ ἄγαλμα αἱ τῆς Ἑστίας ἱέρειαι παρθένοι διὰ μέσης τῆς ἱερᾶς ὁδοῦ ἐς τὴν τοῦ βασιλέως αὐλὴν μετεκόμισαν. κατεφλέχθη δὲ καὶ ἄλλα πλεῖστα τῆς πόλεως

---

[688] Grosso 1964, op.cit.

μέρη <καὶ> κάλλιστα, ἱκανῶν τε ἡμερῶν πάντα ἐπιὸν τὸ πῦρ ἐπεβόσκετο, οὐδὲ πρότερον ἐπαύσατο, πρὶν ἢ κατενεχθέντες ὄμβροι ἐπέσχον αὐτοῦ τὴν ὁρμήν. ὅθεν καὶ τὸ πᾶν ἔργον ἐξεθειάσθη πιστευόντων κατ' ἐκεῖνο καιροῦ τῶν τότε ἀνθρώπων ὅτι γνώμῃ θεῶν καὶ δυνάμει ἤρξατό τε τὸ πῦρ καὶ ἐπαύσατο. συνεβάλλοντο δέ τινες ἐκ τῶν καταλαβόντων, πολέμων σημεῖον εἶναι τὴν τοῦ νεὼ τῆς Εἰρήνης ἀπώλειαν. τὰ γοῦν ἀκολουθήσαντα, ὡς ἐν τοῖς ἑξῆς ἐροῦμεν, ἐκ τῆς ἀποβάσεως τὴν προϋπάρχουσαν φήμην ἐπιστώσατο. πολλῶν δὴ καὶ δεινῶν συνεχῶς κατειληφότων τὴν πόλιν οὐκέτι ὁ Ῥωμαίων δῆμος μετ' εὐνοίας τὸν Κόμοδον ἐπέβλεπεν, ἀλλὰ καὶ τὰς αἰτίας τῶν ἀλλεπαλλήλων συμφορῶν ἐς τοὺς ἐκείνου ἀκρίτους φόνους καὶ τὰ λοιπὰ τοῦ βίου ἀνέφερεν ἁμαρτήματα. οὐδὲ γὰρ ἐλάνθανε τὰ πραττόμενα πάντα, ἀλλ' οὐδὲ αὐτὸς λανθάνειν ἤθελεν· ἃ δὲ πράττων οἴκοι διεβάλλετο, ταῦτα καὶ δημοσίᾳ δεῖξαι ἐτόλμησεν· ἐς τοσοῦτόν τε μανίας καὶ παροινίας προὐχώρησεν, ὡς πρῶτον μὲν τὴν πατρῴαν προσηγορίαν παραιτήσασθαι, ἀντὶ δὲ Κομόδου καὶ Μάρκου υἱοῦ Ἡρακλέα τε καὶ Διὸς υἱὸν αὐτὸν κελεύσας καλεῖσθαι ἀποδυσάμενός τε τὸ Ῥωμαίων καὶ βασίλειον σχῆμα λεοντῆν ἐπεστρώννυτο καὶ ῥόπαλον μετὰ χεῖρας ἔφερεν· ἀμφιέννυτό τε ἁλουργεῖς καὶ χρυσουφεῖς ἐσθῆτας, ὡς εἶναι καταγέλαστον αὐτὸν ὑφ' ἑνὶ σχήματι καὶ θηλειῶν πολυτέλειαν καὶ ἡρώων ἰσχὺν μιμούμενον. τοιοῦτος μὲν δὴ προιὼν ἐφαίνετο, ἤλλαξε δὲ καὶ τῶν ἐνιαυσίων μηνῶν τὰ ὀνόματα, ὅσα μὲν ἀρχαῖα καταλύσας, πάντας δὲ ταῖς ἑαυτοῦ προσηγορίαις ὀνομάσας, ὧν αἱ πλεῖσται ἐς Ἡρακλέα δῆθεν ὡς ἀνδρειότατον ἀνεφέροντο. ἔστησε δὲ καὶ ἀνδριάντας αὐτοῦ κατὰ πᾶσαν τὴν πόλιν, ἀλλὰ μὴν καὶ ἀντικρὺ τοῦ τῆς συγκλήτου συνεδρίου τόξον διηγκυλημένον· ἐβούλετο γὰρ δὴ καὶ τὰς εἰκόνας αὐτῷ φόβον ἀπειλεῖν. τὸν μὲν οὖν ἀνδριάντα μετὰ τὴν ἐκείνου τελευτὴν καθελοῦσα ἡ σύγκλητος Ἐλευθερίας εἰκόνα ἵδρυσεν· ὁ δὲ Κόμοδος μηκέτι κατέχων ἑαυτοῦ δημοσίᾳ θέας ἐπετέλεσεν, ὑποσχόμενος τά τε θηρία πάντα ἰδίᾳ χειρὶ κατακτενεῖν καὶ τοῖς ἀνδρειοτάτοις τῶν νεανιῶν μονομαχήσειν. διαδραμούσης δὲ τῆς φήμης συνέθεον ἔκ τε τῆς Ἰταλίας πάσης καὶ τῶν ὁμόρων ἐθνῶν, θεασόμενοι ἃ μὴ πρότερον μήτε ἑωράκεσαν μήτε ἠκηκόεσαν. καὶ γὰρ διηγγέλλετο αὐτοῦ τῆς χειρὸς τὸ εὔστοχον, καὶ ὅτι ἔμελεν αὐτῷ ἀκοντίζοντι καὶ τοξεύοντι μὴ πταίειν.

'Although he feared a popular uprising and a new attempt upon his life, Commodus nevertheless, at the urging of his advisers, entered the city. Received there with great enthusiasm, he went to the imperial palace, escorted by the people. After undergoing such risks, the emperor trusted no one; he killed now without warning, listening to all accusations without question and paying no heed to those worthy of a hearing. He no longer had any regard for the "good life"; night and day, without interruption, licentious pleasures of the flesh made him a slave, body and soul. Men of intelligence and those who had even a smattering of learning were driven from the palace as conspirators, but the emperor gave enthralled attention to the filthy skits of comedians and actors. He took lessons in driving the chariot and trained to take part in the wild-animal fights; his flatterers praised these activities as proof of his manliness, but he indulged in them more often than befitted an intelligent emperor. In that time of crisis a number of divine portents occurred. Stars remained visible during the day; other stars, extending to an enormous length, seemed to be hanging in the middle of the sky. Abnormal animals were born, strange in shape and deformed of limb. But the worst portent of all, which aggravated the present crisis and disturbed those who employ auguries and omens to predict the future, was this. Although no massing of dark clouds and no thunderstorm preceded it, and only a slight earthquake occurred beforehand, either as a result of a lightning bolt at night or a fire which broke out after the earthquake, the Temple of Peace, the largest and most beautiful building in the city, was totally destroyed by fire. It was the richest of all the temples, and, because it was a safe place, was adorned with offerings of gold and silver; every man deposited his possessions there. But this fire, in a single night, made paupers of many rich men. All Rome joined in mourning the public loss, and each man lamented his own personal loss. After consuming the temple and the entire sacred precinct, the fire swept on to destroy a large part of the city, including its most beautiful buildings. When the temple of Vesta went up in flames, the image of Pallas Athena was exposed to public view — that statue which the Romans worship and keep hidden, the one brought from Troy, as the story goes. Now, for the first time since its journey from Troy to Italy, the statue was seen by men of our time. For the Vestal Virgins snatched up the image and carried it along the Sacred Way to the imperial palace. Many other beautiful sections of the city were destroyed in this fire, which continued to burn for days, spreading in all directions. It was not finally extinguished until falling showers put an end to its raging. For this reason the disaster was held to be of divine origin; in that critical period, men believed that the fire was started and stopped by the will and power of the gods. Some conjectured from these events that the destruction of the temple of Peace was a prophecy of war. And subsequent events, as we shall relate in the books to follow, confirmed this prophecy by actual events. With so many disasters befalling the city in rapid succession, the Roman people no longer looked with favor upon Commodus; they attributed their misfortunes to his illegal murders and the other mistakes he had made in his lifetime. He no longer concealed his activities, nor did he have any desire to keep them secret. What they objected to his doing in private he now had the effrontery to do in public. He fell into a state of drunken madness. First he discarded his family name and issued orders that he was to be called not Commodus, son of Marcus, but Hercules, son of Zeus. Abandoning the Roman and imperial mode of dress, he donned the lion skin, and carried the club of Hercules. He wore purple robes embroidered with gold, making himself an object of ridicule by combining in one set of garments the frailty of a woman and the might of a superman. This was the way he looked in his public appearances. He assigned new names to the months of the year; abolishing the old ones, he called the months after his own list of names and titles, most of which actually referred to Hercules as the manliest of men. He erected statues of himself throughout the city, but opposite the senate house he set up a special statue representing the emperor as an archer poised to shoot, for he wished even his statues to inspire fear of him. The senate removed this statue of Commodus after his death and replaced it with a statue of Freedom. Now the emperor, casting aside all restraint, took part in the public shows, promising to kill with his own hands wild animals of all kinds and to fight in gladiatorial combat against the bravest of the youths. When this news became known, people hastened to Rome from all over Italy and from the neighboring provinces to see what they had neither seen nor even heard of before. Special mention was made of the skill of his hands and the fact that he never missed when hurling javelins or shooting arrows.' (1.13.7-15.1)

ὁ δὲ Κόμοδος ἀσχάλλων τοὺς μὲν ἀπεπέμψατο, αὐτὸς δὲ ἐπανελθὼν ἐς τὸ δωμάτιον ὡς δὴ καθευδήσων (καὶ γὰρ μεσημβρίας εἰώθει τοῦτο ποιεῖν), λαβὼν γραμματεῖον τούτων δὴ τῶν ἐκ φιλύρας ἐς λεπτότητα ἠσκημένων ἐπαλλήλῳ τε ἀνακλάσει ἀμφοτέρωθεν ἐπτυγμένων γράφει, ὅσους χρὴ τῆς νυκτὸς φονευθῆναι. ὧν πρώτη μὲν ἦν

Μαρκία, εἵποντο δὲ Λαῖτός τε καὶ Ἔκλεκτος, ἐπὶ δὲ τούτοις πολὺ πλῆθος τῶν τῆς συγκλήτου πρωτευόντων. τοὺς μὲν γὰρ πρεσβυτέρους καὶ <ἔτι> λοιποὺς πατρῴους φίλους ἀποσκευάσασθαι πάντας ἤθελεν, αἰδούμενος ἔχειν αἰσχρῶν ἔργων σεμνοὺς ἐπόπτας· τῶν δὲ πλουσίων τὰς οὐσίας χαρίσασθαι ἐβούλετο μερίσαι τε ἐς τοὺς στρατιώτας καὶ τοὺς μονομαχοῦντας, τοὺς μὲν ἵνα φυλάττοιεν αὐτόν, τοὺς δὲ ἵνα τέρποιεν. γράψας δὴ <τὸ> γραμματεῖον τίθησιν ἐπὶ τοῦ σκίμποδος, οἰηθεὶς μηδένα ἐκεῖσε εἰσελεύσεσθαι. ἦν δέ τι παιδίον πάνυ νήπιον, τούτων δὴ τῶν γυμνῶν μὲν ἐσθῆτος χρυσῷ δὲ καὶ λίθοις πολυτίμοις κεκοσμημένων, οἷς ἀεὶ χαίρουσι Ῥωμαίων οἱ τρυφῶντες. ὑπερηγάπα δὲ ὁ Κόμοδος αὐτὸ ὡς συγκαθεύδειν πολλάκις. Φιλοκόμοδός τε ἐκαλεῖτο, δεικνυούσης καὶ τῆς προσηγορίας τὴν στοργὴν τὴν ἐς τὸν παῖδα τοῦ βασιλέως. τὸ δὴ παιδίον τοῦτο ἄλλως ἀθῦρον, προελθόντος τοῦ Κομόδου ἐπὶ τὰ συνήθη λουτρά τε καὶ κραιπάλας, εἰσδραμὸν ἐς τὸν θάλαμον ὥσπερ εἰώθει, τὸ γραμματεῖον ἐπὶ τοῦ σκίμποδος κείμενον ἀνελόμενον, ἵνα δὴ παίζειν ἔχοι, πρόεισι τοῦ οἴκου. κατὰ δέ τινα δαίμονα συνήντετο τῇ Μαρκίᾳ. ἡ δὲ (καὶ αὐτὴ γὰρ ἔστεργε τὸ παιδίον) περιπτύξασα καὶ φιλοῦσα <αὐτὸ> τὸ γραμματεῖον ἀφαιρεῖται, δεδοκυῖα δὴ μή τι τῶν ἀναγκαίων ὑπὸ νηπιότητος ἀγνοοῦν παῖζον διαφθείρῃ. γνωρίσασα δὲ τὴν τοῦ Κομόδου χεῖρα, ταύτῃ καὶ μᾶλλον ἐσπούδαζε διεξελθεῖν τὴν γραφήν. ἐπεὶ δὲ εὗρεν αὐτὸ θανατηφόρον καὶ πρὸ ἁπάντων αὐτήν τε μέλλουσαν τεθνήξεσθαι, Λαῖτόν τε καὶ Ἔκλεκτον ἐπακολουθήσοντας, τῶν τε λοιπῶν τοσοῦτον φόνον, ἀνοιμώξασα καθ' ἑαυτήν τε εἰποῦσα "εὖγε, ὦ Κόμοδε. ταῦτ' ἄρα χαριστήρια εὐνοίας τε καὶ στοργῆς <τῆς ἐμῆς> ὕβρεώς τε καὶ παροινίας τῆς σῆς, ἧς ἐτῶν τοσούτων ἠνεσχόμην. ἀλλ' οὐ καταπροίξῃ αὐτὸς μεθύων νηφούσης γυναικός." ταῦτα εἰποῦσα τὸν Ἔκλεκτον μεταπέμπεται. ἔθος δ' εἶχεν αὐτῇ προσιέναι ἅτε τοῦ θαλάμου φύλαξ, ἔτι τε καὶ ἐπὶ συνουσίᾳ αὐτοῦ διεβάλλετο. δοῦσα δὲ τὸ γραμματεῖον "ὅρα" ἔφη "ποίαν μέλλομεν παννυχίζειν ἑορτήν". ὁ δ' Ἔκλεκτος ἀναγνούς, τε καὶ ἐκπλαγείς (ἦν δὲ τὸ γένος Αἰγύπτιος, τολμῆσαί τε ἅμα καὶ δράσαι θυμῷ τε δουλεῦσαι πεφυκώς) κατασημηνάμενος οὖν τὸ γραμματεῖον διὰ τινος τῶν ἑαυτῷ πιστῶν ἀναγνωσθησόμενον πέμπει τῷ Λαίτῳ. ὁ δὲ καὶ αὐτὸς ταραχθεὶς ἀφικνεῖται πρὸς Μαρκίαν ὡς δὴ συσκεψόμενος αὐτοῖς περὶ ὧν ἐκέλευσεν ὁ βασιλεὺς καὶ τοῦ τῶν μονομάχων καταγωγίου· προσποιησάμενοι δὲ περὶ τῶν ἐκείνῳ διαφερόντων σκέπτεσθαι συντίθενται φθάσαι τι δράσαντες ἢ παθεῖν, οὐδὲ καιρὸν εἶναι μελλήσεως ἢ ἀναβολῆς. ἀρέσκει δὴ δοῦναι φάρμακον δηλητήριον τῷ Κομόδῳ, ὑπέσχετο δ' αὐτὸ ῥᾶστα δώσειν ἡ Μαρκία. εἰώθει γὰρ αὐτὴ κιρνᾶναί τε καὶ διδόναι τὴν πρώτην πόσιν, ὡς ἥδιον πίοι παρ' ἐρωμένης. ἐλθόντι δὲ αὐτῷ ἀπὸ τοῦ λουτροῦ ἐμβαλοῦσα ἔς τε κύλικα τὸ φάρμακον οἴνῳ τε κεράσασα εὐώδει δίδωσι πιεῖν. ὁ δ' ὡς συνήθη φιλοτησίαν μετὰ πολλὰ λουτρὰ καὶ γυμνάσια τὰ πρὸς θηρία διψῶν ἔπιεν ἀναισθήτως. εὐθέως δὲ κάρος ἐπέπεσεν αὐτῷ, καὶ ἐς ὕπνον καθελκόμενος ὑπὸ καμάτου <τοῦτο> πάσχειν οἰηθεὶς ἀνεπαύσατο. ὁ δὲ Ἔκλεκτος καὶ Μαρκία πάντας ἀποστῆναι κελεύσαντες ἔς τε τὰ οἰκεῖα ἀπιέναι, ἡσυχίαν δὴ παρεσκεύαζον αὐτῷ. εἰώθει δὲ καὶ ἐπὶ ἄλλων <καιρῶν> τοῦτο πάσχειν ὁ Κόμοδος ὑπὸ κραιπάλης· πολλάκις γὰρ λουόμενος καὶ πολλάκις ἐσθίων οὐδένα καιρὸν εἶχεν ἐς ἀνάπαυσιν ὡρισμένον, ἀλλεπαλλήλοις καὶ διαφόροις συνεχόμενος ἡδοναῖς, αἷς δὴ καταλαβούσῃ ὥρᾳ καὶ ἄκων ἐδούλευεν. ἐπ' ὀλίγον μὲν οὖν ἡσύχασε, περὶ στόμαχον δὲ καὶ κοιλίαν τοῦ φαρμάκου γενομένου ἴλιγγός τε αὐτὸν καταλαμβάνει ἔμετός τε πολὺς ἐπιγίνεται, ἢ τῆς προεγκειμένης τροφῆς ἅμα πότῳ πολλῷ ἐξωθούσης τὸ φάρμακον, ἢ διὰ τὸ προκαταλαμβανόμενον, ὅπερ εἰώθασι βασιλεῖς ἑκάστοτε πρὸ πάσης τροφῆς λαμβάνειν, κώλυμα δηλητηρίων. πλὴν ἀλλὰ πολλοῦ γε τοῦ ἐμέτου ὄντος, φοβηθέντες μὴ πᾶν ἐξεμέσας τὸ φάρμακον ἀνανήψῃ καὶ πάντες ἀπόλωνται, νέον τινὰ ὄνομα

Νάρκισσον, γενναῖόν τε καὶ ἀκμαστήν, πείθουσιν εἰσελθόντα τὸν Κόμοδον ἀποπνῖξαι, μεγάλα δώσειν ἔπαθλα ὑποσχόμενοι. ὃ δ' εἰσδραμὼν παρειμένον αὐτὸν ὑπὸ τοῦ φαρμάκου καὶ μέθης ἀποσφίγξας τὸν τράχηλον φονεύει. τοιούτῳ μὲν τέλει τοῦ βίου ὁ Κόμοδος ἐχρήσατο, βασιλεύσας ἔτη τρισκαίδεκα μετὰ τὴν τοῦ πατρὸς τελευτήν, εὐγενέστατός τε τῶν πρὸ αὐτοῦ γενομένων βασιλέων, κάλλει τε τῶν καθ' αὐτὸν ἀνθρώπων εὐπρεπέστατος αὐταρκέστατός τε συμμετρίᾳ σώματος, εἰ δέ τι δεῖ καὶ περὶ ἀνδρείας εἰπεῖν, οὐδενὸς ἥττων εὐστοχίᾳ τε καὶ εὐχειρίᾳ, εἰ μὴ τὴν τούτων εὐμορίαν αἰσχροῖς ἐπιτηδεύμασι κατῄσχυνεν, ὡς προείρηται.

'Commodus, enraged, dismissed them and retired to his bedroom for a nap (for this was his custom in the middle of the day). First he took a wax tablet — one made from a thin strip of basswood, which grows under the bark of the linden tree — and wrote down the names of those who were to be put to death that night. Marcia's name was at the top of the list, followed by Laetus and Eclectus and a large number of the foremost senators. Commodus wanted all the elder statesmen and the advisers appointed for him by his father, those who still survived, to be put to death, for he was ashamed to have these revered men witness his disgraceful actions. He planned to confiscate the property of the wealthy and distribute it to the soldiers, so that they would protect him, and to the gladiators, so that they would entertain him. After composing his list, Commodus placed the tablet on his couch, thinking that no one would come into his bedroom. But there was in the palace a very young little boy, one of those who went about bare of clothes but adorned with gold and costly gems. The Roman voluptuaries always took delight in these lads. Commodus was very fond of this child and often slept with him; his name, Philocommodus, clearly indicates the emperor's affection for him. Philocommodus was playing idly about the palace. After Commodus had gone out to his usual baths and drinking bouts, the lad wandered into the emperor's bedroom, as he usually did; picking up the tablet for a plaything, he left the bedroom. By a stroke of fate, he met Marcia. After hugging and kissing him (for she too was fond of the child), she took the tablet from him, afraid that in his heedless play he might accidentally erase something important. When she recognized the emperor's handwriting, she was eager to read the tablet. Discovering that it was a death list and that she was scheduled to die first, followed by Laetus and Eclectus and many others marked for murder, she cried out in grief and then said to herself: "So, Commodus, this is my reward for my love and devotion, after I have put up with your arrogance and your madness for so many years. But, you drunken sot, you shall not outwit a woman deadly sober!" She then summoned Eclectus; he was in the habit of visiting her anyway, since he was the bedroom steward, and it was rumored that she was sleeping with him. She handed him the tablet, saying: "See what a party we are to enjoy tonight!" Eclectus read it and was dumfounded (but he was an Egyptian, bold by nature and quick-tempered, a man of action). Sealing the tablet, he sent it off to Laetus by one of his trusted slaves. After reading the tablet, Laetus hurried to Marcia as if to discuss the emperor's orders with her, especially about his proposed stay with the gladiators. And while they pretended to be arguing about this matter, they concluded that they must act first or suffer the consequences, agreeing that it was no time for indecision or delay. They decided to poison Commodus, and Marcia assured them that she could administer a potion with the greatest ease. For it was her custom to mix the wine and give the Emperor his first cup, so that he might have a pleasant drink from the hand of his beloved. When Commodus returned from his bath, she poured the poison into the cup, mixed it with a pungent wine, and gave it to him to drink. Since it was his practice to take a cup of friendship after his many baths and jousts with animals, he drained it without noticing anything unusual. Immediately he became drowsy and stupefied and fell asleep, believing that it was the natural result of his exertions. Eclectus and Marcia ordered all the rest to return to their homes, and made everything quiet for him. Commodus had acted like this on other occasions when overcome by wine. Since he bathed often and drank often, he had no set time for sleeping; in addition, he indulged in all kinds of pleasures, to which he was a willing slave at any hour. For a short time he lay quiet, but, when the poison spread through his stomach and bowels, he became nauseated and began to vomit violently, either because his excessive eating and drinking were expelling the poison, or because he had taken beforehand an antidote for poison, as emperors regularly did before eating or drinking. After much vomiting had occurred, the conspirators, afraid that Commodus would get rid of the poison, recover, and kill them, promised lavish rewards to a powerful young nobleman, Narcissus, if he would strangle the emperor. Narcissus rushed in where the emperor lay overcome by the poisoned wine, seized him by the throat, and finished him off. Such was the fate Commodus suffered, after ruling for thirteen years from the date of his father's death. He was the most nobly born of all the emperors who preceded him and was the handsomest man of his time, both in beauty of features and in physical development. If it were fitting to discuss his manly qualities, he was inferior to no man in skill and in marksmanship, if only he had not disgraced these excellent traits by shameful practices.' (1.17.1-12)

Ἀνελόντες δὲ τὸν Κόμοδον οἱ ἐπιβουλεύσαντες, ὡς ἐν τῷ πρώτῳ συντάγματι τῆς ἱστορίας δεδήλωται, κρύψαι τε τὸ γενόμενον βουλόμενοι, ὡς ἂν τοὺς φυλάσσοντας τὴν βασίλειον αὐλὴν δορυφόρους λάθοιεν, ἐνειλήσαντες στρωμνῇ τινι εὐτελεῖ τὸ σωμάτιον καὶ καταδήσαντες, ἐπιθέντες δὲ δυσὶν οἰκέταις τῶν πιστῶν ἑαυτοῖς, ἐκπέμπουσιν ὡς δή τι σκεῦος τῶν ἐκ τοῦ θαλάμου περισσόν. οἱ δὲ φέροντες διὰ μέσων ἐκφέρουσι τῶν φυλάκων, ὧν οἱ μὲν ὑπὸ μέθης ἐκραιπάλων, οἱ δὲ ἐγρηγορότες κἀκεῖνοι ἐς ὕπνον κατεφέροντο κατεχούσαις τε ταῖς χερσὶ τὰ δοράτια ἐπανεπαύοντο, οἳ δ' οὐ πάνυ τὸ ἐκφερόμενον τοῦ θαλάμου, ὅτι ποτ' εἴη, ἐπολυπραγμόνουν, ἐπεὶ μηδ' αὐτοῖς διέφερε ταῦτ' εἰδέναι. τὸ μὲν οὖν σῶμα τοῦ βασιλέως οὕτως κλαπὲν ἐκκομισθέν τε τῆς αὐλείου θύρας νύκτωρ ὀχήματι ἐπιθέντες ἐς τὸ προάστειον ἀπέπεμψαν. ὁ δὲ Λαῖτος καὶ Ἔκλεκτος ἅμα τῇ Μαρκίᾳ τὸ πρακτέον ἐβουλεύοντο. ἔδοξε δὲ αὐτοῖς περὶ μὲν τοῦ θανάτου φήμην ἐγκατασπεῖραι, ὅτι δὴ αἰφνιδίως τετελευτήκοι ἀποπληξίας ἐπιπεσούσης· καὶ γὰρ ἐνδεχομένων πίστιν ἕξειν ᾤοντο τὴν φήμην προδιαβεβλημένης τῆς ἀκορέστου καὶ ὑπερβαλλούσης ἐκείνου τρυφῆς. πρῶτον δὲ ἔδοξεν αὐτοῖς ἐπιλέξασθαι ἄνδρα πρεσβύτην τινὰ καὶ σώφρονα τὸν διαδεξόμενον τὴν ἀρχήν, ὅπως αὐτοί τε σωθεῖεν καὶ ἀπὸ τῆς πικρᾶς καὶ ἀκολάστου τυραννίδος πάντες ἀναπνεύσειαν. καθ' ἑαυτοὺς δὴ ἀναλογιζόμενοι οὐδένα οὕτως ἐπιτήδειον εὕρισκον ὡς Περτίνακα. ἦν δ' ὁ Περτίναξ τὸ μὲν γένος Ἰταλιώτης, ἐν δὲ πολλαῖς στρατιωτικαῖς τε καὶ πολιτικαῖς εὐδοκιμήσας πράξεσι, πολλὰ δὲ κατὰ Γερμανῶν καὶ τῶν ὑπὸ τὴν ἀνατολὴν βαρβάρων ἐγείρας τρόπαια, μόνος τε περιλειφθεὶς τῶν σεμνῶν πατρῴων τῷ Κομόδῳ φίλων· ὃν οὐκ ἀπέκτεινε, τῶν Μάρκου ἑταίρων τε καὶ στρατηγῶν ἐντιμότατον γενόμενον, ἢ διὰ σεμνότητα αἰδούμενος ἢ ὡς πένητα τηρήσας. ἦν γὰρ αὐτῷ καὶ τοῦτο μέρος τῶν ἐγκωμίων, ὅτι πλεῖστα πάντων ἐγχειρισθεὶς πάντων οὐσίαν εἶχεν ἐλάττονα. πρὸς δὴ τοῦτον τὸν Περτίνακα νυκτὸς ἀκμαζούσης πάντες τε ὕπνῳ κατειλημμένων ἀφικνοῦνται ὁ Λαῖτος καὶ ὁ Ἔκλεκτος ὀλίγους τῶν συνωμοτῶν ἐπαγόμενοι. ἐπιστάντες δὲ αὐτοῦ κεκλεισμένης τῆς οἰκίας ταῖς θύραις διεγείρουσι τὸν φυλάσσοντα. ἀνοίξας δὲ ἐκεῖνος καὶ θεασάμενος στρατιώτας ἐφεστῶτας καὶ Λαῖτον, ὃν ᾔδει ἔπαρχον ὄντα, ἐκπλαγεὶς καὶ ταραχθεὶς <εἰς>αγγέλλει.

'After the conspirators had killed Commodus, as has been described in the first book of our history, they were anxious to keep the deed secret. And so, to prevent the praetorians on guard in the imperial palace from discovering what they had done, they wrapped the emperor's body in bed linen and tied it securely. They gave the bundle to two loyal slaves and sent it out of the palace as if it were no more than laundry, somewhat bulkier than usual. The slaves carried their burden past the guards; some of them were asleep, overcome by wine, others still awake, but dozing off leaning on their spears. The praetorians made no attempt to discover the contents of the bundle carried from the emperor's bedroom, since it was not their concern to look into such things. After the emperor's body had been carried out through the palace gates undetected, it was placed in a wagon and taken to the outskirts of the city. Then Laetus and Eclectus conferred with Marcia about the best course to follow. They decided that an announcement should be made to the effect that the emperor had died suddenly of apoplexy. They were sure that this report would be accepted without question by those who heard it, since his endless and excessive orgies had prepared them for such an outcome. But before doing anything else, the conspirators thought it best to choose a sensible elder statesman as the successor to the throne, both to save themselves and to bring to all enjoyment of a respite from a tyrant so harsh and undisciplined. Discussing the matter among themselves, they found no man so well qualified for the post as a native-born Italian named Pertinax. This Pertinax was famous for his accomplishments, both civil and military; he had won many victories over the Germans and the Eastern barbarians and was the only survivor of the revered advisers appointed for Commodus by his father. Commodus had not had him put to death — this most distinguished of Marcus' companions and generals — either out of respect for his noble qualities or indifference to him as a pauper. And yet his poverty had contributed in no small measure to the universal praise Pertinax enjoyed; for, despite responsibilities which far outweighed those of his colleagues, he was less wealthy than any of them. That night, while all were sleeping, Laetus and Eclectus, accompanied by a few fellow conspirators, came to Pertinax. Standing at the locked gates of his house, they aroused the porter on guard there. When the man awoke and saw the soldiers standing before the gates with Laetus, whom he knew to be the praetorian prefect, he was alarmed and went inside to report to his master.' (2.1.1-5)

The first passage by Herodian (1.13.7-15.1) has been included in order to exhibit the dramatic licence of the author.[689] Many of these aspects (such as the statue of Pallas,[690] and the nature and date of the great fire[691]) have been previously viewed as being either confused o

---

[689] Grosso 1964, *op.cit.*
[690] Heodian 1.14.4.
[691] Herodian 1.14.6.

entirely fictional. All the same, the actual assassination itself (1.17.1-12) is largely high on dramatic tension (if not invention) and very scant on proven detail.[692] This is not said to denigrate the worth of Herodian's account – he simply sought to provide an enthralling characterisation of the event. This is exhibited in the next passage (2.1.1-15) where the account is retold for entirely different literary motives. As mentioned previously, the breadth of these descriptions illustrates the emphasis desired by Herodian – this was the culmination of his first book – a 'fitting' end to a despot, whose reign had not only besmirched the legacy of his illustrious father, but also effected the ensuing phase of Roman politics. While Herodian could simply be neglected as a source for this clearly partial view and also for the way in which he represented such perspectives,[693] the text here reflects more of a commentary about the instability of the Third Century AD.[694] Commodus was an easy scapegoat (unpopular with the élites, non-conforming, and not overtly successful). As mentioned previously, he was not an ideal *princeps*, but he did not cause the instability that was to come either. This is further illustrated through an assessment of the assassination references by Cassius Dio (73.22.1-24.3):

ἀπέθανέ γέ τοι, μᾶλλον δὲ ἀνῃρέθη, οὐκ ἐς μακράν. ὁ γὰρ Λαῖτος καὶ ὁ Ἔκλεκτος ἀχθόμενοι αὐτῷ δι' ἃ ἐποίει, καὶ προσέτι καὶ φοβηθέντες (ἠπείλει γὰρ σφισιν, ὅτι ἐκωλύετο ταῦτα ποιεῖν), ἐπεβούλευσαν αὐτῷ. ὁ γὰρ Κόμμοδος ἀμφοτέρους ἀνελεῖν ἐβούλετο τοὺς ὑπάτους, Ἐρύκιόν τε Κλάρον καὶ Σόσσιον Φάλκωνα, καὶ ὕπατός τε ἅμα καὶ σεκούτωρ ἐν τῇ νουμηνίᾳ ἐκ τοῦ χωρίου ἐν ᾧ οἱ μονομάχοι τρέφονται προελθεῖν· καὶ γὰρ τὸν οἶκον τὸν πρῶτον παρ' αὐτοῖς, ὡς καὶ εἷς ἐξ αὐτῶν ὤν, εἶχε. καὶ μηδεὶς ἀπιστήσῃ· καὶ γὰρ τοῦ κολοσσοῦ τὴν κεφαλὴν ἀποτεμὼν καὶ ἑτέραν ἑαυτοῦ ἀντιθείς, καὶ ῥόπαλον δοὺς λέοντά τέ τινα χαλκοῦν ὑποθεὶς ὡς Ἡρακλεῖ ἐοικέναι, ἐπέγραψε πρὸς τοῖς δηλωθεῖσιν αὐτοῦ ἐπωνύμοις καὶ τοῦτο, "πρωτόπαλος σεκουτόρων, ἀριστερὸς μόνος νικήσας δωδεκάκις" οἶμαι "χιλίους" διὰ μὲν δὴ ταῦτα ὅ τε Λαῖτος καὶ ὁ Ἔκλεκτος ἐπέθεντο αὐτῷ, κοινωσάμενοι καὶ τῇ Μαρκίᾳ τὸ βούλευμα. ἐν γοῦν τῇ τελευταίᾳ τοῦ ἔτους ἡμέρᾳ, ἐν τῇ νυκτί, τῶν ἀνθρώπων ἀσχολίαν περὶ τὴν ἑορτὴν ἐχόντων, φάρμακον διὰ τῆς Μαρκίας ἐν κρέασι βοείοις αὐτῷ ἔδωκαν. ἐπεὶ δ' οὐκ ἠδυνήθη παραχρῆμα ὑπό τε τοῦ οἴνου ὑπό τε τῶν λουτρῶν, οἷς ἀεὶ ἀπλήστως ἐχρῆτο, φθαρῆναι, ἀλλὰ καὶ ἐξήμεσέ τι κἀκ τούτου ὑποτοπήσας αὐτὸ ἠπείλει τινά, οὕτω δὴ Νάρκισσόν τινα γυμναστὴν ἐπέπεμψαν αὐτῷ, καὶ δι' ἐκείνου λούμενον αὐτὸν ἀπέπνιξαν. τῷ μὲν οὖν Κομμόδῳ τοῦτο τὸ τέλος ἐγένετο ἔτη δώδεκα καὶ μῆνας ἐννέα

---

[692] Traupman 1956, *op.cit.*

[693] Herodian has often been overlooked by modern scholars in preference for the more analytical style of Cassius Dio. This is not justified.

[694] Grosso 1964, *op.cit.*

καὶ ἡμέρας τεσσαρεσκαίδεκα ἄρξαντι, ἐβίω δὲ ἔτη τριάκοντα ἓν καὶ μῆνας τέσσαρας· καὶ ἐς αὐτὸν ἡ οἰκία ἡ τῶν ὡς ἀληθῶς Αὐρηλίων αὐταρχοῦσα ἐπαύσατο. πόλεμοι δὲ μετὰ τοῦτο καὶ στάσεις μέγισται συνέβησαν, συνέθηκα δ' ἐγὼ τούτων τὴν συγγραφὴν ἐξ αἰτίας τοιᾶσδε. βιβλίον τι περὶ τῶν ὀνειράτων καὶ τῶν σημείων δι' ὧν ὁ Σεουῆρος τὴν αὐτοκράτορα ἀρχὴν ἤλπισε, γράψας ἐδημοσίευσα· καὶ αὐτῷ καὶ ἐκεῖνος πεμφθέντι παρ' ἐμοῦ ἐντυχὼν πολλά μοι καὶ καλὰ ἀντεπέστειλε. ταῦτ' οὖν ἐγὼ τὰ γράμματα πρὸς ἑσπέραν ἤδη λαβὼν κατέδαρθον, καί μοι καθεύδοντι προσέταξε τὸ δαιμόνιον ἱστορίαν γράφειν. καὶ οὕτω δὴ ταῦτα περὶ ὧν νῦν καθίσταμαι ἔγραψα. καὶ ἐπειδή γε τοῖς τε ἄλλοις καὶ αὐτῷ τῷ Σεουήρῳ μάλιστα ἤρεσε, τότε δὴ καὶ τἆλλα πάντα τὰ τοῖς Ῥωμαίοις προσήκοντα συνθεῖναι ἐπεθύμησα· καὶ διὰ τοῦτο οὐκέτι ἰδίᾳ ἐκεῖνο ὑπολιπεῖν ἀλλ' ἐς τήνδε τὴν συγγραφὴν ἐμβαλεῖν ἔδοξέ μοι, ἵν' ἐν μιᾷ πραγματείᾳ ἀπ' ἀρχῆς πάντα, μέχρις ἂν καὶ τῇ Τύχῃ δόξῃ, γράψας καταλίπω. τὴν δὲ δὴ θεὸν ταύτην ἐπιρρωννύουσάν με πρὸς τὴν ἱστορίαν εὐλαβῶς πρὸς αὐτὴν καὶ ὀκνηρῶς διακείμενον, καὶ πονούμενον ἀπαγορεύοντά τε ἀνακτωμένην δι' ὀνειράτων, καὶ καλὰς ἐλπίδας περὶ τοῦ μέλλοντος χρόνου διδοῦσάν μοι ὡς ὑπολειφομένου τὴν ἱστορίαν καὶ οὐδαμῶς ἀμαυρώσοντος, ἐπίσκοπον τῆς τοῦ βίου διαγωγῆς, ὡς ἔοικεν, εἴληχα, καὶ διὰ τοῦτο αὐτῇ ἀνάκειμαι. συνέλεξα δὲ πάντα τὰ ἀπ' ἀρχῆς τοῖς Ῥωμαίοις μέχρι τῆς Σεουήρου μεταλλαγῆς πραχθέντα ἐν ἔτεσι δέκα, καὶ συνέγραψα ἐν ἄλλοις δώδεκα· τὰ γὰρ λοιπά, ὅπου ἂν καὶ προχωρήσῃ, γεγράψεται. πρὸ δὲ τῆς τοῦ Κομμόδου τελευτῆς σημεῖα τάδε ἐγένετο· ἀετοί τε γὰρ περὶ τὸ Καπιτώλιον πολλοὶ καὶ ἔξεδροι ἐπλανῶντο, προσεπιφθεγγόμενοι οὐδὲν εἰρηναῖον, καὶ βύας ἀπ' αὐτοῦ ἔβυξε, πῦρ τε νύκτωρ ἀρθὲν ἐξ οἰκίας τινὸς καὶ ἐς τὸ Εἰρηναῖον ἐμπεσὸν τὰς ἀποθήκας τῶν τε Αἰγυπτίων καὶ τῶν Ἀραβίων φορτίων ἐπενείματο, ἔς τε τὸ παλάτιον μετεωρισθὲν ἐσῆλθε καὶ πολλὰ πάνυ αὐτοῦ κατέκαυσεν, ὥστε καὶ τὰ γράμματα τὰ τῇ ἀρχῇ προσήκοντα ὀλίγου δεῖν πάντα φθαρῆναι. ἀφ' οὗ δὴ καὶ τὰ μάλιστα δῆλον ἐγένετο ὅτι οὐκ ἐν τῇ πόλει τὸ δεινὸν στήσεται, ἀλλὰ καὶ ἐπὶ πᾶσαν τὴν οἰκουμένην αὐτῆς ἀφίξεται. οὐδὲ γὰρ κατασβεσθῆναι ἀνθρωπίνῃ χειρὶ ἠδυνήθη, καίτοι παμπόλλων μὲν ἰδιωτῶν παμπόλλων δὲ στρατιωτῶν ὑδροφορούντων, καὶ αὐτοῦ τοῦ Κομμόδου ἐπελθόντος ἐκ τοῦ προαστείου καὶ ἐπισπέρχοντος. ἀλλ' ἐπειδὴ πάντα ὅσα κατέσχε διέφθειρεν, ἐξαναλωθὲν ἐπαύσατο.

'And he actually did die, or rather was slain, before long. For Laetus and Eclectus, displeased at the things he was doing, and also inspired by fear, in view of the threats he made against them because they tried to prevent him from acting in this way, formed a plot against him. It seems that Commodus wished to slay both the consuls, Erucius Clarus and Sosius Falco, and on New Year's Day to issue forth both as consul and secutor from the quarters of the gladiators; in fact, he had the first cell there, as if he were one of them. Let no one doubt this statement. Indeed, he actually cut off the head of the Colossus, and substituted for it a likeness of his own head; then, having given it a club and placed a bronze lion at its feet, so as to cause it to look like Hercules, he inscribed on it, in addition to the list of his titles which I have already indicated, these words: "Champion of secutores; only left-handed fighter to conquer twelve times (as I recall the number) one thousand men." For these reasons Laetus and Eclectus attacked him, after making Marcia their confidant. At any rate, on the last day of the year, at night, when people were busy with the holiday, they caused Marcia to administer poison to him in some beef. But the immoderate use of wine and baths, which was habitual with him, kept him from succumbing at once, and instead he vomited up some of it; and thus suspecting the truth, he indulged in some threats. Then they sent Narcissus, an athlete, against him, and caused this man to strangle him while he was taking a bath. Such was the end of Commodus, after he had ruled twelve years, nine months, and fourteen days. He had lived thirty-one years and four months; and with him the line of the genuine Aurelii ceased to rule. After this there occurred most violent wars and civil strife. I was inspired to write an account of these struggles by the following incident. I had written and published a little book about the dreams and portents which gave Severus reason to hope for the imperial power; and he, after reading the copy I sent him, wrote me a long and complimentary acknowledgment. This letter I received about nightfall, and soon after fell asleep; and in my dreams the Divine Power commanded me to write history. Thus it was that I came to write the narrative with which I am at this moment concerned. And inasmuch as it won the high approval, not only of others, but, in particular, of Severus himself, I then conceived a desire to compile a record of everything else that concerned the Romans. Therefore, I decided to leave the first treatise no longer as a separate composition, but to incorporate it in this present history, in order that in a single work I might write down and leave behind me a record of everything from the beginning down to the point that shall seem best to Fortune. This goddess gives me strength to continue my history when I become timid and disposed to shrink from it; when I grow weary and would resign the task, she wins me back by sending dreams; she inspires me with fair hopes that future time will permit my history to survive and never dim its lustre; she, it seems, has fallen to my lot as guardian of the course of my life, and therefore I have dedicated myself to her. I spent ten years in collecting all the achievements of the Romans from the beginning down to the death of Severus, and twelve years more in composing my work. As for subsequent events, they also shall be recorded, down to whatever point it shall be permitted me. Before the death of Commodus there were the following portents: many eagles of ill omen soared about the Capitol and moreover uttered screams that boded nothing peaceful, and an owl hooted there; and a fire that began at night in some dwelling leaped to the temple of Pax and spread to the storehouses of Egyptian and Arabian wares, whence the flames, borne aloft, 2 entered the palace and consumed very extensive portions of it, so that nearly all the State records were destroyed. This, in particular, made it clear that the evil would not be confined to the City, but would extend over the entire civilized world under its sway. For the conflagration could not be extinguished by human power, though vast numbers both of civilians and soldiers carried water, and Commodus himself came in from the suburb and encouraged them. Only when it had destroyed everything on which it had laid hold did it spend its force and die out.' (Dio 73.22.1-24.3)

These passages illustrate a variety of literary motifs and priorities for the author. The length of the account of Commodus' death by Cassius Dio exhibits how important the assassination of the emperor was for the culmination of the anti-Commodus tradition in Book 73. Regardless of the way in which the structure of the *Roman History* was presented, this passage (73.22.1-24.3) is clearly emphasised by the author – Commodus was to be despised and his death was ultimately liberating for the people of Rome. This was of course further emphasised in the anoher passage (74.1.3-2.4) and also indirectly clarified in an additional section (74.2.5-6) by contrasting the relief of the brief reign of Pertinax (and his various successors) with Commodus – an emperor who had the time to become unpopular within a turbulent period. All the same, Commodus is shown as being deserving of such an end. As mentioned previously, whether this is accurate is an entirely different question, but it clearly suited the literary intent of the author. The impact of this account is, however, undeniable. Commodus was been viewed ever since as being entirely corrupt and even deserving of such a horrible death as well. This was also accentuated by the *HA* biographer in their account (*Commodus* 16.1-7; 17.1-20.5), which also exhibits the precursors to the death itself in great detail:

Prodigia eius imperio et publice et privatim haec facta sunt: crinita stella apparuit. vestigia deorum in foro visa sunt exeuntia. et ante bellum desertorum caelum arsit. et repentina caligo ac tenebra in Circo kalendis Ianuariis oborta; et ante lucem fuerant etiam incendiariae aves ac dirae. de Palatio ipse ad Caelium montem in Vectilianas aedes migravit, negans se in Palatio posse dormire. Ianus geminus sua sponte apertus est, et Anubis simulacrum marmoreum moveri visum est. Herculis signum aeneum sudavit in Minucia per plures dies. bubo etiam supra cubiculum eius deprehensa est tam Romae quam Lanuvii. ipse autem prodigium non leve sibi fecit; nam cum in gladiatoris occisi vulnus manum misisset, ad caput sibi detersit, et contra consuetudinem paenulatos iussit spectatores non togatos ad munus convenire, quod funeribus solebat, ipse in pullis vestimentis praesidens. galea eius bis per portam Libitinensem elata est.

'The prodigies that occurred in his reign, both those which concerned the state and those which affected Commodus personally, were as follows. A comet appeared. Footprints of the gods were seen in the Forum departing from it. Before the war of the deserters the heavens were ablaze. On the Kalends of January a swift coming mist and darkness arose in the Circus; and before dawn there had already been firebirds and ill-boding portents. Commodus himself moved his residence from the Palace to the Vectilian Villa on the Caelian hill, saying that he could not sleep in the Palace. The twin gates of the temple of Janus opened of their own accord, and a marble image of Anubis was seen to move. In the Minucian Portico a bronze statue of Hercules sweated for several days. An owl, moreover, was caught above his bedchamber both at Lanuvium and at Rome. He was himself responsible for no inconsiderable an omen relating to himself; for after he had plunged his hand into the wound of a slain gladiator he wiped it on his own head, and again, contrary to custom, he ordered the spectators to attend his gladiatorial shows clad not in togas but in cloaks, a practice usual at funerals, while he himself presided in the vestments of a mourner. Twice, moreover, his helmet was borne through the Gate of Libitina.' (*HA Commodus* 16.1-7)

His incitati, licet nimis sero, Quintus Aemilius Laetus praefectus et Marcia concubina eius inierunt coniurationem ad occidendum eum. primumque ei venenum dederunt; quod cum minus operaretur, per athletam, cum quo exerceri solebat, eum strangularunt. Fuit forma quidem corporis iusta, vultu insubido, ut ebriosi solent, et sermone incondito, capillo semper fucato et auri ramentis inluminato, adurens comam et barbam timore tonsoris. Corpus eius ut unco traheretur atque in

Tiberim mitteretur, senatus et populus postulavit, sed postea iussu Pertinacis in monumentum Hadriani translatum est. Opera eius praeter lavacrum, quod Cleander nomine ipsius fecerat, nulla exstant. sed nomen eius alienis operibus incisum senatus erasit. nec patris autem sui opera perfecit. classem Africanam instituit, quae subsidio esset, si forte Alexandrina frumenta cessassent. ridicule etiam Carthaginem Alexandriam Commodianam togatam appellavit, cum classem quoque Africanam Commodianam Herculeam appellasset. ornamenta sane quaedam Colosso addidit, quae postea cuncta sublata sunt. Colossi autem caput dempsit, quod Neronis esset, ac suum imposuit et titulum more solito subscripsit, ita ut illum Gladiatorium et Effeminatum non praetermitteret. hunc tamen Severus, imperator gravis et vir nominis sui, odio, quantum videtur, senatus inter deos rettulit, flamine addito, quem ipse vivus sibi paraverat, Herculaneo Commodiano. Sorores tres superstites reliquit. ut natalis eius celebraretur, Severus instituit. Adclamationes senatus post mortem Commodi graves fuerunt. ut autem sciretur quod iudicium senatus de Commodo fuerit, ipsas adclamationes de Mario Maximo indidi et sententiam senatus consulti:

"Hosti patriae honores detrahantur. parricidae honores detrahantur. parricida trahatur. hostis patriae, parricida, gladiator in spoliario lanietur. hostis deorum, carnifex senatus, hostis deorum, parricida senatus; hostis deorum, hostis senatus. gladiatorem in spoliario. qui senatum occidit, in spoliario ponatur; qui senatum occidit, unco trahatur; qui innocentes occidit, unco trahatur. hostis, parricida, vere vere. qui sanguini suo non pepercit, unco trahatur. qui te occisurus fuit, unco trahatur. nobiscum timuisti, nobiscum periclitatus es. ut salvi simus, Iuppiter optime maxime, serva nobis Pertinacem. fidei praetorianorum feliciter. praetoriis cohortibus feliciter. exercitibus Romanis feliciter. pietati senatus feliciter. Parricida trahatur. rogamus, Auguste, parricida trahatur. hoc rogamus, parricida trahatur. exaudi Caesar: delatores ad leonem. exaudi Caesar: Speratum ad leonem. victoriae populi Romani feliciter. fidei militum feliciter. fidei praetorianorum feliciter. cohortibus praetoriis feliciter. Hostis statuas undique, parricidae statuas undique, gladiatoris statuas undique. gladiatoris et parricidae statuae detrahantur. necator civium trahatur. parricida civium trahatur. gladiatoris statuae detrahantur. te salvo salvi et securi sumus, vere vere, modo vere, modo digne, modo vere, modo libere. Nunc securi sumus; delatoribus metum. ut securi simus, delatoribus metum. ut salvi simus, delatores de senatu, delatoribus fustem. te salvo delatores ad leonem. te imperante delatoribus fustem. Parricidae gladiatoris memoria aboleatur, parricidae gladiatoris statuae detrahantur. impuri gladiatoris memoria aboleatur. gladiatorem in spoliario. exaudi Caesar: carnifex unco trahatur. carnifex senatus more maiorum unco trahatur. saevior Domitiano, impurior Nerone. sic fecit, sic patiatur. memoriae innocentium serventur. honores innocentium restituas, rogamus. parricidae cadaver unco trahatur. gladiatoris cadaver unco trahatur. gladiatoris cadaver in spoliario ponatur. perroga, perroga: omnes censemus unco trahendum. qui omnes occidit, unco trahatur. qui omnem aetatem occidit, unco trahatur. qui utrumque sexum occidit, unco trahatur. qui sanguini suo non pepercit, unco trahatur. qui templa spoliavit, unco trahatur. qui testamenta delevit, unco trahatur. qui vivos spoliavit, unco trahatur. servis serviimus. qui pretia vitae exegit, unco trahatur. qui pretia vitae exegit et fidem non servavit, unco trahatur. qui senatum vendidit, unco trahatur. qui filiis abstulit hereditatem, unco trahatur. Indices de senatu, delatores de senatu, servorum subornatores de senatu. et tu nobiscum timuisti; omnia scis et bonos et malos nosti. omnia scis, omnia emenda; pro te timuimus. o nos felices, te vere imperante! de parricida refer, refer, perroga. praesentiam tuam rogamus. innocentes sepulti non sunt. parricidae cadaver trahatur. parricida sepultos eruit; parricidae cadaver trahatur."

Et cum iussu Pertinacis Livius Laurensis, procurator patrimonii, Fabio Ciloni consuli designato dedisset, per noctem Commodi cadaver sepultum est. senatus adclamavit: "Quo auctore sepelierunt, parricida sepultus eruatur, trahatur." Cincius Severus dixit: "Iniuste sepultus est. qua pontifex dico, hoc collegium pontificum dicit. quoniam laeta percensui, nunc convertar ad necessaria: censeo quas is, qui nonnisi ad perniciem civium et ad dedecus suum vixit, ob honorem suum decerni coegit, abolendas statuas, quae undique sunt abolendae, nomenque ex omnibus privatis publicisque monumentis eradendum mensesque iis nominibus nuncupandos quibus nuncupabantur, cum primum illud malum in re publica incubuit."

'Because of these things — but all too late — Quintus Aemilius Laetus, prefect of the guard, and Marcia, his concubine, were roused to action and entered into a conspiracy against his life. First they gave him poison; and when this proved ineffective they had him strangled by the athlete with whom he was accustomed to exercise. Physically he was very well proportioned. His expression was dull, as is usual in drunkards, and his speech uncultivated. His hair was always dyed and made lustrous by the use of gold dust, and he used to singe his hair and beard because he was afraid of barbers. The people and senate demanded that his body be dragged with the hook and cast into the Tiber; later, however, at the bidding of Pertinax, it was borne to the Mausoleum of Hadrian. No public works of his are in existence, except the bath which Cleander built in his name. But he inscribed his name on the works of others; this the senate erased. Indeed, he did not even finish the public works of his father. He did organize an African fleet, which would have been useful, in case the grain-supply from Alexandria were delayed. He jestingly named Carthage Alexandria Commodiana Togata, after entitling the African fleet Commodiana Herculea. He made certain additions to the Colossus by way of ornamentation, all of which were later taken off, and he also removed its head, which was a likeness of Nero, and replaced it by a likeness of himself, writing on the pedestal an inscription in his usual style, not omitting the titles Gladiatorius and Effeminatus. And yet Severus, a stern emperor and a man whose character was well in keeping with his name, moved by hatred for the senate — or so it seems — exalted this creature to a place among the gods and granted him also a flamen, the "Herculaneus Commodianus", whom Commodus while still alive had planned to have for himself. Three sisters survived him. Severus instituted the observance of his birthday. Loud were the acclamations of the senate after the death of Commodus. And that the senate's opinion of him may be known, I have quoted from Marius Maximus the acclamations themselves, and the content of the senate's decree:

"From him who was a foe of his fatherland let his honours be taken away; let the honours of the murderer be taken away; let the murderer be dragged in the dust. The foe of his fatherland, the murderer, the gladiator, in the charnel-house let him be mangled. He is foe to the gods, slayer of the senate, foe to the gods, murderer of the senate, foe of the gods, foe of the gods, foe of the senate. Cast the gladiator into the charnel-house. He who slew the senate, let him be dragged with the hook; he who slew the guiltless, let him be dragged with the hook — a foe, a murderer, verily, verily. He who spared not his own blood, let him be dragged with the hook; he who would have slain you, let him be dragged with the hook. You were in terror along with us, you were endangered along with us. That we may be safe, O Jupiter Best and Greatest, save for us Pertinax. Long life to the guardian care of the praetorians! Long life to the praetorian cohorts! Long life to the armies of Rome! Long life to the loyalty of the senate! Let the murderer be dragged in the dust. We beseech you, O Sire, let the murderer be dragged in the dust. This we beseech you, let the murderer be dragged in the dust. Hearken, Caesar: to the lions with the informers! Hearken Caesar: to the lions with Speratus! Long life to the victory of the Roman people! Long life to the soldiers' guardian care! Long life to the guardian care of the praetorians! Long life to the praetorian cohorts! On all sides are statues of the foe, on all side are statues of the murderer, on all sides are statues of the gladiator. The statues of the murderer and gladiator, let them be cast down. The slayer of citizens, let him be dragged in the dust. The murderer of citizens, let him be dragged in the dust. Let the statues of the gladiator be overthrown. While you are safe, we too are safe and untroubled, verily, verily, if in very truth, then with honour, if in very truth, then with freedom. Now at last we are secure; let informers tremble. That we may be secure, let the informers tremble. That we may be safe, cast informers out of the senate, the club for informers! While you are safe, to the lions with informers! While you are ruler, the club for informers! Let the memory of the murderer and the gladiator be utterly wiped away. Let the statues of the murderer and the gladiator be overthrown. Let the memory of the foul gladiator be utterly wiped away. Cast the gladiator into the charnel-house. Hearken, Caesar: let the slayer be dragged with the hook. In the manner of our fathers let the slayer of the senate be dragged with the hook. More savage than Domitian, more foul than Nero. As he did unto others, let it be done unto him. Let the remembrance of the guiltless be preserved. Restore the honours of the guiltless, we beseech you. Let the body of the murderer be dragged with the hook, let the body of the gladiator be dragged with the hook, let the body of the gladiator be cast into the charnel-house. Call for our vote, call for our vote: with one accord we reply, let him be dragged with the hook. He who slew all men, let him be dragged with the hook. He who slew young and old, let him be dragged with the hook. He who slew man and woman, let him be dragged with the hook. He who spared not his own blood, let him be dragged with the hook. He who plundered temples, let him be dragged with the hook. He who set aside the testaments of the dead, let him be dragged with the hook. He who plundered the living, let him be dragged with the hook. We have been slaves to slaves. He who demanded a price for the life of a man, let him be dragged with the hook. He who demanded a price for a life and kept not his promise, let him be dragged with the hook. He who sold the senate, let him be dragged with the hook. He who took from sons their patrimony, let him be dragged with the hook. Spies and informers, cast them out of the senate. Suborners of slaves, cast them out of the senate. You, too, were in terror along with us; you know all, you know both the good and the evil. You know all that we were forced to purchase; all we have feared for your sake. Happy are we, now that you are the emperor in truth. Put it to the vote concerning the murderer, put it to the vote, put the question. We ask your presence. The guiltless are yet unburied; let the body of the murderer be dragged in the dust. The murderer dug up the buried; let the body of the murderer be dragged in the dust."

The body of Commodus was buried during the night, after Livius Laurensis, the steward of the imperial estate, had surrendered it at the bidding of Pertinax to Fabius Cilo, the consul elect. At this the senate cried out: "With whose authority have they buried him? The buried murderer, let him be dug up, let him be dragged in the dust." Cincius Severus said: "Wrongfully has he been buried. And I speak as pontifex, so speaks the college of the pontifices. And now, having recounted what is joyful, I shall proceed to what is needful: I give it as my opinion that the statues should be overthrown which this man, who lived but for the destruction of his fellow-citizens and for his own shame, forced us to decree in his honour; wherever they are, they should be cast down. His name, moreover, should be erased from all public and private records, and the months should be once more called by the names whereby they were called when this scourge first fell upon the state." (*HA Commodus* 17.1-20.5)

The dramatisation of these passages cannot be undermined – they directly impact upon the audience, which was the intent of the *HA* biographer. Again, the emphasis is upon the length and theatricality of the account rather than the historical account. This is exhibited through the use of direct speech – dramatising accounts that would have never been available to the author in the Fourth Century AD. Yet of course these literary methods add to the perceived strength of its legitimacy. While Syme has referred to the *HA* biographer as a 'fraudster',[695] for once I disagree with him (a very rare occurrence). The author simply sought to create a characterisation of various *principes*, regardless of the facts. His style is clearly lacking (and is deserving of such criticism), but these 'historical' faults are also noted in other biographies that are held in much greater esteem, such as Plutarch, and even more importantly Suetonius (or perhaps even Tacitus' *Agricola*). The use of Commodus' assassination as a literary tool by the *HA* biographer was intended in exactly the same fashion.[696] The general implications, however, establish that the account needs to be viewed critically. The author sought to emphasise the deserving nature of Commodus' death, owing to the character's depraved and debauched sensibilities,[697] but as mentioned previously, the *HA* biographer was hardly alone in conveying such a consistent sentiment.

The analysis of Commodus' death by the ancient literary sources was evidently more about textual constructions rather than simply detailing the events. If the latter was important then they would all agree – they do not (aside from referring to a few key figures in the events). This epitomises the difficulties in the literary sources, but they are unfortunately the only available evidence for this particular analysis. All the same, they do agree about his characterisation – Commodus deserved such an unfortunate end. This does not seem to be an entirely accurate assessment though. The general circumstances of the Roman Empire had become increasingly difficult in circumstances that were largely beyond the control of the *princeps* (the northern frontier is a case in point – Marcus Aurelius had spent the vast majority of the final decade of his reign trying to secure this important and vulnerable border). Foreign policy and fiscal matters presented gradually more issues that needed to be addressed, but this

---

[695] Syme 1983, *op.cit.*

[696] Grosso 1964, *op.cit.*

[697] Traupman 1956, *op.cit.*

was evident in previous principates as well. This is not meant to absolve Commodus of all responsibility for the matters of state, but it is important to place his reign within a broader temporal and sociological context. In terms of his assassination, it must also be noted that few of his predecessors in the First Century AD seemingly died of natural causes either.[698] Therefore, it is vital to consider the general nature of Commodus' reign from this point in order to provide an overall assessment of his principate.

Commodus' Dependency upon Others

One of the most consistent themes that comes across in the analysis of Commodus (be it in an ancient assessment or sometimes a modern view) was his ineptitude. While much of this can be attributed to the prevalence of the anti-Commodus characterisation within the ancient literary sources, this issue must be dealt with in more general terms. After all was it possible for one person to deal with the complexity of the Roman Empire in the Second Century AD? Perhaps this was why Marcus Aurelius noted the extremity of such a task and welcomed Lucius Verus as his imperial colleague. The nature of both domestic and foreign politics at this point was so complex that a broader framework (even beyond two *principes*) was necessary. Commodus' representation suffers from this necessity. The swift promotion of the son in AD 175/6 in difficult circumstances (the revolt of Avidius Cassius) and then his removal to the northern frontier was hardly the ideal introduction to the cold face of Roman politics. When this is combined with his general inexperience in this regard (in conjunction with his probable sense of imperial entitlement) it becomes clear that he really needed the support of other influential people in a variety of circumstances (political, military, praetorian aspects are good examples). Marcus Aurelius seemingly put such a network in place, but it is also important to note how Commodus is shown (by the ancient literary sources) as rejecting the 'good' advisors, and promoting the opposite.

In relation to domestic politics, as discussed previously, Commodus was almost completely inexperienced in practical matters. While he probably learnt from the guidance of his father, Marcus Aurelius, and by viewing the workings of the imperial household (and *consilium*), it is impossible to determine how actively he was either taught or involved prior to AD 180. But it is evident that the

---

[698] Grosso 1964, *op.cit.*

joint principate period was of little assistance in a domestic political context – he was not in Rome during this period at all. This leads to the question about where such an inexperienced (and yet 'established') *princeps* could gain support. Judging from the available ancient evidence it becomes evident that Commodus primarily sought the backing of the military and the wider populace (non-élite) in Rome. The aristocratic (and highly influential) classes were seemingly not one of his priorities, which may have been a result of his own personal sense of self entitlement (as the sole surviving son of Marcus Aurelius), but this is difficult to tell for certain. All the same, while this is impossible to prove with any real conviction, the indications are there in the ancient record. It is evident that it was impracticable for him to run the Roman State on his own – so, therefore, he was dependent upon both his *consilium* and his *amici* for advice and guidance. But in turn this also left him seriously exposed to the personal ambitions of such companions and advisors as well.

The ancient literary sources of course accentuate the dependency of Commodus on others in order to clearly establish the weakness of his administration. Nevertheless, every emperor was exposed in such a fashion; both Tiberius and Claudius are excellent examples of such a prior scenario. This simply highlights the extreme pressures of the incumbent system, and yet it also emphasises how the imperial role went beyond one person (and yet only the leading individual would be really be held responsible in the ancient accounts). For Commodus there were two primary protagonists in the texts: Sextus Tigidius Perennis and Marcus Aurelius Cleander. Of course both have been shown to be highly influential leaders of the Praetorian *corps*, in similar (or equally negative) roles to that of Lucius Aelius Sejanus and Quintus Naevius Sutorius Macro. While the tradition within the ancient literary sources of having corrupt Praetorian Prefects under less than 'popular' *principes* was well established, the reality of an emperor depending upon such a person should not be questioned (why else would Vespasian choose his son Titus as prefect after all). The reality of every emperor was the quandary about who to trust. If the ancient sources are to be trusted, Commodus made poor choices – but again this was not unknown previously either. Nevertheless, for the present discussion it is simply pertinent to note his reliance upon such people and concurrently his lack of experience provided even more of a hindrance for him.

The dependency of Commodus Antoninus upon the opinions, advice and actions of others is quite obvious. All the same, this was the reality for any *princeps* – administratively it was an impossible job for any one person in light of the complexity of the issues and problems that would have continually arisen. Despite this, the ancient literary sources use this type of dependency as a means by which Commodus could be depicted as negligent and inattentive to his duties – he was of course instead more inclined towards the benefits of being a *princeps* rather than its responsibilities. It has become evident throughout this study that Commodus was largely inexperienced in the affairs of the capital, which would have been blatantly apparent to his contemporaries. Whether this made him too reliant upon his advisors and other prominent figures, such as the Praetorian Prefects, is a moot point. According to the ancient literary sources he was too susceptible to influence (or at least negligence), but this is a less than objective stand point. They have accentuated the problems he faced and down played his achievements. Therefore, in order to consider this further, the administration of Commodus requires further analysis by using a variety of ancient sources of evidence.

An Analysis of Commodus (Official Policies)

The official policies of Commodus' reign provide an excellent insight into the overall running of the Roman State between AD 180-192. The aim of this section is to generally assess the objectives and limitations of his principate in order to gain an insight into not only the period itself, but also into the nature of the available ancient sources of evidence. In this regard there has been a wide range of focus areas considered. These topics include financial and military aspects, as well as examining both foreign and domestic administrative policies. In order to undertake this effectively the widest possible assortment of ancient evidence has been consulted, as has been attempted throughout the whole of the present study. All the same, the ancient literary sources have been clearly taken as the dominant avenue of information, but, as mentioned previously, this does not always appear to be entirely justified. So, therefore, the present analysis is useful by allowing a further examination and perspective into the anti-Commodus textual tradition. This is most clearly exhibited through the examination of Commodus' financial administration.

The state finances from AD 180-192 can be examined using both numismatic evidence and ancient literary sources. Nevertheless, these disparate avenues of information provide equally disparate perspectives of Commodus' fiscal administration. If the ancient literary sources are to be believed there was a great deal of financial waste and excess during this period, which ultimately led to the fiscal decline and instability of the Third Century AD. This assessment is clearly quite simplistic, but it was certainly in accordance with the descriptions provided in the general anti-Commodus sentiment that dominated these texts. All the same, the weights of silver and gold denominations during the reigns of Marcus Aurelius and Commodus present an image of consistency and stability. There is no indication of extreme depreciation between AD 169-192 (aside from a gradual decline that was more indicative of market forces), thus suggesting responsible fiscal management within difficult circumstances. At this point it is pertinent to note that after Commodus' death the fiscal tactics of both markedly increasing and reducing the percentages of precious metal were used by the ensuing *principes* – to little reward in either regard. Nevertheless, it should also be noted that under both Marcus Aurelius and Commodus the numismatic issues under question had patently reduced in weight when compared to the same issues of the early First Century AD (see Adams 2007), which indicates a general depreciation of Roman currency over time. However, this was not indicative of Commodus' neglect – rather a decline in Rome's fiscal trading position over time.

A similar impression is provided through an examination of the foreign policy implemented by Commodus. The ancient literary sources accentuate the negligence of Commodus in this regard, highlighting how this may have ultimately led to the general weakening of the Roman frontiers (which has been shown not to be the case). This was achieved by them through the wider emphasis being placed upon instability in regions such as Dacia, Britain, and Mauretania on the *limes*. All the same, as mentioned previously, these literary accounts provide very few details about the state affairs despite giving quite lengthy characterisations about both the seriousness of such incursions and the ineptitude of the *princeps* (the *HA* biographer deals with both Dacia and Mauretania in one sentence for example). The successes are also attributed to the generals rather than Commodus – a literary feature that is only applied to 'bad' emperors, despite the exact same process being used by 'good' *principes*). These representations emphasise how Commodus was not involved, except with the 'unjustified' (?) peace declaration on the northern frontier. The undertaking of foreign campaigns (and their successes) was attributed by the early authors to his legates, thus giving Commodus none of the credit. This was, however, a long established tradition by various emperors (since Augustus really), which makes such criticism quite undeserving. Therefore, it seems that Commodus was able to maintain the general integrity of the Roman frontiers overall, despite increasingly difficult circumstances in several areas, particularly on the northern *limes*.

The nature of the pressures on the Roman frontiers meant that the management of military affairs had become increasingly essential, which was clearly of great importance to Commodus. This has been overtly demonstrated through the number of numismatic issues that advertised the harmony (or at least understanding) between the legions and the *princeps*. While this may not have actually been the case, as shown through the possible insurrection of Maternus, these coins do represent how vital military support was to Commodus, and how he sought to maintain such a close relationship. In view of the turbulence of the period from AD 180-192, he does seem to have been somewhat successful in this regard. This is indicated by the general levels of *concordia* between the two parties and the minimal level of rejection of Commodus by the army. This could also be indicated by the ensuing difficulties posed by the legions following his death towards Pertinax (and his successors) in order to maintain their allegiance. So in general terms, Commodus appears to have been quite successful in this regard. All the same, the area in which he had his most severe challenges was clearly in relation to his domestic policies – a domain where much more subtlety than he possessed was required.

When considering how Commodus sought to deal with domestic, political and administrative affairs there are several aspects that can be examined. Firstly, the complexity of the domestic issues surrounding the *princeps* must be acknowledged, which in many ways explains his great dependence upon others (regardless of whether it was justified or not). The wide range of competing self-interests also needs to be recognised, which further complicated these matters for him to address. All of this explains the necessity that existed for his presence in the capital (a topic that he would have been fully aware of). There would have not only been the possibility of internal threats by a variety of competitors, but also a significant number of pressures upon him by various influential interest groups, such as his senatorial and equestrian social peers for example. What comes across is that he was largely out of his depth – such a role required both nuance and subtlety from a leader, which were character traits that he seemingly lacked. This becomes evident even through a critical reading of the ancient literary sources. Whether this was owing to the self interests of his peers, or his lack of experience in the capital itself, or his own personal sense of self importance is a complete moot point – it being probably a combination of all three actually. All the same, what becomes more evident is that he sought popularity throughout the wider community in preference to the respect provided by the social élites, whose support was essential for the general success of his principate.

Therefore, it would appear that the overall assessment of the AD 180-192 period should be largely positive. The frontiers were generally secure and the financial position of the State was relatively stable within the trying circumstances that surrounded beyond the control of the *princeps*. In addition to this, the relationship between Commodus and the military was also relatively stable, thus ensuring another vital support base for the emperor. All the same, it is evident that he faced a far greater challenge in securing his position within the capital itself – the potential list of ambitious (and well connected) replacements among his social peers (and close confidants for that matter) certainly complicated matters for him. How he dealt with such threats was an intricate issue – one that Commodus ostensibly dealt with poorly. The delicate nature of such concerns had been approached previously by most *principes* with both positive and negative outcomes. Commodus was extreme in his response to his perceived threats (reactions that went beyond due process), a result that was not welcome among his élite contemporaries – hence the negative assessment of his principate. Nevertheless, this deals with his general characterisation within the ancient textual corpus, which needs special consideration in relation to how Commodus has been viewed overall – in both antiquity and in modern times.

An Analysis of Commodus (Characterisations)

The representation of Commodus is of course a highly significant feature of the present study. The textual characterisations of him have had a definitive impact upon Commodus' place within the broader historical record. While there are a variety of ancient representations of this *princeps* (archaeological, epigraphic, numismatic for example), the primary focus here has been upon the ancient literary sources, which is largely owing to their dominance as a source of information. While this study has consistently evaluated each literary source critically, it should not be taken that any of them are of no use for an analysis of Commodus Antoninus. The opposite is the case – they are vital. Each ancient author not only reflects their own literary priorities (because they are all different in so many ways), but they also demonstrate the dominance of the over-riding perspective of their times (the anti-Commodus tradition), which was the prevailing sentiment among his social peers during his principate. They reflect his rejection, which in turn allows for the analysis of why this occurred. All the same, this ability for some perspective is only achievable through the analysis of other ancient sources of information, such as numismatics and statue bases. Therefore, some of the predominant literary themes require attention within this study, beginning with one of the most common topics – the unpopularity (or perhaps instability?) of Commodus.

If the ancient literary sources are to be believed in an unequivocal fashion, Commodus was a highly unpopular *princeps*. All the same, this perspective is really only representative of one (aristocratic or influential?) section of the community – the social peers of the emperor. This group was evidently not his greatest priority when it came to endearing himself, which explains their prevailing mutual hostility. While the reasoning behind this antagonism has been postulated over previously within this study, for the present purposes it is simply pertinent to note its existence. Stemming from this it is vital to recognise how the ancient literary sources do not represent the views of either the military or the common (non-élite) people. It is evident that these groups were the primary foci for Commodus' attention seeking popularity. Aristocratic respect was not a priority for him, and his desire for such 'base' support would have also in turn led to their ire as well. Nevertheless, judging from both the response of the army after his death and the continued erection of statues in his honour throughout the empire, he does not appear to have been as unpopular and unstable as the ancient texts would have us believe.

The prevalent characterisations of Commodus Antoninus in the ancient literary sources have focused upon his corruption and indolence consistently. Yet, as has been shown throughout this study, such textual allegations are inherently questionable because of their partiality. Commodus was not an ideal *princeps*, but the authors under question clearly make consistent efforts to present him in the worst light possible – regardless of their historical accuracy (which is evidently not their literary priority). This emphasises their subjectivity and illustrates the predominance of their intended audience as well.

It is difficult to find representations of two more disparate characters in Marcus Aurelius and Commodus. The father is shown as fair, capable and ideal, whereas the son is depicted as the complete opposite (see Adams 2013 for further discussion of the contrast in relation to Marcus Aurelius and Commodus). The reality of the situation was that Marcus knew how to work within the proclivities of Roman domestic politics, whereas Commodus had little idea (or possibly he cared minimally for such details, depending upon the perspective you take on him). How this came about is a debatable point (possibly his training, education, personality, environment are just a few examples), but it is evident that Marcus Aurelius knew how to 'play the game' in the capital. Regardless of the idealism surrounding him, it is also evident that this was not a talent shared by his son, Commodus. The latter had little capacity for the nuance and subtlety required for a 'successful' Roman *princeps*. Yet, as mentioned previously, the administration of Commodus was quite beneficial despite the resulting criticism of him. It appears more than likely that the ancient literary sources sought to fulfil dual literary motives with such representations: the 'depravity' of Commodus accentuated the 'idealism' of Marcus Aurelius and vice versa. Marcus Aurelius was the 'ideal' *princeps* and Commodus' depravity accentuated this – the only sticking point was his parentage, but this was easily overcome by most ancient authors by claiming Commodus was really the son of a gladiator. So at this point these representations require further discussion as examples of their negative constructions. For the purposes of this study, the biography of Commodus in the *Historia Augusta* has been taken as a case in point – one that reflects the overall characterisation of him.

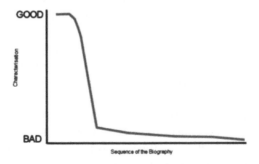

Figure 22 – Structure of a 'Bad' Biography

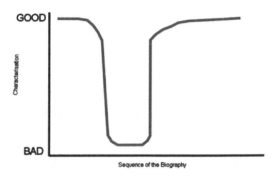

Figure 23 – Structure of a 'Good' Biography

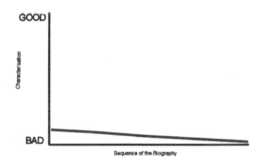

Figure 24 – Structure of Commodus' Biography

This text presents a consistently negative portrayal of Commodus, emphasising his depravity and bloodthirsty nature. A typical negative biography would begin with some relatively positive traits, and then plunge into the depravity of a character in order to accentuate the depravity of the individual and their corruption (thereby establishing their fall from grace) (Fig. 22). This is the opposite of a positive biography where the narrative accentuates positive traits from the outset and for the majority of the narrative, except for a small critical section in the early stages of the text (in order to not only accentuate the author's impartiality, but also emphasise the development of the character – essentially how such defects were overcome) (Fig. 23). The biography of Commodus by the *HA* biographer was of course intrinsically negative. All the same, while this biographical has been noted, the *Vita Commodi* was even more extreme in its negativity (Fig.

24), which not only exhibits the consistency in its negativity towards him, but it also emphasises the lack of nuance on the part of the *HA* biographer as well. The author neglected to use his preference for a Suetonian method by simply (and relentlessly) exhibiting Commodus as an 'evil' emperor. All the same, one of the most fascinating passages in the *Commodus* is Section 17 (see below). This not only deals with the death of Commodus, but it also provides a highly critical assessment of him, which results in a reference to his deification (but this is even criticised by author as being motivated by Septimius Severus' antagonism towards the Senate). As far as the *HA* biographer was concerned, the character of Commodus was not redeemable in any fashion whatsoever, which highlights the force of the anti-Commodus tradition even by the end of the Fourth Century AD.

The characterisation of the AD 180-192 period is hardly positive by any of the ancient literary sources. This quite difficult period was meant to epitomise the negligent and cruel nature of the *princeps*. All the same, as mentioned previously, this perspective is by far too simplistic. The characterisation of Commodus in the ancient literary sources can only be relied upon up to a certain point, judging from the unequivocal negativity in his portrayal by them. Yet such disapproval has not been confirmed by the other sources of ancient evidence (be they archaeological or epigraphic), thus illustrating their partiality. When considering how Commodus has been characterised, it is also imperative to examine the place of this controversial *princeps* within a more general perspective of Roman imperial history. Therefore, at this point the ensuing developments after his death have been analysed as a source of discussion for his wider contextualisation. This is important because it not only illustrates the overall historical circumstance in which the extant sources were being composed (well at least for Herodian and Cassius Dio), but it also allows for a greater understanding of the resulting events that have in turn affected the judgement of Commodus within the historical record.

The Aftermath

It is clear that Commodus Antoninus was perceived as lacking experience during his principate, just as it was noted that he did not prioritise cementing a close relationship with many of his social peers. The difficulties between Commodus and many members of this group was largely owing to both his inability to satisfy ambitions (or more precisely their precious sensibilities) as well as his priorities being focused upon more 'common' (non-élite) avenues of support. This sentiment is implied throughout all of the ancient literary sources, which has resulted in his unpopular depiction. This does not mean that he was not culpable for this social breakdown – in fact it illustrates how he was not a talented leader really at all (through the alienation of such a vital and influential segment of Roman society). These deficiencies have, however, been used by all of the ancient literary sources as a means of blaming Commodus for the ensuing difficulties that occurred following his death. It would be entirely unrealistic to claim that Rome in the Third Century AD was in a settled state, but this seems to have been connected to the negligence of Commodus in the ancient texts. This is not justified. All the same, in order to gain the optimal insight in to this situation the reign of Pertinax needs to be initially examined so that this post-Commodus period can be considered.

Publius Helius Pertinax had succeeded in a well established military career prior to the death of Commodus,[699] but it is clear that his reign was both brief and tumultuous.[700] While he appears to have tried to bring about various fiscal, military and administrative reforms, almost none of them survived him. One of the primary difficulties that he faced was the influence of the Praetorian *corps* – the group that ultimately killed him.[701] He also sought to stabilise the Roman currency, with limited success – after all he reigned for less than three months. There are several factors from his reign that need to be considered for the present purposes of this study. Firstly, the brief reign of Pertinax (and the nature of his demise) illustrates the difficulties that had not only existed during Commodus' reign (military control, social and political factionalism, the influence of the Praetorian Guard as obvious examples), but also how they became exceedingly more problematic after his assassination in AD 192. The difficulties with the Praetorians,[702] internal politics, general military affairs and factionalism were clearly the issues that faced Pertinax upon his appointment as *princeps*. These issues had existed under Commodus, but they became manifestly more prominent as challenges under the reign of Pertinax. The irony here is that in many

---

[699] *HA Pert.* 2.1; 2.4; Dio 73.3.
[700] cf. E. Champlin, "Notes on the Heirs of Commodus", *AJPh* 100.2, 1979, p. 289.
[701] Dio 74.10.
[702] Champlin 1979, *op.cit.*, p. 289.

ways these affairs became worse after the removal of Commodus Antoninus, and yet he was subsequently blamed for it by the ancient literary sources in a variety of ways. All the same, the post-Commodus phase needs to be considered more extensively in order to fully appreciate the historical context of the period – from Didius Julianus until the early reign of Septimius Severus.

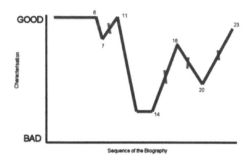

Figure 25 – Structure of Severus' Biography

The instability of the year following the death of Commodus is reflected in the number of competitors for the principate: Pertinax, Didius Julianus, Pescennius Niger, Clodius Albinus and Septimius Severus. Didius Julianus essentially bought the position through the bribery of the Praetorian Guard after Pertinax's assassination, but this was ultimately rejected by the other three imperial aspirants.[703] Ultimately Septimius Severus was victorious, having defeated Pescennius Niger in Cilicia (AD 194),[704] and Clodius Albinus at Lugdunum in AD 197.[705] The high scale of volatility during this period demonstrates many of the difficulties that had confronted Commodus during his principate – such as military influence, the personal ambitions of other influential personages, and the general (or even numerous) issues that faced any *princeps* in light of the tumultuous circumstances at the time. Perhaps the state of affairs at the time are best illustrated by the construction of the *HA* biographer's *vita* (Fig. 25) – there is a clear combination of 'good' and 'bad' elements in this characterisation, but not in a fashion that conforms to either archetypal biographical form (Figs. 22, 23). Septimius Severus was able to

---

[703] Herodian 2.6.4; Dio 74.11.5.

[704] *HA Pesc. Nig.* 5.8.

[705] *HA Severus* 11.

bring stability to the Empire, but it is also clear that the required methods were not always popular:

occidit autem sine causae dictione hos nobiles: Mummium Secundinum, Asellium Claudianum, Claudium Rufum, Vitalium Victorem, Papium Faustum, Aelium Celsum, Iulium Rufum, Lollium Professum, Aurunculeium Cornelianum, Antonium Balbum, Postumium Severum, Sergium Lustralem, Fabium Paulinum, Nonium Gracchum, Masticium Fabianum, Casperium Agrippinum, Ceionium Albinum, Claudium Sulpicianum, Memmium Rufinum, Casperium Aemilianum, Cocceium Verum, Erucium Clarum, Aelium Stilonem, Clodium Rufinum, Egnatuleium Honoratum, Petronium Iuniorem, Pescennios Festum et Veratianum et Aurelianum et Materianum et Iulianum et Albinum, Cerellios Macrinum et Faustinianum et Iulianum, Herennium Nepotem, Sulpicium Canum, Valerium Catullinum, Novium Rufum, Claudium Arabianum, Marcium Asellionem. horum igitur tantorum ac tam inlustrium virorum, nam multi in his consulares, multi praetorii, omnes certe summi viri fuere, interfector ab Afris ut deus habetur. Cincium Severum calumniatus est quod se veneno adpetisset, atque ita interfecit. Narcissum dein, Commodi strangulatorem, leonibus obiecit. multos praeterea obscuri loci homines interemit praeter eos quos vis proelii absumpsit. Post haec, cum se vellet commendare hominibus, vehicularium munus a privatis ad fiscum traduxit. Caesarem dein Bassianum Antoninum a senatu appellari fecit, decretis imperatoriis insignibus. rumore deinde belli Parthici excitus patri matri avo et uxori priori per se statuas conlocavit. Plautianum ex amicissimo cognita eius vita ita odio habuit, ut et hostem publicum appellaret et depositis statuis eius per orbem terrae gravi eum insigniret iniuria, iratus praecipue, quod inter propinquorum et adfinium Severi simulacra suam statuam ille posuisset. Palaestinis poenam remisit quam ob causam Nigri meruerant. postea iterum cum Plautiano in gratiam rediit et veluti ovans urbem ingressus Capitolium petit, quamvis et ipsum procedenti tempore occiderit. Getae minori filio togam virilem dedit, maiori Plautiani filiam uxorem iunxit. ii qui hostem publicum Plautianum dixerant deportati sunt. ita omnium rerum semper quasi naturali lege mutatio est. filios dein consules designavit. Getam fratrem extulit. profectus dehinc ad bellum Parthicum est, edito gladiatorio munere et congiario populo dato. multos inter haec causis vel veris vel simulatis occidit, damnabantur autem plerique, cur iocati essent, alii, cur tacuissent, alii, cur pleraque figurata dixissent, ut "ecce imperator vere nominis sui, vere Pertinax, vere Severus."

He put to death without even a fair trial the following noblemen: Mummius Secundinus, Asellius Claudianus, Claudius Rufus, Vitalius Victor, Papius Faustus, Aelius Celsus, Julius Rufus, Lollius Professus, Aurunculcius Cornelianus, Antonius Balbus, Postumius Severus, Sergius Lustralis, Fabius Paulinus, Nonius Gracchus, Masticius Fabianus, Casperius Agrippinus, Ceionius Albinus, Claudius Sulpicianus, Memmius Rufinus, Casperius Aemilianus, Cocceius Verus, Erucius Clarus, Aelius Stilo, Clodius Rufinus, Egnatuleius Honoratus, Petronius Junior, the six Pescennii, Festus, Veratianus, Aurelianus, Materianus, Julianus, and Albinus; the three Cerellii, Macrinus, Faustinianus, and Julianus; Herennius Nepos, Sulpicius Canus, Valerius Catullinus, Novius Rufus, Claudius Arabianus, and Marcius Asellio. And yet he who murdered all these distinguished men, many of whom had been consuls and many praetors, while all were of high estate, is regarded by the Africans as a god. He falsely accused Cincius Severus of attempting his life by poison, and thereupon put him to death; next, he cast to the lions Narcissus, the man who had strangled Commodus. And besides, he put to death many men from the more humble walks of life, not to speak of those whom the fury of battle had consumed. After this, wishing to ingratiate himself with the people, he took the postal service out of private hands and transferred its cost to the privy-purse. Then he caused the senate to give Bassianus Antoninus the title of Caesar and grant him the imperial insignia. Next, when called away by the rumour of a Parthian war, he set up at his own expense statues in honour of his father, mother, grandfather and first wife. He had been very friendly with Plautianus; but, on learning his true character, he conceived such an aversion to him as even to declare him a public enemy, overthrow his statues, and make him famous throughout the entire world for the severity of his punishment, the chief reason for his anger being that Plautianus had set up his own statue among the statues of Severus' kinsmen and connections. He revoked the punishment which had been imposed upon the people of Palestine on Niger's account. Later, he again entered into friendly relations with Plautianus, and after entering the city in his company like one who celebrates an ovation, he went up to the Capitol, although in the course of time he killed him. He bestowed the toga virilis on his younger son, Geta, and he united his elder son in marriage with Plautianus' daughter. Those who had declared Plautianus a public enemy were now driven into exile. Thus, as if by a law of nature, do all things ever shift and change. Soon thereafter he appointed his sons to the consulship; also he greatly honoured his brother Geta. Then, after giving a gladiatorial show and bestowing largess upon the people, he set out for the Parthian war. Many men meanwhile were put to death, some on true and some on trumped-up charges. Several were condemned because they had spoken in jest, others because they had not spoken at all, others again because they had cried out many things with double meaning, such as "Behold an emperor worthy of his name — Pertinacious in very truth, in very truth Severe." *(HA Severus* 13-14)

Septimius Severus' principate was generally successful, but his more 'controversial' (or stern) decisions certainly reflect the necessity to take a firm approach towards the establishment of his rule at the time.[706] All the same, for the purposes of the present discussion his most pertinent decision was the deification of Commodus,[707] which is attested upon many of the later (post AD 192) statue bases dedicated up until AD 211.[708] According to the *HA* biographer this was only to antagonise a resistant senatorial group, but this seems to have been quite a simplistic explanation by the author. Septimius Severus may have used the tactic of intimidation frequently, but this decision seems to have been more closely associated with the legitimisation of his imperial position – a similar connection to the equally 'unpopular' Nero was made by Galba,[709] Otho,[710] Vitellius,[711] and Vespasian.[712] Nevertheless, they did not deify Nero – Septimius Severus acted as

---

[706] See A.R. Birley, *Septimius Severus: the African Emperor*, London, 1971.
[707] Grosso 1964, *op.cit.*
[708] Hojte 2005, *op.cit.*
[709] Wellesley 1989, *op.cit.*
[710] Levick 1999, *op.cit.*
[711] Wellesley 1989, *op.cit.*
[712] Levick 1999, *op.cit.*

such towards Commodus, thus suggesting that he may not have been as unpopular as he has been described by the early authors. The extant statue bases also indicate that this view was shared by others in the Roman Empire beyond Septimius Severus as well. Commodus was clearly not the tyrant that the ancient literary sources would have us believe – he was not an ideal *princeps*, but stability was evidently maintained from AD 180-192. It is notable how the *HA* biographer produced a 'mixed' representation of Septimius Severus despite his use of similar 'controlling' methods to Commodus, who received an entirely negative from the author.

The period in which Commodus reigned was certainly a challenge, one that would have tested even the most talented and experienced of *principes*. He was not such a person. When the progression of his career is considered he had two major problems to contend with: firstly, an over inflated sense of his own birthright (or entitlement), and secondly, a minimal level of experience at the 'hard end' of an emperor's duties – the realities of internal Roman politics prior to his sole principate. The joint principate sought to aid him in this regard, following from the threat posed by Avidius Cassius, but this period (AD 175/6-180) was spent on the northern frontier, thus giving him little experience in the game play of politics. Watching Marcus Aurelius, his father, in his role as emperor would have been one thing – experiencing it would have been an entirely different matter.

All the same, many of the policies of Commodus were sound in view of the prevailing circumstances. The Empire was stable, the finances were generally steady, the military was under control (for the most part), the ambitious Praetorian Prefects had been removed when necessary, and the provinces were seemingly satisfied with their circumstances. Yet he did not excel at the most important aspect – the engagement with (and placation of) his social peers. This not only affected the capacity of his administration (which resulted in his eventual death), but it also has influenced his place in the historical record. Commodus was not an astute politician – he sought his own gratification and self indulgence by appealing to the 'common' people rather than the people who really 'mattered' – those who ultimately made the decisions in real terms. He sought *popularity* over *respect* within the sphere of Roman domestic politics – an unwise choice with the historian's benefit of hindsight. His self indulgence (and self promotion) incurred nothing but their ire as well. Whether this was justified can be determined through the extant consular lists of AD 181-192 – unlike many of his predecessors (such as good emperors like Vespasian, Titus, Trajan and Hadrian) Commodus did not dominate the consulship either himself personally or through the appointment of his *familia* and *consilium*. He did occasionally use it for his own promotion, but he also did not neglect other social élites either – Septimius Severus himself being a beneficiary. In essence, he was not a talented leader like some of his imperial predecessors, but nor was he a tyrant.

ABBREVIATIONS

AClass	Acta Classica
AJA	American Journal of Archaeology
AJPh	American Journal of Philology
AncSoc	Ancient Society
ANRW	Aufstieg und Niedergang der römischen Welt: Geschichte und Kultur Rom sim Spiegel der neueren Forschung
BAR	British Archaeological Reports
BMC	Coins of the Roman Empire in the British Museum
CIL	*Corpus Inscriptionum Latinorum*
CPh	Classical Philology
CQ	Classical Quarterly
CR	Classical Review
CW	Classical World
G&R	Greece and Rome
HAC	Historia-Augusta-Colloquium
HCP	Harvard Studies in Classical Philology
IG	*Inscriptiones Graecae*
IGR	*Inscriptiones Graecae ad Res Romanas Pertinentes*
ILS	*Inscriptiones Latinae Selectae*
JHS	Journal of Hellenic Studies
JRA	Journal of Roman Archaeology
JRS	Journal of Roman Studies
MDAIR(A)	Mitteilungen des Deutschen Archaeologischen Instituts Römische Abteilung
MEFRA	Melanges École Française de Rome: Antike
MusHel	Museum Helveticum
RIC	Roman Imperial Coinage
TAPA	Transactions of the American Philological Association
YCIS	Yale Classical Studies

BIBLIOGRAPHY

Adams, G.W., 2001, "Licinius Sura, Dio and the Not So Acephalous *ILS* 1022", *Journal of Ancient Civilisations* 16, pp. 5-8.

Adams, G.W., 2005, "Suetonius and his Treatment of the Emperor Domitian's Favourable Accomplishments", *SHT* 6.A.3, http://www.ut.ee/klassik/sht/2005/adams1.pdf

Adams, G.W., 2006, *The Suburban Villas of Campania and their Social Function*, Oxford: Archaeopress.

Adams, G.W., 2007, *Caligula: the Hellenistic Views of a Roman Emperor*, Boca Raton: BrownWalker.

Adams, G.W., 2007, *Rome and the Social Role of Elite Villas in its Suburbs*, Oxford: Archaeopress.

Adams, G.W., 2008, "An Analysis of Antoninus Pius' Frontier Policy in Northern Britain and its Representation of his Principate", *Journal of Ancient Civilizations* 23, pp. 119-37.

Adams, G.W., 2013, *Marcus Aurelius in the Historia Augusta and Beyond*, Lanham: Lexington Books.

Adams, J.N., 1972, "On the Authorship of the *HA*", *CQ* 22, pp. 186-94.

Adams, J.N., 1977, "The Linguistic Unity of the *HA*", *Antichthon* 11, pp. 93-102.

Adembri, B., 2000, *Hadrian's Villa*, Electa: Milan.

Albertini, E., 1965, "The Latin West: Africa, Spain and Gaul", *CAH* XI, pp. 479-510.

Alföldy, G., 1970, "Eine Proskriptionsliste in der *Historia Augusta*", *HAC* 1968/9, pp. 1-11.

Alföldy, G., 1971, "Der Friedensschluss des Kaisers Commodus mit den Germanen", *Historia* 20.1, pp. 84-109.

Alföldy, G., 1977, *Konsulat und Senatorenstand unter den Antoninen: Prosopographische Untersuchungen zur Senatorischen Führungsschicht*, Antiquitas 1.27: Bonn.

Alföldy, G., 2000, "Roman Spain", *CAH* XI, pp. 444-61.

Allison, P.M., 1992, "The relationship between wall-decoration and room-type in Pompeian houses: a case study of the Casa della Caccia Antica", *JRA* 5, pp. 235-49.

Ameling, W., 1997, "Griechische Intellektuelle und das Imperium Romanum: das Biespiel Cassius Dio", *ANRW* 34.3, pp. 2472-96.

Aurigemma, S., 1964, *Villa Adriana near Tivoli*, trans. A.W. Van Buren, Arti Grafiche A. Chicca: Tivoli.

Baldwin, B., 1981, "Ausonius and the *Historia Augusta*", *Gymnasium* 88, p. 438.

Baldwin, B., 1995, "Some Legal Terms in the *Historia Augusta*", *Maia* 47, pp. 207-9.

Barnes, T.D., 1972, "Some Persons in the *Historia Augusta*", *Phoenix* 26.2, pp. 140-82.

Barnes, T.D., 1976, "The *Epitome De Caesaribus* and its Sources", *CPh* 71.3, pp. 258-68.

Barnes, T.D., 1978, *The Sources of the Historia Augusta*, Collection Latomus 155, Latomus Revue d'Etudes Latines: Brussels.

Baynes, N.H., 1924, "The Date of the Composition of the *Historia Augusta*", *CR* 38, pp. 165-9.

Baynes, N.H., 1926, *The Historia Augusta: its date and purpose*, Oxford University Press: Oxford.

Baynes, N.H., 1928, "The *Historia Augusta*: its date and purpose. A reply to Criticism", *CQ* 22, pp. 166-71.

Bellingham, D.C., 1985, "Die Statuarische ausstattung der Villa Hadriana bei Tivoli (review)", *JRS* 75, p. 274-5.

Bennett, J., 2001, *Trajan – Optimus Princeps*, Indiana University Press: Bloomington.

Bergmann, B., 1994, "Painted Perspectives of a villa visit: landscape as status and metaphor", in Gazda, E.K. (ed.), *Roman Art in the Private Sphere*, University of Michigan Press: Ann Arbor, p. 65.

Bird, H.W., 1981, "The Sources of the De Caesaribus", *CQ* 31.2, pp. 457-63.

Bird, H.W., 1984, *Sextus Aurelius Victor: a historiographical study*, Francis Cairns: Liverpool.

Bird, H.W., 1993, *The Breviarium Ab Urbe Condita of Eutropius*, Liverpool University Press: Liverpool.

Bird, H.W., 1994, *Liber De Caesaribus of Sextus Aurelius Victor*, Liverpool University Press: Liverpool.

Birley, A.R., 1971, *Septimius Severus: the African Emperor*, London.

Birley, A.R., 1974, "Kolb, Literarische Beziehungen zwischen Cassius Dio und Herodian (Review)", *JRS* 64, pp. 266-8.

Birley, A.R., 1995, "Indirect Means of tracing Marius Maximus", *HAC* 1992, pp. 57-74.

Birley, A.R., 1997, "Marius Maximus: the Consular Biographer", *ANRW* 34.3, pp. 2678-757.

Birley, A.R., 2000, *Marcus Aurelius: a biography*, Routledge: London.

Birley, E., 1978, "Fresh Thoughts on the Dating of the *Historia Augusta*", *HAC* 1975/6, pp. 99-105.

Bowman, A.K., 1970, "A letter of Avidius Cassius?", *JRS* 60, pp. 20-6.

Bowman, A.K., 1982, "Fronto and Antonine Rome [Review]", *Phoenix* 36.3, pp. 369-71.

Bradford Welles, C., 1936, "A Yale Fragment of the Acts of Appian", *TAPA* 67, pp. 7-23.

Bradley, K.R., 1982, "Fronto and Antonine Rome [Review]", *CJ* 77.4, pp. 369-71.

Brandt, H., 1996, *Kommentar zur Vita Maximi et Balbini der Historia Augusta*, Antiquitas 4.2: Bonn.

Broughton, T.R.S., 1975, "The Priests of the Roman Republic: a study of interactions between priesthoods and Magistracies [Review]", *Gnomon* 47.4, pp. 383-7.

Brunt, P.A., 1973, "The Fall of Perennis: Dio-Xiphilinus 72.9.2", *CQ* 23.1, pp. 172-7.

Bruun, P., 1999, "Coins and the Roman Imperial Government", in Paul, G.M. (ed.), *Roman coins and Public Life under the Empire: E. Togo Salmon Papers II*, University of Michigan Press: Ann Arbor, pp. 19-40.

Burgess, R.W., 2001, "Eutropius v.c. *Magister Memoriae?*", *CPh* 96.1, pp. 76-81.

Callu, J.P., 1987, "*L'Histoire Auguste* de Petrarque", *HAC* 1984/5, pp. 81-115.

Cameron, A., 1998, "Education and Literary Culture", *CAH* 13, pp. 665-707.

Cameron, A., 2001, "The *Epitome De Caesaribus* and the *Chronicle* of Marcellinus", *CQ* 51.1, pp. 324-7.

Cassatella, A., 1990, "Un disegno di pirro Ligorio ed I resti sotto il Triclinio della Domus Flavia", in *Gli Orti Farnesiani sul Palatino*, École Francaise de Rome: Rome, pp. 155-66.

Champlin, E., 1974, "The Chronology of Fronto", *JRS* 64, pp. 136-59.

Champlin, E., 1979, "Notes on the Heirs of Commodus", *AJPh* 100.2, pp. 288-306.

Champlin, E., 1980, *Fronto and Antonine Rome*, Harvard University Press: Cambridge, Mass.

Chastagnol, A., 1964, "Le Problème de *l'Histoire Auguste*: état de la question", *HAC* 1963, pp. 43-71.

Chastagnol, A., 1968, "L'Utilisation des 'Caesars' d'Aurelius Victor dans *l'Histoire Auguste*", *HAC* 1966/7, pp. 53-65.

Clinton, K., 1989, "Hadrian's contribution to the Renaissance of Elusis", in Walker, S. and Cameron, A. (eds.), *The Greek Renaissance in the Roman Empire*, Institute of Classical Studies: London, pp. 56-68.

Cohen, H., 1880-1992, *Descrzjtption historique des monnaies frappees sous l'Empire Romain*, Paris.

Coleman, K.M., 1990, "Fatal Charades: Roman Executions Staged as Mythological Enactments", *JRS* 80, pp. 44-73.

Cumont, F., 1965, "The Frontier Provinces of the East", *CAH* XI, pp. 606-48.

De Blois, L., 1984, "The Third Century and the Greek Elite in the Roman Empire", *Historia*, 33.3, pp. 358-77.

De Blois, L., 1997, "Volk und Soldaten bei Cassius Dio", *ANRW* 34.3, pp. 2650-76.

De Kind, R.E.L.B., 1998, *Houses in Herculaneum: a new view on the town planning and the building of Insulae III and IV*, J.C. Gieben: Amsterdam.

Den Boer, W., 1972, *Some Minor Roman Historians*, Brill: Leiden.

Den Hengst, D., 2002, "The Discussion of Authorship", *HAC* 2000, pp. 187-95.

Dessau, H., 1889, 'Über Zeit und Persönlichkeit der Scriptores Historiae Augustae', *Hermes* 25, pp. 337-92.

Dessau, H., 1916, *Inscriptiones Latinae Selectae*.

Drake, J.H., 1899, "Studies in the Scriptores Historiae Augustae", *AJPh* 20.1, pp. 40-58.

Dudley, D.R., 1967, *Urbs Roma*, Phaidon Press: London.

Duncan-Jones, R., 1965, "An Epigraphic Survey of Costs in Roman Italy", *PBSR* 33, pp. 224-6.

Duncan-Jones, R.P., 1999, "The Monetization of the Roman Empire: Regional Variations in the Supply of Coin Types", in Paul, G.M. (ed.), *Roman coins and Public Life under the Empire: E. Togo Salmon Papers II*, University of Michigan Press: Ann Arbor, pp. 61-82.

Elton, H., 2003, "Commodus: an Emperor at the Crossroads (Review)", *JRS* 93, p. 397.

Esdaile, K.A., 1917, "The Commodus-Mithras of the Salting Collection", *JRS* 7, pp. 71-3.

Fentress, E., Gatti, S., Goodson, C., Hay, S., Kuttner, A. and Maiuro, M., 2006, "Excavations at Villa Magna 2006", *Journal of Fasti Online*. www.fastionline.org/docs/2006-68.pdf.

Fentress, E., Goodson, C., Hay, S., Kuttner, A. and Maiuro, M., 2006, *Excavations at Villa Magna 2006*.

Festy, M., 1999, "Aurélius Victor, source de l'*Histoire Auguste* et de Nicomaque Flavien", *HAC* 1998, pp. 121-34.

Foss, C., 1990, *Roman Historical Coins*, Seaby: London.

Fullerton, M.D., 1986, "Die Statuarische Ausstattung der Villa Hadriana bei Tivoli (review)", *AJA* 90, pp. 249-51.

Gabriel, M.M., 1952, *Masters of Campanian Painting*, H. Bittner: New York.

Gaffney, V., Patterson, H. and Roberts, P., 2001, "Forum Novum-Vescovio: studying urbanism in the Tiber valley", *JRA* 14, pp. 59-79.

Geer, R.M., 1936, "Second Thoughts on the Imperial Succession from Nerva to Commodus", *TAPA* 67, pp. 47-54.

George, M., 1997, "Servus and domus: the slave in the Roman house", in Laurence, R. and Wallace-Hadrill, A. (eds.), *Domestic Space in the Roman World: Pompeii and Beyond*, *JRA* Supp 22: Portsmouth, pp. 15-24.

Gherardini, M., 1974, *Studien zur Geschichte des Kaisers Commodus*, Verband der wissenschaftlichen Gesellschaften Österreichs: Wien.

Gibson, S., DeLaine, J. and Claridge, A., 1994, "The Triclinium of the Domus Flavia: a new reconstruction", *PBSR* 62, pp. 67-100.

Giuliani, C.F., 1977, "Domus Flavia: una nuova lettura", *MDAIR(A)* 84, pp. 91-106.

Goodman, D., Piro, S. and Nishimura, Y., 2002, "GPR Time Slice Images of the Villa of Emperor Trajanus, Arcinazzo, Italy (A.D. 52-117)", *Proceedings of SPIE* 4758, pp. 268-72.

Gordon, A.E., 1983, *Illustrated Introduction to Latin Epigraphy*, University of California Press: Berkeley.

Goudineau, C., 2000, "Gaul", *CAH* XI, pp. 462-95.

Grainger, J.D., 2003, *Nerva and the Roman Succession Crisis of AD 96-99*, Routledge: London.

Green, R.P.H., 1981, "Marius Maximus and Ausonius' *Caesares*", *CQ* 31.1, pp. 226-36.

Grosso, F., 1964, *La Lotta Politica al Tempo di Commodo*, Accademia delle Scienze: Turin

Hahm, D.E., 1963, "Roman Nobility and the Three Major Priesthoods, 218-167 BC", *TAPA* 94, pp. 73-85.

Haines, C.R., 1920, "Fronto", *CR* 34, pp. 14-18.

Hamberg, P.G., 1968, *Studies in Roman Imperial Art*, L'erma di Bretschneider: Rome.

Hammond, M., 1959, *The Antonine Monarchy*, Papers and Monographs of the American Academy in Rome 19: Rome.

Hannah, R., 1986, "The Emperor's Stars", *AJA* 90.3, pp. 337-42.

Hekster, O., 2002, *Commodus: an Emperor at the Crossroads*, J.C. Gieben: Amsterdam.

Hekster, O., 2002, "Of Mice and Emperors: a Note on Aelian 'De Natura animalium' 6.40", *CPh* 97.4, pp. 365-70.

Hellegouarc'h, J., 1999, *Eutrope: abrégé d'Histoire Romaine*, Belles Lettres: Paris.

Hirstein, J., 1998, "L'Histoire du texte de l'*Histoire Auguste*: Egnazio et la Vita Marci", *HAC* 1996, pp 167-89.

Hojte, J.M., 2005, *Roman Imperial Statue Bases: from Augustus to Commodus*, Aarhus University Press: Aarhus.

Honore, T., 1987, "Scriptor Historiae Augustae", *JRS* 77, pp. 156-76.

Hopkins, K., 1980, "Taxes and Trade in the Roman Empire", *JRS* 70, pp. 101-25.

Houston, G.W., 1973, "The Priests of the Roman Republic: a study of interactions between priesthoods and Magistracies [Review]", *CW* 67.1, pp. 51-2.

Howgego, C., 1992, "The Supply and Use of Money in the Roman World 200 BC to AD 300", *JRS* 82, pp. 1-31.

Howgego, C., 1995, *Ancient History from Coins*, Routledge: London.

Hüttl, W., 1975, *Antoninus Pius*, Arno Press: New York.

Idris Bell, H., 1965, "Egypt, Crete and Cyrenaica", *CAH* XI, pp. 649-75.

Jarrett, M.G., 1978, "The Case of the Redundant Official", *Britannia* 9, pp. 289-92.

Jashemski, W.F. and Salza Prina Ricotti, E., 1992, "Preliminary Excavations in the Gardens of Hadrian's Villa: the Canopus Area and the Piazza d'Oro", *AJA* 96, pp. 579-97.

Johne, K.-P., 1976, "Neue Beiträge zur Historia-Augusta-Forschung", *Klio* 58.1, pp. 255-62.

Johne, K.-P., 1977, "Die Epitome de Caesaribus und die *Historia Augusta*", *Klio* 59.2, pp. 497-501.

Kaiser-Raiß, M.R., 1980, *Die stadtrömische Münzprägung während der Allein-herrschaft des Commodus: Untersuchungen zue Selbstdarstellung eines römisches Kaisers*, P.N. Schulten: Frankfurt.

Kalinowski, A., 2002, "The Vedii Antonini", *Phoenix* 56, pp. 109-49.

Keil, J., 1965, "The Greek Provinces", *CAH* XI, pp. 555-605.

Keppie, L. 1991, *Understanding Roman Inscriptions*, Batsford: London.

King, C.E., 1999, "Roman Portraiture: Images of Power?", in Paul, G.M. (ed.), *Roman coins and Public Life under the Empire: E. Togo Salmon Papers II*, University of Michigan Press: Ann Arbor, pp. 123-36.

Kleiner, D.E.E., 1992, *Roman Sculpture*, Yale University Press: New Haven.

Kolb, F., 1972, *Literarische Beziehungen zwischen Cassius Dio und Herodian*, *Antiquitas* Reihe 4.9: Bonn.

Lanciani, R., 1967, *The Ruins and Excavations of Ancient Rome*, Benjamin Blom: New York.

Laurence, R., 1994, *Roman Pompeii: space and society*, Routledge: London.

Leunissen, P.M.M., 1989, *Konsuln und Konsulare in der Zeit von Commodus bis Severus Alexander (180-235 n. Chr.): Prosopographische Untersuchungen zur senatorischen Elite im Römischen Kaisserreich*, J.C. Gieben: Amsterdam.

Levick, B.M., 1992, "Konsuln und Konsulare in der Zeit von Commodus bis Severus Alexander (Review)", *CR* 42.1, pp. 116-17.

Levick, B.M., 1999, "Messages on the Roman Coinage: Types and Inscriptions", in Paul, G.M. (ed.), *Roman coins and Public Life under the Empire: E. Togo Salmon Papers II*, University of Michigan Press: Ann Arbor, pp. 41-60.

Levick, B., 2000, "Greece and Asia Minor", *CAH* XI, pp. 604-34.

MacDonald, W.L. and Pinto, J.A., 1995, *Hadrian's Villa*, Yale University Press: New Haven, 1995.

Mantle, I.C., 2002, "The Roles of Children in Roman Religion", *G&R* 49.1, pp. 85-106.

Mari, Z., 2004a, "La villa di Triano ad Arcinazzo Romano", *Journal of Fasti Online*. www.fastionline.org/docs/2004-1.pdf

Marriott, I., 1979, "The Authorship of the *Historia Augusta*: two computer studies", *JRS* 69, pp. 65-77.

Marshall, P.K., 2001, "Eutropius", *CR* 51.2, pp. 271-2.

Matthews, J.F., 1968, "Marcus Aurelius (Review)", *JRS* 58, pp. 262-3.

Mattingly, H., 1927, *Roman Coins: from the earliest times to the fall of the western empire*, Methuen: London.

Meadows, A. and Williams, J., 2001, "Moneta and the Monuments", *JRS* 91, pp. 27-49

Meckler, M., 1996, "The Beginning of the *Historia Augusta*", *Historia* 45.3, pp. 364-75.

Mellor, R., 1982, "Fronto and Antonine Rome [Review]", *Journal of Philology* 103.4, pp. 459-62.

Metcalf, W.E., 1999, "Coins as Primary Evidence", in Paul, G.M. (ed.), *Roman coins and Public Life under the Empire: E. Togo Salmon Papers II*, University of Michigan Press: Ann Arbor, pp. 1-17.

Millar, F., 1964, *A Study of Cassius Dio*, Oxford University Press: Oxford.

Millar, F., 1966, "La Lotta Politica al Tempo di Commodo (Review)", *JRS* 56, 1966, pp. 243-5.

Momigliano, A., 1954, "Date et destinataire de l'*Histoire Auguste* (Review)", *JRS* 44, pp. 129-31.

Momigliano, A., 1966, "An Unsolved Problem of Historical Forgery: the *Scriptores Historiae Augustae*", in *Studies in Historiography*, London, pp. 143-80.

Mommsen, T., 1890, "Die Scriptores Historiae Augustae", *Hermes* 25, pp. 228-92.

Moulton, W.J., 1919-20, "Gleanings in Archaeology and Epigraphy", *Annual of the American School of Oriental Research in Jerusalem* 1, pp. 66-92.

Muller, A., 1883, "Zur Geschichte des Commodus", *Hermes* 18.4, pp. 623-6.

Murison, C.L., 1999, *Rebellion and Reconstruction*, Scholars Press: Atlanta.

Murison, C.L., 2003, "M. Cocceius Nerva and the Flavians", *TAPA* 133.1, pp. 147-57.

Nixon, C.E.V., 1971, *An Historiographical Study of the Caesares of Sextus Aurelius Victor*, diss. Michigan.

Oliver, J.H., 1950, "Three Attic Inscriptions concerning the Emperor Commodus", *AJPh* 71.2, pp. 170-9.

Oliver, J.H., 1967, "The Sacred Gerousia and the Emperor's Consilium", *Hesperia* 36.3, pp. 329-35.

Ortolani, G., 1998, *Il Padiglione di Afrodite Cnida a Villa Adriana. progetto e significato*, Librerie Maze: Rome.

Packer, J.E., 1998, "Mire exaedificavit: three recent books on Hadrian's Tiburtine villa", *JRA* 11, pp. 583-96.

Paschoud, F., 1999, "Propos sceptiques et iconoclasts sur Marius Maximus", *HAC* 1998, pp. 251-54.

Patterson, H. and Millett, M., 1998, "The Tiber valley Project", *PBSR* 66, pp. 1-20.

Pelling, C., 1997, "Biographical History? Cassius Dio on the Early Principate", in Edwards, M.J. and Swain, S. (eds.), *Portraits: biographical representation in the Greek and Latin Literature of the Roman Empire*, Oxford University Press: Oxford, pp. 117-44.

Penella, R.J., 1976, "S.H.A. Commodus 9.2-3", *AJPh* 97.1, p. 39.

Piro, S., Goodman, D. and Nishimura, Y., 2003, "The Study and Characterization of Emperor Traiano's Villa", *Archaeological Prospection* 10, pp. 1-25.

Pitts, L.F., 1989, "Relations between Rome and the German Kings on the Middle Danube in the First to Fourth Centuries A.D.", *JRS* 79, pp. 45-58.

Platner, S.B., 1962, *A Topographical Dictionary of Ancient Rome*, L'Erma di Bretschneider: Rome.

Portalupi, F., 1961, *Marco Cornelio Frontone*, Giappichelli: Turin.

Potter, T.W., 1991, "Towns and territories in southern Etruria", in Rich, J. and Wallace-Hadrill, A. (eds.), *City and Country in the Ancient World*, Routledge: London, pp. 191-209.

Purcell, N., 1987, "Town in Country and Country in Town", in MacDougall, E.B. (ed.), *Ancient Roman Villa Gardens*, Dumbarton Oaks Colloquium on the History of Landscape Architecture 10: Washington, pp. 187-203.

Raeder, J., 1983, *Die Statuarische Ausstattung der Villa Hadriana bei Tivoli*, P. Lang: Frankfurt.

Raubitschek, A.E., 1949, "Commodus and Athens", *Hesperia Supp.* 8, pp. 279-466.

Rees, R., 1998, "Eutropius", *CR* 48.1, pp. 65-7.

Reynolds, J., 2000, "Cyrenaica", *CAH* XI, pp. 547-58.

Richardson, L. jnr., 1992, *A New Topographical Dictionary of Ancient Rome*, John Hopkins University Press: Baltimore.

Richlin, A., 1992, *The Garden of Priapus: sexuality and aggression in Roman humour*, Oxford University Press: Oxford.

Richlin, A., 2006, *Marcus Aurelius in Love*, University of Chicago Press: Chicago.

Robathan, D.M., 1942, "Domitian's Midas-Touch", *TAPA* 73, pp. 130-44.

Rose, C.B., 1997, *Dynastic Commemoration and Imperial Portraiture in the Julio-Claudian Period*, Cambridge University Press: Cambridge.

Rostovtzeff, M., 1957, *The Social and Economic History of the Roman Empire*, Vols. 1 and 2, Oxford University Press: Oxford.

Rostovtseff, M. and Mattingly, H., 1923, "Commodus-Hercules in Britain", *JRS* 13, pp. 91-109.

Ruger, C., 2000, "Roman Germany", *CAH* XI, pp. 496-513.

Saller, R.P., 1994, *Patriarchy, property and death in the Roman Family*, Cambridge University Press: Cambridge.

Sandys, J.E., 1927, *Latin Epigraphy: an introduction to the study of Latin Inscriptions*, Ares Publishers: Chicago.

Sansone, D., 1990, "The Computer and the *Historia Augusta*: a note on Marriott", *JRS* 80, pp. 174-7.

Satre, M., 2000, "Syria and Arabia", *CAH* XI, pp. 635-63.

Scheid, J. and Huet, V. (eds.), 2000, *La Colonne Aurélienne: autor de la colonne Aurélienne. Geste et image sur la colonne de Marc Aurèle à Rome*, Brepols: Turnhout.

Schlumberger, J., 1974, *Die Epitome de Caesaribus: Untersuchungen zur heidnischen Geschichtsschreibung des 4. jahrhunderts n. Chr.*, C.H. Beck: Munich.

Schmid, W., 1964, "Eutropspuren in der *Historia Augusta*", *HAC* 1963, pp. 123-33.

Schwartz, J., 1968, "Sur la date de l'*Histoire Auguste*", *HAC* 1966/7, pp. 91-9.

Schwendemann, J., 1923, *Der historische Wert der Vita Marci bei den Scriptores Historiae Augustae*, C. Winter: Heidelberg.

Scott, K., 1931, "The Significance of Statues in Precious Metals in Emperor Worship", *TAPA* 62, pp. 101-23.

Scranton, R., 1944, "Two Temples of Commodus at Corinth", *Hesperia* 13.4, pp. 315-48.

Shotter, D.C.A., 1983, "The Principate of Nerva", *Historia* 32.2, pp. 215-26.

Sijpesteijn, P.J., 1988, "Commodus' Titulature in Cassius Dio", *Mnemosyne* 41, pp. 123-4.

Simpson, C.J., 1980, "Ulpius Marcellus Again", *Britannia* 11, pp. 338-9.

Smallwood, E.M., 1966, *Documents Illustrating the Principates of Nerva, Trajan and Hadrian*, Cambridge University Press: Cambridge .

Speidel, M.P., 1993, "Commodus the God-Emperor and the Army", *JRS* 83, pp. 109-14.

Stewart, P., 2003, *Statues in Roman Society: representation and response*, Oxford University Press: Oxford.

Straub, J., 1972, "Cassius Dio und die *Historia Augusta*", *HAC* 1970, pp. 271-85.

Strong, D.E., 1961, *Roman Imperial Sculpture*, Alec Tiranti: London.

Sutherland, C.H.V., 1941, "Roman Coinage from Antoninus to Commodus", *CR* 55.2, pp. 93-5.

Sutherland, C.H.V., 1987, *Roman History and Coinage 44BC-AD69*, Oxford University Press: Oxford.

Swain, S., 1996, *Hellenism and Empire*, Oxford University Press: Oxford.

Syme, R., 1930, "The Imperial Finances under Domitian, Nerva and Trajan", *JRS* 20, pp. 64-5.

Syme, R., 1958, *Tacitus*, Volumes I and II, Oxford University Press: Oxford.

Syme, R., 1964, *Sallust*, University of California Press: Berkeley.

Syme, R., 1964, "Hadrian and Italica", *JRS* 54, pp. 142-9.

Syme, R., 1968, "The Ummidii", *Historia* 17, pp. 72-105.

Syme, R., 1968, "*Ignotus*, the Good Biographer", *HAC* 1966/7, pp. 131-53.

Syme, R., 1968, "Ipse ille patriarcha", *HAC* 1966/7, pp. 119-30.

Syme, R., 1968, *Ammianus and the Historia Augusta*, Oxford University Press: Oxford.

Syme, R., 1970, "The Secondary Vitae", *HAC* 1968/9, pp. 285-307.

Syme, R., 1971, *Emperors and Biography: studies in the Historia Augusta*, Oxford University Press: Oxford.

Syme, R., 1971, "The *Historia Augusta*: a call of clarity", *Antiquitas* 4.

Syme, R., 1972, "The Composition of the *Historia Augusta*: recent theories", *JRS* 62, pp. 123-33.

Syme, R., 1972, "Marius Maximus Once Again", *HAC* 1970, pp. 287-302.

Syme, R., 1972, "The Son of the Emperor Macrinus", *Phoenix* 26.3, pp. 275-91.

Syme, R., 1976, "Astrology in the *Historia Augusta*", *HAC* 1972/4, pp. 291-309.

Syme, R., 1976, "Bogus Authors", *HAC* 1972/4, pp. 311-21.

Syme, R., 1978, "Propaganda in the *Historia Augusta*", *Latomus* 37, pp. 173-92.

Syme, R., 1979, "Ummidius Quadratus, Capax Imperii", *HSCP* 83, pp. 287-310.

Syme, R., 1983, *Historia Augusta Papers*, Oxford University Press: Oxford.

Syme, R., 1983, "Hadrian and Antioch", *HAC* 1979/81, pp. 321-31.

Syme, R., 1987, "Avidius Cassius: his rank, age and quality", *HAC* 1984/5, pp. 207-22.

Syme, R., 1988, "The Cadusii in History and in Fiction", *JHS* 108, pp. 137-50.

Temin, P., 2001, "A Market Economy in the Early Roman Empire", *JRS* 91, pp. 169-81.

Tomei, M.A., 1985, "La Villa detta di Triano ad Arcinazzo", *ArchLaz* 7, pp. 178-84.

Toynbee, J.M.C., 1978, *Roman Historical Portraits*, Thames and Hudson: London.

Traupman, J.C., 1956, *The Life and Reign of Commodus*, PhD Diss., Princeton University.

Vermeule, C., 1975, "The Weary Herakles of Lysippos", *AJA* 79.4, pp. 323-32.

Vinson, M.P., 1989, "Domitia Longina, Julia Titi, and the Literary Tradition", *Historia* 38.4, pp. 431-50.

Wallace-Hadrill, A., 1981, "The Emperor and his Virtues", *Historia* 30.3, pp. 298-323.

Wallace-Hadrill, A., 1988, "The Social Structure of the Roman House", *PBSR* 56, pp. 43-97.

Webb, C.J., 1897, "Fronto and Plutarch", *CR* 11.6, pp. 305-6.

Weber, W., 1965, "The Antonines", *CAH* XI, pp. 325-92.

White, P., 1977, "The Authorship of the *HA*", *JRS* 67, pp. 115-33.

Whittaker, C.R., 2000, "Africa", *CAH* XI, pp. 514-46.

Williams, S., 1985, *Diocletian and the Roman Recovery*, Batsford: London.

Williams, W., 1976, "Individuality in the Imperial Constitutions: Hadrian and the Antonines", *JRS* 66, pp. 67-83.

Wilson, A., 2002, "Machines, Power and the Ancient Economy", *JRS* 92, pp. 1-32.

Woolf, G., 1992, "Imperialism, empire and the integration of the Roman economy", *World Archaeology* 23.3, pp. 283-93.

Zanker, P., 1988, *The Power of Images in the Age of Augustus*, University of Michigan Press: Ann Arbor.

Zernial, H.L., 1986, *Akzentklausel und Textkritik in der Historia Augusta*, Antqituitas 4.18.

CPSIA information can be obtained at www.ICGtesting.com
Printed in the USA
LVOW01s1030080815

449207LV00013B/129/P